A Research Agenda for Environmental Crime and the Law

Elgar Research Agendas outline the future of research in a given area. Leading scholars are given the space to explore their subject in provocative ways, and map out the potential directions of travel. They are relevant but also visionary.

Forward-looking and innovative, Elgar Research Agendas are an essential resource for PhD students, scholars and anybody who wants to be at the forefront of research.

For a full list of Edward Elgar published titles, including the titles in this series, visit our website at www.e-elgar.com.

A Research Agenda for Environmental Crime and the Law

Edited by

RICARDO PEREIRA

Reader in Transnational Law, School of Law and Politics, Cardiff University, UK

TERESA FAJARDO

Professor of International Law and International Relations, University of Granada, Spain

Elgar Research Agendas

Edward Elgar
PUBLISHING

Cheltenham, UK • Northampton, MA, USA

Published by
Edward Elgar Publishing Limited
The Lypiatts
15 Lansdown Road
Cheltenham
Glos GL50 2JA
UK

Edward Elgar Publishing, Inc.
William Pratt House
9 Dewey Court
Northampton
Massachusetts 01060
USA

Authorised representative in the EU for GPSR queries only: Easy Access System Europe – Mustamäe tee 50, 10621 Tallinn, Estonia, gpsr.requests@easproject.com

A catalogue record for this book
is available from the British Library

Library of Congress Control Number: 2025935539

This book is available electronically in the Elgaronline
Law subject collection
https://doi.org/10.4337/9781803929958

MIX
Paper | Supporting responsible forestry
FSC® C013604

ISBN 978 1 80392 994 1 (cased)
ISBN 978 1 80392 995 8 (eBook)
ISBN 978 1 0353 6975 1 (ePub)

Printed and bound by CPI Group (UK) Ltd, Croydon, CR0 4YY

Contents

Contributors

Carolyn Abbot is a Professor of Environmental Law at the University of Manchester and Co-Director of the Manchester Centre for Regulation, Governance and Public Law. Her research centres broadly on environmental regulation. She has written extensively on the theory and practice of regulatory compliance and enforcement in environmental law and, in recent years, has been researching the role of NGOs in the making, implementation and enforcement of environmental law.

Victoria Colvin is a Senior Lecturer at the School of Law, University of Wollongong, Australia. Her research focuses on criminal law and practice, discretionary decision making, accountability in criminal justice, and the law of evidence. Before entering academia, Victoria was a prosecutor with the Criminal Justice Branch of the Attorney General of British Columbia, Canada.

Anna Di Ronco is an Associate Professor at the Department of Legal Studies at the University of Bologna and Senior Lecturer in Criminology at the Sociology Department of the University of Essex. Her research critically addresses dynamics of exclusion and penalisation in the public space, as well as performative, visual and mediated practices of resistance. Her books include *Policing Environmental Protest: Power and Resistance in Pandemic Times* (Bristol University Press, 2023), *Criminology: A Sociological Introduction* (co-authored; Routledge, 4th edn, 2020), and *Harm and Disorder in the Urban Space: Social Control, Sense and Sensibility* (co-edited; Routledge, 2021).

Teresa Fajardo is a Professor of International Law and International Relations at the University of Granada (Spain) and holds a Jean Monnet Chair on EU Climate Diplomacy. She read law at Granada and Poitiers Universities and the Licence Spéciale en Droit Européen at the Institut d'Études Européennes at the Université Libre de Bruxelles. Her research interests lie in the field of international and European environmental law and soft law. She participated in the EU-funded interdisciplinary research project, the European Union Action to Fight Environmental Crime (EFFACE). She has drawn up reports for the European Commission and the European Parliament on wildlife crime. Among her publications are *To Criminalise or Not to Criminalise IUU Fishing: The EU's Choice* (Marine Policy, 2022), and *Biological Diversity and International Law. Challenges for the Post 2020 Scenario* (Springer, 2021).

Michael Faure has a Master of Laws (LLM) from the University of Chicago (1985) and a PhD from the Albert Ludwig Universität Freiburg im Breisgau (1989). He is a Professor of International and Comparative Environmental Law at Maastricht University and a

Professor of Comparative Private Law and Economics at the Erasmus School of Law Rotterdam, both in the Netherlands.

Juan Luis Fuentes Osorio studied law (LLB) at the University of Granada (1996). He continued his postgraduate studies with a scholarship (DAAD) at the Ludwig-Maximiliams Universität München (1999–2001), obtaining a PhD in Criminal Law from the University of Jaén in 2003 and a Masters in Criminology (PGC) from the Universidad Nacional de Educación a Distancia in 2006. He is currently a Senior Lecturer in Criminal Law and Criminology at the University of Jaén. He has published extensively on environmental crime and was a member of the European project, the European Union Action to Fight Environmental Crime (EFFACE), contributing with several reports.

Gabriel Hallevy is a Full Professor at the Faculty of Law, Ono Academic College. He is a world-leading expert in criminal law and in AI law.

Thomas Obel Hansen (LLM (2007), PhD in Law (2010), Aarhus University Law School, Denmark) is the 2023–24 Maria Zambrano Distinguished Researcher with the Department of International Law, Ecclesiastical Law and Philosophy of Law at the Universidad Carlos III de Madrid (Spain). He is a Senior Lecturer in the School of Law at Ulster University and a member of the Transitional Justice Institute (TJI) (UK) since January 2016.

Ludwig Krämer (now retired) was a judge at the Landgericht Kiel (Germany) and served as an official in the environmental department of the EU Commission. He was an Honorary Professor in London (UCL), Bremen, Copenhagen, Brugge and Gent. He published extensively on EU environmental law, most recently *Krämer's EU Environmental Law* (Bloomsbury, 9th edn, 2024).

Sjoerd Lopik is a lawyer (advocaat) and partner in both the Climate Law Practice and the Investigations & Enforcement Practice of De Roos. He represents NGOs, governmental authorities and corporations in matters that relate to climate law and enforcement matters. He also is a PhD candidate at the Institute of Criminal Law and Criminology of Leiden University. His research regards the role of criminal law in the legal response to climate change.

Gary Lynch-Wood is a Senior Lecturer at the University of Manchester and an Associate Professor at the City University of Hong Kong. His research focuses on impacts and responses to regulation and the challenges of designing effective approaches. He has carried out both theoretical and empirical analyses and has published in several leading journals.

Angus Nurse is a Professor of Law and Environmental Justice at Anglia Ruskin University. He was previously Head of Criminology and Criminal Justice at Nottingham Trent University. Angus has research interests in green criminology, criminality, critical criminal justice, environmental law, animal rights and human rights law. His books include *Policing Wildlife* (Palgrave Macmillan, 2015), *Animal Harm: Perspectives on why People Harm and Kill Animals* (Ashgate, 2013), *Miscarriages of Justice: Causes, Consequences and Remedies* (Policy Press, 2018) (co-authored with Sam Poyser and Rebecca Milne), *The Citizen and the State* (Emerald, 2020) and *Wildlife Criminology* (Bristol University Press, 2020) (co-authored with Tanya Wyatt).

Ricardo Pereira is a Reader at Cardiff University, School of Law & Politics, United Kingdom. He holds a PhD in International and European Law from the University of Essex and two LLM degrees in International Law from the University of London. He has acted as a consultant for international and regional organisations and NGOs, including the UNEP, the UNODC, the IUCN and the European Commission, and is currently a member of the IUCN World Commission on Environmental Law. His main research interests lie in environmental and natural resources law, transnational and European criminal law, the law of the sea and human rights law. His other recent editorial roles include the book *The Governance of Criminal Justice in the European Union: Transnationalism, Localism and Public Participation in an Evolving Constitutional Order* (Edward Elgar Publishing, 2020) and a Special Issue on the legal protection of 'The Amazon Rainforest' published by the *Review of European, Comparative and International Environmental Law* (2021, Issue 2).

Stefano Porfido is a postdoctoral fellow at Roma Tre University in Rome, where he investigates the interplay between criminal law and the legal regime governing nature restoration within European law. He holds a PhD from the Sant'Anna School of Advanced Studies in Pisa, focusing on restorative justice for corporate environmental crimes. He has been a visiting scholar at Erasmus University of Rotterdam and later at the Centre for International Environmental Studies—now the Hoffmann Centre for Global Sustainability—at the Geneva Graduate Institute. There, as an affiliate member, he continues his research on corporate sustainable due diligence law in the context of the European Green Deal.

Alberto Quintavalla is an Assistant Professor at Erasmus School of Law and Co-director of the Erasmus Centre of Law and Digitalization. He has been a visiting researcher at the Hebrew University of Jerusalem and the European University Institute. He received the Early Career Award from the Royal Netherlands Academy of Arts and Sciences (KNAW) for his research on AI, the environment and human rights. He is the author of articles in leading journals and the co-editor of *Artificial Intelligence and Human Rights* (Oxford University Press, 2023).

Stephan Sina is a Senior Fellow at Ecologic Institute in Berlin and a specialist lawyer (Fachanwalt) in administrative law. He specialises in climate change law, energy law, environmental criminal law and resources law. He has written numerous studies for governmental agencies, foundations and NGOs, published in specialist journals and books, participated as an expert in parliamentary hearings, and was involved in preparatory work for legislation. He has a PhD in Law from the University of Heidelberg.

Ragnhild Sollund is a Professor of Criminology at the University of Oslo. She has published widely within the field of green criminology, particularly on wildlife crimes and harms. Ten of her 18 books are in the field of green criminology and animal abuse, including *Green Harms and Crimes* (Palgrave Macmillan, 2015), *The Crimes of Wildlife Trafficking. Issues of justice, Legality and Morality* (Routledge, 2019), and *Animal Victimization in Wildlife Trade. Parallel Harms and Crimes* (Routledge, 2025). Before entering this field, she made important contributions to the fields of police racial profiling, migration, and violence. Sollund was partner in the EU-funded project European Union Action to Fight Environmental Crime (EFFACE) (2012–16), and the project leader of *CRIMEANTHROP* (2019–24). She is recipient of the Energy Globe Award (2015) and the Lifetime Achievement Award of the Division of Critical Criminology and Social Justice (DCCSJ) of the American Society of Criminology (2015).

Nigel South PhD FAcSS is an Emeritus Professor of Sociology and Criminology at the University of Essex, UK. He has made various contributions to the development of 'Green Criminology' including co-authoring *Green Cultural Criminology* (Routledge, 2014) and *Water, Crime and Security in the Twenty-First Century* (Palgrave Macmillan, 2018), as well as co-editing the *International Handbook of Green Criminology* (Routledge, 2nd edn, 2020). In 2022 he received the Outstanding Achievement Award from the British Society of Criminology and in 2013 received the Lifetime Achievement Award from the American Society of Criminology, Division on Critical Criminology and Social Justice.

Sarah Wright is a Senior Lecturer with the School of Law at the University of Wollongong, Australia. Sarah's research focus includes environmental crime, compliance and enforcement in environmental law, regulatory theory and effective regulation. Prior to entering academia Sarah worked as a Senior Legal Officer with the NSW Office of Environment and Heritage, which then incorporated the NSW Environment Protection Authority, and also as Tipstaff to the Hon. Justice Nicola Pain of the Land and Environment Court of NSW.

Preface

The triple planetary crises of climate change, biodiversity loss and pollution are among humanity's greatest challenges in the twenty-first century. These existential challenges are further magnified by the rise and growth of environmental crimes and criminality as they have emerged in a wide range of forms and contexts globally. The overarching aim of this *Research Agenda for Environmental Crime and the Law* is to open up new avenues for the study of environmental crime from both the legal and multidisciplinary approaches offered by the different contributions it brings together.

As with any project of such collaborative nature, its successful completion would not be possible without the many actors involved to whom we owe our deepest thanks. First and foremost, we would like to express our gratitude to the contributors to this edited volume for their thought-provoking contributions casting a critical eye on the different problems and solutions relating to the legal protection of the environment. The strength of their arguments and research stems from their academic commitment to the study of environmental crime and, in some cases, also from their experience in combating it as practitioners. It has been a pleasure and a privilege to work with each of you.

We would also like to extend our gratitude to our publisher, Edward Elgar, for embarking with us on this journey to bring this project to fruition. We are especially grateful to Amber Watts and Ben Booth, Senior Commissioning Editors at Edward Elgar. Their support from the outset has contributed greatly to a smooth editing experience. Thanks are also due to the team at Edward Elgar during the book's production process. In particular, we would like to thank copyeditor Michelle Afford and proofreader Joanna Southwell, editorial assistant Ross Harrison and junior desk editor Victoria Bromley, for their help and efficiency throughout the publication process. Lastly, we are indebted to our families and friends for their love and encouragement.

It should be noted that the chapters in this volume reflect developments in the law (to the best of our and the contributors' knowledge!) up until September 2024. Occasionally, some contributors may refer to legal developments that took place in the later part of 2024 or the early part of 2025 before the book's publication.

We hope you will enjoy reading this volume and that it will stimulate new avenues for debates and inspire further research, which has always been our ultimate goal.

The Editors

1 Introduction: a panoramic view of global environmental criminal law research

Ricardo Pereira and Teresa Fajardo

1. Environmental criminal law research: history, approaches and directions

Environmental crime is one of the most profitable and fastest growing areas of international criminal activity. The three main drivers of environmental crime are the growing global demand for environmental goods; the economic benefits arising from environmental crime, which include both the potential for high profits for those engaged in the trade and the desire for access to illegal goods; as well as specific regulatory gaps, which include deficiencies in international and national laws and their enforcement.[1] Organised criminal groups, corporations and individual actors make significant profits from environmental criminality, as estimated by international organisations, national governments and non-governmental organisations.[2]

---

1 R. Pereira, *Environmental Criminal Liability and Enforcement in European and International Law* (Brill, 2015). See generally, C. Schmidt, 'Environmental Crimes: Profiting at the Earth's Expense' in R. White (ed), *Environmental Crime: A Reader* (Willan Publishing, 2009); G. Hayman and D. Brack, *Workshop Report: International Environmental Crime: The Nature and Control of Environmental Black Markets* (The Royal Institute of International Affairs, London 1998).

2 Environmental crime generates around US $110 to $281 billion in criminal gains each year. See the Financial Action Task Force (FATF), *Money Laundering from Environmental Crimes* (FATF, Paris 2021), at https://www.fatf-gafi.org/content/dam/fatf-gafi/reports/Money-Laundering-from-Environmental-Crime.pdf. In their report *The Rise of Environmental Crime*, UNEP and INTERPOL estimated that the value of environmental crime was 26 per cent larger than previous estimates, at $91–258 billion in 2016 compared to $70–213 billion in 2014, at https://www.unep.org/news-and-stories/press-release/unep-interpol-report-value-environmental-crime-26.

Unsurprisingly, there has been considerable academic research addressing the environmental crime phenomenon, particularly by green criminologists and legal scholars, and to a lesser extent by international relations scholars and other social and political scientists.[3] The application of criminal sanctions for enforcement of the so-called environmental rule of law at the international and national levels has also led to the proliferation of legal scholarship dedicated to studying the role of national criminal laws for the protection of the environment.[4]

Although violations of environmental law have traditionally been perceived as regulatory offences of a less serious nature (*malum prohibita*) than other types of serious offences criminalised under national law (*malum in se*), the growth of the 'global environmental consciousness', particularly since the 1970s,[5] has ignited calls for international environmental cooperation to address a common definition of environmental crime, an approximation of penalties and improved cooperation between law enforcement agencies of countries of origin, transit and destination of the proceeds of environmental crime, as well as more effective and dissuasive sanctions to combat environmental crime.

From a historical perspective, the advent of the industrial revolution in the eighteenth century, despite bringing prosperity to some parts of the globe – particularly to the European powers – led to increasing levels of industrial pollution, deforestation and land use change, which had detrimental effects on the environment and human health.[6] This, in turn, led to the response of several European countries introducing legislation in the nineteenth and twentieth centuries to regulate and prevent harmful levels of industrial pollution and to protect certain marine and terrestrial areas.[7] Yet

---

3 See further for example R. White, *Environmental Crime* (Edward Elgar Publishing, Cheltenham, UK and Northampton, MA 2020). This scholarly research is complemented by research and commentaries by law enforcement agency members and practitioners. See for example R. De Rijck, 'Believing in criminal law. On how the European legislator of Directive 2008/99/EC deems strict criminal law necessary for the functioning of environmental legislation, but Member States consider it an expression of their sovereignty', (2013) 4 *Tijdschrift voor Sanctierecht & Onderneming* 1–16, I.S. Moreno, 'Introduction to the Environmental Crimes Issue of the USA Bulletin,' (2012) *US Attorneys' Bulletin*; J.A. Alfaro, 'Towards an Understanding of Consequences of the Prioritization of Environmental Crime in the European Union' (2023) 6 *Cuadernos de la Guardia Civil* 31–48, F. Gudin, 'EU rule of law actors and the environmental crime directive: upholding the law in a new era of ecological challenges' (2024) *ERA Forum* 1–17.

4 See further for example M. Faure and G. Heine, *Criminal Enforcement of Environmental Law in the European Union*, (Kluwer Law International, Netherlands 2005).

5 See the 1972 *Declaration of the United Nations Conference on the Human Environment. Report of the United Nations Conference on the Human Environment*, UN Doc A/CONF.48/14/Rev.1 (1 January 1973).

6 See also, Pereira (2015) (note 1).

7 Including, for example, the German General Industrial Code (1845), the British Waterworks Clauses Act (1845), the French Dangerous Industrial and Commercial

as noted by Michael Faure and Sjoerd Lopik in Chapter 2 of this volume, the history of environmental criminal law can be said to commence in the 1970s when the first 'real' environmental statutes in Europe were adopted, focusing on the actual protection of the environment in the form of 'sectoral laws aimed at the protection of water, air or soil, with criminal law being applied as the driving force behind an administrative system of protection'.[8]

In this vein, according to Andrew Ashworth, the contours of criminal law are '"historically contingent" – not the product of any principled inquiry or consistent application of certain criteria, but largely dependent on the fortunes of successive governments, on campaigns in the mass media, on the activities of various pressure groups, and so forth'.[9] He suggests that the resort to criminalisation is often a reaction of legislators and governments in light of certain catastrophic disasters or as a result of a penal code reform.[10] In particular, the criminalisation of environmental offences in

Activities Act (1917) and the Spanish Water Act (1878). For a discussion, see A. Vercher Noguera, 'The Use of Criminal Law for the Protection of the Environment in Europe: Council of Europe Resolution (77) 28' 10 *Northwestern Journal of International Law & Business* 442, (1990) 442. Moreover, in France, a crime of poaching was introduced to the Law of 15 April 1829 on 'River Fishing'. It has been applied by the courts since 1859 to manufacturers that discharge pollutants into water. K. Tiedemann, 'Theorie et Reforme du Droit Penal de L'Environment: Etude de Droit Penal Compare' (1986) *Revue de Science Criminelle et Droit Penal Compare* 264.

8 M. Faure and S. Lopik, 'Methods for Environmental Criminal Law Research,' Chapter 2. Similarly, as regards environmental criminal law in the US, 'the earliest modern federal felony statutes were not enacted until 1980, with additional environmental criminal legislation promulgated by the United States Congress during the 1990s [and ...] [b]efore 1980, federal criminal provisions for environmental infractions carried only misdemeanor penalties'. R.F. Blomquist, 'The Logic and Limits of Environmental Criminal Law in the Global Setting: Brazil and the United States – Comparisons, Contrasts, and Questions in Search of a Robust Theory' (2011) 25(1) *Tulane Environmental Law Journal* 83. In Australia, 'pollution and the illegal disposal of waste was the first of the environmentally damaging practices to generate public concern and receive formal regulatory attention. Laws were first enacted in Australia in the early 1970s and combined with a broad range of additional statutory tools' (S. Bricknell, *Environmental criminal law in Australia*, AIC Reports Research and Public Policy Series 109 (Australian Institute of Criminology, 2010)).

9 A. Ashworth, 'Is the Criminal Law a Lost Cause?' (2000) 116 *Law Quarterly Review* 225, 226.

10 Indeed, many European states have introduced into their penal codes specific provisions on the protection of the environment: following the example of the German *Strafgesetzbuch* of 1980, an amendment to which introduced a chapter entitled 'Crimes against the Environment', a number of European countries reformed their penal codes. See generally, C. Ringelmann, 'Recent Trends in Environmental Criminal Legislation' (1997) 5 *Eur. J. Crime L. & Crim. Just.* 393, 394–5. See also, Pereira (2015) (note 1).

many countries appears to be 'historically contingent'[11] and coincides with the growing awareness of the importance of preserving environmental values and resources.[12]

With the advent of economic globalisation in the 1990s and the growth of 'global crime',[13] transnational environmental crime (TEC) has increasingly been treated as a priority policy area, leading to the growth of legal and socio-legal scholarship dedicated to the study of TEC.[14] As noted by Abbot and Lynch-Wood in Chapter 3 of this volume in their analysis of transnational corporate environmental crime, the term TEC captures multiple offences and forms 'a category of crime in a socio-normative rather than a strictly legal sense'.[15] Yet they note that 'alongside lax enforcement and low penalties if laws are enforced, national legal responses to TEC may therefore do little to combat TEC activity'.[16] In the context of transnational organised wildlife crime, Angus Nurse in Chapter 8 of this volume explains that 'organised crime groups take advantage of global markets, continued demand for wildlife products, and a comparatively weak enforcement regime relative to that in place for other serious global trafficking commodities such as drugs and weapons'.[17] Hence, from a legal perspective, current research has provided evidence of the (in)effectiveness of existing sanctions regimes and strategies commonly applied by enforcement bodies to combat national and transnational environmental crime.

Despite the urgency of the global environmental crisis, there is no consensus on a definition of environmental crime across United Nations (UN) bodies.[18] In general,

---

11 Ashworth (2000) (note 9), at 225.

12 The adoption of the EU Ship-Source Pollution Directive 2005/35/EC and the Council Framework Decision 2005/667/JHA on ship-source pollution crimes in response to the *Erika* oil tanker disaster in 1999 off the coast of France, and particularly the *Prestige* oil tanker disaster in 2002 off the coasts of Spain and Portugal, are examples of reactive legislation.

13 See further, T. Hall and V. Scalia (eds), *A Research Agenda for Global Crime* (Edward Elgar Publishing, Cheltenham, UK and Northampton, MA 2019).

14 See further for example L. Elliott and W.H. Schaedla, *Research Handbook of Transnational Environmental Crime* (Edward Elgar Publishing, Cheltenham, UK and Northampton, MA 2016); Pereira (2015) (note 1); A. Farmer, M. Faure and G.M. Vagliasindi (eds), *Environmental Crime in Europe* (Hart Publishing, 2018).

15 C. Abbot and G. Lynch-Wood, Chapter 3 Transnational Environmental Crime Across Global Supply Chains – A Place for Due Diligence? in this volume. See also, L. Elliott and W.H. Schaedla, 'Transnational Environmental Crime: Excavating the Complexities – An Introduction' in Elliott and Schaedla (2016) (note 14), p.4.

16 Abbot and Lynch-Wood, ibid. They argue that in some jurisdictions, laws to address TEC are inadequate, and these crimes may be regarded as victimless and therefore low priority. See also, J. Ayling, 'Prevention of Transnational Environmental Crime and Regulatory Pluralism' in P. Drahos (ed), *Regulatory Theory: Foundations and Applications* (ANU Press, 2017).

17 See A. Nurse, Chapter 8 The Global Illegal Wildlife Trade Crisis in this volume.

18 See further T. Fajardo and R. Pereira's Chapter 14 'International Institutions and the Fight against Transnational Environmental Crimes' in this volume. On proposed

States tend to prefer to refer in international forums to 'crimes that affect the environment' or 'environment-related crimes'. Even though environmental crimes are part of and one of the main drivers of the triple planetary crises – climate change, biodiversity loss and pollution – in many legal systems they are still subordinated to the traditional crimes to which they are related, such as corruption, fraud and money laundering, insofar as they are easier to prosecute and obtain a conviction for. In most countries, environmental crimes are still 'not taken seriously'.[19] In many cases, environmental crimes are only ancillary offences to other traditional and principal crimes, and their prosecution is subordinated to the leading case (which may concern primarily other crimes, such as financial crimes). Yet, as public awareness of environmental issues increases, there are growing calls for (serious) environmental offences not to be regarded as mere regulatory offences (or *mala prohibita*), but 'real' crimes (*mala in se*).[20] Moreover, as noted by Juan Luis Fuentes in Chapter 6 of this volume, there is no doubt that the complexity of environmental legislation and of the concrete cases prosecuted requires police, forensic, prosecutorial and judicial specialisation.[21]

The above challenges have culminated in scholarly research and policy debates regarding law reform, such as proposals for the creation of a crime of 'ecocide' under international law[22] and for effective (criminal and/or administrative) penalties to address new and emerging environmental challenges such as illegal waste shipment,[23] climate

---

definitions of environmental crime in the literature, see for example M. Clifford, *Environmental Crime: Enforcement, Policy and Social Responsibility* (Gaitherburg, Aspen 1998), at 26; and Y. Situ and D. Emmons, *Environmental Crime: The Criminal Justice System's Role in Protecting the Environment* (Sage Publications, 2000), at 4.

19 See T. Fajardo, 'The European Union's Approach in the Fight against Wildlife Trafficking: Challenges Ahead' (2016) 19(1) *Journal of International Wildlife Law & Policy* 1–21.

20 See also, S. Bell, D. McGillivray, O. Pedersen, E. Lees and E. Stokes, *Environmental Law* (OUP, 2024), Chapter 8.

21 J.L. Fuentes Osorio, Chapter 6 The Effectiveness of Environmental Criminal Law Enforcement in this volume.

22 See T. Hansen's Chapter 4 Towards a New Agenda for Ecocide Norms-Adoption and Enforcement in this volume. See also for example F. Mégret, 'The Problem of an International Criminal Law of the Environment' (2011) 36(2) *Colum. J. Envtl. L.* 195–257; R. Pereira, 'After the ICC Office of the Prosecutor 2016 Policy Paper on Case Selection and Prioritisation: Towards an International Crime of Ecocide?' (2020) 31 *Criminal Law Forum* 2.

23 See L. Bisschop, 'Illegal Trade in Hazardous Waste' in Elliott and Schaedla (2016) (note 14); R. Pereira, 'Towards Effective Implementation of the EU Environmental Crime Directive? The Case of Illegal Waste Management and Trafficking Offences' (2017) 26 *Review of European, Comparative and International Environmental Law* 2, 147–62 and C. Brennan, 'The Enforcement of Waste Law in Northern Ireland: Deterrence, Dumping and the Dynamics of Devolution' (2016) 28 *Journal of Environmental Law* 471–96.

change,[24] or the extraction of mineral resources in the deep seabed or outer space.[25] This provides the backdrop for a global research agenda on environmental crime and the law, as will be discussed in the next sections.

1.1 The global geographical distribution of, and approaches for, environmental criminal law research

Environmental criminal law research has been led by research institutions[26] primarily in the Global North, particularly by scholars affiliated with academic institutions in the United States (US),[27] the United Kingdom (UK),[28] Australia[29] and the European Union (EU) Member States.[30] In many instances, this type of scholarly research tends to be published in academic journals and publishing houses of international standing, thus ensuring wider distribution and dissemination of environmental crime research.[31] Some

---

24 See further S. Sina's Chapter 11 Climate Change and Criminal Justice in this volume. See also for example R. Kramer, *Carbon Criminals, Climate Crimes (Critical Issues in Crime and Society)* (Rutgers University Press, 2020).

25 See United Nations Office on Drugs and Crime, *Responding to Illegal Mining and Trafficking in Metals and Minerals: A Guide to Good Legislative Practices* (UNODC, Vienna 2023), available at https://sherloc.unodc.org/cld/uploads/pdf/Illegal_Mining_and_Trafficking_in_Metals_and_Minerals_E.pdf; and Isabel Feichtner, Mining for Humanity in the Deep Sea and Outer Space: The Role of Small States and International Law in the Extraterritorial Expansion of Extraction, *Leiden Journal of International Law* (2019), 32, 255–274.

26 We use the term 'research institutions' primarily to refer to higher education institutions, although we recognise that private bodies such as consultancies and think tanks also conduct relevant environmental crime or environmental crime-related research.

27 See for example R. Lazarus, 'Meeting the Demands of Integration in the Evolution of Environmental Law: Reforming Environmental Criminal Law' (1993) 83 *Georgetown Law Journal*; M. Clifford, *Environmental Crime: Enforcement, Policy and Social Responsibility* (Gaitherburg, Aspen 1998).

28 A. Ogus and C. Abbot, 'Sanctions for Pollution: Do we have the Right Regime?' (2002) 14(3) *Journal of Environmental Law* 289. M. Watson, 'The Use of Criminal and Civil Penalties to Protect the Environment: A Comparative Study' (2006) 15(4) *European Energy and Environmental Law Review* 108–13; M. Watson, 'Organised Crime and the Environment: The British Experience' (2005) 14(8/9) *European Energy and Environmental Law Review* 207–13.

29 See further S. Wright and V. Colvin's Chapter 7 Enforceable Undertakings as an Alternative to Prosecution in Australian Environmental Law Enforcement in this volume. See also, Bricknell (2010) (note 8).

30 A. Vercher Noguera (1990) (note 7), at 442; A. Vercher Noguera, 'Some Reflections on the Use of Criminal Law for the Protection of the Environment' (2002) 10 *Env. Liability* 3, 107; K. Tiedemann (1986) (note 7); C. Ringelmann, 'Recent Trends in Environmental Criminal Legislation' (1997) 5 *Eur. J. Crime L. & Crim. Just.* 393, 394–5. F. Comte and L. Krämer (eds), *Environmental Crime in Europe: Rules and Sanctions* (Europa Law Publishing, Groningen 2004).

31 Even though often they are not published in open access format. Environmental criminal law research typically tends to be published in specialist environmental law, criminal law and justice, and international or comparative law academic journals, in

environmental criminal law studies in Europe have been carried out in cooperation with regional organisations or enforcement agencies, for example, the work conducted by the Norwegian Center for Global Analysis (RHIPTO) in coordination with the United Nations Environmental Programme (UNEP) and the International Criminal Police Organization (INTERPOL),[32] and the one conducted by the Institute for Transnational Legal Research (METRO) in coordination with European Union Network for the Implementation and Enforcement of Environmental Law (IMPEL);[33] and may be funded by and carried out in coordination with the European Commission, particularly as it prepared a legislative instrument for harmonisation of environmental criminal law of the EU Member States.[34] The new EU Environmental Crime Directive 2024/1203 itself was preceded by preliminary studies and assessments and backed up by research on the challenges faced by particular EU Member States[35] when implementing the previous 2008/99 Environmental Crime Directive.[36]

---

scholarly books and as technical reports for international and national organisations or NGOs.

32 See C. Nellemann, R. Henriksen, A. Kreilhuber, D. Stewart, M. Kotsovou, P. Raxter, E. Mrema and S. Barrat (eds), *The Rise of Environmental Crime – A Growing Threat to Natural Resources Peace, Development and Security*, A UNEP-INTERPOL Rapid Response Assessment (UNEP and RHIPTO Rapid Response–Norwegian Center for Global Analyses, 2016), available at www.rhipto.org.

33 M. Faure and G. Heine, 'Criminal Enforcement of Environmental Law in the European Union' (IMPEL Network, July 2000). IMPEL is an EU non-profit association of the environmental authorities of the Member State acceding and candidate countries for the implementation and enforcement of environmental law. See http://ec.europa.eu/environment/impel/. This study was later published as M. Faure and G. Heine, *Criminal Enforcement of Environmental Law in the European Union* (Kluwer Law International, 2005).

34 See, for example Milieu and Huglo Lepage, *Summary Report: Study on measures other than criminal ones in cases where Environmental Community Law has not been respected in the EU Member States'* (20 September 2004), 52 (B4-3040A/2003/369724/MAR/A.3).

35 See, for example J.L. Fuentes Osorio, T. Fajardo, R. Faria et al. (2020), *Estudio sobre el carácter disuasorio, efectivo y proporcional de las sanciones penales impuestas en España y Portugal en delitos contra el Medio Ambiente y su adecuación a la Directiva 2008/99/EC sobre protección del medio ambiente a través del derecho penal*, SEO/BirdLife, Report prepared in the framework of Project LIFE Guardianes de la Naturaleza, funded by the European Commission (2020), 144.

36 See further, for example Commission Working Document, Evaluation of the Directive 2008/99/EC of the European Parliament and of the Council of 19 November 2008 on the protection of the environment through criminal law ('Environmental Crime Directive'), Brussels, 28.10.2020 SWD(2020)259 final; and Milieu (Law & Policy Consulting), *Study to supply the Impact Assessment of the Directive 2008/99/EC on the protection of the environment through criminal law*, JUST/2020/JACC/FW/CRIM/0122 (9 December 2021), available at https://commission.europa.eu/system/files/2022-02/study_final_report_en.pdf. See also in the context of the EFFACE project, for example V. Mitsilegas, M. Fitzmaurice, E. Fasoli and T. Fajardo, *Analysis of International Legal*

Increasingly, the global environmental crisis and global equity and environmental justice discourses have shifted the focus of environmental crime research to the countries in the Global South and, in some cases involving cooperation between research institutions in both the Global North and the Global South, particularly in the context of green criminology research.[37] This includes, for example, research that has addressed environmental crime prevention and control strategies and challenges in a transnational context[38] or in particular Global South jurisdictions, for example China,[39] Indonesia,[40] Brazil,[41]

Instruments Relevant in the Fight Against Environmental Crime (EFFACE, July 2014). See further http://efface.eu.

[37] See, for example D.R. Goyes (ed), *Green Crime in the Global South: Essays on Southern Green Criminology* (Palgrave Macmillan, Switzerland 2023).

[38] See further, C. Abbot and G. Lynch-Wood, Chapter 3 Transnational Environmental Crime Across Global Supply Chains – A Place for Due Diligence? in this volume; and T. Fajardo and R. Pereira, International Institutions and the Fight Against Transnational Environmental Crimes Chapter 14 also in this volume. See also e.g. G.L. Elliott and W.H. Schaedla (eds.), *Research Handbook of Transnational Environmental Crime* (Edward Elgar, 2016); L. Elliot, 'Cooperation on Transnational Environmental Crime: Institutional Complexity Matters' 26 *Review of European, Comparative and International Environmental Law*, 2; G. Broussard, 'Building an Effective Criminal Justice Response to Wildlife Trafficking: Experiences from the ASEAN Region' 26 *Review of European, Comparative and International Environmental Law*, 2; and G. Rose, 'Australian Law to Combat Illegal Logging in Indonesia: A Gossamer Chain for Transnational Enforcement of Environmental Law', 26 *Review of European, Comparative and International Environmental Law.*

[39] M. Lu and M. Faure, 'Does the tiger have teeth? A critical examination of the toolbox approach of environmental law enforcement in China' (2021) 31 *Review of European, Comparative & International Environmental Law* 89–102; B. Liu, 'Criminal justice cooperation to combat transnational wildlife crime: An examination of cooperation between China and Africa' (2022) 32 *Review of European, Comparative & International Environmental Law* 119–35; Y. Jiao, 'Greater China and Transnational Environmental Crime: Understanding Criminal Networks and Enforcement Responses' in Elliott and Schaedla (2016) (note 14).

[40] A. Wibisana, M.G. Faure and R. Majory, 'Error in personam: Confusion in Indonesia's environmental corporate criminal liability' (2021) 32(2) *Criminal Law Forum* 247–84; M. Faure, 'Towards a New Model of Criminalization of Environmental Pollution: The Case of Indonesia' in M. Faure and P. Niessen (eds), *Environmental Law in Development: Lessons from the Indonesian Experience* (Edward Elgar Publishing, Cheltenham, UK and Northampton, MA 2006).

[41] See, for example M. Raftopoulos and J. Morley, 'Ecocide in the Amazon: The Contested Politics of Environmental Rights in Brazil' (2020) 24 *International Journal of Human Rights* 1, 616; and L.K. McAllister, 'On Environmental Enforcement and Compliance: A Reply to Professor Crawford's Review of *Making Law Matter. Environmental Protection and Legal Institutions in Brazil*' (2009) 40 *George Washington International Law Review* 649.

Colombia,[42] and Ecuador,[43] the Democratic Republic of Congo,[44] Nigeria[45] or, more widely, in specific Global South regions, such as Southeast Asia/ASEAN and South Asia,[46] Latin America,[47] and Africa/the African Union.[48]

Resource-related constraints and the lack of access to research funding are among the main challenges facing environmental criminal law research, a problem which most prominently affects Global South research institutions.[49] Moreover, although national environmental criminal law frameworks are well established in some jurisdictions,[50] this is not the case for the majority of countries, particularly in the Global South, where the

---

42 See, for example R. Pereira, B. Sjöstedt and T. Krause, 'The Environment and Indigenous People in the Context of the Armed Conflict and Peacebuilding Process in Colombia: Implications for the Special Jurisdiction for Peace and International Criminal Justice' (CAPAZ Policy Brief, 2021).

43 See, for example C. Lambert, 'Environmental Destruction in Ecuador: Crimes against Humanity under the Rome Statute?' (2017) 30 *Leiden Journal of International Law* 707.

44 See, for example S. Mandiefe Piabuo, P.A. Minang, C.J. Tieguhong, D. Foundjem, F. Nghobuoche, 'Illegal logging, governance effectiveness and carbon dioxide emission in the timber-producing countries of Congo Basin and Asia' (2021) 23 *Environment, Development and Sustainability* 14176–96.

45 See, for example J. Nwazi, 'An Evaluation of Environmental Criminal Liability and Enforcement in Nigeria' (2022) 30 *Afr. J. Int'l & Comp. L.* 323.

46 See, for example J. Lin, 'Tackling Southeast Asia's Illegal Wildlife Trade' (2005) *9 SYBIL* 191–208; and S. Sinha, 'Wildlife trade in South Asia' in Elliott and Schaedla (2016) (note 14). See on environmental cooperation in ASEAN more generally, L. Elliott, 'ASEAN and Environmental Cooperation: norms, interests and identity' (2003) 16 *The Pacific Review* 1.

47 See, for example M. Ungar, 'Prosecuting Environmental Crime: Latin America's Policy Innovation' (2017) *8 Latin American Policy* 63; D.R. Goyes, H. Mol, A. Brisman and N. South (eds), *Environmental Crime in Latin America: The Theft of Nature and the Poisoning of the Land* (Palgrave Macmillan, 2016).

48 See the ECO-SOLVE Programme funded by the EU and conducted by the Global Initiative Against Transnational Organized Crime, and its report *Exposing elite protection and corruption in environmental crime across Africa* (March 2024), available at https://globalinitiative.net/wp-content/uploads/2024/03/Exposing-elite-protection-and-corruption-in-environmental-crime-across-Africa-ECO-SOLVE-March-2024.pdf; and D. Lambrechts, 'Reflections from Africa: Limited State Capacity and the Rise of Environmental Organised Crime' in S.L. Smith and L. Sahramaki (eds), *Research Handbook on Environmental Crimes and Criminal Enforcement* (Edward Elgar Publishing, Cheltenham, UK and Northampton, MA 2024).

49 It appears that further evaluation is needed on whether national Research Councils and other national or regional funding bodies prioritise environmental crime research. On funding for environmental law research, see further M. Lee and C. Abbot, 'Philanthropy and Environmental Law' (2024) 51 *Journal of Law and Society* 3.

50 See, for example Brazil's Law no. 9605 on environmental crime (1998); Colombia's Law no. 2111 on environmental crimes (2021); and Ecuador's Comprehensive Organic Criminal Code, Law no. 180, Title IV, chapter four 'Offences against the environment and nature or Pasha Mama' (2014).

legal frameworks and governance for environmental law enforcement generally tends to be weaker. This is a reflection of the fact that there is currently no global environmental crime convention harmonising national environmental criminal law;[51] and as we discuss in Chapter 14 of this volume, relatively few international institutions currently have a mandate to specifically tackle environmental crime. Even when they do, in most cases this is primarily exercised through soft-law instruments in the form of guidelines and recommendations to national governments and law enforcement agencies (LEAs).[52]

In the context of TEC, a comprehensive research analysis requires an evaluation of the legal frameworks in both consumer markets and the source countries of the products of illegal trade. Therefore, as discussed by Faure and Lopik in Chapter 2 of this volume, not only empirical research but also comparative legal research can provide scholars with an important analytical framework for their findings.[53] They further suggest that:

> Research in the field of environmental criminal law often benefits from comparative legal analyses. Comparative law has various benefits. Not only can it enhance the understanding of one's own legal system by contrasting it with that of others, it may also reveal potential improvements based on the strengths of other jurisdictions. In addition, comparative law has been used as a tool to facilitate harmonisation of law between states.[54]

The transnational element characteristic of environmental crime research and the comparative law methodologies that may be applicable to this type of research, therefore, call for effective cooperation between Global North and Global South research institutions. In this context, there is also a need for further policy-oriented environmental crime research, as argued by Ludwig Krämer in Chapter 5 of this volume.[55] Krämer argues that with regards to capacity building for biodiversity crime research, researchers should aim to '… set up joint ventures, research teams, empirical research undertakings, joint data collection mechanisms […] at a global level and strive to overcome, at the same time, the language barrier';[56] and he further contends that 'closer cooperation of researchers with public authorities at national and transnational level is necessary'.[57] Moreover, effective collaboration between researchers,

---

51 See T. Fajardo and R. Pereira, Chapter 14 International Institutions and the Fight Against Transnational Environmental Crimes in this volume.

52 Ibid.

53 See M.G. Faure and S.J. Lopik, Chapter 2 Methods for Environmental Criminal Law Research in this volume.

54 Ibid.

55 See L. Krämer, Chapter 5 Biodiversity Crime in this volume. Another related debate concerns the impact of scholarly research on decision-making by judicial and law and policy-making authorities. In the European Court of Human Rights context, see Kanstantsin Dzehtsiarou and Niccolo Ridi, 'The Use of Scholarship by the European Court of Human Rights' 3 *International and Comparative Law Quarterly,* 73, 2024 pp. 707–746.

56 L. Krämer Chapter 5 Biodiversity Crime in this volume.

57 Ibid.

non-governmental organisations (NGOs), and other key stakeholders appears essential for the production of comprehensive and inclusive environmental crime research. Therefore, policy-oriented environmental crime research must be prioritised and properly funded to help bring meaningful changes to the law and policy and enforcement practices at the international and national level.

Despite noting the significance of policy-oriented research, this is not to dismiss the value of scholarly environmental crime research that engages with (legal or criminological) theory. In this regard, it is notable that there has been less engagement with theory in environmental criminal law scholarship,[58] than has been the case with green criminology research, which has a stronger record of engagement with theoretical approaches to environmental crime (as evidenced by three chapters in this volume).[59] These theoretical perspectives help to build the foundations and overarching frameworks for studying environmental crime. Moreover, interdisciplinary approaches combining legal, socio-legal and green criminologist approaches and methods are crucial for the development of environmental criminal law research, thereby building on the foundations and perspectives from several disciplines, as argued by Anna Di Ronco and Nigel South in Chapter 9 of this volume.[60]

2. International organisations and environmental criminal law research: global outlook and prospects for future research

International cooperation between organisations and agencies such as those of the UN, INTERPOL, and the EU, together with the different national law enforcement agencies, has allowed for a qualitative leap in the gathering of intelligence on

---

58 With some notable exceptions in the socio-legal literature on environmental crime, particularly in the context of ecocide, see, for example E. Cusato and E. Jones, 'The "Imbroglio" of Ecocide: A Political Economic Analysis' (2024) 37 *Leiden Journal of International Law* 42–61; and M. Kooijman, 'From Anthropos to Oikos in International Criminal Law: A Critical-Theoretical Exploration of Ecocide as an "Ecocentric" Amendment to the Rome Statute' in D. Dam-de Jong and F. Amtenbrink (eds), *Netherlands Yearbook of International Law 2021*, 52 (Springer, 2023). See also Gabriel Hallevy's proposal for a theoretical framework for the imprisonment of corporations for environmental damage in Chapter 13 Imprisonment as an Alternative to Financial Penalties on Corporate Entities for Environmental Offenses in this volume.

59 See A. Nurse's Chapter 8 on The Global Illegal Wildlife Trade Crisis in this volume (who engages with more-than-human/posthumanist theory); A. Di Ronco and N. South's Chapter 9 Environmental Harms, Ecocidal Trends and Restorative Responses: Some Interdisciplinary Directions (who embraces Environmental Restorative Justice as a framework for the study of environmental crime); and R. Sollund's Chapter 10 A Green Criminology Perspective on Animal Rights (who endorses multi-species justice theory) in this volume.

60 See A. Di Ronco and N. South's Chapter 9 Environmental Harms, Ecocidal Trends and Restorative Responses: Some Interdisciplinary Directions in this volume.

transnational environmental criminality. In fact, inter-agency and inter-institutional cooperation has evolved to adapt to each national or regional context, while recognising the symbiotic relationship between environmental crimes and other transnational and organised crimes that are ancillary or related to those crimes. However, there is still no global environmental crime treaty nor is there a definition of environmental crime that States have accepted as a common frame of reference. Ultimately, any attempt by international organisations to make progress in the fight against environmental crime is subject to the consent, participation and funding by their member states. The absence of a global environmental organisation[61] has contributed to the limited institutionalisation and fragmentation of policies relating to international cooperation in the fight against environmental crime. As a result, multi-level, soft, sectoral and fragmented governance has developed, which at the normative level articulates common policies through soft-law instruments such as strategies, manuals and guidelines for action and, at the operational level, has led to the setting up of both formal and informal networks for enhanced cooperation. Thus, despite the lack of an express mandate in their constitutive treaties, international organisations have developed functions relating to environmental crime and global policies for awareness raising and the prevention and prosecution of crimes associated with planetary environmental crises. In addition, they have contributed to the design of frameworks for common action to promote the enforcement by States of commitments derived from global norms and for the implementation of soft-law instruments. For instance, the UN and its programmes and agencies such as the UNEP and the United Nations Office on Drugs and Crime (UNODC) have catalysed normative efforts, while operational efforts aimed at enhancing and coordinating the work of the national law enforcement agencies have been developed by INTERPOL at the international level[62] and by Europol and Eurojust at the regional level.[63] It is anticipated that the levels of

---

61 The UNEP is a UN programme and hence not a fully-fledged UN organisation or agency. On proposals for a UN environment organisation, see, for example F. Biermann, 'Strengthening Green Global Governance in a Disparate World Society: Would a World Environment Organisation Benefit the South?' (2002) *International Environmental Agreements: Politics, Law and Economics* 297–315. On UNEP's contribution to environmental crime research, see in particular UNEP, *The State of Knowledge of Crimes that have Serious Impacts on the Environment* (2018), available at https://wedocs.unep.org/bitstream/handle/20.500.11822/25713/knowledge_crime_envImpacts.pdf?isAllowed=y&sequence=1.

62 See further, INTERPOL, National Environmental Security Task Force, *Bringing Compliance and Enforcement Agencies Together to Maintain Environmental Security* (2014); and the INTERPOL website https://www.interpol.int/Crimes/Environmental-crime/Our-response-to-environmental-crime.

63 See Europol, *Environmental Crime in the Age of Climate Change*, Threat Assessment (2022), available at https://www.europol.europa.eu/cms/sites/default/files/documents/Environmental%20Crime%20in%20the%20Age%20of%20Climate%20Change%20-%20Public%20report_5.pdf; and Eurojust, *Strategic Project on Environmental Crime Report* (2014), available at https://www.eurojust.europa.eu/publication/strategic-project-environmental-crime. See further, V. Mitsilegas and F. Giuffrida, *The Role of EU*

intitutional and inter-agency cooperation will grow in future in an effort to combat transnational environmental crime.

The environmental crime studies carried out by international organisations, such as UNODC and INTERPOL,[64] are essential for informing scholarly environmental criminal law research. These studies include crucial data on prosecution and enforcement, as well as environmental crime trends such as new online marketplaces used for illegal trade and the application of new or emerging technologies,[65] which provide invaluable resources for researchers working in the field of environmental crime. Moreover, as we discuss in Chapter 14 of this volume,[66] in addition to legislative guides and other environmental crime studies,[67] UNODC's recent research provides the first global overview of where offences against the environment are criminalised, covering nine specific sectors: deforestation and logging, mining, air pollution, noise pollution, soil pollution, water pollution, illegal fishing, waste and wildlife trafficking.[68]

NGOs not only participate at the international and national levels in the normative and operational actions of States and international organisations, but also act as the 'eyes and ears on the ground'. For instance, they have convened an Independent Expert Panel in 2021 to propose a definition of ecocide,[69] proposed a new protocol to the Palermo Convention on Transnational Organised Crime to fight illegal wildlife

Agencies in Fighting Transnational Environmental Crime: New Challenges for Eurojust and Europol (Brill, 2017).

64 See C. Nellemann, R. Henriksen, A. Kreilhuber, D. Stewart, M. Kotsovou, P. Raxter, E. Mrema and S. Barrat (eds), *The Rise of Environmental Crime – A Growing Threat to Natural Resources Peace, Development and Security,* a UNEP-INTERPOL Rapid Response Assessment, UNEP and RHIPTO Rapid Response–Norwegian Center for Global Analyses, available at https://www.unep.org/resources/report/rise-environmental-crime-growing-threat-natural-resources-peace-development-and.

65 See further S. Porfido and A. Quintavalla's Chapter 12 Artificial Intelligence and Environmental Crime in this volume.

66 T. Fajardo and R. Pereira's Chapter 14 International Institutions and the Fight Against Transnational Environmental Crimes in this volume.

67 See further, https://www.unodc.org/unodc/en/environment-climate/resources.html.

68 UNODC, *Global Analysis on Crimes that Affect the Environment – Part 1: the Landscape of Criminalization* (United Nations publication, Vienna 2024) https://css.unodc.org/documents/data-and-analysis/Crimes%20on%20Environment/ECR_1.Legislative_Review.pdf; see also: UNODC, *Global Analysis on Crimes that Affect the Environment - Part 2a: Forest Crimes: Illegal Deforestation and Logging* (United Nations publication, 2025), https://www.unodc.org/documents/data-and-analysis/Crimes%20on%20Environment/ECR25_P2a_Deforestation.pdf.

69 See the proposed definition of ecocide in 2021 by the Independent Expert Panel convened by Stop Ecocide International, available at https://www.stopecocide.earth/legal-definition. See further, T. Hansen's Chapter 4 Towards a New Agenda for Ecocide Norms Adoption and Enforcement in this volume.

trafficking[70] and have taken on the task of training LEAs in the countries of origin, transit and destination of environmental crimes.[71] Therefore, non-state actors from civil society organisations[72] complement States in their fight against environmental crime through the exercise of different operational functions, ranging from the collection and processing of information on the emergence of new environmental crimes to the investigation and disclosure of the *modus operandi* of criminal groups, for example, on the internet.[73] Through NGO participation, the UN bodies and agencies gain invaluable support in terms of legitimacy, intelligence-sharing[74] and scientific knowledge.[75]

3. Introduction to *A Research Agenda for Environmental Crime and the Law*: scope, objectives and overview of the chapters

This *Research Agenda on Environmental Crime and the Law* has two central aims: 1) to evaluate the current state and direction of research in the field of environmental criminal law, identifying priority research areas and future trends in academic research; and 2) to provide not only a fresh evaluation of the current state of the law, but also to probe the likely evolution of the law, taking account of current and new global environmental threats. The book was designed to be visionary and provocative. With this in mind, this *Research Agenda* will examine ontological questions such as the place of criminal law within the overarching system of sanctions for environmental law enforcement; which breaches of the law ought to be criminalised and the optimal types and levels of penalties entailing deterrent effects; and how far the criminal law should be reserved for the most serious violations of environmental law and only applied as a last resort (or *ultimum remedium*). Although this volume will be primarily

70 See the End Wildlife Crime initiative's proposed a draft protocol on illicit wildlife trafficking to the 2003 UN Organised Crime Convention, available at https://endwildlifecrime.org/untoc-wildlife-protocol/#:~:text=Statement%20of%20purpose,States%20Parties%20to%20that%20end.

71 See, for example the work of the Wildlife Justice Commission at https://wildlifejustice.org/about-us/.

72 See A. Colás, *International Civil Society* (Polity, 2002).

73 See, for example NGO engagement with LEAs in the Programme UNITE funded by the EU with the participation of the French Gendarmerie (OCLAESP), the Italian Carabinieri, the Guardia Civil (SEPRONA), the Hungarian and Slovak police forces and the NGOs IFAW, WWF Hungary, WWF France, WWF Belgium and TRAFFIC's in-kind support, https://www.uniteproject.eu/.

74 See T. Fajardo, 'La sociedad civil internacional y el multilateralismo inclusivo en la CoP26 de Glasgow' (2022) *Anuario de la Facultad de Derecho de la Universidad Autónoma de Madrid* 157–81.

75 See, for example the Intergovernmental Science-Policy Platform on Biodiversity and Ecosystem Services (IPBES) reports, the Red List of the International Union for Conservation of Nature (IUCN), and the criteria that they establish to characterise environmental harm and crimes.

focused on the role of the (criminal/environmental) law for environmental protection, it also recognises the multi-disciplinarity of the study of environmental crime and hence several contributions in this volume cross disciplinary boundaries, probing the criminological and socio-legal contexts in which environmental criminals operate.

This *Research Agenda* brings together leading authors in the environmental crime field from different disciplines who convey the complex nature of this type of crime, and is organised according to three broad-ranging research strands or themes, as follows: Part I – Methodologies for and the state-of-the-art in environmental criminal law research; Part II – Green criminology and multi-disciplinary approaches to environmental crime; and Part III – Pushing the boundaries of legal and socio-legal research: new and emerging themes in environmental criminal law. We now turn to presenting an overview of each chapter in the three Parts of this volume.

3.1 Part I – Methodologies for and the state-of-the-art in environmental criminal law research

This Part examines existing research methodologies and the state-of-the-art in environmental criminal law research. The methodologies considered in this Part include historical methods, comparative law research, empirical research, socio-legal research, and law and economics methods. It also examines the current trends and themes that tend to inform legal research in this area, including law enforcement against TECs in the context of transnational business activities, and the prospects and challenges for the prosecution of ecocide and biodiversity crime at the international and national level. Moreover, this Part evaluates existing initiatives and measures aimed at harmonising environmental criminal law in particular jurisdictions (such as the EU), and the effectiveness of the national legal frameworks for law enforcement against environmental offences.

In the first chapter in this Part, Michael Faure and Sjoerd Lopik[76] discuss the main methodologies currently applied for environmental criminal law research, in particular the historical approach, comparative law, empirical research (including socio-legal research), and law and economics methods.

Initially, by adopting a historical approach, they note that the first 'real' environmental laws, that is, focusing on the actual protection of the environment, were sectoral laws aimed at the protection of water, air or soil, with criminal law as the driving force behind an administrative system of protection. According to the authors, as these first environmental statutes in Europe date back to the 1970s, so does the history of environmental criminal law.

They then argue that research in the field of environmental criminal law often benefits from comparative legal analyses and that comparative law has various benefits.

76 M.G. Faure and S.J. Lopik, Chapter 2 Methods for Environmental Criminal Law Research in this volume.

They note that not only can it enhance the understanding of one's own legal system by contrasting it with that of others, but it may also reveal potential improvements based on the strengths of other jurisdictions. In addition, they note that comparative law has been used as a tool to facilitate the harmonisation of law between states.

The authors also consider the role of law and economics methods. According to the authors, law and economics studies focus on trade-offs: to reduce crime, a law and economics approach recommends increasing the probability of detection of breaches of the law and/or the harshness of the punishment for such breaches. They suggest that in conducting environmental criminal law research, no one method is necessarily more suitable than another and that the appropriate method will largely depend upon the research questions posed. They further suggest that, in reality, one will often need to employ an integrated, holistic approach in which several (and in some cases maybe even all) of the discussed approaches are combined.

In the next chapter, Carolyn Abbot and Gary Lynch-Wood[77] consider the potential contribution that legitimate private enterprises could make to the TEC regulatory endeavour. They note that, alongside lax enforcement and low penalties if laws are enforced, national legal responses to TEC may do little to combat TEC activity. Hence, they argue that, as they hold considerable influence, private enterprises could play an enhanced role in detecting and disrupting TEC activity across global supply chains. Moreover, the authors argue that corporate due diligence is emerging as an important development in mitigating corporate environmental harms and human rights violations, reflecting the role that private enterprises can play, as regulatory surrogates, in identifying adverse risks and impacts occurring across supply chains. They suggest that mandatory due diligence is an important step forward but that more defined and direct measures may be required to support traditional criminal law enforcement responses to cross-border environmental crime.

Also taking a transnational law perspective, in the next chapter, Thomas Obel Hansen[78] discusses current proposals to achieve more meaningful justice for serious environmental crimes, in particular by exploring the feasibility of recent proposals for expanding accountability for environmental crimes such as the ecocide proposal tabled by the Independent Panel of Experts (IEP) in 2021. He suggests that current debates about ecocide norms adoption and enforcement continue to be heavily steered towards international criminal law – and the International Criminal Court (ICC) system, in particular. The author notes that a wide range of countries and nations in Europe, the Americas and Central Asia have already passed national legislation, or bills have been introduced before national parliaments, to criminalise acts that to

77 C. Abbot and G. Lynch-Wood, Chapter 3 Transnational Environmental Crime Across Global Supply Chains – A Place for Due Diligence? in this volume.

78 T. Hansen, Chapter 4 Towards a New Agenda for Ecocide Norms Adoption and Enforcement in this volume.

varying degrees resemble parts of the 2021 IEP ecocide proposal. He argues that advocates must consider how ecocide can remain attractive in the years ahead, and researchers would need to further explore which legal modalities work particularly well from the perspective of effective enforcement.

Also focusing on specific categories of environmental crimes, in the next chapter, Ludwig Krämer[79] examines the role of criminal law in protecting the environment, particularly in the context of biodiversity crimes. He argues that, in general, the criminal law does not effectively protect the impairment of protected areas, as many impairing acts are permitted by public authorities and criminal sanctions appear to be quantitatively insufficient, hardly ever addressing impairing actions by public authorities themselves and being neither sufficiently effective nor dissuasive. Moreover, he notes that an administrative permit may easily be obtained, and authorities initiate or at least tolerate activities in protected areas that are detrimental to biodiversity, such as logging, mining, construction or industrial developments. He proposes a series of recommendations on how research in the field of biodiversity crimes could be strengthened, in particular by exploring avenues for better regulation, better application of legal provisions, improved capacity building, further cooperation and improved communication between researchers and key stakeholders. Moreover, he recommends that the social and political contexts of biodiversity crime are considered and that a more policy-oriented research agenda for biodiversity crime is developed.

In the next chapter, Juan Fuentes Osorio[80] analyses the effectiveness of environmental criminal law enforcement with a focus on specific jurisdictions, particularly the EU and its Member States. He reflects on specific criticisms of the effectiveness of environmental criminal law and its enforcement in those contexts and evaluates whether those criticisms are reasonably justified. He argues that environmental crimes must be prioritised by law enforcement authorities who must commit themselves to developing adequate and coordinated national strategies in the fight against environmental crime.

The author argues that the dispersion and fragmentation of environmental administrative regulations makes it difficult to establish whether a conduct is prohibited or whether it has exceeded the authorisation limits and hence hinders the ability of national legislators, judges and prosecutors in having a holistic vision of the unlawful conducts and applicable sanctions. As regards sentencing and enforcement, he argues that the greater likelihood of conviction does not imply a greater likelihood of a defendant being sentenced to a prison term, receiving a heavy fine or having a severe disqualification order imposed by the courts. Moreover, the author contends that the imposition of lenient penalties by the courts, which are not proportionate to the seriousness of the environmental crime and which are not supplemented by additional penalties and measures such as confiscation of proceeds of crime or reparation of the

79 L. Krämer, Chapter 5 Biodiversity Crime in this volume.

80 J.L. Fuentes Osorio, Chapter 6 The Effectiveness of Environmental Criminal Law Enforcement in this volume.

damage to the environment, may reduce the deterrent effect of environmental criminal law. He suggests that this is because the low level of penalties for environmental crimes can be perceived, from a rational economic perspective, as an acceptable cost of doing business.

In the last chapter in this Part, also addressing environmental law enforcement frameworks, Sarah Wright and Victoria Colvin[81] analyse the role of Enforceable Undertakings (EUs) as a new tool for regulators to facilitate an appropriate response to breaches of environmental law in Australia. They note that EUs were 'invented in Australia' in the early 1990s as an enforcement tool in the trade practices area and are now available to many Australian regulators, including environmental regulators, with similar mechanisms adopted in other jurisdictions (such as the UK). As explained by the authors, EUs allow an alleged offender to offer proposed terms to a regulator that, if accepted, will generally settle an alleged breach and avoid a prosecution. Hence, they suggest that EUs are a form of 'contractually-based' enforcement which, if breached, can be upheld through civil proceedings. Based on a five-year study covering the financial years from 2018–19 to 2022–23 involving selected regulatory agencies in New South Wales, they argue that EUs have replaced prosecutions in a significant proportion of matters in Australia, particularly for organisations (including companies and certain public bodies) for which nearly half had alleged breaches dealt with through EUs. However, they also suggest that individuals are more likely to be prosecuted and thereby subject to the associated stigma of a criminal conviction.

Despite noting that EUs can include a wide range of 'innovative outcomes' addressing matters such as environmental remediation and projects for the benefit of the environment and communities, they suggest that EUs will not be an appropriate enforcement response in all cases, either because the regulatory agency considers the proposed terms inadequate, or because the circumstances may dictate that prosecution is the appropriate response in the public interest.

3.2 Part II – Green criminology and multi-disciplinary approaches to environmental crime

Part II of the book is centred on green criminology and multi-disciplinary approaches to environmental crime. In light of the significant role played by green criminologists in the study of environmental crime, as was noted above, this Part aims to address key green criminology debates and approaches to tackling environmental crime. The common approach in all three chapters in this Part is the understanding that environmental crime should be broadly construed to include environmental harm which may not (yet) be criminalised or declared illegal in particular national legal systems, and that a harm-based approach provides the foundational perspective from which to conduct green criminology research. They may also adopt an 'ecocentric' or biocentric approach for the protection of nature and animal rights.

---

81 S. Wright and V. Colvin, Chapter 7 Enforceable Undertakings as an Alternative to Prosecution in Australian Environmental Law Enforcement in this volume.

In the first chapter in this Part, Angus Nurse[82] assesses the state of the current global illegal wildlife trade (IWT) crisis, providing both green criminologist and legal insights into the extent of the crisis and making recommendations for lawmakers, policymakers and key stakeholders for addressing the current crisis. He argues that, in many respects, wildlife trafficking aligns closely with the criminological gaze, incorporating discussion of organised crime, corruption, transnational crime, the behaviour of offenders and the failures of governance and enforcement mechanisms. As a result, wildlife trafficking is a developing area of criminological scholarship and a core concern of green criminology.

The author argues that there is need for further research to consider how best to influence consumer behaviour to eliminate the consumption of illegal wildlife products through effective demand reduction strategies. Policymakers also need to consider approaches that might strengthen the effectiveness of law enforcement and deterrence, for example by raising awareness of the legal framework for protection of wildlife from illegal trade and any penalties that may be applicable under national laws for the sale and consumption of illegal wildlife products. He contends that addressing the illegal trade in wildlife requires a more holistic approach situated within preventative and restorative principles rather than a primarily retributive justice approach.

In the next chapter in this Part, Anna Di Ronco and Nigel South[83] draw upon an interdisciplinary body of work to describe some of the environmental crimes and ecocidal trends that have not diminished but have gathered pace since the mid-twentieth century, largely because they have not been taken seriously, or have strategically been ignored by states and corporations alike. They further argue that despite the numerous international environmental treaties in force regionally and globally, they are frequently weak in scope, enforcement and effectiveness because states tend to be reluctant to limit their sovereignty.

In order to address those challenges, they propose an 'Environmental Restorative Justice' (ERJ) approach to tackling environmental crimes, which finds its roots in many Indigenous cultures and cosmologies and which holds the central belief that humans and nature are fundamentally interconnected and interdependent. This approach opposes the typically Western, anthropocentric view that nature belongs to human domination and is a commodity for human consumption and exploitation. They note that some countries have institutionalised ERJ and have introduced it into their legal and criminal justice systems, and in the past two decades specialist environmental courts were established in some jurisdictions, which have experimented with using restorative justice conferences and sentencing. They argue that while ERJ is mostly focused on repairing past harms, it also activates a process of capacity building within affected communities that enables them to (re)construct relations – both

82 A. Nurse, Chapter 8 The Global Illegal Wildlife Trade Crisis in this volume.

83 A. Di Ronco and N. South, Chapter 9 Environmental Harms, Ecocidal Trends and Restorative Responses: Some Interdisciplinary Directions in this volume.

within them and with nature – and prevent future harms. More generally, drawing on a number of interdisciplinary projects discussed by the authors in their chapter, they argue that many among us have in our 'inner worlds' the 'seeds' of ecocentric cosmologies, which – if allowed to germinate and grow – could enable people to become allies or guardians of nature and defend it legally or through activist practices.

Developing on the green criminology approaches to environmental crime, in the next chapter in this Part, Ragnhild Sollund[84] aims to present the ways in which the rights of animals are regarded within the growing field of criminology commonly referred to as green criminology (or eco-global criminology) and to show why such perspectives are crucial in the present nature crisis and in view of the increasing knowledge we have obtained about the abilities of non-human animals.

She notes that often environmental crimes, including animal abuse and wildlife crimes, are responded to with administrative sanctions such as fines. Yet when it comes to corporate environmental crimes, such administrative sanctions often lack a deterrent effect because they are simply a cost that corporations will pass on to consumers. She then argues that green criminologists, therefore, sought to engage also with harms that are leniently criminalised or not criminalised because of the weakness of environmental law. She argues, therefore, that a harms perspective is therefore central to green criminological study, with an emphasis on critical victimology that encompasses non-human victims of harm. Thus, she claims that the perspectives of green criminology are essential in the analysis of harms committed against the natural environment and the non-human beings who are part of it, since a legal perspective alone is too limited to encapsulate all serious types of environmental and animal harm.

3.3 Part III – Pushing the boundaries of legal and socio-legal research: new and emerging themes in environmental criminal law

The chapters in this Part tend to follow a common approach in that they address new and emerging environmental threats or innovative aspects of environmental crime research that tend to push the boundaries of the discipline or that may be underexplored in the literature, including the inter-relationship between climate change and criminal justice; the interconnections between artificial intelligence and environmental crime; a proposed theoretical framework for the imprisonment of corporations for environmental offences; and, finally, the current and emerging future role of international institutions in the fight against transnational environmental crimes.

In the first chapter in this Part, Stephan Sina[85] analyses why criminal law does not play a substantial role in current discussions on mitigating climate change, and whether

84 R. Sollund, Chapter 10 A Green Criminology Perspective on Animal Rights in this volume.
85 S. Sina, Chapter 11 Climate Change and Criminal Justice in this volume.

this could and should be changed. He notes that an assessment of the current state of enforcing climate mitigation obligations reveals that, as a rule, neither EU law nor national legal systems oblige Member States to introduce criminal sanctions for the infringement of climate mitigation laws. However, he argues that there are strong arguments for the criminalisation of serious breaches of mitigation laws, although the fact that individual greenhouse gas (GHG) emissions contribute to climate change only to a modest extent makes it difficult to identify which violations are to be considered serious.

Drawing upon the approach applied by Satzger and von Maltitz (2021)[86] for an autonomous climate criminal law, he argues that, with progressing climate change, violations of climate mitigation obligations will be perceived as more serious offences and thus increasingly treated as criminal offences. Therefore, he considers that the role of criminal law in achieving climate justice is likely to grow from its current modest role of primarily securing compliance with mitigation administrative law obligations to a potentially more autonomous role in light of the increase in global warming and the quest for climate neutrality.

In the following chapter, Stefano Porfido and Alberto Quintavalla[87] examine the interplay between artificial intelligence (AI) and environmental crime. They outline the advances in surveillance and crime prediction that have been brought into contemplation by the advent of AI, and examine the benefits of AI with a particular focus on the role of AI algorithms in combatting environmental crimes and in improving corporate compliance with environmental obligations. They also unpack some of the tensions that the rise of AI will engender, in particular those that pertain to political control.

The authors note that technological breakthroughs have fundamentally shaped the criminal justice system. For instance, the expansion of enforcement agencies' investigative powers has led to calls for the fundamental guarantees of the legal rights of defendants to be strengthened and thus ensuring that trials are fair. They further note that in the enforcement of environmental criminal law, AI systems are used, inter alia, to classify data, detect anomalies in environmental indices, and identify the areas that illegal loggers and poachers are most likely to target. Therefore, they argue that AI finds uses across the whole spectrum of environmental crimes, primarily by enhancing monitoring and surveillance, and that its employment has been particularly fruitful in wildlife, ocean and land conservation.

Despite the identified benefits of AI in combatting environmental crimes, they argue that there are considerable risks associated with AI. In particular, AI could facilitate the commission of environmental crimes, such as when illegal loggers and poachers

86 H. Satzger and N. von Maltitz, Das Klimastrafrecht – ein Rechtsbegriff der Zukunft, Zeitschrift für die gesamte Strafrechtswissenschaft (ZStW), 133 (2021).

87 S. Porfido and A. Quintavalla, Chapter 12 Artificial Intelligence and Environmental Crime in this volume.

are able to use AI surveillance systems to avoid areas that the authorities are likely to be monitoring. Moreover, they argue that the capacity of AI systems to interpret data about environmental harm and even to predict its occurrence underscores its critical role in shaping criminalisation processes. According to the authors, this role of AI can become particularly problematic because of the well-documented shortcomings of AI, which include biased input data, lack of transparency and interpretability, and human rights concerns. Ultimately, they argue that a flawed AI system can distort reality, and decisions about criminalisation that are based on such distortions can produce even greater social and environmental harm.

In the next chapter, Gabriel Hallevy[88] starts by discussing the limited effectiveness of financial punishments on corporations and then explores the theoretical legal basis for the imposition of imprisonment on corporations as an alternative to financial punishments for corporate environmental damage. The author argues that there is a theoretical basis for imposing imprisonment as an appropriate corporate criminal punishment for environmental harm and that, in many instances, it is theoretically possible to convert certain non-financial (physical) penalties typically applicable to natural persons to legal entities. Drawing upon the judicial practices in selected jurisdictions, he argues that imprisonment can be applied not only to humans but also to corporate offenders, even though imprisonment was originally designed as a punishment for human offenders. He further argues that, due to the limited effectiveness of financial punishments on corporations, there is no legal justification for domestic courts to continue applying primarily financial penalties for environmental offences. He substantiates this argument by noting that modern criminal law enables courts to impose a range of non-financial penalties both on human offenders and corporations. Moreover, he argues that punishing corporations with imprisonment (which the author distinguishes from incarceration) would enable courts to act in a much more flexible way than financial penalties allow since they would have the power to match an appropriate penalty to the circumstances of the case and taking into account both the *in-rem* and *in-personam* characteristics of corporate defendants.

In the final chapter of this Part and the volume, Teresa Fajardo and Ricardo Pereira[89] review the specific functions assigned to a selection of international and regional organisations and the informal networks created between them and national LEAs to fight TEC. They examine the mandates that selected international institutions have received through fragmented regulatory frameworks in which TEC is addressed at the international and regional levels in the form of multilateral environmental agreements (MEAs) and soft-law instruments, such as UN General Assembly (UNGA) and the UN Economic and Social Council (ECOSOC) resolutions. The authors note that the growing interest of international institutions in fighting environmental crimes depends, to a large extent, on their respective mandates to oversee the implementation

---

88 G. Hallevy, Chapter 13 Imprisonment as an Alternative to Financial Penalties for Corporate Entities for Environmental Damage in this volume.

89 T. Fajardo and R. Pereira, Chapter 14 International Institutions and the Fight against Transnational Environmental Crimes in this volume.

of and compliance with environmenmental law as reflected in existing MEAs and soft-law instruments, through the provision of twofold political and normative action. Yet they note that when most of these international and regional organisations were created, the environment was not yet a common concern for States, so only after reform of their founding treaties or an extensive and teleological interpretation of their mandates was it possible to expand their competences and capabilities in order to deal with environmental offences. They further note that, in light of the limited normative competences enjoyed by most international organisations, they engage in international norm-promoting activity of varying intensity and require effective collaboration with both State and non-State actors to carry out their functions. Moreover, they argue that since international organisations are instrumental to the interests of States, it is necessary to expand their competences and resources so that, with autonomy, they can pursue the common interests of humanity and the global environment.

PART I

Methodologies for and the state-of-the-art in environmental criminal law research

2

Methods for environmental criminal law research

Michael Faure and Sjoerd Lopik

1. Introduction

Due to numerous serious environmental crises, the past decade has seen a significant increase in public interest in environmental matters. Policymakers search for possible ways to prevent biodiversity loss, limit climate change and avert other environmental disasters. Environmental law, including environmental criminal law, is one of the tools that politicians can employ for these aims. Researching and understanding environmental criminal law requires an analytical framework of research methods. The aim of this chapter is to provide (future) scholars in environmental criminal law with an overview of a number of such methods. We will provide a descriptive analysis of the most important methods that have so far been used in environmental criminal law research.

This chapter aims to equip scholars with the necessary tools and insights for conducting research in environmental criminal law. In order to do so, we will first provide a high-level overview of the history of environmental criminal law, including certain recent developments (section 2). Thereafter, we will define which legal interests and values may be protected by environmental criminal law, as this is crucial for understanding this field of law (section 3). Following this, we will describe three of the most important research methods for environmental criminal law scholars, namely comparative legal research (section 4), law and economics research (section 5) and empirical methods (section 6). We will explain the main features, advantages and limitations of each of these methods, as well as how they can be applied to issues of environmental criminal law. Finally, we will conclude by suggesting how these methods can be combined and complemented to produce rigorous and innovative research on environmental criminal law (section 7).

The aim of this chapter is to give a brief introduction to the main research methods that can be used for environmental criminal law research and to evaluate the comprehensiveness and diversity of one's own research. On that note, this chapter does not provide detailed instructions on how to apply each method, but rather offers a general overview of their strengths, limitations and purposes. Given the nature of the chapter, we do not exhaustively describe how certain research methods should be employed. For researchers who do wish to use a certain method, we have striven to include a rich body of footnotes that provide further assistance on that specific method.

2. History of environmental criminal law

To understand the research questions and challenges in any field of law, it is helpful to situate them within their historical context. As Rubin stated:

> To begin by saying, 'We can assume that the Hittites and the Aztecs had the same conception of law that we do', would be obviously wrong. In fact, it would be risible. But when scholars analyse the law of our own society, they generally assume that the same concept of law that prevailed in premodern times is equally applicable to the very different society, and different forms of government, that exists today. That may not be as risible, but it is just as wrong.[1]

Environmental criminal law, though a relatively new branch of law, is not immune to this problem. In fact, environmental criminal law has already undergone significant developments over time. To put the current system of environmental criminal law in perspective, researchers in this field must be aware of the historical factors that have shaped its emergence and evolution.

In many countries, environmental statutes originally emerged from statutes aimed at the protection of workers. These statutes focused, in other words, on the safety of the workforce within a factory. For example, a Belgian Act of 5 May 1888 required owners of dangerous or unhealthy installations to possess a permit. Non-compliance with the conditions of this permit was criminalised.[2] Hence, the primary goal of these old statutes was not the preservation of the environment, but rather the protection of the workforce. The first environmental law cases often related to nuisance law and dealt with conflicts between neighbours in which, for example, one was emitting smoke, affecting the enjoyment of an adjacent property. These types of conflicts in practice mainly concerned property law, although environmental pollution could have been at the origin of the conflict. Those early environmental disputes could already be seen in the 1960s, for example in Belgium.[3]

---

1 E.L. Rubin, 'From Coherence to Effectiveness: A Legal Methodology for the Modern World' in R. van Gestel, H.W. Micklitz and E.L. Rubin, *Rethinking Legal Scholarship: A Transatlantic Dialogue* (Cambridge: Cambridge University Press, 2017), p. 310.

2 M. Faure and M. Visser, *De strafrechtelijke bescherming van het leefmilieu in België, Duitsland en Nederland. Modellen van strafbaarstelling en hun bewijsrechtelijke implicaties* (Antwerp: Intersentia, 1999), p. 22.

3 M. Faure, *Umweltrecht in Belgien. Strafrecht im Spannungsfeld von Zivil- und Verwaltungsrecht* (Freiburg im Breisgau: Max Planck Institut für Ausländisches und Internationales Strafrecht, 1992), pp. 256–8.

The first 'real' environmental laws, that focused on the actual protection of the environment, were sectoral laws aimed at the protection of water, air or soil, with criminal law as the driving force behind an administrative system of protection.[4] As these first environmental statutes in Europe date back to the 1970s, so does the history of environmental criminal law.

At that time, criminal law was mostly used as a backup option for the enforcement of certain administrative environmental laws. The focus of environmental criminal law, therefore, was not primarily on penalising environmental damage, but rather on penalising violations of administrative duties. Many scholars criticised this so-called administrative dependency of environmental criminal law. Even in cases of severe environmental damage, environmental criminal law could not be enforced as long as no administrative obligations were violated. In practice, this meant that many polluters could hide behind their permits, even if they knew their actions would cause major damage to the environment. A second feature of this area of law at that time was that criminal law was often the only way to enforce those administrative laws. In many cases, administrative fines or civil sanctions were not available to respond to environmental violations. This was problematic, as it led to an over-reliance on criminal law. The prevailing view in academia was that criminal law ought to be a method of last resort (*ultimum remedium*), to be used only in cases where other methods do not suffice. Criminal law being the only method of enforcement available at that time was clearly at odds with this principle.[5]

Such critiques of environmental criminal law were later (partly) responded to in many jurisdictions. One of these developments was the abandonment of the system of absolute administrative dependency by many European countries. This led to the protection of the environment by a more autonomous criminal law. Put differently, criminal liability could now also arise if no administrative obligations were violated.[6] Furthermore, criminal law would often no longer be the only method for responding to violations of environmental obligations. Many countries introduced a 'toolbox approach' or 'pyramid approach' in which criminal law was just one of the various ways in which a government could respond to violations of environmental statutes. To a certain extent, decriminalisation took place and administrative law, in some cases,

---

4 M. Faure, 'The Revolution in Environmental Criminal Law in Europe' (2017) 35(2) *Virginia Environmental Law Journal* 321–56, pp. 327–8.

5 See further M.G. Faure, 'Environmental Criminal Liability: The Long and Winding Road towards an Effective Environmental Criminal Law System in the EU' in M. Peeters and M. Eliantonio, *Research Handbook on EU Environmental Law* (Cheltenham, UK and Northampton, MA: Edward Elgar Publishing, 2020), and M.G. Faure, 'The Development of Environmental Criminal Law in the EU and its Member States' (2017) 26(2) *RECIEL* 139–46.

6 We will further consider these forms of criminal accountability in section 3 of this chapter.

even became the only way in which governments could react to such violations. These changes have shaped the current state of environmental criminal law in Europe.[7]

To gain a comprehensive understanding of the historical development of environmental criminal law, researchers should also examine the influence of international and European law. When environmental criminal law emerged in the 1970s, international law and European law played no role whatsoever, since criminal law was an area solely within the power of individual nation states. However, there was a significant body of European administrative environmental law. European harmonisation of environmental criminal law only began in the late 1990s.[8] From a European Union (EU) perspective, inter alia, the Environmental Crime Directive should be taken into account. A revised version of that Directive was adopted by the EU in 2024.[9] With respect to environmental criminal law, researchers should also consider the legislative work done by the Council of Europe. A Council of Europe Convention on the Protection of the Environment through Criminal Law of 4 November 1998 was probably one of the first attempts to create a comprehensive system for the protection of the environment through criminal law.[10] Unfortunately, this convention never entered into force as a result of a lack of ratifications. However, the Council of Europe has started new negotiations for the adoption of a convention with the same objective.[11] Additionally, the resolutions of the United Nations on environmental crime may be relevant for researchers at the international level.[12]

Researchers should also examine recent debates and developments relating to environmental criminal law to get a holistic view of this field of law. In response to growing public interest in environmental issues, various initiatives have emerged or are underway to reform existing or to create new legal instruments in this area. An example of this is the legislative initiative for the criminalisation of ecocide. Ecocide is a term coined by the United States (US) biologist Galston in 1970 to characterise the use of napalm by the US army during the Vietnam War. From a legal perspective, ecocide is a criminal offence that aims to punish the most severe forms of environmental destruction. For the meaning of the term 'severe', many initiatives look to the definition provided in Article 1(1) of the Environmental Modification Convention (ENMOD), which speaks of 'widespread, long-lasting or severe effects'. Attempts to

7 See further M.G. Faure (n 5).
8 Ibid.
9 Directive (EU) 2024/1203.
10 The text can, inter alia be found in M. Faure and G. Heine, *Environmental Criminal Law in the European Union: Documentation of the Main Provisions with Introductions* (Freiburg im Breisgau: Max Planck Institute for Foreign and International Criminal Law, 2000), pp. 397–406.
11 See further, https://search.coe.int/cm/Pages/result_details.aspx?ObjectID=0900001680a91ebb.
12 See, for example, Resolution 10/6 (Preventing and combating crimes that affect the environment falling within the scope of the United Nations Convention against Transnational Organized Crime).

include ecocide as an offence under international criminal law date back to the 1970s, but the topic gained renewed momentum in 2010 when British lawyer Polly Higgins presented a draft international law of ecocide to the United Nations Law Commission.[13]

The ecocide debate has moved from the international to the national level in recent years.[14] Several European countries have recently adopted a crime of ecocide in their criminal codes, while many others have seen the start of the legislative process to make ecocide a crime. In 2021, France made ecocide a crime after a much-discussed legislative process. The French ecocide law was toned down significantly compared to earlier versions.[15] The Belgian legislature adopted a crime of ecocide in February 2024.[16] Meanwhile, ecocide has also gained attention from political parties in other countries that are considering or already drafting domestic laws on the topic. For example, the Dutch Animal Party (*Partij voor de Dieren*) filed a proposal for an ecocide law with the Dutch legislature in November 2023. The proposal received serious criticism from the Dutch Council of State, which found the proposal to be in violation of the *lex certa* requirements of criminal law.[17]

Another development of the last decade is the fast-growing amount of climate legislation, which often includes criminal sanctions for non-compliance. Most countries have pledged to pursue the goal of the Paris Climate Agreement, which requires them to take measures to (significantly) reduce their greenhouse gas (GHG) emissions. One of the ways in which countries try to give substance to their promises is by enacting environmental laws. These cover areas such as car emissions, the Emission Trading System, and energy efficiency obligations for businesses.[18] Such laws are often part of

---

13 For an overview of international criminal law initiatives, see A. Greene, 'The Campaign to Make Ecocide an International Crime: Quixotic Quest or Moral Imperative' (2019) 30(3) *Fordham Environmental Law Review* 1–48, and R. Pereira, 'After the ICC Office of the Prosecutor 2016 Policy Paper on Case Selection and Prioritisation: Towards an International Crime of Ecocide?' (2020) 31 *Criminal Law Forum* 179–224.

14 See also T. Hansen's Chapter 4 Towards a New Agenda for Ecocide Norms Adoption and Enforcement in this volume.

15 Article L231-1 en L231-3 Code de l'environnement. This law was adopted via Loi n° 2021–1104 du 22 août 2021 portant lutte contre le dérèglement climatique et renforcement de la résilience face à ses effets.

16 As a starting point, see Resolutie van de Belgische Kamer van Volksvertegenwoordigers van 29 juni 2021, Doc 55 1429/002, available at www.lachambre.be/FLWB/PDF/55/1429/55K1429002.pdf. The final provision can be found in Article 128, Book II of the Nieuw Strafwetboek.

17 Council of State 27 March 2024, W16.23.00358/II.

18 See the Dutch article S.J. Lopik and S.H. Stax, 'Klimaatverandering en strafrecht: een verkenning' (2020) 3 *BoomStrafblad* 117–26. Also see S.J. Lopik, 'A criminal law response to climate change: positive obligations under the ECHR?' *Strasbourg Observers*, 4 April 2023, available at https://strasbourgobservers.com/2023/04/04/a-criminal-law-response-to-climate-change-positive-obligations-under-the-echr.

the European Green Deal.[19] The authors are not aware of any studies that examine the general state of (criminal) enforcement of these climate laws in Europe.[20] However, there are signals that indicate inadequate enforcement in certain areas. For instance, various researchers have pointed out areas for improvement in the supervision and enforcement of the regulations regarding the European Emission Trading System.[21]

3. Protecting legal interests and values

The development of environmental criminal law in Europe has been strongly influenced by German legal doctrine, especially the idea that criminal law should safeguard specific values and interests that the law deems worthy of protection (*Rechtsgüter*). To analyse environmental criminal law provisions, it is essential first to identify which interests they aim to protect. According to the prevailing view in environmental criminal law literature, there should be different kinds of criminal law provisions that offer varying degrees of protection to the environment. In that regard, most countries employ different categories of offences: abstract endangerment crimes, concrete endangerment crimes, autonomous crimes and/or a combination of all three.[22] We will discuss these four models since they are vital to understanding European environmental criminal law provisions.

Abstract endangerment offences aim to sanction violations of administrative legislation, rather than to directly respond to environmental pollution. They rely on the existing framework of environmental law, where administrative authorities set limits on emissions and require licences for certain activities. If companies violate these limits or licences, they may face criminal prosecution. The protection of the environment under these offences is indirect, as criminal law can only come into play once administrative law has been violated. Many abstract endangerment offences punish violations of obligations such as paperwork requirements or operations or emissions

---

19 Communication from the European Commission COM(2019) 640 final. See also A. Pingen, 'Commission Proposal for Better Protection of the Environment by Means of Criminal Law', *EUCrim*, 29 January 2022, available at https://eucrim.eu/news/commission-proposal-for-better-protection-of-the-environment-by-means-of-criminal-law/#:~:text=The%20proposal%20aims%20to%20make,the%20disturbance%20of%20ecological%20balance.

20 See also S. Sina's Chapter 11 Climate Change and Criminal Justice in this volume.

21 See, for example, M. Peeters, 'Inspection and Market-Based Regulation through Emissions Trading: The Striking Reliance on Self-Monitoring, Self-Reporting and Verification' (2006) 2(1) *Utrecht Law Review* 177–95.

22 For an overview, see M. Faure, 'Towards a new model of criminalization of environmental pollution: the case of Indonesia' in M. Faure and N. Niessen (eds), *Environmental law in development. Lessons from the Indonesian experience* (Cheltenham, UK and Northampton, MA: Edward Elgar Publishing, 2006), pp. 195–200. M. Faure and G. Heine, *Criminal Enforcement of Environmental Law in the European Union* (The Hague: Kluwer Law International, 2005).

without the required licence. Abstract endangerment offences in themselves generally offer insufficient possibilities to ensure environmental protection, since companies that comply with administrative law can still cause serious harm to the environment. Nevertheless, these provisions may play a role in the protection of the environment, as having to comply with administrative rules may reduce the likelihood of environmental damage. Furthermore, because of these provisions, environmental agencies have more sufficient data for their supervisory tasks of monitoring whether companies comply with their information obligations emanating from environmental law.[23]

Concrete endangerment offences differ from abstract ones in that they require evidence of a threat of harm to the environment resulting from an unlawful act. Therefore, concrete endangerment provisions are more directly concerned with the protection of the environment, whereas abstract provisions often primarily seem to protect the administrative legal order. Concrete endangerment offences are generally seen as more serious provisions than their abstract counterparts. Accordingly, the former generally come with higher penalties. It is important to note that for concrete endangerment offences, actual environmental harm is not required. For punishment, it is sufficient that the suspect created the danger of such harm.[24]

Lastly, some countries have a form of autonomous environmental criminal offences in their criminal law systems.[25] These offences target the most severe cases of environmental pollution, regardless of any administrative decisions or regulations. The idea is that the damage caused by such pollution is so great that it cannot be justified by complying with administrative rules. These offences eliminate the so-called 'permit shield', which means that legal subjects cannot avoid liability by arguing that they were emitting in accordance with their permits if such emissions cause a certain level of harm. These offences may therefore raise questions from a rule of law viewpoint, since a government may prosecute companies (or their directors and officers) for emissions that they were allowed to undertake based on administrative law. Therefore, these criminal provisions require clear and additional explanations on when such accountability may occur.[26]

Several jurisdictions use a combination of the three models described above. As mentioned above, these offences reflect different levels of environmental harm. While abstract endangerment offences mostly serve administrative interests, concrete endangerment offences are more clearly linked to protecting humans or the environment. Conversely, autonomous crimes most prominently intend to defend those

23 S.F. Mandiberg and M.G. Faure, 'A Graduated Punishment Approach to Environmental Crimes: Beyond Vindication of Administrative Authority in the United States and Europe' (2009) 34(2) *Columbia Journal of Environmental Law* 447–511.

24 Ibid.

25 For an overview, see A. Di Landro, 'Models of environmental criminal law, between dependence on administrative law and autonomy' (2022) 31(5) *European Energy and Environmental Law Review* 272–97, 290–7.

26 S.F. Mandiberg and M.G. Faure (n 23).

human interests and environmental values. Although it has often been argued that adequate protection of the environment requires a combination of these three types of offences, not all countries currently have such a combination.[27] The autonomous model in particular is quite rare. For example, the Dutch legal system only recognises abstract and concrete endangerment offences, but no autonomous environmental offences, even though various scholars have suggested that the Netherlands should introduce them.[28]

In this respect, the EU 2024 Environmental Crime Directive is of relevance. This new Directive requires Member States to adopt an environmental criminal offence that can, under certain circumstances, lead to accountability, even though the suspect had an environmental licence for the conduct concerned. Punishment for licenced activities can take place if that licence was obtained fraudulently or by corruption, extortion or coercion. The same applies if such authorisation is in manifest breach of relevant substantive legal requirements.[29] EU Member States have two years to implement this Directive (until 21 May 2026). This means that they are under an obligation to start adopting a criminal provision which is more like the abovementioned autonomous environmental criminal offences. For several EU Member States, this requires a transformation of their environmental criminal law systems.

4. Comparative legal research

Research in the field of environmental criminal law often benefits from comparative legal analyses. Comparative law has various benefits. Not only can it enhance the understanding of one's own legal system by contrasting it with that of others, but it may also reveal potential improvements based on the strengths of other jurisdictions. In addition, comparative law has been used as a tool to facilitate harmonisation of law between states.[30] In doing comparative research, scholars will benefit from considering the models of environmental crimes set out in section 3 of this chapter. Since these models capture the main features of the environmental criminal statutes of many countries, they are a useful framework or starting point for comparative analyses.

---

27 M.G. Faure, 'Criminal liability for exploitation of natural resources' in S. Alam, J.H. Bhuiyan and J. Razzaque, *International Natural Resources Law, Investment and Sustainability* (London: Routledge, 2017) and M.G. Faure, 'Revolution in Environmental Criminal Law in Europe' (2017) 35 *Virginia Environmental Law Journal* 321–56.

28 See, for example, I.M. Koopmans, *De strafbaarstelling van milieuverontreiniging: een rechtsvergelijkende studie naar de administratief afhankelijke structuur van het milieustrafrecht* (Arnhem: Gouda Quint, 1996).

29 Article 3(1) Directive (EU) 2024/1203.

30 M. Van Hoecke, 'Methodology of Comparative Legal Research' (2015) 12 *Law and Method* 1–35, p. 2. For an overview of this research method, see M. Siems, *Comparative Law* (Cambridge: Cambridge University Press, 2022) and M. Reimann and R. Zimmermann, *The Oxford Handbook of Comparative Law* (Oxford: Oxford University Press, 2006).

The methods to be used for comparative legal analyses are not settled. Some researchers state that it is 'an informal, almost intuitive, knowledge process',[31] while others use more explicit and clearly defined research methods.[32] It has often been noted that there is little agreement on the methods for such analyses. Legal literature has, however, identified various methods that researchers can employ for comparative legal research. Some of these methods are:

- the functional method, which examines how legal systems address certain practical problems and achieve similar or different outcomes;
- the structural method, which explores the underlying structures and principles of legal systems and their similarities and differences;
- the analytical method, which focuses on legal concepts and their meanings and applications across legal systems; and
- the historical method, which traces the development and evolution of law and legal institutions over time.[33]

Scholars should familiarise themselves with the strengths and limitations of each method and the criteria and sources they use to compare legal systems. These methods are not mutually exclusive, and researchers may combine them to suit their research objectives.[34]

Besides determining the goal of the comparative endeavour and the methods to use, comparative law researchers must also decide which legal systems they will examine. The researcher's knowledge of language often plays an important role in this respect. This explains why there is a relatively high volume of comparative research concerning law in English-speaking countries. However, English translations of legal texts are increasingly available, making it easier to perform analyses of laws from non-English-speaking jurisdictions. Furthermore, an international team can be a solution to achieving a more complete analysis. Before conducting comparative research, scholars should thus ask themselves whether they, or their research group as a whole, can sufficiently familiarise themselves with the desired legal system's language and culture.[35]

Lastly, researchers must choose exactly what they will compare through their methods and between their jurisdictions of choice. For example, only comparing legislation will often be insufficient. Scholars must generally also take into account the way in which legislation is interpreted in court and how it is put into practice. Fully comparing law-in-context requires a large amount of information on the countries

---

31 E. Morgera, 'Global Environmental Law and Comparative Legal Methods' (2015) 24(3) RECIEL 254–64, p. 262.
32 M. Van Hoecke (n 30).
33 Ibid., pp. 8–21.
34 Ibid.
35 Ibid., pp. 3–5.

of interest, which may be challenging to find. Researchers should therefore clearly indicate what sources and perspectives they have used to come to their conclusions.

It has been noted that comparative law has been shifting from a nation-state focus towards having a more global dimension.[36] This means that, in addition to domestic law, comparative law researchers are increasingly studying international and European legal instruments. The influence of such legal documents, especially from the EU, on the environmental criminal law systems of the Member States, is growing. When conducting a comparative legal study in this respect, international and European texts can be compared with their effects at the domestic level. In this way, scholars may also identify whether states have complied with their international obligations.

Comparative legal research can thus provide scholars with an analytical framework for their findings. As the methods described above may seem rather theoretical, scholars may benefit from studying practical examples of such research. These can be found in comparative law journals, such as the *American Journal of Comparative Law*, or even comparative environmental law journals, such as *Comparative Environmental Law and Regulation*.[37]

5. Law and economics research

Law and economics research uses microeconomics to analyse the law. The approach to crime and criminal law is largely based on the work of Nobel laureate Gary Becker in the 1960s.[38] The basic premise of law and economics is that the law, through introducing certain costs and benefits, can influence the behaviour of rational actors (*the homo economicus*).[39] For all kinds of actors, including companies, individuals and government agencies, the benefits of making certain choices must be weighed against their costs. Law and economics studies thus focus on trade-offs. To reduce crime, a law and economics approach recommends increasing the probability of detection of breaches of the law and/or the harshness of the punishment in the event of such breaches.[40] Since the chances of one being caught for environmental crimes are currently low (see

36 E. Morgera (n 31).

37 Also see handbooks on comparative environmental law, such as E. Lees and J.E. Viñuales (eds), *The Oxford Handbook of Comparative Environmental Law* (Oxford: Oxford University Press, 2019).

38 G.S. Becker, 'Crime and punishment: an economic approach' (1968) 76(2) *The Journal of Political Economy* 169–217.

39 M.G. Faure and R.A. Partain, 'Environmental Crime' in M.G. Faure and R.A. Partain, *Environmental Law and Economics: Theory and Practice* (Cambridge: Cambridge University Press, 2019), p. 216.

40 For an overview of this method, see F. Parisi, *The Oxford Handbook of Law and Economics: Volume 1: Methodology and Concepts* (Oxford: Oxford University Press, 2017).

section 6 of this chapter), a law and economics approach in most jurisdictions would suggest severe sanctions to deter (potential) violators.

Arguably, environmental criminal law is one of the legal areas most suited to applying a law and economics approach. In the context of environmental crimes, it is often assumed that violators are rational in their behaviour, for example in cases of illegal hunting, unlawful emissions or deforestation. This fits well with the 'trade-off' assumptions of a law and economics model, which may be why there has been considerable research in the field of environmental law and economics.[41] To a certain extent, it may be true that environmental crime is committed deliberately by actors who first weigh up the costs and benefits of their actions. At the very least, this premise may serve as a useful starting point to review which sanctions to employ in response to environmental damage. The choices of potential lawbreakers are, however, not the only focus of the cost-benefit analysis in a law and economics model. Scholars may also find this approach suitable for analysing the costs of enforcement compared to its benefits. These costs include, inter alia, the costs of supervision, catching a suspect, legal proceedings and enforcing sanctions.[42] Such costs may be weighed against the benefits of crime reduction. Combining these approaches, a comprehensive study of environmental crime following Becker's model could allow scholars to study the actions of both potential violators and regulators.

In environmental cases, possibilities for criminal enforcement often coexist with those for administrative enforcement.[43] This brings additional potential questions to the table when it comes to a law and economics approach, since a cost-benefit analysis can be performed between the two enforcement regimes. Research shows that, from a law and economics perspective, it is most effective for states to employ a system that combines both administrative and criminal enforcement. Generally, administrative sanctions are easier and cheaper to impose than criminal law sanctions. Criminal enforcement is often associated with sanctions that have more impact, including non-monetary sanctions such as imprisonment.[44]

Given the fact that both the probability of detection and the level of potential sanctions for environmental crime are generally low (see section 6 of this chapter), one would expect a large number of environmental law violations based on the law and economics model. Corporations can often make significant economic gains from such violations, while the chances of facing severe penalties tend to be very low. Nevertheless, it

---

41 See, for example, M.G. Faure and R.A. Partain, *Environmental Law and Economics: Theory and Practice* (Cambridge: Cambridge University Press, 2019).

42 M.G. Faure and R.A. Partain (n 39), p. 217.

43 See on the choice between administrative and criminal enforcement, M. Faure and K. Svatikova, 'Criminal or Administrative Law to Protect the Environment?' (2012) 24(2) *Journal of Environmental Law* 253–86.

44 M.G. Faure and R.A. Partain (n 39), p. 214.

has been found that many corporations do comply with environmental legislation.[45] This has been referred to as the Harrington Paradox. This paradox may be explained by the fact that violations are often dealt with during regulatory conversations, in which regulatory agencies agree not to enforce or prosecute based on an instructive conversation with the violator. Furthermore, the potential costs for companies that violate environmental statutes consist of more than just the monetary sanctions such as fines and prohibitions against participating in public tenders. Reputational damage and the unpleasant experience of being the subject of (criminal) proceedings may also have a deterrent effect.[46] The reputational stakes for companies may be high since environmental criminal cases often lead to significant media attention, such as in the case of the diesel emissions scandal and the Deepwater Horizon oil spill.

Law and economics studies can be categorised by distinguishing between the traditional and the new law and economics perspectives. The traditional perspective focuses on topics such as market regulation, competition law and taxation. It sees economics as a tool to design efficient policies and legislation. The new perspective, on the other hand, views economics as a science of human behaviour. It emphasises the role of economic incentives in influencing behaviour, while the traditional perspective relies more heavily on prescriptive and coercive measures. Behavioural economics may be especially relevant in research addressing climate change, as it can help in understanding how to induce behavioural change among various actors, both companies and individuals, aimed at reducing their GHG emissions.[47]

6. Empirical methods

Empirical methods are ways of acquiring knowledge based on observation, measurement, modelling or data analysis, rather than pure logic or authority. Empirical methods aim to produce objective and verifiable evidence to support or refute claims about legal phenomena. For a long time, many European countries had little information available on the extent of environmental crime.[48] However, in the past decade, information availability has improved significantly. Various Member States of the EU and

---

45 There are also findings that point towards higher percentages of non-compliance; see, for example, Netherlands Court of Audit, *Enforcing in the Dark* (30 June 2021), available at https://english.rekenkamer.nl/publications/reports/2021/06/30/enforcing-in-the-dark.

46 M.G. Faure and R.A. Partain (n 39), p. 221.

47 O. Lobel, 'A Behavioural Law and Economics Perspective: Between Methodology and Ideology when Behavioural Sciences Meet Law' in R. van Gestel, H.W. Micklitz and E.L. Rubin, *Rethinking Legal Scholarship: A Transatlantic Dialogue* (Cambridge: Cambridge University Press, 2017), pp. 476–98 and M.G. Faure and R.A. Partain, 'Introduction' in M.G. Faure and R.A. Partain, *Environmental Law and Economics: Theory and Practice* (Cambridge: Cambridge University Press, 2019), p. 6.

48 See for example, M.A. Cohen, 'Empirical Research on the Deterrent Effect of Environmental Monitoring and Enforcement' (2000) 30 *Envt'l L Rep* 10, 245.

the EU itself regularly publish findings regarding the state of environmental crime and the prosecution thereof.[49] These findings can be used by scholars employing empirical methods in their research, which are often combined with one or more of the aforementioned methods of environmental criminal law research.[50] The problem is, however, that data collection systematically only takes place in a few Member States, not all data are publicly available and that, moreover, the methods of data collection diverge, resulting in comparisons often being impossible. Most empirical methods consist of an analysis of numbers that revolve around, for example, pollution, compliance and sanctions. However, such methods may also consist of interviews, including survey-questionnaires.

Empirical methods can also encompass analyses of the extent to which supervision and enforcement take place in the field of environmental criminal law. While the EU Member States are obliged to criminalise environmental harm, it still often seems quite easy for violators to evade responsibility under criminal law. Indeed, the EU does not have an environmental agency that enforces such legislation or may impose enforcement thereof upon Member States.[51] A first problem when assessing the degree of enforcement in Member States (including the number of inspections, inspectors, fines, and so on) is that such data often seem to be lacking.[52] There may, for example, be data on the number of decisions of a criminal court and (if at all) on the number of sanctions imposed. What is often lacking is an overview of the total number of installations to be inspected and the number of inspectors available to monitor environmental compliance. Moreover, empirical research regarding environmental pollution and environmental law compliance is also complicated by the fact that environmental data are often self-reported by companies subject to environmental statutes. Therefore, there may be an incentive for the compiler of such data to ensure that they reflect positively on the company, in other words that the amount of pollution is low and the level of compliance is high. Furthermore, as already mentioned, it should be noted that there is no harmonisation of the format of the data between Member States, which makes it even harder to make comparisons between countries.

---

49 See for example, Netherlands Court of Audit, *Enforcing in the Dark* (30 June 2021), available at https://english.rekenkamer.nl/publications/reports/2021/06/30/enforcing-in-the-dark. See also European Union Action to Fight Environmental Crime (EFFACE), *Fighting Environmental Crime in Germany: A Country Report* (2014), available at https://efface.eu/sites/default/files/EFFACE_Fighting%20Environmental%20Crime%20in%20Germany_0/index.pdf.

50 For a general overview of such research methods, see P. Cane and H.M. Kritzer (eds), *The Oxford Handbook of Empirical Legal Research* (Oxford: Oxford University Press, 2010); and L. Epstein and A.D. Martin, *An Introduction to Empirical Legal Research* (Oxford: Oxford University Press, 2014).

51 It should be noted that the European Commission may, under certain circumstances, commence proceedings against Member States based on Article 258–260 TFEU.

52 M.G. Faure, 'The Development of Environmental Criminal Law in the EU and Its Member States' (n 5).

The European Directive 2008/99/EC on the protection of the environment through criminal law[53] did not include any provisions concerning data collection and was, for that reason, criticised in the literature.[54] In 2024, the EU adopted a new version of this Directive, as was discussed previously in this chapter.[55] Article 22 of this new version requires Member States to ensure that a system is in place for the recording, production and provision of data on the reporting, investigative and judicial stages in relation to certain environmental criminal offences. This is likely to improve the amount of information available for empirical research methods. In addition to this new Directive, Recommendation 2001/331/EC of 4 April 2001 had already provided for minimum criteria for environmental inspections in the Member States and for a duty to collect such data.[56] However, since this was only a Recommendation, there has been hardly any compliance with this obligation.[57]

It has been proven through empirical methods that violations of environmental provisions in many cases go unpunished, as Member States often have no adequate legal form of enforcement in place (as already mentioned in section 5 above). The number of inspections per company seems to be limited, which often results in environmental violations not being discovered. If such violations are discovered, dismissal rates are often high, which can be seen in countries such as the United Kingdom (UK) and Belgium.[58] Consequently, the probability that violators of environmental laws will be prosecuted is low. Research regarding enforcement in Belgium, for example, indicated that the chance of being prosecuted after an environmental violation was below 1 per cent.[59] However, there are indicators that the chances of enforcement are higher under administrative environmental law.[60] Furthermore, it has been shown that serious cases are more likely to be prosecuted.[61] This confirms the hypothesis formulated in the law and economics section that public prosecutors prefer to focus on a few egregious cases and to dismiss others.[62]

Empirical methods help researchers to examine which sanctions are imposed in environmental criminal law cases. Studies on fines for environmental violations indicate

53 [2008] OJ L 328.
54 M.G. Faure, 'Environmental Criminal Liability: The Long and Winding Road towards an Effective Environmental Criminal Law System in the EU' (n 5), pp. 248–63.
55 Directive (EU) 2024/1203.
56 [2001] OJ L 118.
57 See further on the importance of this Recommendation, F. Blanc and M.G. Faure, 'Smart Enforcement in the EU' (2020) 23(11) *Journal of Risk Research* 1405–23.
58 M.G. Faure (n 27), 'The Revolution in Environmental Criminal Law in Europe'. Also see M.G. Faure and R.A. Partain (n 39), p. 218.
59 M.G. Faure and K. Svatikova (n 43).
60 M.G. Faure (n 4), pp. 339–42.
61 M.G. Faure and R.A. Partain (n 39), p. 218.
62 This issue arises in regimes where the principle of opportunity applies. In those where the principle of legality prevails, such a decision would not be possible, or it could be, on the other hand, due to a lack of resources to prosecute offences.

average levels that are likely to be insufficient to deter large corporations.[63] In practice, it seems that monetary sanctions are the default option for environmental matters. Generally, imprisonment is only imposed in cases of fraud or very serious environmental harm.[64] Furthermore, empirical methods can determine which subject of law is prosecuted after violations. Environmental pollution is often caused by corporate actors or persons acting on their behalf. This gives rise to the question of who should be targeted in a criminal prosecution: the employees actually committing such offences, the corporations they work for or the directors or managers of these corporations. There are indications in environmental criminal law research that a combination of monetary sanctions for the corporation and separate sanctions for individuals involved is most effective.[65] There is also interesting empirical research on the effectiveness of various enforcement models. Traditionally, economists would favour a harsh deterrence approach, with severe sanctions and high certainty of the imposition thereof. However, criminological research shows that many environmental violations are committed out of ignorance rather than intentionally.[66] If that is the case, an information strategy, following a compliance approach, might be more effective than a harsh deterrence approach. Generally, empirical research has indicated that a higher probability of detection (inter alia by improving inspection and monitoring efforts) has a higher deterrent effect than a severe expected sanction.[67]

7. Conclusion

In this chapter, we have indicated that there are different ways in which environmental crime and environmental criminal law can be approached. Obviously, in conducting environmental law research, no one method is necessarily more suitable than another. The appropriate method will largely depend upon the research questions posed. Moreover, in reality one will often need to employ an integrated, holistic approach in which several (and in some cases maybe even all) of the discussed approaches are combined. One could, for example, start with the dogmatic approach (presented in section 3) and analyse what specific values and legal interests are protected through the different legal provisions found in each legal system. In addition, one could analyse to what extent the various degrees of protection of environmental interests can be found in previous legislation that may no longer be in force, adopting a historical approach (as suggested in section 2). Moreover, there may be important differences

63 See, for example, M.G. Faure and R.A. Partain (n 39), p. 219.
64 Ibid., p. 223.
65 Ibid., pp. 225–7.
66 H.M. Princen and R.M.M. Vossen, 'Naleving en handhaving van regelgeving – loont het de moeite?' (2003) 29(9) *Justitiële Verkenningen* 54–69. We note that ignorance of the law generally is not a legal defence for the commission of crimes.
67 M.A. Cohen, 'Criminal law as an instrument of environmental policy: theory and empirics' in A. Hayes (ed), *Law and Economics of the Environment* (Cheltenham, UK and Northampton, MA: Edward Elgar Publishing, 2001), pp. 198–216.

between the ways in which various legal systems use criminal law to protect the environment, thus offering scope for a critical comparative perspective (section 4).

One of the crucial questions for economists and environmental scholars is to what extent different formulations of environmental crime provide both adequate protection of the environment and appropriate deterrent effects and incentives for compliance. That is one of the crucial questions of the law and economics approach that was presented in section 5. To conclude, in many research projects, the different theoretical approaches and doctrinal methods will have to be complemented by an empirical perspective. This can provide useful insights on the relationship between the inputs in environmental law enforcement on the one hand, and the output (in compliance terms) and the outcome (in terms of reaching improved environmental quality) on the other hand.

Finally, we do realise that environmental criminal law is only one of the many different methods that can be employed to remedy environmental harm. A crucial question is therefore what place environmental criminal law takes in the toolbox together with other instruments such as administrative and private law remedies.[68] In that respect, the contribution of criminal law will probably be modest, but nevertheless still an important one. Precisely for that reason, it remains important to pay attention to the various research methods, as these can make a significant contribution to gaining insights into the effectiveness of environmental criminal law.

---

68 See also S. Wright and V. Colvin's Chapter 7 Enforcement Undertakings as an Alternative to Prosecution in Australian Environmental Law Enforcement in this volume.

3

Transnational environmental crime across global supply chains: a place for due diligence?

Carolyn Abbot and Gary Lynch-Wood

1. Introduction

The planet faces severe challenges. Biodiversity and ecosystem services are, as is well reported, in decline.[1] Whilst global trade has created economic opportunities, driving growth and wealth generation, it has led to significant and negative impacts on nature and people.[2] Historically, international trade was dominated by goods produced in one country being distributed to consumers abroad. Now, approximately 70% of worldwide trade takes place in global value chains[3] where the stages of production – extraction to disposal – occur across countries and continents.[4] These complex global value chains, traversing national boundaries and involving multiple actors, have created new avenues and opportunities for transnational environmental crimes (TECs).

1 The global rate of species extinction is significantly higher than the average over the past ten million years and is set to accelerate, with approximately 25% of species already threatened with extinction. Intergovernmental Science-Policy Platform on Biodiversity and Ecosystem Services (IPBES), *The Global Assessment Report on Biodiversity and Ecosystem Services: Summary for Policy Makers* (2019), 11–12, available at https://www.ipbes.net/sites/default/files/inline/files/ipbes_global_assessment_report_summary_for_policymakers.pdf (last accessed 13 June 2024).

2 Ibid, 13.

3 Global value chains and global supply chains are different but interrelated concepts, with value chains aimed at enhancing competitive advantage. In this chapter, we largely use the concept of 'supply chain'. See Chiara Macchi, *Business, Human Rights and the Environment: The Evolving Agenda* (T.M.C. Asser Press, Netherlands 2022), 2.

4 OECD, *Trade Policy Implications of Global Value Chains* (2020), available at https://www.oecd.org/trade/topics/global-value-chains-and-trade/ (last accessed 13 June 2024).

Responsibility for TEC regulation and its enforcement ultimately rests with individual states and national agencies (for example police bodies, environmental regulators, port authorities). It is perhaps therefore unsurprising that there are significant differences in legal frameworks, including approaches to corporate criminal liability, and varying operational enforcement capacities. Julie Ayling notes how, in some jurisdictions, laws to address TEC are inadequate, and these crimes may be regarded as victimless and therefore low priority.[5] Alongside lax enforcement and low penalties if laws are enforced, national legal responses to TEC may therefore do little to combat TEC activity.[6] Combined with the fact that TEC takes place within a complex and shifting environment that raises extraterritoriality problems if one state is seen interfering in another's jurisdictional affairs, there is a glaring challenge for regulatory governance.

In this chapter, we consider the potential contribution that legitimate private enterprises could make to the TEC regulatory endeavour. Holding considerable influence across global supply chains, private enterprises could play an enhanced role in detecting and disrupting TEC activity. Borrowing from the regulation literature, their wealth, knowledge, capacity, and economic positioning within supply chains make them well placed to act as 'regulatory surrogates' and support the state in fighting TEC.[7] One way the state can harness the surrogate regulatory function of private enterprises may be emerging already, if slowly, which is mandatory due diligence.[8]

Due diligence has its origins in the United States (US) Securities Act of 1933. While imposing strict civil liability on persons who made untrue statements and omissions of material fact in a securities registration statement, there was a defence of 'reasonable investigation'.[9] The approach has been extended to other corporate and commercial domains, including acquisitions and mergers, and has now emerged as a tool for addressing corporate harms to human rights and the environment. Guidelines and soft law instruments such as the Organisation for Economic Co-operation and Development (OECD) *Guidelines for Multinational Enterprises*[10] and the associated

---

5 Julie Ayling, 'Prevention of Transnational Environmental Crime and Regulatory Pluralism' in Peter Drahos (ed), *Regulatory Theory: Foundations and Applications* (ANU Press, 2017).

6 Ibid.

7 There is no ideal way of determining a firm's influence or power within a supply chain. Legal measures often use employee numbers and/or turnover as a proxy. For recent approaches, see further section 6.

8 There are some notable examples of targeted due diligence requirements in the TEC space, for example the EU Timber Regulations (Regulation 995/2010). In this chapter, we are exploring an emerging set of measures which potentially have far greater economic and environmental reach.

9 Securities Act of 1933, section 11, available at https://www.govinfo.gov/content/pkg/COMPS-1884/pdf/COMPS-1884.pdf (last accessed 6 June 2024).

10 OECD, *OECD Guidelines for Multinational Enterprises on Responsible Business Conduct* (2023), available at https://www.oecd.org/investment/mne/ (last accessed 13 June 2024).

OECD *Due Diligence Guidance*[11] have evolved at the international level and represent an important step in the development of voluntary due diligence for social harms. However, it is the non-binding UN Guiding Principles on Business and Human Rights (UNGPs),[12] presented to the international community in 2011 and which offered an alternative, bottom-up approach to the global corporate human rights problem, that have been the main impetus for *mandatory* due diligence laws at national and regional levels.[13] These developments must at least be of interest owing to the close association between TEC activity and human rights abuses, and the acknowledgement in part of the literature that certain aspects of TEC indicate a lack of corporate due diligence.[14] TEC impacts local resources, affects health and livelihoods, drains state resources through corruption, and so forth.[15] That '[h]uman rights abuses and environmental crime often go hand in hand'[16] leads to the conclusion that addressing one just might go some way to addressing the other. In this chapter we explore some important and recent developments in mandatory due diligence regulation and reflect upon whether these initiatives are capable of mobilising private enterprises in helping to combat aspects of TEC.

The next section briefly considers the nature and scope of TEC. Then, in section 3, we turn to the dynamics of TEC activity that complicate the compliance and criminal

---

11 See OECD, *OECD Due Diligence Guidance for Responsible Business Conduct* (2018), available at https://www.oecd.org/investment/due-diligence-guidance-for-responsible-business-conduct.htm (last accessed 13 June 2024).

12 United Nations, *Guiding Principles on Business and Human Rights: Implementing the United Nations 'Protect, Respect and Remedy' Framework* (2011), available at https://www.ohchr.org/sites/default/files/documents/publications/guidingprinciplesbusinesshr_en.pdf (last accessed 13 June 2024).

13 The draft treaty on Business and Human Rights at the Human Rights Council represents an interesting development at the international level, one which, Macchi argues, would not have been possible before Ruggie's 'protect, respect and remedy' framework. The draft treaty defines state obligations relating to the impacts of business activities and includes a requirement that states, in preventing human rights abuses, shall require businesses to carry out human rights due diligence (Article 6). The latest draft text is available at https://www.ohchr.org/en/hr-bodies/hrc/wg-trans-corp/session10 (last accessed 10 June 2024). See generally Macchi (n 3) Ch 7.

14 See, for example Lieselot Bisschop, 'Illegal Trade in Hazardous Waste' in Lorraine Elliott and William H. Schaedla (eds), *Handbook of Transnational Environmental Crime* (Edward Elgar Publishing, Cheltenham, UK and Northampton, MA 2016).

15 Matthew Hall, *Exploring Green Crime: Introducing the Legal, Social and Criminological Contexts of Environmental Harm* (Palgrave MacMillan, UK 2015); Daan P. van Uhm and William D. Moreto, 'Corruption Within the Illegal Wildlife Trade: A Symbiotic and Antithetical Enterprise' (2018) 58(4) *British Journal of Criminology* 864, 885.

16 The Global Initiative Against Transnational Organised Crime, *The Global Response to Transnational Organized Environmental Crime* (January 2014), 5, available at https://globalinitiative.net/wp-content/uploads/2019/04/TGIATOC-The-Global-Response-to-Transnational-Organized-Environmental-Crime-web.pdf (last accessed 13 June 2024).

enforcement process at the domestic level, focusing primarily on private enterprise involvement. Section 4 introduces the concept of due diligence and considers its emergence in voluntary frameworks at the international level. Section 5 explores how the UNGPs have intensified the political appetite for mandatory measures in relation to human rights. Then, in section 6, we review emerging mandatory due diligence frameworks in France, Germany and at the European Union (EU) level, and reflect on their scope for dealing with TEC activities across supply chains. The concluding section suggests that mandatory due diligence is an important step forward, but that more defined and direct measures may be required to support traditional criminal law enforcement responses to cross-border environmental crime.

2. The scope and extent of transnational environmental crime

There is no universally agreed definition of TEC,[17] possibly because it occurs within a highly complex institutional and economic landscape. Generally speaking, it involves 'the movement across borders of species, resources, and pollutants in contravention of domestic law or in violation of prohibition or regulation regimes established by multilateral environmental agreements'.[18] International and regional environmental law (and relevant principles such as the no-harm and prevention principles) are important to the development of national legislation to combat TEC.[19] TEC is, however, a crime primarily at the national level, but with transnational dimensions, with acts and omissions (if ever detected and brought into the criminal justice system) subject to criminal procedures, penalties and sanctions. It is the cross-border, global and international dimension of TEC that distinguishes it from environmental crimes committed solely at the domestic level.

TEC is a concept that captures multiple offences and forms 'a category of crime in a socio-normative rather than a strictly legal sense.'[20] It can be conceived as operating across two broad categories: trafficking in natural resources and species (for example

---

17 See discussion in, for example, Rob White, *Transnational Environmental Crime: Toward an Eco-Global Criminology* (Willan Publishing, 2011) Ch 1.

18 Lorraine Elliott, 'Fighting Transnational Environmental Crime' (2012) 66(1) *Journal of International Affairs* 87, 89.

19 With some notable exceptions, existing multilateral environmental agreements do not provide any detail on the creation of domestic mechanisms in criminal law. For example, the Basel Convention on the Control of Transboundary Movements of Hazardous Wastes and their Disposal, Article 4 paragraph 3, considers illegal traffic in hazardous and other wastes to be criminal but leaves the design of criminal law mechanisms to nation states. See generally Gregory Rose, 'International Jurisdictional Challenges in the Suppression of Transnational Environmental Crime' in Elliott and Schaedla (n 14).

20 Lorraine Elliott and William H. Schaedla, 'Transnational Environmental Crime: Excavating the Complexities – An Introduction' in Elliott and Schaedla (n 14), 4.

illegally logged timber, endangered species) and trafficking in hazardous substances (for example ozone-depleting substances, waste).[21] These activities give rise to considerable and well-documented environmental and human health impacts. For instance, wildlife trafficking presents a serious threat to species and biodiversity,[22] the trade in illegally logged or stolen timber is a major cause of deforestation, resulting in the loss of species and habitats, and waste trafficking can contaminate both land and water and negatively affect human health and communities. Yet, the impacts of TEC extend beyond the environment and human health. The sheer range and scale of actors involved in TEC activities, a matter we turn to in section 3, speak to the much broader impact of TEC on sustainable development and environmental security.[23] Indeed, the control of TEC appeals to several of the Sustainable Development Goals (for example responsible production and consumption, life on land, sustainable communities),[24] with the loss of income through legitimate trade in, for instance, natural resources hampering economic development and exacerbating income inequalities.[25]

As noted earlier, environmental crime is not defined as an international crime. Rather, it relies on offences in domestic law that give effect to key international environmental treaties, including the 1973 Convention on International Trade in Endangered Species of Wild Fauna and Flora (CITES) and the 1989 Basel Convention on the Control of Transboundary Movements of Hazardous Waste and their Disposal. Despite the ongoing development of these existing multilateral environmental agreements, and an increase in funds allocated to the disruption of TEC networks, it remains a significant challenge and one that will inevitably worsen. After all, an increased scarcity of natural resources will, in all likelihood continue to attract transnational criminal activities.[26] Current estimates suggest the scale of environmental crime, in terms of

21 Glen Wright, 'Conceptualising and Combating Transnational Environmental Crime' (2011) 14 *Trends in Organised Crime* 332, 333.

22 For instance, the pangolin (a scaly anteater), listed in Appendix I of CITES, is one of the world's most targeted animals for illegal trade. With its meat being considered a delicacy and its scales and claws used in traditional medicines, over one million have been killed and trafficked in the past decade. See, for example, Christian Nellemann et al. (eds), *The Rise of Environmental Crime: A Growing Threat to Natural Resources, Peace, Development and Security*, a UNEP-INTERPOL rapid response assessment (UNEP, 2016), 43–5, available at https://www.unep.org/resources/report/rise-environmental-crime-growing-threat-natural-resources-peace-development-and (last accessed 13 June 2024). Also see, in this volume, Ludwig Krämer, Chapter 5 Biodiversity Crime and Angus Nurse, Chapter 8 The Global Illegal Wildlife Trade Crisis.

23 See, for example, Meredith L. Gore et al, 'Transnational environmental crime threatens sustainable development' (2019) 2 *Nature Sustainability* 784.

24 See generally https://sdgs.un.org/goals (last accessed 13 June 2024).

25 For a detailed and current account of the impacts of environmental crime, see UNEP, *The State of Knowledge of Crimes that Have Serious Impacts on the Environment* (2018), section 1.3, available at https://www.unep.org/resources/publication/state-knowledge-crimes-have-serious-impacts-environment (last accessed 13 June 2024).

26 Daan van Uhm and Rick Nijman, 'The Convergence of Environmental Crime With Other Serious Crimes: Subtypes Within the Environmental Crime Continuum' (2022)

annual loss of resources, is likely to be in the region of $91–259 billion, a rise of 26% from 2014 estimates.[27] It is fourth in the table of the most lucrative crimes globally, behind drug smuggling, counterfeiting and human trafficking, and has an annual growth rate of at least 5–7%, although for some species and commodities it may be as high as 21–28%.[28] In light of these figures, it seems an opportune moment to reflect upon whether alternative approaches to TEC prevention can assist in addressing the problem.

3. Transnational environmental crime as a law enforcement problem

The complexities of TEC are well known and indicate that multiple regulatory approaches are needed.[29] Take supply and demand drivers as an example. These vary depending on the TEC activity. Illegal trade in wildlife is largely demand-driven, with consumer or cultural preferences playing an important role in the trade of these 'lootable commodities'.[30] Illegal trade in hazardous waste tends to be supply-driven, clearly incentivised by the desire for low-cost waste disposal.[31] The use of direct regulation (underpinned by criminal liability) may be less effective at addressing the push and pull factors that influence different TEC activities, and would fail to provide positive incentives to influence, for instance, consumer demands.[32] Nevertheless, if well-designed and properly enforced, such an approach would have to be part of the regulatory mix. It can have both a general and specific deterrent impact and send a strong moral signal about the wrongfulness of such activities. The 'policing' of TEC is, however, complicated. As argued by Glen Wright, although much can be learnt from attempts to combat transnational organised crime more broadly, TEC is unique and multifaceted and requires a series of tailored enforcement responses.[33] We focus, in this section, on an important feature of TEC that further complicates the design of effective regulation, namely the plurality of potential offenders that operate across TEC networks. Private enterprises occupying key positions within global supply chains may of course be involved in illicit TEC activity. But for those acting lawfully, it is their position in supply chains that provides opportunities to address TEC activities, thereby complementing state approaches to compliance and enforcement of TEC laws.

19(4) *European Journal of Criminology* 542.

27 Nellemann et al. (n 22), 20. See also UNEP (n 25).

28 UNEP (n 25), 39.

29 See, for example White (n 17), Ch 1; Wright (n 21); Ayling (n 5).

30 Elliott and Schaedla (n 20), 5.

31 Ibid, 6.

32 See further Daniel W.S. Challender and Douglas C. MacMillan, 'Transnational Environmental Crime: More Than an Enforcement Response' in Elliott and Schaedla (n 14).

33 Wright (n 21).

TEC networks are broad, diverse and complex. They involve both legitimate and illegitimate actors, individuals (both opportunistic and organised), large-scale criminal organisations and more loosely organised groups, corrupt officials and private enterprises.[34] Individuals or networks of individuals – including poachers, smugglers and exporters/importers – may be involved in a range of offences from relatively low-scale to more serious crimes and may be embedded in a chain of environmental criminal activity. There are criminal networks that have been actively engaging in unlawful activities (in, say, drug trafficking) for some time but then turn to TEC activity for new sources of income.[35] In fact, much TEC is embedded in organised crime networks and shares some of the broader characteristics of transnational organised crime.[36] It is also not uncommon for corrupt government officials to facilitate TECs, with one report noting that 'along supply chains and at the source of many natural resource markets, corruption manifests itself along a spectrum from low-legal bribery to grand corruption'.[37] In some countries, the corruption and bribery associated with TEC is endemic, undermines attempts to embed 'good governance [and corrodes] the institutions of the state and compromise core values such as the rule of law'.[38] The range of perpetrators working within these criminal networks will vary according to both the type and scope of the offence(s) and the geographical dimension of their operations.

---

[34] Ibid, 338.

[35] A recent strategic report from INTERPOL that considers the nexus between organised crime and pollution crime found, from a study of 27 pollution crime cases (19 of which related to transnational crimes), that the perpetrators could be classified into two categories: centralised criminal groups and mafia clans, and decentralised networks and chains of individual suspects. These groups not only specialise in specific TEC activities such as wildlife trafficking or waste disposal but include well-known organised criminal groups involved in other forms of illicit activity such as human trafficking. See INTERPOL, *Strategic Report: The Nexus Between Organised Crime and Pollution Crime* (June 2022), 19–21, available at https://www.interpol.int/en/Crimes/Environmental-crime/Pollution-crime (last accessed 13 June 2024).

[36] The UN Convention against Transnational Organized Crime (15 November 2000) and associated Protocols (commonly referred to as the Palermo Convention) are the main international instruments in the fight against transnational organised crime.

[37] Global Initiative Against Transnational Organized Crime, *Expanding the Toolkit to Tackle Organized Environmental Crime: Recommendations for the G7 Ministers* (June 2021), 5, available at https://globalinitiative.net/wp-content/uploads/2021/06/Expanding-the-toolkit-to-tackle-organized-environmental-crime-Recommendations-for-the-G7-ministers-GITOC.pdf (last accessed 13 June 2024). Drawing on INTERPOL's report on pollution crime (n 35), a key characteristic of the 27 cases included in the study is the ability of criminal organisations to infiltrate public officials at both the local and national levels who may, for instance, facilitate criminal activity by providing confidential information, altering official documentation or inhibiting enforcement action.

[38] Elliott (n 18), 94.

Private enterprises, the focus of this chapter, are also involved with TEC for a variety of reasons and in different ways. Owners and operators of legitimate companies may knowingly and intentionally turn to illicit criminal activity to reduce production costs, the risk of which will inevitably increase as, for example, waste disposal costs rise or raw material costs increase. A recent Europol assessment of environmental crime notes that waste crimes have traditionally been committed by criminals disposing of waste on behalf of companies seeking to avoid costs associated with legal waste disposal.[39] The notorious and much-reported Trafigura case in 2006 provides a notable example.[40] Beyond any direct and deliberate involvement in TEC activity, private enterprises may also unwittingly find themselves complicit through their corporate relationships with other seemingly legitimate firms in the global supply chain. As noted by Meredith Gore and colleagues, multinational corporations 'relying on the development of, and manufacturing from, natural resources can have legal supply chains exploited by TEC offenders …'.[41] In short, at any point in the global supply chain, private enterprises may be involved in TEC, from the company that forges documents that signal a consignment of legitimate chemicals mixed with banned ozone-depleting substances, to the manufacturer that receives timber from a logging company that exceeds quotas.[42]

Given the complexity of the global supply chain and the multiplicity of geographically dispersed legitimate private enterprises that participate, identifying TEC activity is a significant challenge for law enforcement. First, supply chains are not necessarily designed for transparency. Private enterprises and suppliers often fear that divulging too much information would undermine competitiveness or expose them to criticism.[43] Second, illicit markets may operate alongside and become concealed within

---

39 Europol, *Environmental Crime in the Age of Climate Change* (2022), available at https://www.europol.europa.eu/cms/sites/default/files/documents/Environmental_Crime_in_the_Age_of_Climate_Change_threat_assessment_2022.pdf (last accessed 13 June 2024).

40 Trafigura, a private, multinational independent oil trading company, dumped dangerous and toxic waste created by the 'caustic washing' of gasoline blend stocks (this washing took place at sea with the resultant waste stored in the slop tanks of the *Probo Koala* tanker) at several sites in the city of Abidjan in the Ivory Coast. Trafigura had arranged for the slop waste to be unloaded and treated by a local company called Tommy Ltd, which had been incorporated ten days before the arrival of the tanker. For a useful summary, see Environmental Justice Organisations, Liabilities and Trade (EJOLT), 'The Trafigura Case' (August 2015), available at http://www.ejolt.org/2015/08/trafigura-case/ (last accessed 13 June 2024).

41 Gore et al. (n 23), 785.

42 See, for example the discussion of 'sham recyling' of e-waste in Reece Walters and Maria Angeles Fuentes Loureiro, 'Waste Crime and the Global Transference of Hazardous Substances: A Southern Green Perspective' (2020) 28 *Critical Criminology* 463.

43 Alexis Bateman and Leonardo Bonanni, 'What Supply Chain Transparency Really Means', *Harvard Business Review* (20 August 2019), available at https://hbr.org/2019/08/what-supply-chain-transparency-really-means (last accessed 13 June 2024).

licit markets. Illegally logged timber is often mixed in with shipments of legally sourced and traded wood, which makes it difficult to combat the illegal trade.[44] This highlights the vulnerability of legitimate businesses across the supply chain. Third, and closely linked to the previous point, criminal networks are operationally sophisticated. Take transnational waste crime. Over the past ten years, criminals have operated directly within the legal waste management sector[45] and have used legitimate businesses, with relevant licences and authorisations, to store, transfer and dispose of waste. For example, Lieselot Bisschop, in her illuminating discussion of illegal trade in hazardous waste, notes that e-waste may unknowingly be sold to illegal waste collectors, signalling a lack of due diligence in waste management processes.[46] The challenges for legitimate enterprises extend beyond transnational waste crimes. For instance, the illegal trade in molluscs on the European food market generates profits of several million euros annually. The criminal network will ultimately sell the molluscs to legal fishmongers, with fraudulent documents labelling the molluscs as originating from permitted areas.[47]

Even multinational corporations are not immune from exposure to TEC in the global supply chain. It was revealed recently that Ikea had for some years sold children's furniture made from wood linked to illegal logging in protected Russian forests.[48] A two-year investigation by the US Environmental Investigation Agency, a non-governmental organisation (NGO), led to accusations that a major Austrian timber company supplying DIY stores across Europe had offered to buy illegal timber. The report alleges Holzindustrie Schweighofer willingly and knowingly accepted illegally harvested timber and that it had used a bonus system to incentivise additional cutting.[49] Yet, given that the company sources its timber from over 1000 different suppliers, it would be a significant task to exclude illegally sourced timber from its supply

44 Sophie Saydan, 'Criminality and Costs: The Human Toll of Transnational Environmental Crime' in Elliott and Schaedla (n 14), 95–6.
45 Europol (n 39), 13–14.
46 Bisschop (n 14).
47 Europol (n 39), 32–3.
48 Jane Dalton, 'Ikea Sold Children's Furniture "Made of Illegally-Logged Russian Wood"', *The Independent* (16 July 2021), available at https://www.independent.co.uk/climate-change/news/ikea-children-furniture-illegal-wood-b1884276.html last accessed 13 June 2024. As noted in Global Initiative Against Transnational Organised Crime (n 37), 5–6: '[A]longside the legitimate trade in timber comes an insatiable illegal trade resulting in deforestation on a mass scale and timber traded in vast quantities, laundered through countries, relabelled and sold into industry across the globe.'
49 Environmental Investigation Agency, *Stealing the Last Forest: Austria's Largest Timber Company, Land Rights, and Corruption in Romania* (October 2015), available at https://us.eia.org/report/st/#:~:text=EIA's%20report%2C%20Stealing%20the%20Last,illegalities%20prevailing%20in%20Romania's%20forests (last accessed 13 June 2024). Article 3(2)(p) of the recently enacted Directive 2024/1203 of 11 April 2024 on the protection of the environment through criminal law is drafted to bring this type of activity into domestic criminal law.

chain. The important point to note is that these legitimate businesses may be vehicles for TEC.

4. An introduction to due diligence

The previous section gives a brief insight into the complexity of TEC. Global supply chains, working across jurisdictional boundaries, present opportunities for offenders to engage in TEC activity. It is therefore important to think creatively about ways of strengthening the state's hand in TEC detection and prevention and explore a more pluralistic approach to regulation which uses 'combinations of instruments invoking first, second and third parties rather than the state alone'.[50] By leveraging their resources and influence, and encouraging them to take greater agency over their adverse impacts (including environmental impacts), private enterprises could play a more significant role.[51] In short, they could act as 'regulatory surrogates'.[52]

One means of co-opting the influence of private enterprises is through due diligence. This could provide a way of ensuring that companies operating within supply chains maintain standards of good practice. But what is due diligence and what does it involve? Due diligence is a preventative and risk-based tool for assisting and improving decisions. Broadly, it refers to the actions an entity can be expected to take to prevent harm, that is, to ensure a future or ongoing activity is feasible or safe, that it meets required standards, or that reasonable care is used to eliminate or minimise negative outcomes.[53] Due diligence can involve a review or audit of relevant economic, legal or social circumstances, and may include information gathering, background searches, record keeping, performance appraisals and data evaluation. It can be undertaken prior to a transaction or activity to determine whether it should proceed (for example business transactions such as a corporate merger). Or it can be performance-based and ongoing to establish if an in-progress pursuit conforms to standards (for example to assess whether it is compliant or meets norms or industry values).

Whilst due diligence was traditionally used for decision making in relation to more narrowly defined commercial developments such as acquisitions, its reach has been extended significantly. Due diligence frameworks now address a broader range of issues (including environment and human rights), where the purpose is to mitigate or

50 Neil Gunningham, 'Integrating Management Systems and Occupational Health and Safety Regulation' (1999) 26 *Journal of Law and Society* 192, 214.
51 See generally Ayling (n 5).
52 For an overview of the literature, see Carolyn Abbot, 'Bridging the Gap: Non-State Actors and the Challenges of Regulating New Technology' (2012) 39(3) *Journal of Law and Society* 329.
53 Due diligence norms are definitionally complex. For an insightful discussion of due diligence and 'adverse environmental impact' see Colin Mackie, 'Due Diligence in Global Value Chains: Conceptualizing "Adverse Environmental Impact"' (2021) 30(3) *RECIEL* 297.

avoid adverse social impacts associated with commercial and industrial operations. In the social domain, due diligence has, at least until recently, tended to be a voluntary undertaking, with external stakeholders (consumers, investors and commercial parties, for example) placing increased pressure on firms to 'freely' engage in responsible social, human rights and environmental practices, and to improve risk management processes. Guidelines and soft law instruments have been developed to assist and enhance the process and to make due diligence frameworks more rigorous. For example, the OECD *Guidelines for Multinational Enterprises* (MNE Guidelines), recently updated in June 2023, provide the leading normative guidance on responsible business conduct.[54] Under General Policy 11, enterprises should 'carry out risk-based due diligence … to identify, prevent and mitigate actual and potential adverse impacts …'. Building on the MNE Guidelines, the OECD *Due Diligence Guidance for Responsible Business Conduct* was adopted in June 2018, becoming the first government-backed reference to due diligence applying to all businesses and sectors.[55] Specific guidance is provided for high-impacting sectors such as minerals, extractives, agriculture, clothing and footwear. Although the OECD framework is not legally binding, it has instilled among governments and other stakeholders a common understanding of due diligence for responsible conduct. Furthermore, despite its voluntary nature, numerous firms have acted on the Guidance with a view to embedding due diligence processes.[56]

In many respects, the MNE Guidelines are also progressive from a governance perspective, moving beyond a purely self-regulatory approach by requiring states to establish National Contact Points (NCPs) for Responsible Business Conduct. The purpose of these NCPs is twofold, namely '"to promote awareness and uptake of the Guidelines … [and to] contribute to the resolution of issues that arise in relation to the implementation of the Guidelines in specific instances'.[57] NCPs are non-judicial grievance mechanisms that offer a non-adversarial approach to conflict resolution and may involve mediation between parties. Although NCPs have the potential to promote the effective implementation of the Guidelines, most are under-resourced, lack visibility and are 'largely toothless, with governments and NCPs refusing to adopt both essential carrots and sticks to encourage meaningful engagement and outcomes'.[58] Despite

---

54 OECD (n 10).

55 OECD (n 11).

56 Stefano Spinaci, 'Corporate Sustainability Due Diligence: How to Integrate Human Rights and Environmental Concerns in Value Chains' (European Parliament, May 2023), available at https://www.europarl.europa.eu/RegData/etudes/BRIE/2022/729424/EPRS_BRI(2022)729424_EN.pdf (last accessed 13 June 2024).

57 OECD (n 10), 56.

58 Marian G. Ingrams, 'The 2023 Update of the OECD Guidelines sets Stronger Standards for Companies but Weak Expectations for Governments – High and Lowlights from the New Text' (2023) 8 *Business and Human Rights Journal* 427, 432. For further discussion of NCPs, see Kari Otteburn and Axel Marx, 'Seeking Remedies for Corporate Human Rights Abuses: What is the Contribution of OECD National Contact Points?' in Axel Marx et al. (eds), *Research Handbook on Global Governance, Business and*

challenges in implementation, the global reach of NCPs has the potential to make a meaningful contribution to human rights and environmental abuses. Given that their remit extends to transnational cases where, for instance, the company subject to a complaint is domiciled in one country but the victims are in another, they could play an important role in addressing TEC.

Despite these developments, both the OECD MNE Guidelines and the Due Diligence Guidance are, as mentioned, non-binding and have often proved ill-suited to tackling complex challenges posed by global supply chains.[59] To what extent can companies be trusted to engage in a process and use valuable resources when there are no obligations to do so? If companies do engage, how far will their commitments go, and how likely are they to 'greenwash'? Such questions, coupled with increasing social and environmental problems, have led to the emergence of mandatory due diligence frameworks, some of which have links to TEC. One of the most significant developments has been in the area of human rights, which, as mentioned above, could have implications for TEC. New and emerging legal due diligence obligations have been stimulated, to some extent, by the UNGPs.[60] The Principles are broad in scope, going beyond due diligence, as they encourage states to adopt a mix of mandatory and voluntary approaches (for example guidance, incentives, sanctions, liability)[61] to tackling corporate human rights abuses. That said, and following a lengthy process, national and regional legal due diligence standards are emerging as one of the primary tools for achieving the objectives of the UNGPs. We now turn to the Principles and consider some of the emerging legal frameworks.

Human Rights (Edward Elgar Publishing, Cheltenham, UK and Northampton, MA 2022); Karin Buhmann, 'Confronting Challenges to Substantive Remedy for Victims: Opportunities for OECD National Contact Points under a Due Diligence Regime Involving Civil Liability' (2023) 8 *Business and Human Rights Journal* 403.

59 Macchi (n 3), Ch 5, and Lise Smit et al., *Study on Due Diligence Requirements Through the Supply Chain* (European Commission Publications Office, 2020), Section IV, available at https://op.europa.eu/en/publication-detail/-/publication/8ba0a8fd-4c83-11ea-b8b7-01aa75ed71a1/language-en (last accessed 13 June 2024).

60 Much has been written about the Guiding Principles. See for example John Ruggie, Caroline Rees, and Rachel Davis, 'Ten Years After: From UN Guiding Principles to Multi-Fiduciary Obligations' (2021) 6 *Business and Human Rights Journal* 179; Rashmi Venkatesan, 'The UN Framework on Business and Human Rights: A Workers' Rights Critique' (2019) 157 *Journal of Business Ethics* 635; Matthew Murphy and Jordi Vives, 'Perceptions of Justice and the Human Rights Protect, Respect, and Remedy Framework' (2013) 116 *Journal of Business Ethics* 781; Björn Fasterling and Geert Demuijnck, 'Human Rights in the Void? Due Diligence in the UN Guiding Principles on Business and Human Rights' (2013) 116 *Journal of Business Ethics* 799.

61 Ibid, Ruggie, Rees and Davis (n 60), 189.

5. The UN Guiding Principles: towards (mandatory) due diligence

The UNGPs have become an authoritative statement in policy on the responses to corporate human rights abuses.[62] Particularly during the 1990s, there were growing concerns over the harmful impacts of corporate activities. Set against a backdrop of increased liberalisation of international trade rules, growing numbers of economically and politically powerful multinational corporations and increases in foreign direct investment in developing economies, the concerns were laid bare by notable examples of abuse (for example sweatshops and the apparel and footwear industries in Asia).[63] In short, the criticisms of globalisation and an increasingly dominant corporate sector were leading to pressures for action regarding corporations and global supply chains.

Building on the (later abandoned) 2003 UN Norms on Transnational Corporations and Other Business Enterprises with Regard to Human Rights,[64] John Ruggie, a Harvard University professor who had been instrumental in establishing the UN Global Compact, was appointed as Special Representative of the Secretary-General (SRSG) in 2005. He was given a broad mandate to identify issues and standards of corporate responsibility and his work eventually spread over three phases. From 2005, there was a mapping and research exercise that considered the scope of abuses across states and firms. The second phase, in 2008, saw the presentation of a new framework for safeguarding rights.[65] This framework had three normative pillars: the *State duty to protect* against human rights abuses by third parties, the *business responsibility to respect* rights, and access to judicial and non-judicial *remedies*. The framework was widely endorsed by stakeholders, including states and corporations. The mandate of SRSG was extended for a third operational phase, to 2011, so that the framework could

---

62 See Surya Deva and David Bilchitz (eds), *Human Rights Obligations of Business: Beyond the Corporate Responsibility to Respect?* (Cambridge University Press, Cambridge 2013).

63 See, James Harrison, 'Establishing a Meaningful Human Rights Due Diligence Process for Corporations: Learning from Experience of Human Rights Impact Assessment' (2013) 31 *Impact Assessment and Project Appraisal* 107; Josh Greenberg and Graham Knight, 'Framing Sweatshops: Nike, Global Production, and the American News Media' (2004) 1(2) *Communication and Critical/Cultural Studies* 151.

64 See David Weissbrodt and Muria Kruger, 'Norms on the Responsibilities of Transnational Corporations and Other Business Enterprises with Regard to Human Rights' (2003) 97 *American Journal of International Law* 901; Pini Pavel Miretski and Sascha-Dominik Bachmann, 'The UN "Norms on the Responsibility of Transnational Corporations and Other Business Enterprises with Regard to Human Rights": A Requiem' (2012) 17 *Deakin Law Review* 5.

65 UNGPs (n 12).

be developed.[66] This eventually led to the full report on the UNGPs, which was presented in 2011.

Briefly, the UNGPs aim to provide substance and direction to the three normative pillars of *state duty, business responsibilities* and *remedies*. They set out what states should do to protect rights and how private enterprises could respect them by acting responsibly. Never intended to signal the end of the process, the Principles were to be understood in their dynamic dimension and capacity over time to advance new norms, practices, and targeted and coordinated actions.[67] The first pillar provides that states have the primary duty to protect against corporate human rights abuses within their jurisdiction. It is seldom mentioned, but it is nevertheless explicit within the text that environmental laws, and the appropriate enforcement of such laws, are germane to business respect for human rights. States should therefore 'consider whether such laws are currently being enforced effectively, and if not, why this is the case and what measures may reasonably correct the situation'.[68] What is more, to meet their duties, states should consider the introduction of regulatory or other such measures (for example due diligence) if regarded appropriate for the national context and they should consider additional measures if an enterprise is owned or controlled or receives substantial support and services from the state. The second pillar concerns the responsibility of business to respect human rights within and across its operations, which, as has been made clear, should include avoiding adverse human rights impacts through environmental harm.[69] Again, while companies are given a range of responsibilities, the usefulness of due diligence as a potential business tactic is outlined in some detail in the UNGPs. It is stressed under Principle 15, for example, that businesses should have in place policies and processes appropriate to their circumstances, including a 'human rights due diligence process to identify, prevent, mitigate and account for how they address their impacts'. Principle 17 elaborates on the parameters of due diligence, emphasising how the proper process should include assessing actual and potential impacts, integrating and acting upon findings, tracking responses, and communicating how any impacts are addressed. While it is acknowledged that due diligence processes will be context-sensitive, depending on issues such as business size and scale, a robust approach should cover impacts deriving from a company's activities, operations, products, services as well as business relationships. The third pillar relates to access to judicial and non-judicial remedies. Clearly, robust

66 Astrid Sanders, 'The Impact of the "Ruggie Framework" and the United Nations Guiding Principles on Business and Human Rights on Transnational Human Rights Litigation', LSE Law, Society and Economy Working Papers 18/2014, available at https://papers.ssrn.com/sol3/papers.cfm?abstract_id=2457983 (last accessed 12 June 2024).

67 César Rodríguez-Garavito, cited in Ruggie, Rees and Davis (n 60).

68 UNGPs (n 12), 5. This is the commentary to Principle 3 of the UNGPs.

69 On this link between business, human rights and the environment, see United Nations Human Rights Special Procedures, *Framework Principles on Human Rights and the Environment* (2018).

due diligence processes would provide access to appropriate state- and non-state-based resolutions and sanctions.

Due diligence is undeniably an important feature of the UN framework and the response to corporate human rights abuses. It has been described as a norm of expected conduct,[70] as rooted in a transnational social norm rather than an international legal norm,[71] and as going 'beyond the corporate governance standard of risk management to include a whole range of purposes'.[72] John Ruggie and colleague John Sherman suggest due diligence 'serves to meet a company's social license to operate, not its legal license', and that it exists over and above legal requirements and 'applies irrespective of what states do or do not do'.[73] It is, however, the legal responses that we are interested in and which need further consideration. The Principles do not impose legal requirements on states or businesses, nor are they capable of doing so due to their non-binding status. Yet, owing to the UNGPs and their impacts on the discourse and topography of human rights politics and policy, there is considerable momentum for a more robust set of actions and an increasing regulatory focus on business and human rights (for example reporting). Importantly, there is now, in several jurisdictions, an emerging suite of legal due diligence measures.[74] In view of the highlighted association between environment and human rights and the fact that the environment is explicitly part of the UNGPs, it is important to consider the changing legal landscape and to reflect on whether it is capable of addressing aspects of the TEC problem.

6. Emerging legal frameworks for mandatory due diligence

Despite not providing an obligation on states to implement legislative measures on due diligence, it is clear that the UNGPs have started to influence national and regional laws.[75] A brief survey of developments reveals a slowly shifting landscape,

---

70 Office of the High Commissioner for Human Rights, *Corporate Human Rights Due Diligence: Emerging Practices, Challenges and Ways Forward: Summary of the report of the Working Group on Business and Human Rights* (2018), available at https://www.ohchr.org/sites/default/files/Documents/Issues/Business/ExecutiveSummaryA73163.pdf (last accessed 13 June 2024).

71 John Ruggie and John Sherman III, 'The Concept of "Due Diligence" in the UN Guiding Principles on Business and Human Rights: A Reply to Jonathan Bonnitcha and Robert McCorquodale' (2017) 28 *European Journal of International Law* 921, 923.

72 Olga Martin-Ortega, 'Human Rights Due Diligence for Corporations: From Voluntary Standards to Hard Law at Last?' (2014) 32 *Netherlands Quarterly of Human Rights* 44, 56.

73 Ruggie and Sherman (n 71), 923–4.

74 Ruggie, Rees and Davis (n 60).

75 Surya Deva, 'Mandatory Human Rights Due Diligence Laws in Europe: A Mirage for Rightsholders?' (2023) 36 *Leiden Journal of International Law* 389; Markus Krajewski, Kristel Tonstad and Franziska Wohltmann, 'Mandatory Human Rights Due Diligence in Germany and Norway: Stepping, or Striding, in the Same Direction?' (2021) 6 *Business and Human Rights Journal* 550.

with several jurisdictions (for example Finland, Switzerland, Australia, Italy, Norway) having implemented – or being in the process of or having committed themselves to implementing – laws that adopt a due diligence model in the human rights and environmental context. That said, these models are far from uniform in terms of substance, reach and method. They can be general, lacking specificity and focus (for example no explicit reference to crime), and are thus questionable not only in terms of the extent to which they align with the expectations of the UNGPs[76] but also with regard to whether they are able to tackle specific and complex problems such as TEC. A comprehensive evaluation of all developments is not possible in this chapter, so this section outlines three particular examples of corporate due diligence legislation from France, Germany and the EU. While the models share some common features, there are some important differences, and all three models, we argue, are limited in their application to TEC.

Inspired in part by the UNGPs, the 2017 French Duty of Vigilance law, although a tort-based as much as a regulatory measure, creates a programme of legal liability.[77] It was an important milestone with France becoming the first state to enact such a law. The law requires large companies to establish, implement and publish an effective vigilance plan that includes reasonable vigilance measures capable of identifying risks and preventing severe impacts on 'human rights and fundamental freedoms, health and safety of persons and the environment'.[78] The companies directly affected are those incorporated or registered in France for two consecutive fiscal years that either employ at least 5 000 people themselves and through their French subsidiaries or employ at least 10 000 people themselves and through their subsidiaries located in France and abroad.[79] Foreign companies with 10 000 employees worldwide, which are not headquartered in France, are beyond the law's scope, even if some of their employees are employed by French subsidiaries. Estimates suggest that over 150 companies are affected, and these companies are required to identify impacts not only resulting from their own activities, but also from companies they control and subcontractors and suppliers with whom they have established commercial relationships.[80] In terms of substance, companies must develop a plan outlining appropriate measures taken to prevent and avoid human rights and environmental harms caused by business activities. Business activities are not defined and are therefore left broad and open-ended. The vigilance plan should map and assess risks within the business and across supply chains, set out mitigation measures, develop (in partnership with trade unions) an alert mechanism, and establish a monitoring scheme to evaluate the effectiveness of implementation. A notable feature of the due diligence law is that firms are required to publicly disclose plans during the development process, a move designed to enable stakeholder engagement.

---

76 Smit (n 59).

77 Duty of Vigilance of Parent and Instructing Companies Law No. 2017-399.

78 Duty of Vigilance Law Article 1.

79 Ibid; Deva (n 75).

80 Duty of Vigilance Law Article 1.

The seemingly extensive reach of the French due diligence obligations across the supply chain reflects a surrogacy approach to regulation, but it is not without its challenges and limitations, including its application to TEC. The law applies, inter alia, to 'environmental damage' with no attempt to further define the scope of due diligence in that context. Furthermore, and consistent with both the German and EU due diligence models discussed further below, there is no reference to damage caused by environmental crime (at either the domestic or the transnational level) or indeed the impact of environmental crime on human rights. Whilst the French law is broad enough to capture TEC, in the sense that it is not excluded, firms have discretion to select the scope and scale of their vigilance and disclosure measures, and evidence suggests that corporations are indeed adopting a rather restrictive approach and 'have a long way to go to establish adequate due diligence systems'.[81] There are, of course, enforcement and liability mechanisms. Although there is no state body charged with ensuring the implementation of the law, a person with a legitimate interest can send a formal notice to any company who, they allege, has failed to publish or has published an inadequate plan, with the court being the ultimate arbiter of non-compliance. Furthermore, any person who can establish an interest can seek damages for harm if a company fails to comply with its vigilance obligations. Holding corporations to account, however, remains challenging. Whilst both these mechanisms provide for legal accountability and therefore may have an indirect impact on the combatting of TEC, their effectiveness will be determined by the availability (or not) of a well-informed and willing 'complainant' who has the resources to use the legal avenues provided.[82] Furthermore, given the historic lack of transparency within and across supply chains, information is power in this regard; the 'politics of knowledge that are embedded in highly asymmetrical constellations of power represent a major hurdle, both in relation to corporate reporting and to litigation cases against [corporations]'.[83]

Germany has also been at the forefront of legal developments in corporate due diligence and has adopted a similar, though at the same time different, approach. Interestingly, not only did the German Federal Government decide to adopt national legislation, but it also urged and worked towards binding rules at a EU level (see below). In terms of national legislation, the Act on Corporate Due Diligence Obligations in Supply Chains (the Supply Chain Act) came into effect on 1 January 2023. It was, again, an important and ambitious milestone, for it provided new standards on responsible corporate practices, including binding due diligence rules on certain corporations within the supply chain.[84] The potential reach of the Supply Chain Act is wider than that of the French law. It is targeted at companies that have their headquarters or a

81 Almut Schilling-Vacaflor, 'Putting the French Duty of Vigilance Law in Context: Towards Corporate Accountability for Human Rights Violations in the Global South?' (2021) 22 *Human Rights Review* 109, 123.

82 Deva (n 75).

83 Schilling-Vacaflor (n 81).

84 The Act, in section 2(5), defines the supply chain as all products and services of an enterprise and as including all steps – in Germany and abroad – necessary to deliver these goods and services, from extraction to delivery.

branch in Germany. Initially (from 2023), it covered firms that have 3000 or more employees; from 2024 this was reduced to 1000 or more. Smaller firms are not directly affected, although the law will have an indirect effect if they supply to a larger German company (albeit the Act's regulatory reach in this regard is somewhat limited).[85] The measure is estimated to directly affect around 3000 companies.[86]

In contrast to the French Duty of Vigilance law, the Supply Chain Act provides a greater level of legal detail on the precise scope of the due diligence obligations in relation to human rights and environment-related risks. Section 3 sets out nine due diligence obligations, and further details on each of these are provided in sections 4 through to 10. The obligations include establishing a risk management system, designating within the company a responsible person or persons, establishing complaints procedures, and reporting on the fulfilment of obligations and on how the enterprise assesses the impact and effectiveness of any measures. Where risks are identified in the course of carrying out due diligence, the enterprise must take preventative measures without undue delay.[87] In the case of an actual or imminent violation of a human rights-related or environment-related obligation, the company must take 'appropriate remedial action to prevent, end or minimise the extent of the violation'.[88] If a company is found to be non-compliant, there are several enforcement and liability mechanisms. In contrast with the French provision, a state body, the Federal Office for Economic Affairs and Export Control, has monitoring and enforcement obligations under the Act.[89] An enterprise with an annual turnover of more than €400 million can be given an administrative fine of up to 2% of global annual turnover. A firm fined more than €175000 can be excluded from public contracts for up to three years. Civil processing (a 'special capacity to sue') is also part of the enforcement process. Trade unions and non-governmental bodies can litigate on behalf of affected people, although the costs, time and information asymmetries will again act as significant hurdles even if they were to pursue risks and impacts relating to TEC.

The question then is what does this mean for TEC? As with the French Duty of Vigilance law, there is no obligation on enterprises to identify environmental crime, or indeed TEC. We can also draw attention to certain provisions of the Act which may weaken any impact it may have on combatting TEC. First, in contrast to the French law, the Supply Chain Act provides more legal detail on the nature and scope

---

85 See section 9, which states that due diligence obligations in regard to indirect suppliers only arise where an enterprise has 'substantiated knowledge' of a human rights or environment-related violation.

86 See, for example 'The German Supply Chain Act: Navigating third-party risks through effective due diligence', LSEG (21 April 2023), available athttps://www.lseg.com/en/insights/risk-intelligence/the-german-supply-chain-act-navigating-third-party-risks-through-effective-due-diligence#:~:text=Starting%201%20January%202023%2C%20the,as%20any%20likely%20reputational%20damage (last accessed 6 June 2024).

87 Supply Chain Act, section 6.

88 Supply Chain Act, section 7.

89 Supply Chain Act, section 19.

of business risks, but the approach to environment-related risks is set out 'in a very limited manner'.[90] In defining such risks, the Act lists three international conventions, namely the 2013 Minamata Convention on Mercury, the 2001 Stockholm Convention on Persistent Organic Pollutants and the 1989 Basel Convention on the Control of Transboundary Movements of Hazardous Wastes. While activities prohibited under all three international agreements have the potential to fall within our definition of TEC, the measure raises questions over the extent to which corporations can effectively be held to account for these global standards. We suggest that while the German law extends corporate due diligence to these particular environmental risks, it does so with rules that are vague and lacking proper definition. Outside of that prescriptive list, the environment is only protected indirectly as it relates to human rights where, for instance, water pollution 'denies a person access to safe and clean drinking water'.[91] The Act 'fails to effectively protect ecological concerns from the environmentally damaging influences of entrepreneurial activity in the supply chain' and therefore its impact on TEC is diluted.[92]

It could be argued that by providing specific references to international conventions with a TEC dimension, the Supply Chain Act is at least a step forward. Here, we would make two interrelated observations. First (and most obviously), there are numerous TECs that are not covered by the German law directly. Second, we can also reflect on whether listing conventions in this way will encourage enterprises to focus exclusively on those conventions, thereby narrowing the potential scope of due diligence. Perhaps unsurprisingly, German NGOs and labour unions have, as a result, called for a more general environmental clause in the Act, similar to the provisions of the French Duty of Vigilance Law.[93]

Finally, the developments that have taken place in several European states have paved the way for mandatory due diligence measures in the EU.[94] In one of the most significant regulatory developments, given its geographical scope and potential reach into the corporate domain, the European Directive on corporate sustainability and due diligence (CSDDD) epitomises the view that companies can play a more positive role in protecting both the environment and human rights through enhanced governance of their value chains and those with whom they have established business

---

[90] Krajewski, Tonstad and Wohltmann (n 75).

[91] For details, see Supply Chain Act, section 2(9).

[92] Anne-Christin Mittwoch and Fernanda Luisa Bremenkamp, 'The German Supply Chain Act – A Sustainable Regulatory Framework for Internationally Active Market Players?' (2023) 55 *Review of European and Comparative Law* 189, 198.

[93] See Lillie Hafner and Hendrik Simon, 'A Gap between Social and Ecological Rights: A Commentary after One Year of the German Supply Chain Due Diligence Act', PRIF Blog (4 April 2024), available at https://blog.prif.org/2024/04/04/a-gap-between-social-and-ecological-rights-a-commentary-after-one-year-of-the-german-supply-chain-due-diligence-act/ (last accessed 6 June 2024).

[94] Krajewski, Tonstad and Wohltmann (n 75).

relationships.[95] Designed to harmonise legal frameworks across Member States and ensure a greater degree of legal certainty, it reinforces the association between sustainability, human rights and sound environmental management and governance.[96] While the level of ambition was weakened during the negotiation process, particularly in relation to employee and turnover thresholds amid concerns over its impact on a struggling European economy,[97] it nevertheless represents an important step forward. At a basic level, the law requires certain companies with activities in the EU to conduct due diligence in their own operations and across their supply chains. The law will apply progressively, starting in 2027 with companies with over 5000 employees and worldwide turnover higher than €1.5 billion, moving eventually, in 2029, to companies with 1000 employees and worldwide turnover higher than €450 million.[98] It will also apply to non-EU companies if they have a net turnover of more than €450 million, as well as companies that have franchising and licencing agreements, in the EU. Under Article 5, 'Member States shall ensure that companies conduct risk-based human rights and environmental due diligence' by carrying out certain designated actions, including the integration of due diligence processes into their policies and risk management systems and identification, prevention and remediation of potential adverse impacts.

Overall, the CSDDD's approach to due diligence shares much with the German model, discussed above, as does the Directive's approach to the definition of 'adverse environmental impact' in Article 3, which adopts a two-pronged approach. First, it considers adverse impacts from breach of a prohibition that is 'causing any measurable environmental degradation' such as water or air pollution. However, this broad provision applies only where such breaches impact human rights such as where water pollution 'denies a person access to safe and clean drinking water'.[99] Second, it covers adverse impacts from breaches of prohibitions and obligations included in environmental instruments listed in Annex Part II. From a TEC perspective, the list of environmental instruments in the Annex is more extensive than in the German model and includes conventions such as the Convention on Biological Diversity (CBD), CITES and the Montreal Protocol. On enforcement, a dual approach is taken that includes civil liability and administrative oversight.[100] Each Member State is obliged to nominate one or more supervisory

95 Directive 2024/1760 of the European Parliament and the Council of 13 June 2024 on corporate sustainability due diligence.

96 See, for example, CSDDD, Recital 16.

97 The Commission originally defined the threshold for a large company as having 500 employees and a worldwide turnover of €150 million. This has since been revised (see main text).

98 CSDDD, Articles 2(1) and 37 (transitional measures).

99 See CSDDD, Annex, Part 1, paragraphs 15 and 16.

100 Interestingly, it has been suggested that due diligence obligations should be underpinned by criminal liability. See further Beatriz Albuquerque, 'The Interplay Between Environmental Crime and Corporate Sustainability Due Diligence: Seizing the Opportunity to Connect the Dots' (2024) 15(2) *New Journal of European Criminal Law* 209.

authorities responsible, among other duties, for investigating and responding to concerns, initiating investigations and conducting inspections if there are suspected breaches.[101] There is the potential for significant administrative sanctions to be levied against companies that fail to comply, and the sanctions should not be 'less than 5% of the net worldwide turnover of the company in the financial year preceding that of the decision to impose the fine'.[102] Article 29 provides for civil remedies for victims.

Again, there is little doubt that the CSDDD is an important development since it draws into the regulatory domain significant corporate power and influence, both financial and persuasive, and urges companies to adopt a more proactive and preventative approach. Yet, whether it can fully address complex problems such as TEC is open to question. As we note above, the definition of 'adverse environmental impact' explicitly includes international instruments with clear and direct relevance to TEC. However, under Article 9 of CSDDD, where it is 'not feasible to prevent, mitigate, bring to an end or minimise all identified adverse impacts at the same time and to their full extent' companies shall 'prioritise' certain adverse impacts. The effect of Article 9, whilst in many respects a corporate reality, inevitably means that the impacts of TEC may need to be assessed alongside other human rights and environmental impacts and may be prioritised, or not.[103] This also adds a further layer of complexity to both state and third-party oversight of the due diligence requirements in that an assessment needs to be made on a) the extent to which it is feasible to mitigate adverse impacts and if not, b) whether identified impacts have been properly prioritised.[104] Another concern, which is not peculiar to the EU measure, is that while many small and medium enterprises will only be indirectly affected, there will be many that will not be affected at all, regardless of the risks they pose. Size may be, and often is, a determinant of the level of impact. But given the breadth, diversity and complexity of TEC activities, discussed in section 2 above, TEC may take place in areas of commercial activity that are beyond the scope of the due diligence obligations.

7. Concluding remarks

TEC has embedded itself, directly and indirectly, in global supply chains. Current estimates as to scale and scope suggest that existing regulatory approaches are having a

---

101 CSDDD, Articles 24 and 25.

102 CSDDD, Article 27. The EU Environmental Crime Directive (n 49), Article 7 adopts a similar approach to the financial penalties that can be imposed on legal entities committing offences covered by the Directive. These penalties are based on a percentage of turnover or a fixed amount.

103 The Danish Institute for Human Rights, *The EU Corporate Sustainability Due Diligence Directive: Maximising Impact Through Transposition and Implementation* (2024).

104 Human rights impact assessment frameworks may be an important reference point in this regard. See further, Danish Institute for Human Rights, 'Human Rights Impact Assessment: Guidance and Toolbox' (2020). https://www.humanrights.dk/sites/humanrights.dk/files/media/document/DIHR%20HRIA%20Toolbox_Welcome_and_Introduction_ENG_2020.pdf.

limited impact on combatting illegal activity. This chapter has considered an important development in mitigating corporate harms, namely due diligence, a preventative measure that reflects the role private enterprises can play, as regulatory surrogates, in identifying adverse risks and impacts occurring across supply chains. Despite some of the highlighted concerns around, for instance, the economic impact of due diligence measures on productivity and the risk that firms may adopt more defensive approaches to controlling supply chain activities, due diligence measures are clearly gaining significant traction, especially in the Global North. In view of the persuasive influence of the UNGPs, the dominant focus of policy and subsequent legal developments has been on human rights. But human rights harms, as we have noted, often involve environmental harms, with TEC being one example owing to the potential impact it can have on local resources and livelihoods. These emerging measures clearly reflect the real and tangible links between human rights and the environment.

The question for us is whether these measures go far enough; whether they are sufficiently targeted or well-structured to address TEC activity. We have highlighted several concerns and weaknesses (for example specificity, lack of reference to crime, prioritisation) that could have a limiting effect, although this would, of course, be contingent on the extent to which companies embrace their obligations. Given the relatively general nature of the new obligations, and the discretion given to firms in implementing the requirements, we believe a more focused approach is likely to be required: an approach that embeds, in due diligence, more specific and direct obligations that require businesses to identify TEC taking place in their supply chain. We can see examples of this more targeted approach across a number of different criminal activities that in and of themselves have serious human rights implications and would therefore fall within the scope of the emerging due diligence frameworks discussed in the previous section. Take the UK Modern Slavery Act 2015 as an example, which requires certain firms to prepare an annual slavery and human trafficking statement. Importantly, slavery and human trafficking is defined as conduct that constitutes an offence under the Act itself. Whilst the Act states that firms *may* include due diligence processes in their business and supply chain (so due diligence is not mandatory), it does reflect the potential for due diligence to apply to certain specific criminal offences at the domestic level. The effectiveness of a more targeted approach would, of course, differ depending on the nature of the TEC and the perpetrators involved: not all TEC takes place within the direct reach of global supply chains and there are significant networks of smaller supply chain activities that are unlikely (due to the economic burden) to fall within any due diligence framework. Importantly, due diligence will always need to sit alongside more traditional criminal law enforcement responses that ultimately depend on the existence of robust, domestic measures and well-resourced regulators.[105] Nevertheless, it could, given political commitment and corporate willingness, play an enhanced role in combatting TEC.

105 On criminal law and administrative law enforcement, see in this volume, Juan Fuentes Osorio, Chapter 6 The Effectiveness of Environmental Criminal Law Enforcement, and Sarah Wright and Victoria Colvin, Chapter 7 Enforceable Undertakings as an Alternative to Prosecution in Australian Environmental Law Enforcement.

4 Towards a new agenda for ecocide norms adoption and enforcement

Thomas Obel Hansen

1. Introduction[1]

This chapter discusses current proposals to achieve more meaningful justice for serious environmental crimes. It takes a particular interest in exploring the feasibility of recently made suggestions for expanding accountability for environmental crimes, including through the ecocide proposal tabled by the Independent Panel of Experts (IEP) in 2021.[2] On that note, the chapter discusses the prospects for ecocide norms adoption and enforcement both at International Criminal Court (ICC) level and in national jurisdictions. To contextualize this debate, the chapter also pays attention to other recent developments that seek to expand environmental crimes accountability, particularly in situations of armed conflict.

1 This publication presents an outcome of the author's appointment as the 2023–24 Maria Zambrano Distinguished Researcher with Universidad Carlos III de Madrid ('Ministerio de Ciencia, Innovación y Universidades' y a la 'Convocatoria de la Universidad Carlos III de Madrid de Ayudas para la recualificación del sistema universitario español para 2021–2023, de 31 de mayo de 2022 en base al Real Decreto 289/2021, de 20 de abril de 2021, por el que se regula la concesión directa de subvenciones a universidades públicas para la recualificación del sistema universitario español). The chapter is written in the context of the research project 'Making Peace with Nature and Making Nature a Key for Peace' (PaxNatura), funded by the Spanish Ministry of Science and Innovation (Ref.: PID2022-1424842022/ PID2022-142484NB-C21), led by Prof Montserrat Abad Castelos (Universidad Carlos III de Madrid).

2 Independent Expert Panel for the Legal Definition of Ecocide, 'Commentary and Core Text' (June 2021), <https://static1.squarespace.com/static/5ca2608ab914493c64ef1f6d/t/60d1e6e604fae2201d03407f/1624368879048/SE+Foundation+Commentary+and+core+text+rev+6.pdf> accessed 25 June 2024.

Rather than elaborating on the pros and cons of the legal definition of ecocide – an important theme already subject to intensive debate in the scholarship[3] – or other more technical aspects of ecocide prosecution, the key focus of this chapter concerns identifying and discussing more systemic issues pertaining to ecocide norms adoption and enforcement in relevant legal regimes. On that basis, the chapter seeks to reflect on what a future agenda for ecocide norms adoption and enforcement – and, more broadly, environmental crimes accountability – could look like. Accordingly, the chapter's main contribution to scholarly debate and advocacy strategies concerns a broader 'system' approach to identify opportunities and challenges to advancing environmental crimes accountability, in particular for the type of conduct and associated actors broadly covered by the ecocide proposal.[4]

With some notable exceptions,[5] debates about ecocide norms adoption and enforcement continue to be heavily steered towards international criminal law – and the ICC system in particular. The main observation made in this chapter is that, from the perspective of producing more meaningful and comprehensive accountability outcomes for ecocide and other serious environmental crimes, that focus may be disproportionate, and it is helpful to instead pay increased attention to legal avenues outside the ICC system, specifically national jurisdictions, including their ability to exercise jurisdiction over environmental crimes with extraterritorial dimensions. Whereas ecocide norms adoption under the ICC Statute will be characterized by a struggle and environmental crimes prosecution at ICC level faces numerous hurdles, the picture emerging from national jurisdictions in recent years is, in many ways, one of proactiveness and progress. In plain words, why not seek to build further on what appears

[3] On the debate around the *definition* of ecocide, see by way of example Kevin Heller, 'Skeptical Thoughts on the Proposed Crime of "Ecocide" (That Isn't)' (*Opinio Juris*, 23 June 2021) <https://opiniojuris.org/2021/06/23/skeptical-thoughts-on-the-proposed-crime-of-ecocide-that-isnt/> accessed 25 June 2024; Donna Minha, 'The Proposed Definition of the Crime of Ecocide: An Important Step Forward, but Can Our Planet Wait?' (*EJIL:Talk!*, 1 July 2021), <https://www.ejiltalk.org/the-proposed-definition-of-the-crime-of-ecocide-an-important-step-forward-but-can-our-planet-wait/> accessed 25 June 2024; Jérôme de Hemptinne, 'Ecocide: an Ambiguous Crime?' (*EJIL: TALK!*, 29 August 2022), <https://www.ejiltalk.org/ecocide-an-ambiguous-crime/> accessed 25 June 2024.

[4] The chapter draws, in part, on arguments made in previous publications by the author on this topic, but seeks to elaborate on some of the arguments previously made, and on that basis, to reflect on a future research and advocacy agenda on ecocide. For the previous publications, see Thomas Obel Hansen, 'Prosecuting Ecocide: The Norms-Adoption/Enforcement Paradox' (*Just Security*, 22 June 2023) <https://www.justsecurity.org/87009/prosecuting-ecocide-the-norms-adoption-enforcement-paradox/> accessed 25 June 2024, and Thomas Obel Hansen, 'Accountability for Environmental Crimes in Conflict Zones: Why Expanding the International Criminal Court's Jurisdiction is Not the Best Solution' (2024) 56(3) NYU J Int L & Pol 879.

[5] See, for example Darryl Robinson, 'Ecocide — Puzzles and Possibilities' (2022) 20 J Int'l Crim Just 320.

to 'work', rather than what will likely prove a time-consuming and complex process with limited prospects for productive outcomes?

The chapter proceeds as follows: first, it outlines the IEP ecocide proposal in light of other recent initiatives to advance environmental crimes accountability, especially in situations of armed conflict; next, the chapter sets out key perspectives in the scholarship about ICC environmental crimes prosecution and, in that regard, identifies what it refers to as a 'norms adoption/enforcement paradox' in international criminal law; the chapter then proceeds to a discussion of the prospects for *norms adoption* at ICC level and nationally, which is followed by a discussion of the prospects for *norms enforcement* both within the ICC system and in national jurisdictions. Throughout this analysis, the chapter seeks to raise questions and make suggestions for a future research and advocacy agenda on ecocide and for advancing accountability for serious environmental crimes more generally. These points are summarized and further elaborated in the conclusions.

2. The IEP ecocide proposal in light of other initiatives to expand environmental crimes accountability

Convened by the Stop Ecocide organization, an Independent Expert Panel (IEP), which involved acknowledged international criminal law and environmental law experts, tabled its proposal in June 2021 to include ecocide as the fifth crime in the ICC Statute.[6] The proposal defines ecocide as 'unlawful or wanton acts committed with knowledge that there is a substantial likelihood of severe and either widespread or long-term damage to the environment being caused by those acts'.[7] The proposal – which covers environmental harm both in armed conflict and peacetime – defines the core terms as follows:

- 'Wanton' means with reckless disregard for damage that would be clearly excessive in relation to the social and economic benefits anticipated.
- 'Severe' means damage that involves very serious adverse changes, disruption, or harm to any element of the environment, including grave impacts on human life or natural, cultural, or economic resources.
- 'Widespread' means damage that extends beyond a limited geographic area, crosses state boundaries, or is suffered by an entire ecosystem or species or a large number of human beings.
- 'Long-term' means damage which is irreversible or which cannot be redressed through natural recovery within a reasonable period of time.

---

6 For commentaries on the process and expectations concerning implementation, see, for example Christina Voigt, '"Ecocide" as an International Crime: Personal Reflections on Options and Choices' (EJIL:TALK!, 3 July 2021) <https://www.ejiltalk.org/ecocide-as-an-international-crime-personal-reflections-on-options-and-choices/> accessed 25 June 2024.

7 See Independent Expert Panel for the Legal Definition of Ecocide (n 2).

- 'Environment' means the earth, its biosphere, cryosphere, lithosphere, hydrosphere, and atmosphere, as well as outer space.[8]

As the IEP notes, the proposed definition creates two main thresholds for prohibited conduct: 1) there must exist a substantial likelihood that the relevant conduct, which can include both acts and omissions, will cause severe and either widespread or long-term damage to the environment; 2) there must be proof that the acts are unlawful or wanton. Accordingly, 'with these two thresholds, the prosecution would need to prove a substantial likelihood of causing severe and either widespread or long-term damage through acts or omissions that are either unlawful or wanton'.[9]

The main objective of the Stop Ecocide campaign, which facilitated the work of the IEP, is to have the proposed ecocide crime adopted as a crime in the ICC Statute.[10] That being said, the Stop Ecocide campaign appears to pay increased attention, more recently, to the adoption of national legislation that relies on the IEP proposal to criminalize environmental harm, likely as a reflection that this element of the campaign agenda is progressing particularly well.[11]

The IEP ecocide proposal must be appreciated in light of a range of other recent initiatives to address existing accountability gaps for environmental crimes, especially in conflict zones. First, it should be emphasized that although the current debate about ecocide tends to focus predominantly on the IEP proposal, suggestions have previously been made to make ecocide a crime under international law. A notable early example involves the work led by Richard Falk in the early 1970s for the adoption of an 'International Convention on the Crime of Ecocide'.[12] Multiple other suggestions for making ecocide an international crime have since been made.[13] More recently, the UCLA Promise Institute has suggested a definition of ecocide, which in some important ways departs from the IEP definition,[14] but one that appears to have gone largely off the radar since Stop Ecocide launched the IEP initiative.

---

8 Ibid.

9 Ibid.

10 Stop Ecocide, 'Making Ecocide a Crime', <https://www.stopecocide.earth/making-ecocide-a-crime> accessed 25 June 2024.

11 Stop Ecocide, 'Leading States', <https://www.stopecocide.earth/leading-states> accessed 25 June 2024.

12 Richard Falk, 'Environmental Warfare and Ecocide—Facts, Appraisal, and Proposal' (1973) 4 *Bulletin of Peace Proposals* 80. See also the influential work by Polly Higgins, Damien Short, and Nigel South, 'Protecting the Planet: A Proposal for a Law of Ecocide' (2013) 59 Crime, Law Soc Chang 251.

13 See, for example Mark Gray, 'The International Crime of Ecocide' (1996) 26 *California Western International Law Journal* 2; Anja Gauger et al., 'Ecocide is the Missing 5th Crime Against Peace, Human Rights Consortium' (University of London, 2012).

14 UCLA Promise Institute for Human Rights Group of Experts, 'Proposed Definition of Ecocide' (2021), <https://ecocidelaw.com/wp-content/uploads/2022/02/Proposed-Definition-of-Ecocide-Promise-Group-April-9-2021-final.pdf> accessed 1 August 2024. For a discussion of other previous attempts to define ecocide and introduce

A separate recent initiative for advancing protection against environmental crimes in situations of armed conflict involves the International Committee of the Red Cross (ICRC) 2020 guidelines on the protection of the natural environment in armed conflict, intended as a reference tool for states, other parties to armed conflicts, and other actors interpreting and applying international humanitarian law.[15] To the extent that national authorities take the ICRC guidelines into account in drafting and revising military manuals (a question, it should be added, that deserves additional investigation), this would be a major achievement from the perspective of protection of the environment in armed conflict.

Furthermore, the International Law Commission (ILC) adopted, in 2022, the draft principles on protection of the environment in relation to armed conflicts, endorsed by the United Nations (UN) General Assembly. The ILC Draft Principles take a holistic approach to cover situations of armed conflict, including international and non-international armed conflict, as well as pre- and post-conflict situations.[16] The principles are not intended to rewrite international humanitarian law, but nonetheless entail a level of innovation, especially concerning accountability for business enterprises.[17] Principle 10 addresses the responsibility of states to regulate multinational corporations within a due diligence framework, whereas Principle 11 specifically creates a responsibility for States to hold multinational corporations liable for environmental damage occurring in conflict zones.[18] How national jurisdictions come to reflect these principles is vital – and something that merits further scrutiny.

As Karen Hulme notes, both the ICRC guidelines and the ILC principles acknowledge the continued role of international environmental law during armed conflict, while noting that the interaction between international humanitarian law and international

the concept as a crime under international criminal law, see, for example Anastacia Greene, 'The Campaign to Make Ecocide an International Crime: Quixotic Quest or Moral Imperative?' (2019) 30 Fordham Env L R 1.

15 International Committee of the Red Cross, *Guidelines on Protection of Natural Environment in Armed Conflict* (2020), <https://www.icrc.org/en/publication/4382-guidelines-protection-natural-environment-armed-conflict> accessed 25 June 2024.

16 The ILC draft principles take a broad and holistic approach to the concept of armed conflict, which is helpful in the context of addressing environmental crimes. See International Law Commission, *Draft Principles on Protection of the Environment in Relation to Armed Conflicts* (2022) (hereinafter *ILC Draft Principles*). Concerning the significance of the holistic approach, see, for example, Karen Hulme and Elizabeth B. Hessami, 'New Legal Protections for the Environment in Relation to Armed Conflict' (IUCN, 16 July 2022), <https://www.iucn.org/story/202207/new-legal-protections-environment-relation-armed-conflict> accessed 25 June 2024.

17 See Marie Jacobsson and Marja Lehto, 'Protection of the Environment in Relation to Armed Conflicts – An Overview of the International Law Commission's Ongoing Work' (2020) 10(1) Goettingen J Int L 27.

18 See further Britta Sjostedt and Anne Dienelt, 'Enhancing the Protection of the Environment in Relation to Armed Conflicts – The Draft Principles of the International Law Commission and Beyond' (2020) 10(1) Goettingen J Int L 13.

environmental law needs further clarification.[19] Considerations relating to interplay between international humanitarian law, international criminal law, and international environmental law are similarly key to the debate about how to operationalize ecocide as an international crime, which raises issues that need additional exploration.[20]

In another significant development for environmental crimes accountability, the European Union (EU) adopted a new environmental crimes directive in 2024, which provides a comprehensive list of environmental offenses that EU Member States are compelled, under Article 3(3), to introduce as 'qualified' criminal offenses in national law.[21] The adoption of the qualified offenses in the EU directive, which in some ways resembles the IEP ecocide proposal, was (for good reason) welcomed by environmental campaigners.[22] The directive follows on from extensive debate concerning how to advance accountability for environmental crimes within the EU framework. The EU should be lauded for taking such a solid approach to the criminalization of environmental crimes (including noting that the qualified criminal offences can 'encompass conduct comparable to "ecocide"' (Recital 21)). As discussed further below, the directive, arguably makes it less significant from an enforcement perspective in a European context if ecocide is adopted as a crime under the ICC Statute. Even if the directive emphasizes the need for cross-border cooperation (Recital 3), however, the label of 'international crime' under the ICC Statute would come with additional state obligations relating, for example, to state cooperation. The adoption of the EU directive, considered in the broader context of ecocide proposals and national legislation, raises interesting questions around norms-complementarity and synergy.

Taken together, the developments outlined here are evidence of the normative elevation of environmental harm as a serious crime, reflected both in national legal systems and various international and regional instruments. However, the multiple approaches to advancing legal accountability for environmental crime also raise

---

19 Karen Hulme, 'Using International Environmental Law to Enhance Biodiversity and Nature Conservation During Armed Conflict' (2022) 20(5) J Int'l Crim Just 1155.

20 Jérôme de Hemptinne, 'Concluding Observations on the Influence of International Environmental Law over International Criminal Law' (2023) 20(5) J Int'l Crim Just 1287; Robinson (n 5) 317–8.

21 Directive of the European Parliament and of the Council on the protection of the environment through criminal law 2024/1203 and replacing Directives 2008/99/EC and 2009/123/EC. See also European Commission, Directorate-General for Environment, 'New Environmental Crime Directive comes into force' (20 May 2024), <https://environment.ec.europa.eu/news/new-environmental-crime-directive-comes-force-2024-05-20_en> accessed 25 June 2024.

22 Stop Ecocide, 'EU Council Votes to Criminalise Cases Comparable to Ecocide' (26 March 2024) <https://www.stopecocide.earth/2024/eu-council-votes-to-criminalise-cases-comparable-to-ecocide/> accessed 25 June 2024. Concerning previous regulation in the EU framework, see further Ricardo Pereira, 'Towards Effective Implementation of the EU Environmental Crime Directive? The Case of Illegal Waste Management and Trafficking Offences' (2017) 26(2) Rev of Eur, Comp and Int Env L 147.

profound questions concerning the tools available to consolidate serious environmental harm as a form of universally accepted crime (and whether that should be in the form of an international crime, a transnational crime, or something else),[23] as well as questions relating to the credibility and legitimacy of various enforcement regimes, issues that will be elaborated below in this chapter.

3. The broader debate about ICC environmental crimes prosecution

a. To amend the ICC Statute … or not?

International criminal and environmental law scholars have engaged in a lasting debate concerning how the ICC's capacity to investigate and prosecute environmental crimes in different forms could be strengthened. As Rachel Killean observes in a particularly insightful piece, suggested approaches to enhance accountability for environmental crimes broadly fall into two camps: one holding that there is a need for a new legal category for environmental crimes at ICC level, and the other holding that it is possible to promote accountability for environmental crimes within the existing legal framework – and, so to speak, 'green' the ICC without making statutory changes.[24]

To start with the latter perspective, scholars point to options that could be further explored within the existing statutory framework of the ICC and on that basis sometimes reject calls for expanding the Court's jurisdictional basis over environmental crimes. Kai Ambos, for example, argues that:

> It is doubtful whether a new, stand-alone core crime is needed to better protect the environment. It is arguably more sensible, especially from a practical point of view, to further develop in case law those elements in the existing international core crimes which have an environmental ingredient and on which the draft definition of ecocide partly draws.[25]

Commentaries of this nature often seek to suggest concrete modalities for the prosecution of environmental crimes within the existing ICC legal framework, including with reference to Article 8(2)(b)(iv) and sometimes other war crimes provisions, as a crime against humanity, or even as genocide.[26] Of course, this all assumes a willing-

---

23 See also Robinson (n 5) 321.

24 Rachel Killean, 'From Ecocide to Eco-Sensitivity: "Greening" Reparations at the International Criminal Court' (2021) 25 Int J Hum Rights 323.

25 Kai Ambos, 'Protecting the Environment through Criminal Law?' (*EJIL:TALK!*, 29 June 2021), <www.ejiltalk.org/protecting-the-environment-through-international-criminal-law> accessed 25 June 2024.

26 Concerning prosecuting environmental crime as a war crime, see, for example Matthew Gillett, 'Eco-Struggles: Using International Criminal Law to Protect the Environment During and After Non-International Armed Conflict' in Carsten Stahn, Jens Iverson and Jennifer Easterday (eds), *Environmental Protection and Transitions*

ness and capacity in general within the ICC system to advance criminal accountability for environmental crimes. The prosecutor's reference to environmental harm in the 2016 policy paper on case selection and prioritization is sometimes read as evidence of exactly that.[27] On that note, it is also worth flagging that the Office of the Prosecutor (OTP) launched a consultation process in 2024 concerning the development of a new OTP policy paper to advance accountability for environmental crimes under existing provisions in the ICC Statute.[28]

In contrast, those who argue that a new legal category for environmental crimes is needed tend to be less optimistic about the ability of the ICC system as it is currently constructed to adequately handle environmental crimes.[29] These commentators often point to the narrow construction of relevant provisions, in particular the so-called first 'ecocentric' war crimes provision laid down in Article 8(2)(b)(iv) of the ICC Statute, which, in their view, severely limits the prosecutor's ability to successfully prosecute environmental crimes.[30] Commentators subscribing to this view therefore tend to assume that statutory limitations constitute the predominant explanation for why the ICC Prosecutor has to date, not charged any suspects with environmental crimes (even if environmental harm or destruction has sometimes been referenced in other

---

from Conflict to Peace (OUP 2017). Concerning environmental crimes prosecution as a crime against humanity, see, for example Jessica Durney, 'Crafting a Standard: Environmental Crimes as Crimes Against Humanity Under the International Criminal Court' (2018) 24 Hastings Env L J 413. Concerning prosecuting environmental crimes as genocide, see Martin Crook and Damien Short, 'Marx, Lemkin and the Genocide–Ecocide Nexus' (2014) 18 Int J Hum Rights 298.

27 International Criminal Court, Office of The Prosecutor, *Policy Paper on Case Selection and Prioritisation* (15 September 2016). For a discussion of the 2016 Policy Paper, including an understanding of its prospects for advancing prosecution of actors responsible for environmental crimes, see, for example Ricardo Pereira, 'After the ICC Office of the Prosecutor's 2016 Policy Paper on Case Selection and Prioritisation – Towards an International Crime of Ecocide?' (2020) 31 Crim L Forum 179; Nadia Bernaz, 'An Analysis of the ICC Office of the Prosecutor's Policy Paper on Case Selection and Prioritization from the Perspective of Business and Human Rights' (2017) 15 J Int'l Crim Just 527.

28 Although it is interesting to note that the prosecutor also points to the need in that regard to consider other legal frameworks, including 'applicable environmental treaties, rules of customary international law, and the jurisprudence of other international and national courts'. See International Criminal Court, Office of The Prosecutor, 'The Office of the Prosecutor launches public consultation on a new policy initiative to advance accountability for environmental crimes under the Rome Statute' (16 February 2024).

29 See, for example Ammar Bustami and Marie-Christine Hecken, 'Perspectives for a New International Crime Against the Environment: International Criminal Responsibility for Environmental Degradation under the Rome Statute' (2021) 11(1) Goettingen J Int L 145.

30 See, for example Jessica Lawrence and Kevin Heller, 'The Limits of Article 8(2)(b)(iv) of the Rome Statute, the First Ecocentric Environmental War Crime' (2007) 20 Geo Int Env L Rev 61.

charges brought by ICC prosecutors).[31] Accordingly, to remedy existing accountability gaps for environmental crimes, scholars subscribing to this view express a desire to expand the ICC's jurisdictional basis for prosecuting environmental crimes committed in war and peacetime – and the ICC's potential adoption of ecocide as the fifth ICC Statute crime has become central to these debates.[32]

b. The 'norms adoption/enforcement paradox' in international criminal law

The two main perspectives discussed above both assume that the ICC system should feature as a central component – often *the* central component – of efforts to further advance accountability for serious environmental crimes. Arguably, the widespread consensus that the ICC system should be a primary point of entry for advancing environmental crimes accountability has to do with many scholars apparently taking for granted, in more general terms, the superiority of the ICC system in the context of norms adoption – and with it, the desirability of *expanding* criminalization at the ICC level.[33] Perhaps because of that inclination, proponents of expanding jurisdiction for particular crimes or actors seem to sometimes downplay insights from critical international criminal law scholarship about the pitfalls of the ICC system in terms of its conditions of operation and ability to actually enforce relevant norms.

By way of example, proponents of altering the ICC's legal basis to enable the Court to prosecute business enterprises and other legal persons sometimes assume that, if the ICC Statute is amended to permit such prosecutions, they will then automatically occur in a meaningful way, leaving aside the broader conditions of the ICC system that have resulted in a rather limited enforcement record over the past 20 years concerning norms already having the status of crimes in the ICC Statute.[34] As another example, the adoption of the crime of aggression within the ICC legal framework – pursued for many years and ultimately succeeding with an agreed definition in 2010 (with activation of the crime by 2018) – has been surrounded by (often high) expectations that if only norms adoption would happen, that would create a silver bullet towards norms enforcement.[35] So far, however, no charges have been brought for the

---

31 See Gillett (n 26).

32 See, for example Robinson (n 5); Carolyn Stock, 'A Fifth core crime: Crime of ecocide as a new puzzle of the international criminal law' (2023) 1(1) Yearbook of Int & Eur Crim & Procedural L 248–84; Liana Georgieva Minkova, 'The Fifth International Crime: Reflections on the Definition of "Ecocide"' (2023) 25(1) J Genocide Research 62.

33 See similarly Robinson (n 5).

34 See, for example Mordechai Kremnitzer, 'A Possible Case for Imposing Criminal Liability on Corporations in International Criminal Law' (2010) 8 J Int'l Crim Just 909.

35 See, for example Andreas Zimmermann, 'Amending the Amendment Provisions of the Rome Statute: The Kampala Compromise on the Crime of Aggression and the Law of Treaties' (2012) 10(1) J Int'l Crim Just 209–27; Carrie McDougall, *The Crime of Aggression under the Rome Statute of the International Criminal Court* (CUP, Cambridge 2021).

crime of aggression at the ICC level – and current debates about accountability for that crime, for example in the context of Russia's invasion of Ukraine, increasingly focus on alternative accountability avenues.[36]

The present author refers to the tendencies outlined here as a 'norms adoption/enforcement paradox' in international criminal law.[37] The essence of that paradox is that international criminal law – and the ICC system specifically – continues to be seen by many as the most central vehicle for norms adoption concerning serious crimes, even if the efforts needed to achieve norms adoption in international criminal law may often be disproportionate to the expected accountability outcomes due to substantial enforcement challenges at the ICC level.

In the context of environmental crimes accountability, the 'norms adoption/enforcement paradox' may result in what is a desirable outcome for the protection of the environment, and, more broadly, to the further building of the environmental rule of law – namely, advancing legal accountability for actors who violate these norms – being pursued at least partially under the wrong expectations.[38] In other words, the actual performance of the ICC to date, in terms of delivering meaningful accountability outcomes, demonstrates profound obstacles concerning the Court's ability to enforce accountability norms – especially, as we shall see below, with regard to issues that clash with the perceived interests of key actors in the current Western-led global order. It is therefore crucial to keep in mind the 'norms adoption/enforcement paradox' in the specific context of ICC prosecution of environmental crimes, since the most serious of such crimes frequently implicate powerful entities with a stake in the perceived economic and strategic interests of states that are particularly influential in the global order as currently constructed.[39]

36 See, for example Gaiane Nuridzhanian, 'International Enough? A Council of Europe Special Tribunal for the Crime of Aggression' (*Just Security*, 3 June 2024), <https://www.justsecurity.org/96320/council-of-europe-ukraine-tribunal/> accessed 25 June 2024.

37 The concept of a norms adoption/enforcement paradox in international criminal law was first set out in Hansen 'Prosecuting Ecocide…' (n 4) and elaborated further in Hansen 'Accountability for Environmental Crimes…' (n 4).

38 Ibid.

39 See, for example Daniëlla Dam-de Jong and Saskia Wolters, 'Through the Looking Glass: Corporate Actors and Environmental Harm beyond the ILC' (2020) 10 Goettingen J Int L 111.

4. The feasibility of adopting the ecocide proposal at ICC level and nationally, respectively

a. Norms adoption in the ICC system

A wide range of states have expressed support for the IEP ecocide proposal's adoption at ICC level.[40] Notwithstanding that support – and the centrality that the ecocide proposal has recently achieved in the international criminal law agenda – adoption of the IEP proposal in its current form in the ICC Statute will nonetheless face serious obstacles. At the most basic level, it needs emphasizing that any ICC Statute amendment process is a complex and time-consuming one, which creates a high bar for success and necessarily involves compromise to balance different interests and demands among States.[41]

A central reason why such an amendment process is likely to prove extraordinarily challenging for the ecocide proposal in the context of possible consideration at the Assembly of States Parties (ASP) level is that some key players in the global order will likely prove disinclined to ultimately support an amendment which, if adopted in its current proposed form, would not only substantially expand the Court's jurisdiction over environmental crimes, but also the types of *actors* that could potentially be subject to ICC jurisdiction. Such opposition is grounded in the simple fact that some key stakeholders ultimately prefer an ICC system that continues to focus on the types of crimes and actors it has *effectively* prosecuted to date, namely core atrocity crimes committed in conflict zones in the Global South.

Such claims concerning states' preferences are rarely articulated in such clear terms, but, when they are, it is telling of the expectations of certain states regarding what, in their view, the ICC is intended for. A clear example of this concerns statements made by United Kingdom (UK) officials in the context of the ICC's Iraq/UK preliminary examination, which clarified the UK Government's view that the ICC must be careful not to 'act as a human rights monitoring organisation for the whole world … it must focus on its core and essential task', tasks implied to concern the prosecution of core atrocity crimes committed in conflicts in the Global South.[42] The United States (US),

40 See Kate Mackintosh and Lisa Oldring, 'Watch This Space: Momentum Toward an International Crime of Ecocide' (*Just Security*, 5 December 2022, <https://www.justsecurity.org/84367/watch-this-space-momentum-toward-an-international-crime-of-ecocide/> accessed 25 June 2024. See also Stop Ecocide, 'Leading States', <https://www.stopecocide.earth/leading-states> accessed 25 June 2024.

41 See, for example Zimmermann (n 35).

42 See UK Government (FCO), 'Statement by Andrew Murdoch, Legal Director to the International Criminal Court Assembly of States Parties, at its 17th Session in The Hague' (5 December 2018), <https://www.gov.uk/government/speeches/uk-statement-to-icc-assembly-of-states-parties-17th-session> accessed 25 June 2024.

not a State Party to the ICC Statute, has indicated similar preferences.[43] Another clear indication of how some influential states perceive the ICC's role in the global order occurred in the context of the ICC Prosecutor requesting warrants of arrest for Israeli leaders for conduct in the ongoing 2023–24 Gaza War, with ICC Prosecutor Karim Khan explaining in an interview with CNN that 'I've had some elected leaders speak to me and they were very blunt [that] this Court is built for Africa and for thugs like Putin'.[44] A central point in the often advocacy-oriented or highly legal-technical debate about accountability for environmental crimes at ICC level is therefore that some key players in the Western-led global order – including State Parties like the UK and non-State Parties such as the US – prefer an ICC system that continues to focus on core atrocity crimes committed in the Global South or by states such as Russia, seen to challenge the current Western-led global order.

While the type of sentiments mentioned above is likely to provide an underlying explanation for opposition to a potential expansion of ICC jurisdiction to cover ecocide, states opposing the suggestions made for jurisdictional expansion over environmental crimes typically rely on other arguments, especially relating to the *prioritization of resources*, when articulating why, in their view, ecocide should not be adopted as an ICC Statute crime.[45] While the US appears to have not taken an official position on the ecocide proposal or other suggestions for expanding ICC jurisdiction over environmental crimes at the time of writing, the US will likely seek to counter any efforts to that effect, since the ICC's adoption of the ecocide proposal would probably be perceived to expand the Court's ability to exercise jurisdiction over US citizens, including US military personnel and business representatives.[46]

---

43 See for example US Government (State Department), 'Press Release: Antony Blinken, Secretary of State, Ending Sanctions And Visa Restrictions Against Personnel Of The International Criminal Court' (2 April 2021), <https://www.state.gov/ending-sanctions-and-visa-restrictions-against-personnel-of-the-international-criminal-court/> accessed 25 June 2024.

44 CNN, 'Exclusive: ICC Chief Prosecutor explains why he's seeking arrest warrants for leaders of Hamas and Israel' (20 May 2024), <https://edition.cnn.com/videos/tv/2024/05/20/amanpour-icc-karim-khan-arrest-warrants-hamas-netanyahu.cnn> accessed 25 June 2024.

45 See, for example UK Parliament, 'Ecocide', *Hansard*, HL, Vol 814 (21 July 2021), <https://hansard.parliament.uk/Lords/2021-07-21/debates/3AD1BE27-B0A5-4C68-9A39-0E6566E63FCF/Ecocide> (UK Government representatives expressing a priority to improve the ICC's 'ability to prosecute existing crimes against humanity before we create new ones', further noting that 'the significant amendment that would be required to establish a crime of ecocide is not only likely to distract from reform of the international court … it would also be extremely difficult to secure the agreement of all state parties and could occupy international negotiators for many years'.

46 Concerning US opposition to ICC jurisdiction and activity with the potential to target US citizens, see, for example Sara Ochs, 'The United States, the International Criminal Court, and the Situation in Afghanistan' (2019) 95 Notre Dame L Rev 89.

Accordingly, some key players in the global order will almost certainly oppose, or seek to substantially water down, an ICC amendment process involving expanded environmental crimes jurisdiction. Should such an amendment process be initiated, the ultimate outcome could therefore likely be some form of 'compromise' solution which provides for more modest jurisdictional expansion, or one that comes with significant caveats for actually prosecuting the ecocide crime. Such an outcome could potentially be the biggest risk for environmental justice, because how the ICC frames ecocide would serve as a reference point and could possibly lead some states to adopt less comprehensive ecocide legislation than what is currently the trend, as is explored below in the chapter.[47]

Another important point to consider in the context of norms adoption at ICC level is that, even when international law instruments have been expanded to include provisions for the prosecution of environmental crimes, experience shows that this is no guarantee that the relevant states will ratify an amendment, even if they worked collaboratively to conclude an amendment text. A clear example of this involves the 2014 Malabo Protocol, which would grant the African Court of Justice and Human Rights jurisdiction over 'illegal exploitation of natural resources', but the Protocol has not yet entered into force since, at the time of writing, only a single Member State has ratified it.[48] Might a possible amendment process at the ICC level involving ecocide run into similar challenges where perhaps only a group of 'proactive' states ratify the amendment? If so, are these states likely to primarily involve those already showing commitment to outlawing ecocide, including by having already provided for the criminalization of the types of acts amounting to ecocide in national law? If the answer to these questions is likely to be yes, how much of a difference would it then make, from the perspective of actual accountability outcomes for serious environmental crimes, if an ICC amendment process commences and potentially succeeds (in that regard also considering the ICC's complementarity principle)?

To summarize: any ICC amendment process is complex, time-consuming, and bound to result in compromises – and any amendment process specifically seeking to expand the ICC's jurisdiction over environmental crimes is bound to be extraordinarily complex. Even if an ecocide crime should be ultimately adopted in the ICC Statute, it is no guarantee that individual states will ratify the amendment. The fact that resistance is to be expected should the IEP ecocide proposal be formally considered by the ICC ASP does, of course, not by itself imply that the efforts of ecocide campaigners in this regard should be put to rest. It is a reflection, however, that it is worth keeping in

---

47 This point is originally made in Hansen 'Prosecuting Ecocide…' (n 4).

48 See further Daniëlla Dam de Jong and James Stewart, 'Illicit Exploitation of Natural Resources' in Charles Jalloh and Kamari Clarke (eds), *The African Court of Justice and Human and Peoples' Rights* (CUP, Cambridge 2019); Nicole de Silva 'The Malabo Protocol's 10th Anniversary Revives Advocacy for an African Criminal Court' (*EJIL:TALK!*, 25 December 2024), <https://www.ejiltalk.org/the-malabo-protocols-10th-anniversary-revives-advocacy-for-an-african-criminal-court/> accessed 14 March 2025.

mind when considering other options for norms adoption, as will be explored in the following sections.

b. Norms-adoption in national legal systems

Solid legal frameworks permitting the prosecution of environmental crimes are now in place in many countries, though much work remains to be done to achieve more progress. Many of the more recently introduced legal frameworks for prohibition and prosecution of environmental crimes claim to draw substantially on the IEP ecocide proposal. Even if the level of resemblance with the IEP proposal clearly varies and may, in some cases, be overstated,[49] in a sense, 'the ecocide wave is already here', as Darryl Robinson phrases it.[50] But that wave is being driven by developments in national jurisdictions, not by international courts as many ecocide campaigners had initially imagined. This presents an interesting dynamic – also worth exploring outside the ecocide context – concerning how an international advocacy campaign may end up achieving its main goal, perhaps even more effectively than initially hoped for, but through different processes than first imagined.

Certain countries are seen to be particularly influential in driving the ecocide wave. Belgium, for one, often said to take the lead in a European context on environmental crimes legislation, adopted a new penal code in February 2024, which specifically includes recognition of the crime of ecocide.[51] Ecocide campaigners were enthusiastic about the development, with a Stop Ecocide representative noting: 'Belgium has demonstrated strong leadership … with prominent voices like that of Belgium leading the way, tangible progress is being made internationally, particularly so in Europe'.[52] A wide range of other European countries and nations – such as The Netherlands, Scotland, England, Italy, Spain, Iceland, France, and Ukraine – have already passed national legislation, or bills have been introduced before national parliaments, to criminalize acts that, to varying degrees, resemble parts of the IEP ecocide proposal.[53]

49 See, for example Kevin Heller, 'Belgium Set to Criminalise Ecocide (Kinda Sorta)' (*Opinio Juris*, 8 November 2022), <http://opiniojuris.org/2022/11/08/belgium-set-to-criminalise-ecocide-kinda-sorta/> accessed 25 June 2024.

50 Darryl Robinson, 'The Ecocide Wave is Already Here: National Momentum and the Value of a Model Law' (*Just Security*, 23 February 2023), <https://www.justsecurity.org/85244/the-ecocide-wave-is-already-here-national-momentum-and-the-value-of-a-model-law/> accessed 25 June 2024.

51 Maïthé Chini, 'Belgium becomes first in EU to recognise ecocide as international crime' (*The Brussels Times*, 23 February 2024), <https://www.brusselstimes.com/937229/belgium-becomes-first-in-eu-to-recognise-ecocide-as-international-crime-tbtb> accessed 25 June 2024.

52 Stop Ecocide, 'Belgium Becomes First European Country To Recognise Ecocide As International Level Crime', <https://www.stopecocide.earth/2024/belgium-becomes-first-european-country-to-recognise-ecocide-as-international-level-crime> accessed 25 June 2024.

53 Stop Ecocide, 'Leading States', <https://www.stopecocide.earth/leading-states> accessed 25 June 2024. See also Rachel Killean and Damien Short, 'Scoping Domestic

Strengthened environmental crimes legislation has also been introduced, or appears to be on track, in many countries in other regions of the world, including the Americas where countries such as Brazil, Chile, Peru, and Mexico are pushing ahead with ecocide legislation, and several countries in Central Asia have already had ecocide legislation in place for a period of time.[54]

This surge in national ecocide and, more broadly, strengthened environmental crimes legislation is, in its own right, encouraging from an environmental justice perspective – and gives reasons to consider how it can be sustained to promote other countries following suit. Introducing ecocide legislation has clearly become 'hot'. Advocates must consider how it can remain attractive in the years ahead, and researchers and policymakers alike would need to further explore which legal modalities work particularly well from the perspective of effective enforcement.

The national surge also gives reason to reflect on the argument often made by proponents of expanding the jurisdiction of environmental crimes (and several other types of jurisdiction) at the ICC level, namely that a key benefit of criminalization in the ICC Statute concerns an expected drop-down effect whereby states will provide for similar criminalization in domestic legislation.[55] Add to that, the EU's adoption of the new environmental crimes directive which, as discussed above, requires EU Member States to criminalize much of the same conduct entailed in the IEP ecocide proposal, even if Article 3(3) of the directive concerning qualified offenses only applies to the offenses listed in Article 3(2). This suggests that, rather than primarily focusing on ICC adoption of the ecocide crime and the potential drop-down effects, additional efforts should be made to further encourage solid criminalization and enforcement options at the national level.

On that note, scholars such as Darryl Robinson have suggested that drafting an ecocide 'model law' – understood as 'a declaration or document' entailing 'a recommended definition and related provisions, while allowing for national variation and experimentation' – could present a productive way forward.[56] This suggestion merits further exploration, but a crucial first step involves conducting comparative research into these national legislative developments to better understand what factors are decisive in national processes concerning adoption of ecocide legislation; how ecocide norms adoption 'spreads' between different jurisdictions across time and space; and what specific definitions and relevant institutional set-ups are best equipped to facilitate meaningful accountability.

Legal Framework for Ecocide in Scotland' Report for the Environmental Rights Centre for Scotland (ESRC) (March 2024), <https://www.ercs.scot/wp/wp-content/uploads/2024/04/Scoping-a-Domestic-Legal-Framework-for-Ecocide-in-Scotland_April24_online.pdf> accessed 25 June 2024.

54 Ibid.

55 By way of example, this argument is made with regard to the crime of aggression in Annegret Hartig, *Making Aggression a Crime under Domestic Law* (Springer 2023).

56 Robinson (n 50).

To summarize: national legal frameworks permitting the prosecution of serious environmental crimes, to varying degrees resembling the IEP ecocide proposal, have recently been introduced – or are underway – in numerous national jurisdictions. Norms adoption of ecocide is therefore in many ways 'on track' – only, as it happens, that track involves national legislative developments, rather than taking the form of a top-down, international court-led process. Taking all of this into account, it seems a reasonable assumption that focusing on further expanding the legal basis in various national jurisdictions presents the most feasible route towards achieving a solid legal basis for more meaningful and comprehensive accountability for environmental crimes, especially because – as we shall see in the following section – national jurisdictions also likely present the most feasible base for the enforceability of ecocide crime and other serious environmental crimes.

5. The feasibility of *enforcing* the ecocide proposal at ICC level and nationally, respectively

a. Norms enforcement in the ICC system

It is first worth recapping what has, to date, *not* occurred at ICC level, namely the formal investigation of various forms of environmental harm, including that outlined in various Article 15 communications.[57] For instance, despite serious environmental crimes clearly being committed in the contexts of ongoing ICC investigations in Ukraine and Palestine and suggestions made by numerous commentators as to how the ICC could prosecute these within the current legal framework,[58] environmental crimes charges in these conflicts remain off the table at the time of writing.

Part of the explanation for the environmental crimes enforcement gap at the ICC level may have to do with the high thresholds in current ICC Statute provisions, pointed to by some commentators, as noted above in this chapter. Another factor to consider concerns the scientifically-oriented nature of environmental harm investigations, which the ICC system at present may experience challenges handling, a factor likely exacerbated by general resource restraints in the ICC system.[59] That said, it appears that even when the most serious environmental crimes are committed in armed conflict, there is 'something more' that has so far held ICC prosecutors back from actively pursuing charges for environmental crimes. That 'something more' may have to do with the fact that, in any investigation, there is a form of 'competition' between crimes subject to prosecution, each associated with activists' calls for inclusion in charges and – so far – environmental crimes have seemingly not made it to the top of that list,

57 Caitlin Lambert, 'Environmental Destruction in Ecuador: Crimes Against Humanity under the Rome Statute?'(2017) 30 Leiden J Int'l L 707.

58 See further Caitlyn Johnson, 'The ICC and Environmental Protection: Prosecuting Environmental War Crimes in Ukraine' (2024) 14(2) J of Nat Security Law & Policy 287.

59 See, for example Hemptinne (n 3).

perhaps in part because, as discussed elsewhere in this chapter, certain key stakeholders in the ICC system have pressed for the Court to continue to focus on core atrocity crimes.

For the purposes of the arguments set out in this chapter, it is also worth noting that the prosecutor has, to date, *not* brought charges against representatives of business enterprises or other economic actors for potential complicity in ICC Statute crimes, despite previously expressed commitments by the OTP to do exactly that, and despite receiving various Article 15 communications to that effect.[60] Indeed, based on consultations with ICC staff, some scholars observe 'a widespread reluctance' among Court staff to pursue charges against businesspersons (the ICC Statute does not permit the prosecution of corporate entities, but the persons representing them could potentially be prosecuted for crimes involving such entities to the extent the representatives carry personal responsibility).[61]

Of course, the focus and priorities of any accountability regime can change over time (and the OTP consultation process launched in 2024 concerning a new policy paper on environmental crimes mentioned above may indeed be evidence of such a change gradually occurring within the OTP). For now, however, a basic observation is that, despite long-lasting encouragement from various sides, the OTP has neither pursued charges specifically for environmental crimes in the context of relevant existing provisions in the ICC Statute, including Article 8(2)(b)(iv), nor pursued charges against a specific type of actor often implicated in serious environmental crimes, namely representatives of business enterprises.

How, then, is the potential ICC adoption of the ecocide proposal, or other forms of substantial jurisdictional expansion over environmental crimes, likely to impact norms enforcement at ICC level concerning environmental harm and the type of actors that the OTP might pursue in that regard? For sure, should the ASP decide to adopt ecocide as a crime under the ICC Statute or in other ways substantially expand the Court's jurisdiction over environmental crimes, this would be a strong signal to the OTP concerning the priorities of State Parties. This would undoubtedly add pressure on the OTP to 'do something' to demonstrate its capacity to advance environmental crimes accountability in practice.

However, the expectation that we are going to witness a wide range of cases being brought for different types of environmental harm associated with ecocide will likely disappoint. At the most basic level, the 'ICC is already over-loaded and struggling with the crimes currently under its jurisdiction', and consequently the ICC is likely to

60 See further Donna Minha, 'The Possibility of Prosecuting Corporations for Climate Crimes before the International Criminal Court: All Roads Lead to the Rome Statute?' (2020) 41 Michigan J Int L 491.

61 Nicola Palmer and Tomas Hamilton, 'Legal Humility and Perceptions of Power in International Criminal Justice' (2022) 23(3) Int Crim L Rev 1–27.

'handle few, if any, ecocide cases in any given decade'.[62] In simple terms, any ecocide crime enforcement at ICC level is almost certainly bound to be very limited in terms of the *scope of enforcement*.

What is more, the *type of offenders* most commonly associated, in public opinion, with ecocide are executives in large business enterprises operating out of Global North countries, involved in, for example, massive pollution or unlawful extraction of natural resources, or the political leaders who are complicit in, and draw advantage from, these and other types of environmental crimes.[63] Yet, *successful* prosecution of environmental crimes at ICC level is much more likely to occur in the context of low- or mid-level members of armed groups with direct responsibility for crimes negatively affecting the environment in combat situations. The OTP might even at some point seek to *pursue* accountability for other more high-profile types of actors and/or crimes committed in different contexts, but, if so, such efforts are less likely to produce actual accountability outcomes.[64]

It is useful here to dig a bit deeper into the expectations and assumptions of many supporters of ICC adoption of ecocide as a crime: the ecocide proposal is seen by many of its supporters as important not only because it would permit the ICC to increasingly focus on environmental crimes, but also because it is seen to permit focus on a specific category of offenders that are deemed particularly important for the ICC to target, namely powerful elites in the Global North – and, by extension, the potential to help to 'decolonize' international law.[65] However, as this author has previously argued, a jurisdictional expansion which *permits* increased focus on crimes that often involve particularly powerful interests and actors does not, in itself, *facilitate* that such powerful actors are held to account.[66] As Adam Branch and Liana Minkova phrase it, the ICC has tended to 'align with existing structures of global political and economic power instead of challenging those structures'.[67] Whenever it has sought to challenge these structures, the Court is 'corrected' and accountability outcomes have not been achieved.

In the past, ICC prosecutors have at times *attempted* to pursue accountability for crimes perpetrated by actors aligned with particularly powerful players in the global system, such as the militaries of Western powers, as happened in the Afghanistan investigation (alleged war crimes by US armed forces and the Central Intelligence

62 Robinson (n 5).
63 Stop Ecocide, 'What is ecocide', <https://www.stopecocide.earth> accessed 25 June 2024.
64 A point further elaborated in Hansen, 'Accountability for Environmental Crimes…' (n 4).
65 See Robinson (n 5). See also Adam Branch and Liana Minkova, 'Ecocide, the Anthropocene, and the International Criminal Court' (2023) 37 Ethics Int Affairs 51, 54.
66 Hansen, 'Accountability for Environmental Crimes…' (n 4).
67 Branch and Minkova (n 65).

Agency (CIA)) and the Iraq/UK preliminary examination (alleged war crimes by the UK armed forces). Whenever that has happened, the ICC has experienced significant pushback and, ultimately, the Court has been unable to produce accountability outcomes for these types of actors.[68] Add to that, whenever the territorial government subject to specific ICC activity resists this, the Court has continuously run into significant challenges which tend to outdo its ability to produce accountability outcomes, as happened, for example in the Kenya investigation.[69] These fundamental conditions of the ICC system are, regrettably, unlikely to fundamentally change in the context of potential adoption of ecocide as an ICC crime.

Insofar as the ICC continues to produce accountability outcomes mainly in the type of contexts and for the type of actors that it has successfully prosecuted to date (that is, members of non-state armed groups for crimes committed in conflict zones in the Global South), this is unlikely to satisfy the aspirations and demands of ecocide campaigners and other environmentalists.[70]

b. Norms enforcement in national legal systems

The developments in environmental criminal law discussed in this chapter must be considered in light of many national jurisdictions having put in place legislation permitting some form of extraterritorial application of accountability law. This involves various forms of extraterritorial application of criminal law, often under universal jurisdiction principles,[71] but, in some cases, also extraterritorial application of tort law and due diligence legislation, which, in the case of business enterprises, often provides for comparable accountability outcomes in terms of the relevant sanctions (though the expressive value of such accountability outcomes may be different from criminal law ones).[72] It needs emphasizing, in this regard, that there is increased backing in international guidelines and soft law instruments for states to apply universal jurisdiction principles to environmental crimes.[73] Going forward, further consolidating these trends seems vital for advancing meaningful accountability for environmental crimes, already because the most serious of such crimes frequently come with some form of transnational perspective.

---

68 See further Ochs (n 46); Thomas Obel Hansen, 'Accountability for British War Crimes in Iraq? Examining the Nexus between International and National Justice Responses' in Morten Bergsmo and Carsten Stahn (eds), *Quality Control in Preliminary Examination: Reviewing Impact, Policies and Practices* (TOAEP, 2018).

69 See, for example Thomas Obel Hansen, 'The International Criminal Court in Kenya: Three Defining Features of a Contested Accountability Process and Their Implications for the Future of International Justice' (2012) 18(2) Australian J Hum Rights 187.

70 See similarly Branch and Minkova (n 65).

71 See further Máximo Langer and Mackenzie Eason, 'The Quiet Expansion of Universal Jurisdiction' (2019) 30 Eur J Int L 779.

72 See further Dam-de Jong and Wolters (n 39).

73 See, for example International Congress on Universal Jurisdiction, 'Madrid-Buenos Aires Principles On Universal Jurisdiction', https://fibgar.org/upload/proyectos/35/en/principles-of-universal-jurisdiction.pdf accessed 25 June 2024.

The most obvious alternative to the ICC system, in terms of enforcement of ecocide and other forms of environmental crimes, therefore involves national courts' exercise of jurisdiction, including various forms of extraterritorial application of accountability law over environmental crimes. Such efforts have, in the past, faced many of the same obstacles pointed out in the analysis of the ICC above – resulting in difficulties holding to account the type of actors most responsible for environmental harm. For one, pushback from influential states has occurred whenever other states have attempted to pursue accountability for crimes committed outside their territory by the agents of such states, often undermining such attempts (and in some cases even leading to changes in the relevant states' legal frameworks for exercising universal jurisdiction).[74] Extraterritorial application of accountability law is therefore by no means immune to the types of pressure from influential players in the international system already discussed in this chapter. Indeed, whereas universal jurisdiction cases in European courtrooms covering, for example, core atrocity crimes in Rwanda and Syria, regularly produce accountability outcomes, cases targeting officials associated with more powerful states tend not to, precisely because of pushback by the states concerned.[75]

The above being said, in the context of achieving greater accountability outcomes for environmental crimes in conflict zones, national courts' extraterritorial application of accountability law has some basic advantages over the ICC system. For one, national jurisdictions can – and do, in fact, sometimes – apply these legal frameworks to a range of actors who have not been subject to ICC jurisdiction. Criminal prosecution of business actors for crimes committed extraterritorially is a particularly important issue in this regard, given what was discussed above concerning the additional layers of economic interest and extraterritoriality surrounding environmental crimes. As demonstrated by recent cases in some European jurisdictions, domestic authorities (often prompted by non-governmental organizations (NGOs)) have, in some situations, pursued criminal cases against business representatives with alleged responsibility for environmental crimes with extraterritorial dimensions.[76] Furthermore, whereas only a few states traditionally allowed for criminal liability for corporations as legal persons, this trend has now reversed, with many states – unlike the ICC – permitting criminal prosecution of corporations as legal entities.[77] Although existing practice concerning extraterritorial prosecution of corporate actors as legal entities

74 By way of example, this happened in Spain. See Montserrat Abad Castelos, 'The End of Universal Jurisdiction in Spain?' (2013–14) 18 Spanish Yearbook Int L 223. See more generally Katherine Gallagher, 'Universal Jurisdiction in Practice' (2009) 7 J Int Crim Just 1087.

75 See Wolfgang Kaleck, 'From Pinochet to Rumsfeld: Universal Jurisdiction in Europe 1998-2008' (2009) 30 Michigan J Int L 927.

76 For a further discussion of these cases, see Hansen, 'Accountability for Environmental Crimes…' (n 4).

77 For a further discussion of these developments, see Hansen, 'Accountability for Environmental Crimes…' (n 4). See further Eric Engle, 'Extraterritorial Corporate Criminal Liability: A Remedy for Human Rights Violations?' (2006) 20 J Civil Rights

appears to have rarely focused directly on environmental harm, and not all of them have been successfully prosecuted, there is potential for increased reliance on extraterritorial jurisdiction principles to bring criminal cases against corporate entities for serious environmental crimes.

Domestic courts' extraterritorial application of tort law presents another potentially rewarding accountability avenue for corporate actors' responsibility for environmental crimes in conflict zones. On that note, recent practice from Canada and some European jurisdictions has established that corporations operating out of the relevant country may be sued in tort for human rights violations abroad.[78] The current interpretation of the US Alien Torts Claim Act (ATCA) creates significant barriers for pursuing environmental crimes, but this could potentially change in the future.[79] Developments in tort law could potentially be boosted by the relevant normative developments discussed above, including support in the ILC Draft Principles on protection of the environment in relation to armed conflicts for enhancing accountability for business actors, as well as the increased attention, facilitated by the ecocide campaign, on the need for expanding criminalization of environmental crimes.

To summarize, national enforcement of environmental crimes legislation continues to be surrounded by numerous challenges,[80] but some of these challenges could perhaps be addressed by relying on innovative approaches, including the extraterritorial application of legislation covering environmental crimes, and also covering crimes committed by business enterprises.

6. Towards a new research agenda in ecocide

The analysis in this chapter suggests that the IEP ecocide proposal is valuable from a range of perspectives. That value, however, is not mainly to be found in the prospect of adoption at ICC level and effective enforcement by the Court, as most proponents

---

& Eco Dev 287; Sufyan Droubi, 'Transnational Corporations and International Human Rights Law' (2016) 6 Notre Dame J Int Comp L 119.

[78] See William Dodge, 'Supreme Court of Canada Recognizes Corporate Liability for Human Rights Violations' (*Just Security*, 26 March 2020) <https://www.justsecurity.org/69349/supreme-court-of-canada-recognizes-corporate-liability-for-human-rights-violations/> accessed 25 June 2024. On corporate due diligence obligations, see further Carolyn Abbot and Gary Lynch-Wood's Chapter 3 Transnational Environmental Crime Across Global Supply Chains – A Place for Due Diligence? in this volume.

[79] See further Christopher Ewell et al., 'Has the Alien Tort Statute made a Difference?: A Historical, Empirical, and Normative Assessment' (2022) 107 Cornell L Rev 1205.

[80] See further, Juan Fuentes Osorio's Chapter 6 The Effectiveness of Environmental Criminal Law Enforcement and Sarah Wright and Victoria Colvin's Chapter 7 Enforceable Undertakings as an Alternative to Prosecution in Australian Environmental Law Enforcement in this volume.

of the proposal suggest. Rather, the main value should be found in the fact that the tabling of the proposal and the consequent debate have brought about increased attention to the need to promote accountability for crimes with serious, negative implications for the environment. More concretely, the tabling of the ecocide proposal has seemingly induced many states to strengthen accountability frameworks for environmental crimes at the domestic level – and may likely induce more states to do so going forward.

The symbolic or 'expressive' value of making ecocide the fifth ICC crime should not be understated, but neither should the challenges that will likely be encountered trying to adopt and potentially enforce the ecocide norm at the ICC level. Of course, doing one thing does not preclude the other, but, in terms of priorities, it is worth keeping in mind the observations made in this chapter concerning both the complexities that an ICC amendment process is likely to encounter, and the ICC's ability to meaningfully enforce accountability for serious environmental crimes.

The surge in expanded national environmental crimes legislation – now often referenced as ecocide legislation – is noteworthy and in many ways a development that can be attributed to the tireless efforts of ecocide campaigners and increased popular support for environmental crimes prosecution. National enforcement is still surrounded by numerous challenges – and many are expected to remain in the time ahead. Yet, some of these challenges could supposedly be addressed by encouraging innovative solutions, including the extraterritorial application of environmental crimes legislation, also with regard to business enterprises.

Moving forward, the research and advocacy agenda surrounding ecocide and environmental crimes accountability more generally will have to deal with profound questions, key among them are:

- *Norms adoption*: What factors determine (relative) success in terms of national processes concerning adoption of ecocide and related environmental crimes legislation, and how do these compare in different contexts?
- *Norms dissemination*: How is ecocide norms adoption 'spreading' across different jurisdictions in time and space, and what actors and factors drive this development?
- *Norms form and symbolism*: To what extent, and why, is it significant what form the ecocide norm takes, for example, the shape of an international crime, a transnational crime, simply a crime reflected in various national criminal codes, or maybe something new and different, yet to be captured in legal doctrine?
- *Norms monopoly or plurality*: Is it desirable to work towards a singular, uniform understanding of the ecocide norm, or might a level of pluralism offer benefits, and, if so, within what boundaries?
- *Standards for measuring effective norms enforcement*: Besides obvious quantitative factors, what are the criteria that should guide perceptions of 'success' for ecocide norms enforcement (type of conduct, type of actors, and type of sanctions)?
- *Norms complementarity and synergy*: How can the various developments in law relating to environmental crimes accountability occurring in recent years

– including, most notably, the tabling of the IEP ecocide proposal, the ICRC guidelines and ILC principles, and the EU's new environmental crimes directive – be constructed to complement each other to create more synergy?

Bibliography

Abad Castelos, Montserrat, 'The End of Universal Jurisdiction in Spain?' (2013–14) 18 Spanish Yearbook Int L 223.

Ambos, Kai, 'Protecting the Environment through Criminal Law?' (*EJIL:TALK!*, 29 June 2021), <www.ejiltalk.org/protecting-the-environment-through-international-criminal-law> accessed 25 June 2024.

Bernaz, Nadia, 'An Analysis of the ICC Office of the Prosecutor's Policy Paper on Case Selection and Prioritization from the Perspective of Business and Human Rights' (2017) 15 J Int'l Crim Just 527.

Branch, Adam and Liana Minkova, 'Ecocide, the Anthropocene, and the International Criminal Court' (2023) 37 Ethics Int Affairs 51.

Bustami, Ammar and Marie-Christine Hecken, 'Perspectives for a New International Crime Against the Environment: International Criminal Responsibility for Environmental Degradation under the Rome Statute' (2021) 11(1) Goettingen J Int L 145.

Chini, Maïthé, 'Belgium becomes first in EU to recognise ecocide as international crime' (*The Brussels Times*, 23 February 2024), <https://www.brusselstimes.com/937229/belgium-becomes-first-in-eu-to-recognise-ecocide-as-international-crime-tbtb> accessed 25 June 2024.

Crook, Martin and Damien Short, 'Marx, Lemkin and the Genocide–Ecocide Nexus' (2014) 18 Int J Hum Rights 298.

Dam-de Jong, Daniëlla and James Stewart, 'Illicit Exploitation of Natural Resources' in Charles Jalloh and Kamari Clarke (eds), *The African Court of Justice And Human and Peoples' Rights* (CUP, Cambridge 2019).

Dam-de Jong, Daniëlla and Saskia Wolters, 'Through the Looking Glass: Corporate Actors and Environmental Harm beyond the ILC' (2020) 10 Goettingen J Int L 111.

Dodge, William, 'Supreme Court of Canada Recognizes Corporate Liability for Human Rights Violations' (*Just Security*, 26 March 2020), <https://www.justsecurity.org/69349/supreme-court-of-canada-recognizes-corporate-liability-for-human-rights-violations/> accessed 25 June 2024.

Droubi, Sufyan, 'Transnational Corporations and International Human Rights Law' (2016) 6 Notre Dame J Int Comp L 119.

Durney, Jessica, 'Crafting a Standard: Environmental Crimes as Crimes Against Humanity Under the International Criminal Court' (2018) 24 Hastings Env L J 413.

Engle, Eric, 'Extraterritorial Corporate Criminal Liability: A Remedy for Human Rights Violations?' (2006) 20 J Civil Rights & Eco Dev 287.

Ewell, Christopher et al., 'Has the Alien Tort Statute made a Difference?: A Historical, Empirical, and Normative Assessment' (2022) 107 Cornell L Rev 1205.

Falk, Richard, 'Environmental Warfare and Ecocide—Facts, Appraisal, and Proposal' (1973) 4 *Bulletin Of Peace Proposals* 80.

Gallagher, Katherine, 'Universal Jurisdiction in Practice' (2009) 7 J Int'l Crim Just 1087.

Gillett, Matthew, 'Eco-Struggles: Using International Criminal Law to Protect the Environment During and After Non-International Armed Conflict' in Carsten Stahn, Jens. Iverson and Jennifer Easterday (eds), *Environmental Protection and Transitions from Conflict to Peace* (OUP, Oxford 2017).

Gauger, Anja et al., 'Ecocide is the Missing 5th Crime Against Peace, Human Rights Consortium' (University of London, 2012).

Gray, Mark, 'The International Crime of Ecocide' (1996) 26 *California Western International Law Journal* 2.

Greene, Anastacia, 'The Campaign to Make Ecocide an International Crime: Quixotic Quest or Moral Imperative?' (2019) 30 Fordham Env L R 1.

Hansen, Thomas Obel, 'Accountability for British War Crimes in Iraq? Examining the Nexus between International and National Justice Responses' in Morten Bergsmo and Carsten Stahn (eds), *Quality Control in Preliminary Examination: Reviewing Impact, Policies and Practices* (TOAEP, 2018).

Hansen, Thomas Obel, 'Accountability for Environmental Crimes in Conflict Zones: Why Expanding the International Criminal Court's Jurisdiction is Not the Best Solution' (2024) 56 NYU J Int L & Pol 879.

Hansen, Thomas Obel, 'Prosecuting Ecocide: The Norms-Adoption/Enforcement Paradox' (*Just Security*, 22 June 2023), <https://www.justsecurity.org/87009/prosecuting-ecocide-the-norms-adoption-enforcement-paradox/> accessed 25 June 2024.

Hansen, Thomas Obel, 'The International Criminal Court in Kenya: Three Defining Features of a Contested Accountability Process and Their Implications for the Future of International Justice' (2012) 18(2) Australian J Hum Rights 187.

Hartig, Annegret, *Making Aggression a Crime under Domestic Law* (Springer, 2023).

Heller, Kevin, 'Belgium Set to Criminalise Ecocide (Kinda Sorta)' (*Opinio Juris*, 8 November 2022), <http://opiniojuris.org/2022/11/08/belgium-set-to-criminalise-ecocide-kinda-sorta/> accessed 25 June 2024.

Heller, Kevin, 'Skeptical Thoughts on the Proposed Crime of "Ecocide" (That Isn't)' (*Opinio Juris*, 23 June 2021), <https://opiniojuris.org/2021/06/23/skeptical-thoughts-on-the-proposed-crime-of-ecocide-that-isnt/> accessed 25 June 2024.

Hemptinne, Jérôme de, 'Concluding Observations on the Influence of International Environmental Law over International Criminal Law' (2023) 20(5) J Int'l Crim Just 1287.

Hemptinne, Jérôme de, 'Ecocide: an Ambiguous Crime?' (*EJIL:TALK!*, 29 August 2022), <https://www.ejiltalk.org/ecocide-an-ambiguous-crime/> accessed 25 June 2024.

Higgins, Polly, 'Damien Short and Nigel South, Protecting the Planet: A Proposal for a Law of Ecocide' (2013) 59 Crime, Law Soc Chang 251.

Hulme, Karen and Elizabeth B. Hessami, 'New Legal Protections for the Environment in Relation to Armed Conflict' (IUCN, 16 July 2022), <https://www.iucn.org/story/202207/new-legal-protections-environment-relation-armed-conflict> accessed 25 June 2024.

Hulme, Karen, 'Using International Environmental Law to Enhance Biodiversity and Nature Conservation During Armed Conflict' (2022) 20(5) J Int'l Crim Just 1155.

Jacobsson, Marie and Marja Lehto, 'Protection of the Environment in Relation to Armed Conflicts – An Overview of the International Law Commission's Ongoing Work' (2020) 10(1) Goettingen J Int L 27.

Johnson, Caitlyn, 'The ICC and Environmental Protection: Prosecuting Environmental War Crimes in Ukraine' (2024) 14(2) J of Nat Security Law & Policy 287.

Kaleck, Wolfgang, 'From Pinochet to Rumsfeld: Universal Jurisdiction in Europe 1998-2008' (2009) 30 Michigan J Int L 927.

Killean, Rachel, 'From Ecocide to Eco-Sensitivity: "Greening" Reparations at the International Criminal Court' (2021) 25 Int J Hum Rights 323.

Kremnitzer, Mordechai, 'A Possible Case for Imposing Criminal Liability on Corporations in International Criminal Law' (2010) 8 J Int Crim Just 909.

Lambert, Caitlin, *Environmental Destruction in Ecuador: Crimes Against Humanity under the Rome Statute?* (2017) 30 Leiden J Int'l L 707.

Langer, Máximo and Mackenzie Eason, 'The Quiet Expansion of Universal Jurisdiction' (2019) 30 Eur J Int L 779.

Lawrence, Jessica and Kevin Heller, 'The Limits of Article 8(2)(b)(iv) of the Rome Statute, the First Ecocentric Environmental War Crime' (2007) 20 Geo Int Env L Rev 61.

Mackintosh, Kate and Lisa Oldring, 'Watch This Space: Momentum Toward an International Crime of Ecocide' (*Just Security*, 5 December 2022), <https://www.justsecurity.org/84367/watch-this-space-momentum-toward-an-international-crime-of-ecocide/> accessed 25 June 2024.

McDougall, Carrie, *The Crime of Aggression under the Rome Statute of the International Criminal Court* (CUP, Cambridge 2021).

Minha, Donna, 'The Possibility of Prosecuting Corporations for Climate Crimes before the International Criminal Court: All Roads Lead to the Rome Statute?' (2020) 41 Michigan J Int L 491.

Minha, Donna, 'The Proposed Definition of the Crime of Ecocide: An Important Step Forward, but Can Our Planet Wait?' (*EJIL:TALK!*, 1 July 2021), <https://www.ejiltalk.org/the-proposed-definition-of-the-crime-of-ecocide-an-important-step-forward-but-can-our-planet-wait/> accessed 25 June 2024.

Minkova, Liana Georgieva, 'The Fifth International Crime: Reflections on the Definition of "Ecocide"' (2023) 25(1) J Genocide Research 62.

Nuridzhanian, Gaiane, 'International Enough? A Council of Europe Special Tribunal for the Crime of Aggression' (*Just Security*, 3 June 2024), <https://www.justsecurity.org/96320/council-of-europe-ukraine-tribunal/> accessed 25 June 2024.

Ochs, Sara, 'The United States, the International Criminal Court, and the Situation in Afghanistan' (2019) 95 Notre Dame L Rev 89.

Palmer, Nicola and Tomas Hamilton, 'Legal Humility and Perceptions of Power in International Criminal Justice' (2022) 23(3) Int Crim L Rev 1–27.

Pereira, Ricardo, 'After the ICC Office of the Prosecutor's 2016 Policy Paper on Case Selection and Prioritisation – Towards an International Crime of Ecocide?' (2020) 31 Crim L Forum 179.

Pereira, Ricardo, 'Towards Effective Implementation of the EU Environmental Crime Directive? The Case of Illegal Waste Management and Trafficking Offences' (2017) 26(2) Rev of Eur, Comp and Int Env L 147.

Robinson, Darryl, 'Ecocide — Puzzles and Possibilities' (2022) 20 J Int'l Crim Just 320.

Robinson, Darryl, 'The Ecocide Wave is Already Here: National Momentum and the Value of a Model Law' (*Just Security*, 23 February 2023), <https://www.justsecurity.org/85244/the-ecocide-wave-is-already-here-national-momentum-and-the-value-of-a-model-law/> accessed 25 June 2024.

Sjostedt, Britta and Anne Dienelt, 'Enhancing the Protection of the Environment in Relation to Armed Conflicts – The Draft Principles of the International Law Commission and Beyond' (2020) 10(1) Goettingen J Int L 13.

Stock, Carolyn, 'A Fifth core crime: Crime of ecocide as a new puzzle of the international criminal law' (2023) 1(1) Yearbook of Int & Eur Crim & Procedural L 248–84.

Voigt, Christina, '"Ecocide" as an International Crime: Personal Reflections on Options and Choices' (*EJIL:TALK!*, 3 July 2021), <https://www.ejiltalk.org/ecocide-as-an-international-crime-personal-reflections-on-options-and-choices/> accessed 25 June 2024.

Zimmermann, Andreas, 'Amending the Amendment Provisions of the Rome Statute: The Kampala Compromise on the Crime of Aggression and the Law of Treaties' (2012) 10(1) J Int'l Crim Just 209–27.

5 Biodiversity crime

Ludwig Krämer

The protection of biodiversity covers the protection of living organisms as well as habitats of fauna and flora species (ecosystems).[1] The Convention on Biodiversity (CBD) contains neither a list of species nor habitats that it intends to protect; in theory, thus, all living organisms and all habitats are protected under the Convention, including domesticated and 'pest' animals (fleas, mosquitos, and so on). When international environmental agreements refer to the protection of species, though, they normally list the species they intend to protect.[2] The agreements on protected areas also describe, with some precision, the areas which come under the protection of the agreement, or leave it to the contracting parties to identify the areas that shall be protected.

A typical feature of environmental law is the interdependency of national and international protection provisions. Already in 1972, when international discussions on environmental law and policy started, the United Nations (UN) formulated the states' 'sovereign right to exploit their own resources pursuant to their own environmental policy'.[3] This principle was repeated in 1992 and has been generally accepted. There is consensus that fauna and flora species form part of such natural resources.

Theoretically, it would be possible to overcome the question of national sovereignty and legally consider species as a 'common heritage of mankind'. However, such an approach would call into question the basics of international environmental law, that is, the national sovereignty over species and natural areas. It has not yet even been suggested by any state or international organisation. Some further reflections in this regard will be made below.

The national sovereignty over fauna and flora species also has consequences for the discussion of 'biodiversity crime'. That term is not defined. In international

---

1 Convention on Biological Diversity, Rio 1992, Article 1.

2 Convention on the Regulation of Whaling, Washington 1946; Convention on Wetlands of International Importance, especially as Waterfowl Habitat, Ramsar 1971; Convention on the Conservation of European Wildlife and Natural Habitats, Bern 1979.

3 Declaration of the United Nations Conference on the Human Environment, Stockholm 1972, Principle 21. Repeated as Principle 2 in the Declaration on Environment and Development, Rio 2002. Repeated in Article 3 of the CBD.

discussions, it signifies the loss of biodiversity due to the harvesting or trade of species or the impairment of protected areas contrary to international agreements or national law.[4] Again, thus, international environmental agreements refer back to national law regarding when an activity is to be considered a 'crime'. Such an activity may, under the relevant national law, be sanctioned by either criminal or administrative sanctions.[5] When administrative sanctions are foreseen or applied, national legal literature does not normally speak of a 'crime'. This means that the same activity, for example the illegal killing of an animal, may be qualified either as an administrative or as a criminal offence. As the term 'biodiversity crime', in the way it has been used in some of the international environmental law discourses, appears to classify *all* activities that are contrary to national law as 'crimes', this term can thus be misleading and should better be replaced by narrower and more legally precise terms, such as 'biodiversity-related offence' or 'environmental offence'.

Crime and protected areas

As regards biodiversity harm due to the impairment of areas, only a limited number of international environmental agreements protect areas.[6] The agreements leave it to the contracting parties to provide for sanctions in cases of an impairment of a protected area, but abstain from specifying whether the sanctions should be of criminal or administrative character. The difference between the two forms of sanctions is that criminal law implies a stronger social disapproval of the act in question. According to the general principle *nullum crimen sine lege* (a criminal act must have explicitly been so identified by a legislative act),[7] impairments of protected areas can only be sanctioned by criminal law when national legislation has explicitly foreseen this; even legislative silence in this regard does not allow the qualification of an impairing activity as a 'crime'.

European Union (EU) law provided in the beginning that certain areas for birds or for other explicitly-listed fauna and flora species and certain natural habitats that were

---

4 United Nations Office on Drugs and Crime (UNODC), *World Wildlife Crime Report* (Vienna 2020), p. 9. Communication from the Commission to the European Parliament, the Council, the European Economic and Social Committee and the Committee of the Regions EU Action Plan against Wildlife Trafficking, COM(2016) 87, p. 3.

5 Directive 2008/99/EC of the European Parliament and of the Council of 19 November 2008 on the protection of the environment through criminal law [2008] OJ L 328, p. 28, requires the 27 EU Member States to qualify certain acts as criminal actions, punishable by criminal law sanctions. Additionally, the Convention against Transnational Organised Crime, Palermo 2000, asks the contracting parties to qualify certain activities as criminal acts, without referring, though, to environmental acts.

6 Ramsar Convention (n 2), Bern Convention (n 2), UNESCO, Convention concerning the Protection of the World's Cultural and Natural Heritage, Paris 1972.

7 See, for example, the European Convention on Human Rights, Article 7: 'No one shall be held guilty of any criminal offence... which did not constitute a criminal offence under national or international law at the time when it was committed.' The global validity of this principle in some legal systems – for example, in China or Russia – is not certain.

protected should normally not be impaired by human activities.[8] In 2008, EU Directive 2008/99 required EU Member States to legally qualify 'any conduct which causes the significant deterioration of a habitat within a protected site' as a criminal offence;[9] this provision referred to the some 27 000 areas in the EU which are at present listed as protected areas by EU law (Natura 2000). It is the only provision in international law that requires criminal sanctions for the impairment of a protected area.

There is a large scientific consensus that habitat destruction and fragmentation are the biggest threats to biodiversity worldwide. Such destruction or fragmentation is due to deforestation, land use change, urbanisation, infrastructure projects (roads, pipelines, and so on), and other factors which are influenced by demographic development, demands for food supply, trade, or tourism. In view of the impossibility of protecting all the national natural environments, most countries designated specific areas (national parks, national monuments, and so on) to be particularly protected. Activities that might impair such areas require an administrative permit.

The problem for biodiversity in this approach is that not all areas that need protection are actually identified and designated as protected areas by national authorities. Moreover, an administrative permit may easily be obtained; and authorities initiate, or at least tolerate, activities in protected areas that are detrimental to biodiversity, such as logging, mining, construction, or industrial developments. The granting of an administrative permit has the consequence that the permitted activity can no longer be qualified as a 'crime', as it is not illegal. It depends almost entirely on national law and its enforcement, if and to what extent measures to maintain the conservation status of protected areas are adopted and what kind of sanctions are applied in cases of non-compliance.

An attempt to protect natural areas was made through efforts to develop legislation according to which plans, programmes, or projects of some importance had to be assessed as to their environmental impact before they could be permitted. However, such legislation remained largely limited to the Global North,[10] concentrated – apart from EU law – on transnational impacts and left the details of the plans and projects and the intensity of assessment required largely to the national authorities. Also, a negative outcome in an environmental impact assessment does not as such prevent the

---

8 Council Directive 79/409/EEC of 2 April 1979 on the conservation of wild birds [1979] OJ L 103, p. 1; this Directive was later replaced by Directive 2009/147/EC of the European Parliament and of the Council of 30 November 2009 on the conservation of wild birds [2010] OJ L 20, p. 7. Council Directive 92/43/EEC of 21 May 1992 on the conservation of natural habitats and of wild fauna and flora [1992] OJ L 206, p. 7.

9 Directive 2008/99 (n 5), Article 3(h). Directive (EU) 2024/1203 of the European Parliament and of the Council of 11 April 2024 on the protection of the environment through criminal law and replacing Directives 2008/99/EC and 2009/123/EC [2024] OJ L 2024/1203, Article 3 (2) (q) repeated this provision with almost the same wording.

10 See United Nations Economic Commission for Europe, Convention on the Environmental Impact Assessment in a Transboundary Context, Espoo 1991.

authorities from permitting the completion of the plan or project. Again, the sanctions for non-compliance with the legislation were left to national law.

In general, criminal law does not effectively protect the impairment of protected areas, as many impairing acts are permitted by public authorities. Criminal sanctions appear to be quantitatively insufficient, hardly ever address impairing actions by public authorities themselves, and are neither sufficiently effective nor dissuasive.

The scarce data[11] available on this issue, confirm this conclusion. International or global statistics on illegal impairments of protected areas are completely lacking. The United Nations Environment Programme (UNEP) reports on environmental crimes, which are published from time to time, do not specifically refer to the impairment of protected areas.[12] The EU's publications on the implementation of the Environmental Crime Directive 2008/99 ('ECD') did not even mention the number of cases in Member States that came under the scope of the Article 3(h) criminal offence concerning the significant deterioration of a habitat within a protected site, but limited themselves to indicating the maximum imprisonment sentences and the maximum financial sanctions for natural and legal persons established by national law,[13] and underlined that several Member States did not even recognise criminal responsibility of legal persons.[14] Studies on biodiversity crimes mandated by the EU Commission were likewise silent on data concerning protected areas.[15] National research was also inconclusive: for example, the regular national reports on forest fires in Europe mentioned that about 40 per cent of the fires affected areas which were protected under the EU Natura 2000 system, and that about nine out of ten fires were caused by human – intentional or negligent – activity.[16] The percentage of intentional fires – which are clearly 'deliber-

---

11 See generally Council of the EU, *Report on the eighth round of informal evaluation of environmental crime* Document 14065 of 11 November 2019, p. 23: 'There is a lack of information on the entire flow of cases from the administrative authorities, police, public prosecutors' offices and courts, and environmental crime cannot be tracked in a single statistical system so as to provide an overall picture of this criminal phenomenon.'

12 See, for example, UNEP-Interpol, *The Rise of Environmental Crime* (Nairobi, 2016).

13 European Commission: Directorate-General for Environment, *Combating environmental crimes and related infringements – Environmental compliance assurance – Guidance document* (Publications Office of the European Union, 2021); Commission Staff Working Document Evaluation of the Directive 2008/99/EC of the European Parliament and of the Council of 19 November 2008 on the protection of the environment through criminal law (Environmental Crime Directive), SWD (2020) 259.

14 SWD (2020) 259 (n 13), pp. 39 and 233; these countries are Bulgaria, Germany, Greece, Latvia, and Sweden.

15 Milieu, *Evaluation study on the implementation of Directive 2008/99* (Bruxelles, 2014). European Union Action to Fight Environmental Crime (EFFACE), *Environmental crime and the EU. Synthesis of the research project 'EU acts to fight environmental crime'* (Luxembourg, 2016).

16 European Commission: Joint Research Centre, *Forest fires in Europe, Middle East and Africa 2020* (Publications Office of the European Union, 2021).

ate impairments' of a protected area – varied between 3 per cent in Bulgaria and 48 per cent in Poland; and for negligent causation of fires, between 27 per cent in Germany and 70 per cent in Finland.[17] No further details on convictions, acquittals, and so on were published; everybody agreed that the identification of causes of fires was very complicated and that generally not enough staff were available for such investigations.

An in-depth report by the European Parliament on the situation in the United Kingdom (UK) did not address the impairment of protected areas, and a study from 2020 on wildlife crimes was also silent on protected areas.[18] A very detailed study by the United Nations Office on Drugs and Crime (UNODC) in 2021, which again did not refer to the impairment of protected areas, concluded that '(A)n accurate measuring of UK wildlife crime… is currently not possible'.[19] Similarly, studies on the situation of wildlife crime in France, Spain and Portugal did not refer to the impairment of protected areas.[20] A study on Germany indicated that, between 2010 and 2019, between 19 and 45 cases concerning the impairment of a protected area had been brought to the attention of public authorities,[21] without, however, indicating how often these cases had led to criminal convictions or acquittals. Statistics from other EU countries are not available.

A good illustration of the difficulties in classifying the impairment of a protected area as a crime is a case decided by the Court of Justice of the EU (CJEU) in 2021.[22] In that case, farmers had, at least since 2010, abstracted water in the protected area of Donana (Spain) without permission in order to grow agricultural products. This led to a serious impairment of the protected area. The regional government turned a blind eye to these activities and even intended, in order to satisfy the agricultural community and for electoral reasons, to legalise this abstraction of water. The CJEU found a breach of EU provisions to protect the Donana area; however, this did not lead the regional government to consider the farming activities as a 'crime' and open investigations.

Overall, it is fair to assume that the number of crimes concerning protected areas is small. This comes as no surprise when one considers the underlying reasons. Indeed,

---

17 Ibid, pp. 15 and 71.

18 Directorate General for Internal Policies: Policy Department Economic and Scientific Policy, *Wildlife crime in the United Kingdom* (Luxembourg, 2016), PE 578.963:7; Link Wildlife and Countryside, *Wildlife Crime in 2020 – England and Wales* (2021).

19 United Nations Office on Drugs and Crime (UNODC), *Wildlife and Forest Crime. Analytical Toolkit Report* (2021).

20 Service Statistique Ministeriel de la Sécurité Interne (France), L*es atteintes à l'environnement enregistrées par la police et la gendarmerie entre 2016 et 2021. Premier état de lieu* (Paris, 2021), p. 9. J.L Fuente Osorio and T. Fajardo del Castillo, *El carácter disuasorio, efectivo y proporcional de las sanciones penales impuestas en Espana y Portugal en delitos contra el medio ambiente* (Madrid and Lisbon, 2020).

21 Umweltbundesamt (ed), *Umweltdelikte 2019* (Dessau-Rosslau, 2021) pp. 71 and following.

22 *Commission v Spain* (C-559/19) EU:C:2021:512.

the shrinking, or even the disappearance, of protected areas occurs, in particular, through agricultural management measures, urbanisation, infrastructure projects or pollution. Most of these measures are based either on administrative permission to execute the planned activity or the activity not being explicitly prohibited. A granted permission or the absence of an explicit prohibition automatically eliminates the criminal character of the activity and qualifies it at best as an administrative offence. In other words, the reduction or the loss of protected areas is marked most of all by deliberate administrative action or administrative inertia at the local, regional or national level.

Any research concerning criminal activities with regard to protected areas would have to begin at the national level, list the protected areas, then examine the theory and practice of granting permissions to impair the protected area by reducing its size or by permitting constructions or other activities, and qualify the unauthorised impairment as illegal. It would have to examine the activity of all members of the enforcement chain – administrative authorities, police, prosecutors, courts – and examine whether the respective national system of protecting areas from unauthorised actions is in fact effective, dissuasive and proportional, and successful in stopping or significantly slowing down the loss of protected areas. Such research is particularly challenging – for example, the question of on what basis and by whom permits are granted in African countries to reduce a habitat for elephants or lions, or under what conditions such impairments are tolerated, is not an easy one to answer. Another part of the research might examine whether it makes sense to list protected areas and permits or unjustified tolerances to impair them in a global list. Such a global list of protected areas was established by the Internation Union for Conservation of Nature (IUCN), a global environmental network organisation. The criteria for the inclusion of an area in this list depend on compliance with certain standards that were fixed by the IUCN.[23] An impairment of a listed area does not necessarily constitute a crime; rather, this depends on the question of whether the relevant national law explicitly qualifies the impairing activity as illegal.

Research difficulties multiply when the different approaches of states are examined. First, a careful examination would have to be undertaken to identify which areas are protected by law and whether the unauthorised impairment of a protected area is explicitly prohibited. Next, the system of permitting activities would have to be studied in detail to assess the influence of tacit permits, general, unspecified permits, and the geographical dimension of a permit. The activities of the members of the enforcement chain would also have to be examined, as well as the convictions and acquittals in the respective states or regions.

23 By 2022, this list incuded 261766 areas, see https://IUCN.org/our-union/commissions/world-commission-protected-areas (15 July 2022). The criteria do not establish how the 'protection' status is reached or taken away, what happens in case of an impairment, who assesses the appropriate management of the site, what constitutes a significant impairment, and so on.

The overall complexity of such research raises a further research question: whether the unauthorised impairment of a protected area should really be sanctioned by criminal law. The majority of protected area losses are due to explicit or tacit agreements (permits) by the competent local, regional or national authorities, who only exceptionally face criminal prosecution. The political will to apply zero tolerance to impairments of protected areas exists hardly anywhere. To this must be added the general problems of criminal procedures: they normally take a long time; evidence is difficult to establish; police officers, prosecutors and courts have a considerable amount of discretionary power, which can be relatively easily used *in extenso*, as the victim – the environment – has no voice; administrative inertia or negligence is rarely sanctioned by criminal law; and demographic, political, social and economic considerations frequently influence decisions.

Research would also have to examine the question of whether the 'island' approach to protected areas is the most appropriate one. Under this approach, only those areas that have been granted the status of 'protected area' by national law receive particular attention. The CBD mentions 'protected areas or areas, where special measures need to be taken to conserve biological diversity',[24] which is not very helpful. In practice, though, attention is concentrated on classified areas.[25] Research would have to investigate alternatives to the limitations of protected areas.

Taking species from the wild and wildlife trafficking

The CBD aims at the protection of all fauna and flora species but does not contain a list of protected species. Thus, it does not contribute to the question of when the taking of a specimen of a species from the wild constitutes a 'crime'. Other international agreements on the conservation of fauna or flora species enumerate the species that are protected[26] and provide that the contracting parties shall, through their national legislation, provide for sanctions that apply in cases of a breach of the obligation to protect species and which are preventative, dissuasive, and proportionate.

---

[24] CBD, Article 8. In EU law, the CJEU also granted the status of a protected area to areas that needed to be protected but had not been protected under national law; see Commission of the *European Communities v Kingdom of Spain* (C-355/90) EU:C:1993:331 and the 'Cyprus snake' case *European Commission v Republic of Cyprus* (C-340/10) EU:C:2012:143.

[25] The Council of Europe Convention on Landscapes (CETS No. 176, Florence, 2000), is broader but remains rather general as to the protection requirements.

[26] Ramsar Convention; Bonn Convention; Montego Convention; the Whaling Convention mentions 'whales' in general and it is disputed whether this term includes all cetaceans.

The taking of animals or plants from the wild has seen considerable development.[27] Animals or plants are taken to prepare traditional medicines, animals as pets, as tourist trophies, as a form of hunting for sport, for food, for collection purposes, or for commercial activities. Demand in Asia and Europe reached such dimensions that trade in fauna and flora specimens or their derivatives has become a lucrative global business. A UNEP-Interpol study estimated the value of illegal wildlife trafficking at US $7–23 billion per year, to which must be added the value of forestry crimes (illegal logging, illegal timber trade) at US $51–152 billion per year and the value of illegal fishing, estimated at US $11–24 billion per year.[28] The increased taking of species from the wild and the international trade influenced – together with the loss of habitats – the decline of species: some nine million specimens were traded per year between 1975 and 1985, while some 100 million were traded between 2005 and 2014.[29] The World Wildlife Fund (WWF) estimated the decline of animal species – mammals, birds, fish, amphibians, reptiles – between 1970 and 2016 at 68 per cent.[30]

In 1973, the international community adopted an international agreement – the Convention on International Trade in Endangered Species of Wild Fauna and Flora (CITES) – to fight the illegal wildlife trade, though, it has no effect vis-à-vis third parties and thus does not have the effect of making trafficking illegal in non-State Parties to CITES. Significantly, CITES asks contracting parties to 'penalise trade in, or possession of, species' that come under the agreement, but does not specify that the sanctions should be of a criminal character;[31] such a decision is left to the law of each contracting party. In 2018, about 18 000 specimens of endangered species had been

27 See also Angus Nurse's Chapter 8 The Global Illegal Wildlife Trade Crisis in this volume.

28 UNEP-Interpol, *The rise of environmental crime. A growing threat to natural resources, peace, development and security* (Nairobi, 2017), p. 7. See also Commission Communication COM(2016) 87 (n 4) and Commission Staff Working Document Analysis and Evidence in support of the EU Action Plan against Wildlife Trafficking Accompanying the document Communication from the Commission to the European Parliament, the Council, the European Economic and Social Committee and the Committee of the Regions EU Action Plan against Wildlife Trafficking, SWD(2016) 38.

29 Intergovernmental Science-Policy Platform on Biodiversity and Ecosystems Services (IPBES), *Global assessment report on biodiversity and ecosystem services* (Bonn, 2019), p. 489.

30 WWF, *Living Planet Report 2020* (Gland, 2020), p. 16. The decline is different from one continental region to the other: WWF indicates a decline of 94 per cent in Latin America and the Caribbean, 65 per cent in Africa, 45 per cent in Asia-Pacifico, 33 per cent in North America, and 24 per cent in Europe and Central Asia. See also IPBES (n 29), pp. 417 and following.

31 Ibid, Article VIII. Resolution 11.3 of the Conference of the CITES Agreement requested contracting parties to make 'illicit trafficking in protected species involving organised criminal groups' a serious crime.

the subject of seizures for illegal trafficking, with a value of some US $260 million.[32] However, it is estimated that only about 10 per cent of the illegal wildlife trade concern trade in endangered species falling under the scope of CITES.[33] The Convention covers, at present, some 6000 animals and 30 000 plants, which are listed in different, constantly updated annexes to the Agreement. Contracting parties may also ban or restrict trade of other species such as in the case of endangered endemic species that are not listed by CITES and national trafficking activities may be subject to seizures. Contracting parties do not systematically report on their national implementation and enforcement systems or the applied administrative or criminal sanctions, prosecutions, convictions and acquittals.[34] Detailed research on the enforcement system of each of the 183 parties to CITES and its effectiveness in practice is completely lacking.

EU law went two significant steps further. First, it adopted a Regulation on trade in endangered species, which was somewhat more stringent than CITES, and was directly applicable in all EU Member States and thus did not need to be implemented by national legislations.[35] Second, it adopted Directive 2008/99 on Environmental Crime, which provided that the unlawful taking of animals from the wild had to be classified as a criminal offence; the same classification as a criminal offence was required for the unlawful trading in specimens of protected fauna and flora species.[36] The new Environmental Crime Directive 2024/1203 maintained this system of sanctions and even added other new offences.

Trade in endangered species is only part of a much larger international trade in fauna and flora species generally, where legal rules such as international agreements, regional, and national legislation hardly exist at all. The attitude towards wild animals in different parts of the world, due to cultural traditions, religious influence,

---

32 International Consortium on Combating Wildlife Crime (ICCWC) (grouping the CITES Secretariat, Interpol, UNODC, the World Bank Group, and the World Customs Organisation), *Annual report 2020 – Together against wildlife crime* (Geneva, 2021).

33 Convention on Trade in Endangered Species, Washington 1973 (CITES Agreement).

34 See, however, the reporting obligations of EU Member States under Directive 2024/1203 (n 9), Articles 22(4) and 25.

35 Council Regulation (EEC) No 3626/82 of 3 December 1982 on the implementation in the Community of the Convention on international trade in endangered species of wild fauna and flora [1982] OJ L 384, p. 1; this Regulation was replaced by Council Regulation (EEC) No 338/97 of 9 December 1996 on the protection of species of wild fauna and flora by regulating trade therein [1997] OJ L 61, p. 1.

36 Directive 2008/99 (n 5), Article 3(f): '(The unlawful) killing, destruction, possession or taking of specimens of protected wild fauna and flora species' shall be classified as a criminal offence. Article 3(g): '(The unlawful) trading in specimens of protected fauna and flora species or part or derivatives thereof' shall be classified as a criminal offence. Both provisions were not to apply when the acts concerned a negligible quantity and had a negligible impact. The Proposal for a Directive of the European Parliament and of the Council on the protection of the environment through criminal law and replacing Directive 2008/99/EC, COM(2021) 851, did not propose to significantly change these provisions.

consumption habits, and keeping animals as pets, could only, with great difficulty, be overcome via international agreements, other legal instruments, or administrative practice. Efforts to approach the problem through the establishment of lists of endangered fauna and flora species often come too late to prevent the decline of a species. However, this is also due to a notorious lack of human and financial resource – public or private – in dealing with this matter.

The practical consequences of the system of national provisions which sanction the harvesting and trade that is contrary to national law are likewise largely unknown. For Spain, Juan Fuentes Osorio and Teresa Fajardo del Castillo reported that there are some 700 cases of illegal taking or killing of animals per year; yet it is not clear whether these cases are limited to the taking of species from the wild.[37] In Germany, 135 administrative procedures were undertaken in 2018, and 204 in 2019; at the same time, 15 and 44 criminal investigation procedures were started respectively in these two years. While about 60 per cent were successfully completed, the number of convictions is not known.[38] For the UK, the UNODC reported 416 wildlife crime convictions between 2011 and 2020, but reported at the same time that, of 54 cases of wildlife crimes which were brought to the attention of the prosecution offices in 2018–19, only 17 were actually prosecuted and only 11 led to a conviction.[39] Another study reported that for 2019–2020 there were 121 confirmed crimes of illegal hunting, with 55 convictions. With regard to illegal fishing, that study reported 2,025 confirmed criminal offences between 2016 and 2020, with 341 convictions.[40]

Any research on the situation in different countries would have to start by clarifying which unauthorised activities are covered,[41] and then identify the respective national system of administrative and criminal sanctions, as well as the practice of all the members of the enforcement chain at local, regional, and national levels. The research would not only have to consider non-compliance with the CITES provisions, but also unauthorised trade in other non-endangered species. Furthermore, future studies should also look beyond international trade activities by considering domestic trade and, finally, the illegal taking, capturing, and killing of species, as well as illegal logging.[42]

The practical difficulties in achieving a significant reduction in unauthorised activities might be illustrated by the taking of birds in the EU. EU legislation since 1979 has

37 Fuentes Osorio and Fajardo del Castillo (n 20), p. 63.

38 Umweltbundesamt (n 21), p. 85.

39 UNODC (n 4), pp. 47 and 58.

40 Link Wildlife and Countryside (n 18), pp. 13 and 22.

41 For example, Fuentes Osorio and Fajardo del Castillo (n 20) group under the heading 'fauna and flora [impairment]' illegal hunting, animal welfare infringements, illegal fishing, and illegal trafficking.

42 See UNODC (n 4), p. 7. EU Directive 2024/1203 (n 9), Article 3 (2) (p) now adds illegal trade in forest commodities as a criminal offence.

protected all wild European birds.[43] Since 2008, the illegal taking or killing of birds has been considered a criminal act and punishable as such.[44] In two studies published in 2016 and 2019, an environmental organisation published figures on the illegal taking and killing of birds in the EU, which amounted to more than 14 million birds per year.[45] Of course, only a fraction of the acts concerning the taking and killing appear as a 'crime' in the statistics of the EU Member States: many cases remain unknown to the public authorities, the number of specimens affected is considered negligible, numerous cases are considered part of the cultural tradition of the country[46] or, even when enough evidence is available, are sanctioned with an administrative fine.

The Commission itself admitted that the exact extent of wildlife crime and its development since the adoption of ECD 2008/99 is unknown and that there was little evidence that illegal trade in wildlife was significantly reduced as a consequence of the Directive: '[I]t might be concluded that the Directive did not achieve its objective to reduce environmental crime'.[47] Thus, ECD 2008/99 was replaced by ECD 2024/1203.[48]

Wildlife crime could thus be defined as the taking of fauna and flora species from the wild, contrary to applicable international or national legislation. In view of the demand, trade in animals and plants has reached a dimension that increases the risk

---

43 Directive 79/409 (n 8).

44 Directive 2008/99 (n 5), Article 3(f).

45 A. Brochet a.o. (for BirdLife International), *Preliminary assessment of the scope and scale of illegal killing and taking of birds in the Mediterranean region* (Bird Conservation International, Cambridge, 2016), p. 1; A. Brochet et al. (for BirdLife International), *Illegal killing and taking of birds in Europe outside the Mediterranean: assessing the scope and scale of a complex issue* (Bird Conservation International, Cambridge, 2019), p. 10. The figures for the different countries were (mean values): Austria 3900, Belgium 60 200, Bulgaria 37000, Croatia 510000, Cyprus 2.3 million, Czechia 12 800, Denmark 31 300, Estonia 6300, France 522 000, Finland 7600, Germany 100 000, Greece 704 000, Hungary 14 000, Ireland 3200, Italy 5.6 million, Latvia 2500, Lithuania 3100, Luxembourg 0, Malta 108 000, Netherlands 13 200, Poland 18 400, Portugal 133 000, Romania 99 700, Slovakia 5700, Slovenia 254 000, Spain 3.9 million, Sweden 58 600, UK 7300. The figures were, with approval, quoted by European Commission: Directorate-General for Environment, *Combating environmental crime and related infringements – Environmental Quality Assurance – Guidance document.* (Publications Office of the European Union, 2021), p. 35.

46 See *Commission v Malta* (C-557/15) EU:C:2018:477 and *Association One Voice and Ligue pour la protection des oiseaux v Ministre de la Transition écologique et solidaire* (C-900/19) EU:C:2021:211. In those cases, Malta and France passionately defended the right of Member States to permit, for traditional reasons, the taking of birds in a way that was incompatible with Directive 2009/147 (n 8), but were unsuccessful before the Court of Justice of the EU.

47 SWD(2021) 259 (n 13), pp. 54 and 55. The Commission's proposal to review Directive 2008/99, COM (2021) 851 (n 36), suggested continuing to treat trade in specimens of species listed in Regulation 338/97 (n 35) as a crime, unless the trade concerned negligible quantities.

48 Directive 2024/1203 (n 9).

for species. This becomes obvious with regard to specific animals, such as elephants, rhinos, pangolins, great apes, and parrots as well as some plants (such as tropical wood).

In 2016, the EU Commission adopted an action plan to combat wildlife trafficking for the years 2016 to 2020.[49] The plan consisted of 12 general objectives and 32 specific actions,[50] which aimed at improving the global situation concerning wildlife trafficking. In 2022, this action plan was revised; 69 actions were proposed under four general objectives.[51] The Commission also made an assessment of the earlier action plan, which was cautiously optimistic.[52] Further research might be critical to follow the implementation of the new action plan and examine which past actions were successful, which actions were a failure, and what general lessons can be learnt from the action plans – for example, whether there should be an international action plan adopted under CITES.

Another way forward could be to increase the protection of plants and species. Apart from the CBD, there are no other international agreements on the protection of biodiversity generally, including all plants and animals.[53] The protection in other agreements only contains positive lists of some species. During the last decades, concerns have increased that animals are sentient beings and should thus not be exposed to unnecessary suffering. Such concerns developed into suggestions that we should renounce the consumption of meat or animal products in general (vegetarian and vegan movements), particularly in industrialised Western countries; yet differentiation between wild and domesticated animals or animals bred in captivity is not

---

49 Commission Communication (n 4), COM(2016) 87.

50 The 12 objectives were: (1) reduce demand and supply of wildlife products, (2) ensure benefits for rural communities, (3) increase business sector engagement, (4) tackle corruption associated with wildlife trafficking, (5) ensure better implementation, (6) increase capacities to combat wildlife trafficking, (7) fight organised crime more effectively, (8) improve international cooperation, (9) support developing countries more effectively, (10) coordinate actions better, (11) address the security dimension of trafficking, (12) strengthen multilateral efforts.

51 Communication from the Commission to the European Parliament, the Council, the European Economic and Social Committee and the Committee of the Regions Revision of the EU action plan against wildlife trafficking, COM(2022) 581. The four general objectives were (1) prevent wildlife trafficking and address its root causes; (2) strengthen the legal and policy framework; (3) enforce regulations and policies effectively; and (4) strengthen global partnerships.

52 Commission Staff Working Document Evaluation of the EU action plan against wildlife trafficking Accompanying the document Communication from the Commission to the European Parliament, the Council, the European Economic and Social Committee and the Committee of the Regions Revision of the EU action plan against wildlife trafficking, SWD(2022) 354.

53 The International Plant Protection Convention, Rome 1997, protects cultivated and wild plants by preventing the introduction and spread of pests, thus serving human interest.

generally made. As far as can be seen, though, no country has, until now, introduced legislation that legally protects all animals from being taken or killed, or imposes a vegetarian or vegan diet.

Any research on introducing a globally applicable right for animals should examine to what extent such a right would correspond with the religious, cultural, and societal traditions of different countries. As the current international environmental legal framework is strongly influenced by Western countries, the Christian religion might have had considerable influence on the development of the law.[54] Research should examine to what extent other religions have influenced, or are influencing, the attitudes of countries towards the taking of animals (and plants) from the wild. This applies particularly in economically less wealthy countries in Asia, Africa, or Latin America, where animal products are an important source of protein for human consumption, research would also have to examine the impacts and consequences of substituting animal products in the food supply of the populations in those regions.

Research could usefully examine to what extent the approach of giving rights to animals might reduce the taking and killing of animals. Some authors argue for giving rights only to those animals able to suffer pain. Others consider the general cognitive abilities of animals to be decisive. Researchers would also have to explain whether any differentiation among animals is 'man-made' and thus, despite all arguments to the contrary, arbitrary. Further research might also examine the question of whether pest animals, such as termites, fleas, mosquitoes, or rats, should also obtain protection, and to what degree. Further, the question of whether it is compatible with the rights of animals for humans to use animals for scientific research would be relevant.

More fundamental research would have to discuss the arguments raised by some researchers who are of the opinion that animals who can suffer equally to humans should be accorded the same concern and legal protection as humans; and hence that non-human animals are bearers of rights and entitled to justice. This would lead to the consequence that all animal killing, hunting, and fishing would be a violation of animal rights. Some go so far as to conclude that '[T]o the degree that CITES contributes to species extinction, CITES definitely deserves to be linked to organized state corporate crime'.[55] This assessment is not shared here; rather, CITES – which only deals with animal welfare during the international transport of animals – is considered to have significantly contributed to reducing trade in endangered species. However, further research might usefully explore this issue in more detail.

---

54 See the Bible, Genesis 1.28 (God's instruction to man): 'Be fruitful and multiply; fill the earth and subdue it: have dominion over the fish of the sea, over the birds of the air and over every living that moves on the earth.'

55 See, for example, R. Sollund, 'Wildlife Trade and Law Enforcement: A Proposal for Remodelling of CITES: Incorporating Species Justice, Ecojustice and Environmental Justice' (2022) 66 *International Journal of Offender Therapy and Comparative Criminology* 1017.

Some authors who adhere to 'green criminology' sometimes claim that it should no longer be a country that decides whether killing, hunting, or fishing is permitted and under what conditions. Rather, in the name of 'animal rights', it should be decided once and for all that these activities are a crime and have to be sanctioned. This means that the taking of animals from the wild is not only illegal when it conflicts with international or national law; it is always illegal. Under this approach, the whole concept of wildlife crime would have to be rethought and reshaped.

This position, which is not legal practice in any country in the world, comes into conflict with the above-mentioned basic principle of international environmental law that it is states that have the sovereign right to dispose of their natural resources – and this includes animals and plants.[56] The CBD, the Bern Convention, and other international agreements would have to be replaced by new agreements that take account of the rights of animals. Additionally, trade and transport agreements, food supply measures, fishing conventions, agricultural, pharmaceutical, and other agreements would have to be reformulated or repealed in order to accommodate the rights of animals. Further research would have to explore to what extent there is a realistic prospect that such an approach is pursued by the legal, political, and economic authorities at the international and national levels, in particular by states, and whether legally binding international agreements can be adopted.

Linked to the rights of animals as sentient beings is the evolution of considerations that give parts of nature rights of their own. The movement started in New Zealand, where legislative acts declared the river Whanganui and the natural area Te Urewera to be legal entities with rights of their own. Ecuador, Bolivia, and Colombia introduced rights of nature into their national constitutions, and courts in India, Bangladesh, and other countries followed the example of New Zealand[57] in recognising rights of nature to rivers.

The legal discussion considering whether nature, or parts of nature, has rights of its own, which may be defended in court, has not come to a standstill. From such rights of nature, it is only a small step to argue that living organisms such as animals (and plants) have rights of their own, which may be defended in court; the publications of Sollund and numerous other green criminologists evidence this. Research should further explore this path and examine in particular the practice of administrative authorities and courts in Bolivia, Ecuador, and Colombia. Researchers might look into the question of whether such rights should be limited to animals and not include plants, how far such rights should go (should that right include the right to live in a protected habitat?), whether animals bred in captivity or domesticated animals (cows,

---

56 Principle 2 of the Rio Declaration on Environment and Development (1992). The text of the declaration can be found at: https://www.un.org/en/development/desa/population/migration/generalassembly/docs/globalcompact/A_CONF.151_26_Vol.I_Declaration.pdf.

57 See the overview in United Nations, Harmony with Nature, *Rights of Nature Law and Policy*, harmonywithnatureun.org/unDocs (accessed 29 August 2022).

pigs, dogs, and so on) should have rights (and, how far such rights should reach), whether weaker animals (zebras, gnus) should enjoy protection against predators (lions), and so on. The next question would be who decides what is good for nature or, in this discussion, for animals: New Zealand – followed by Colombian, Indian, and Bangladeshi courts – ordered the appointment of guardians for the specific protected area (river), who should take the necessary decisions. It is as yet unclear, though, what happens if a person drowns in a river (should the river be liable?), if hydroelectric power impairs the river flow but is vital for the adjacent population, or what happens, when the guardians make 'bad' decisions. Finally, researchers would have to deal with the argument that all decisions on animal rights or on the rights of rivers, natural parks, and so on are man-made and do not necessarily let prevail the interests of the animal or part of nature in question.[58]

Other efforts in international environmental law that could usefully be explored by research include attempts to introduce a new crime of 'ecocide'.[59] At present, the International Criminal Court[60] is responsible for deciding whether certain particularly serious acts – war crimes, crimes against humanity, genocide, and crimes of aggression – amount to international crimes. Some lawyers suggest extending the jurisdiction of the International Criminal Court to 'ecocide' which was defined by an expert group[61] as 'unlawful or wanton[62] acts committed with knowledge that there is a substantial likelihood of severe and either widespread or long-term damage to the environment caused by those acts'. Research could examine the precarious state of the International Criminal Court itself, which is questioned by several African states and whose Statute was not ratified by, among others, Russia and the United States. Further research might also examine the question of whether the draft definition of 'ecocide' is sufficiently precise, the impact such a crime would have on the taking of animals and plants, whether the limitation to very serious cases would not just concentrate on organised crime activities, and whether the Court's resources would be able to also handle environmental criminal cases.

Concluding remarks

More generally, it is suggested that the following areas should be further explored in the context of research on biodiversity crimes:

58 See the story of the orca, Morgan: M.V. Spiegl, A. Trouborst and I.N. Visser, 'Mission creep in the application of wildlife law: the progressive dilution of legal requirements regarding a wild-born orca kept for "research" purposes' (2019) 28(3) *RECIEL* 328.

59 See also Thomas Obel Hansen's Chapter 4 Towards a New Agenda for Ecocide Norms – Adoption and Enforcement in this volume.

60 Rome Statute of the International Criminal Court, Rome 1998.

61 Independent Expert Panel for the Legal Definition of Ecocide, June 2021.

62 The Expert Panel stated: '"Wanton" means with reckless disregard for damage which would be clearly excessive in relation to social and economic benefits anticipated.'

(1) *Better regulation:* The core of legislation on biodiversity is placed at the national level; EU and international texts play, at best, a supportive role. Research should point out in concrete terms where national legislation has loopholes, allows its bypassing, gives too much discretion to enforcement bodies (police agents, judges, and so on), omits to cover parts of fauna and flora species, or generally prevents the loss of biodiversity at the national level.

Research that follows the above-mentioned approach by green criminologists, according to which any capturing or killing of animals impairs their animal rights and is a crime, could usefully study the impact of such a concept on international environmental law. International (environmental) law is mostly formed by consensus. A consensus to limit the trade in endangered species enabled the adoption, and enables the regular updating, of CITES. Research might explore whether the prohibition of capturing, killing, and trading of all animals, as apparently proposed by some green criminology scholars, would be able to obtain the necessary international consensus. Such research would also have to take into consideration the political, cultural, economic, social, and legal problems that approach would raise, as well as its impact on the basic principle of international environmental law and policy, according to which states have the sovereign right to exploit their own natural resources, provided they do not impair the rights of other states.

(2) *Better application of legal provisions:* Research should explore how national legislation can be better aligned in order to ensure effective and dissuasive sanctions for impairments. Empirical research should try to find out why actual actions taken by members of the enforcement chain are insufficient in many cases and show what positive results may be reached by better application; in doing that, it might orient itself on the guidance published by the International Consortium on Combating Wildlife Crime (ICCWC) on effective law enforcement of wildlife and forest crime.[63] There should also be greater transparency regarding the collection of data on biodiversity crime, as a change in the behaviour of both legal and natural persons can only be obtained by demonstrating results from empirical data and communicating those results to the public at large.

(3) *Capacity building:* There is a general concern about the lack of human and financial resources in the fight against wildlife crime. The lack of capacity leads to prolonged procedures, cases that are not pursued, corruption incidents, increased fraud, unjustified dismissals of persons, frustrations in the enforcement chain, and so on. Capacity building also has importance for researchers: unless they are able to set up structures with researchers in other parts of the world besides Europe and North America, they stand almost no chance of changing the global approach to biodiversity crime. Therefore, they should try to set up joint ventures, research teams, empirical research undertakings, joint data collection mechanisms, and so on at a global level and strive to overcome, at the same time, the language barrier.

---

63 ICCWC, *Indicator framework for combating wildlife and forest crime* (Geneva, 2016).

(4) *Cooperation:* Closer cooperation of researchers with public authorities at the national and transnational levels is necessary. The international phenomenon of biodiversity crime requires an *international* response. The reluctance of states to establish effective international bodies to fight wildlife crime makes cooperation below the institutional level all the more important. While an individual case of illegal trafficking might not appear serious enough for it to be handled under the criminal law, the combined effects of biodiversity crimes – some €8–20 billion has been estimated in biodiversity-related damage per year leading to increased biodiversity loss globally – should clarify the need to effectively combat such activities and resort to the criminal law. Research cooperation must also include closer collaboration with environmental organisations. Such organisations as WWF, Trade Records Analysis of Flora and Fauna in Commerce (TRAFFIC), Greenpeace, and International Fund for Animal Welfare (IFAW), often have invaluable data and possess pragmatic and realistic experiences in the fight against biodiversity crime. Relying on their knowhow could help to spread the message on successes (and failures) in that fight.

(5) *Communication:* The more concerns about the state of the environment are voiced in public, the more likely it is that the levels of environmental protection will improve. Tigers, eagles, orcas, or fish have no voice and cannot formulate their concerns. Researchers should therefore abandon their often-practised splendid isolation, lend a voice to biodiversity, and communicate its problems to the public at large, drawing attention to the ongoing, increasing loss of biodiversity and fostering a shared sense of responsibility. The effectiveness of research in this field is dependent on transparency in data and findings regarding biodiversity crime. Future research should also consider national successes and failures, the impact of actions and inertia, the availability of data, the number of incidents, and applicable sanctions.

(6) *Social and cultural issues:* In many parts of the world, the consumption or selling of live or dead wild animals is practised to ensure subsistence. Research must address the possibility of offering alternatives to the local (indigenous) population and also explain why, for example the consumption of fish is acceptable but of sharks or turtles is not. It will have to examine the question of whether biodiversity loss of (endangered) species is a Western, but not a universal, concern and whether there are alternatives.

(7) *Political will:* There is a limited chance to change the actual global trends in biodiversity loss, unless the political authorities at the local, provincial and national levels are convinced that biodiversity loss is a serious planetary problem and that wildlife crime significantly contributes to this loss. There is too much inertia, passivity, or even open support for or complacency by public authorities with regard to wildlife crime. Clear policy orientation is necessary, which influences day-to-day decision making on biodiversity issues and, in the long term, changes the political approach to biodiversity crime.

An empirical, concrete, and practice-oriented research on biodiversity crime, which goes beyond the general recommendations of UNEP,[64] UNODC, the European Commission, or other international bodies, is the challenge for the years to come. Indeed, there tends to be overall agreement on general issues: biodiversity crimes are increasing, they constitute a threat to sustainable development, and efforts to stop crime should increase. Researchers must devise their research in a way that ensures their findings are taken note of by policymakers and practitioners, and so that the general awareness of the biodiversity crisis increases, with the ultimate aim of bringing meaningful changes to the present approach to tackling biodiversity crime.

64 UNEP, *The environmental crime crisis* (Nairobi, 2014), p. 98.

6 The effectiveness of environmental criminal law enforcement

Juan Luis Fuentes Osorio

I. Introduction

The effectiveness of enforcing environmental criminal law,[1] understood as its capacity to prevent harm to natural systems and flora and fauna, or at least to contribute to reducing the number and intensity of these harms, has been questioned. On the one hand, environmental criminal law has been criticised for not having an impact on the underlying social problem. On the other hand, it is also pointed out that factors linked to the way environmental offences and penalties are drafted and the reluctance of the public administration and other institutions entrusted with the prosecution of environmental harm to punish offenders can reduce the likelihood of conviction. Moreover, it has been stressed that the penalties imposed for environmental crime are usually lenient.[2] These factors reduce the preventative capacity of environmental criminal law, since potential offenders of this type of crime are rational actors who calculate the positive and negative consequences that may derive from their actions.[3] According to a cost-benefit analysis, the potential offender will refrain from damaging the environment when the perceived costs (likelihood of conviction and severity of the sanction) outweigh the benefits. Conversely, if the risk of detection, prosecution

1 This work has been carried out in the framework of the research project 'Estrategias transversales para la prevención de la delincuencia económica y la corrupción' (Ref. PID2021-23028OB-I00). The views expressed in this chapter are the author's own.

2 See for example White, 2010; Billiet and Rousseau, 2014; Fajardo Del Castillo, 2016; Gerstetter et al., 2016; Faure, 2017a, 2017b; Pereira, 2017; Perilongo and Corn, 2017; Fuentes Osorio, 2017a, 2021a, 2021b; European Commission, 2019, 2021a, 2021b; Council of the European Union, 2019a, 2019b; Fuentes Osorio and Fajardo Del Castillo, 2020, 2021; Nurse, 2022; Europol, 2022.

3 See Europol, 2022, p. 7.

and punishment for the environmental crime is low and it also means a saving in production costs, a rational offender would choose to commit this type of offence.[4]

In the following pages I intend to reflect on specific criticisms of the effectiveness of environmental criminal law enforcement and evaluate whether or not those criticisms are reasonably justified. To this end, the chapter is structured in three sections. In section II, I will consider whether environmental law enforcement can be effective within the dominant economic systems. While recognising the limits of environmental law enforcement in this scenario, this chapter finds that the deterrent effects of environmental criminal law may prevent future environmental offences. In this context, section III focuses on identifying and evaluating the obstacles that reduce the probability of conviction for environmental damage. Finally, section IV focuses on the factors that reduce the probability of courts imposing severe sanctions on environmental offenders.

At the outset, it should be noted that one of the difficulties in conducting research on this topic lies in issues around the reporting of environmental infringements (a question which will not be addressed in this chapter). In particular, there is a lack of data (or alternatively, a lack of open access to information) when it comes to environmental criminal prosecutions and environmental law enforcement more generally.[5] To overcome this problem, the new Environmental Crime Directive 2024/1203 ('NECD')[6] states that 'to effectively tackle the environmental criminal offences defined in this Directive, it is necessary that competent authorities in the Member States collect accurate, consistent and comparable statistical data on those offences'.[7] Since this chapter places considerable emphasis on developments in the European Union (EU) and its Member States, the potential impact of the NECD on national environmental criminal law enforcement will also be considered.

II. Effective environmental criminal law in an international industrial society?

Before considering the relevant issues concerning the effective enforcement of environmental criminal law in sections III and IV, this section will make some general observations concerning the effectiveness of environmental criminal law more generally.

4 See critically, European Commission, 2021b, p. 106.

5 See critically, Council of the European Union, 2019a, p. 21; Gerstetter et al., 2016, p. 29; Faure, 2017a, p. 145, 2017b, p. 317; Farmer et al., 2017, p. 331; Perilongo and Corn, 2017, pp. 249 and following; Fuentes Osorio and Fajardo Del Castillo, 2021, pp. 40 and following; Colas Turégano and Morelle Hungría, 2021, p. 28; Colantoni et al., 2022, p. 56; Alfaro Moreno, 2023, p. 38.

6 The new Directive 2024/1203 of the European Parliament and of the Council on the Protection of the Environment through Criminal Law and Replacing Directives 2008/99/EC and 2009/123/EC (NECD).

7 NECD, Preamble 66, see also Articles 17, 22 and 23.

Environmental criminal law is often applied to address environmental issues that impact beyond a specific national jurisdiction. In fact, it can deal with global problems arising from the dominant production model, such as climate change, biodiversity loss, or pollution.[8] These can hardly be solved only by domestic policies adopted by states that may perceive environmental policies as having a negative impact on their socio-economic model.[9] Today, states are obliged to reconcile two often conflicting interests: economic development and the protection of the environment.[10] In this balancing act, the economic interest normally takes precedence.[11] Environmental law, with an anthropocentric approach, often does not actually protect natural resources, like water, flora, or fauna, but instead regulates their exploitation. It is a permit-to-damage system,[12] the limits and conditions of which are stipulated mainly by weighing in the socio-economic benefits of environmental damage. Consequently, although environmental criminal law can sometimes be a reactive instrument for attributing liability for attacks on the environment, it cannot punish most environmental damage which is legally permissible under the so-called allowable risk (*erlaubtes Risiko*).[13]

This preponderance of economic considerations has other manifestations in state practices. Some examples include the refusal by certain states to accept binding international restrictions or their delay or failure in meeting national or international environmental commitments.[14] It also explains the emergence of arguments raised to justify environmental damage, generally known as 'neutralisation techniques'[15] or, alarmingly, warnings that ecological protection jeopardises economic growth and the survival of cultural identity and traditional lifestyles.[16]

In this context, criminal law assumes the expressive-instrumental function of underlining the social value of the environment (that is making society aware of its importance and the need to internalise respectful behaviours towards it) and gives visibility to some particularly serious violations of environmental law and the response of the criminal justice system to them. In this way, the impression is given that the environmental problem has been resolved (or at least is being properly addressed), but

---

8 See in this volume, Stephan Sina's Chapter 11 Climate Change and Criminal Justice and Ludwig Krämer's Chapter 5 Biodiversity Crime.

9 Despite the adoption of the 2015 UN Sustainable Development Goals and many states having signed declarations or treaties recognising the principle of sustainable development.

10 See Ost, 1996, pp. 99 and following.

11 See Fajardo Del Castillo and Campins Eritja, 2021, pp. 7 and following; Nurse, 2022, pp. 333 and following.

12 See Ost, 1996, p. 105, who uses the concept 'permit-to-pollute system'.

13 On this concept see Pastor Muñoz, 2021, pp. 16 and following.

14 See Fajardo Del Castillo and Campins Eritja, 2021, pp. 10 and following.

15 See on the use of neutralisation techniques in relation to environmental harm, Enticott, 2011, pp. 203 and following and Varona, 2023, pp. 70 and following. See also, on the role of restorative justice in environmental crimes, White, 2017, pp. 129 and following; Nurse, 2022, pp. 337 and following.

16 See Colantoni et al., 2022, p. 55.

transmitting the erroneous message that only illegal harm endangers the environment, that the most serious transgressions are criminally sanctioned, and that the creation of criminal offences is a necessary and sufficient mechanism of environmental protection. However, this symbolic function hides the fact that environmental criminal law arguably has more of a legitimising effect on the environmental damage allowed than a dissuasive one.[17] It also conceals the fact that the state does not seek to address these challenges or that it does not have the capacity to do so.

It is not surprising, thus, that the issue of environmental damage does not play a significant role in most states' criminal justice policy agendas. This lack of interest in environmental criminal justice, which is reflected in limited efforts by states to adopt and apply administrative and criminal environmental laws, prosecute environmental infringements and crimes, and allocate the necessary resources to do so, increases when the ideology of governments is pro-industrial and liberal.[18] There is no doubt that, as stressed by the European Commission, 'there will be no lasting improvement in tackling transgressions if the state does not put the fight against environmental crime high on the enforcement agenda, both nationally and cross-border across the EU'.[19] This need for prioritisation of environmental crimes requires a change in the attitude of the state, which must commit itself to developing adequate and coordinated national strategies in the fight against environmental crime.[20] The NECD calls for progress in this direction[21] and demands that 'member States shall establish and publish a national strategy on combatting environmental criminal offences [by three years from the date of entry into force of this Directive] … [They must] ensure that their national strategy is reviewed and updated at regular intervals which are no longer than five years'.[22]

Similarly, this general lack of state interest in environmental criminal justice is reflected in the insufficient development of other preventative policies. In general, 'primary' prevention measures would seek to increase social awareness through educational and publicity actions. Then, 'secondary' prevention actions would facilitate the reporting of environmental damage by civil society[23] and protect journalists and members of non-governmental organisations (NGOs) against abusive reports and legal actions.[24] The NECD recognises this need and therefore stresses that environmental defenders, victims, and whistleblowers must be supported by reinforcing the protection of persons who report environmental criminal offences.[25]

17 See Barrett et al., 2018, p. 546.
18 See White, 2010, p. 372; South, 2016, p. 3.
19 European Commission, 2021a, p. 2.
20 See Alfaro Moreno, 2023, pp. 33 and following.
21 See also Colantoni et al., 2022, p. 66.
22 NECD, Article 21.
23 See Leavitt et al., 2021, pp. 1258 and following, pp. 1267 and following.
24 On the distinction between primary, secondary, and tertiary preventative strategies, see, for example, Larrauri, 2015, pp. 83 and following.
25 See NECD, Preamble, 54–56, and Articles 14, 16.

III. The probability of conviction for environmental crimes

The threat of a sanction is stronger the more likely it is to be imposed.[26] However, the probability of being criminally convicted for causing environmental damage is negatively affected by the presence of a set of obstacles related to the drafting and structure of criminal offences and penalties, as well as the performance of the institutions in charge of the formal prosecution of these offences. This decline in the 'certainty' of being punished for environmental crime is a factor that can influence potential environmental offenders by reducing their subjective perceptions of the risk of prosecution, conviction, and punishment.[27]

It should also noted that the cost of formal sanctions associated with a crime depends on the certainty and promptness of conviction and the severity of the sanction. These are variables that have objective and subjective perspectives. For example, it has been suggested that the offender's subjective perception of the likelihood of conviction will be more relevant than the actual (objective) likelihood of conviction.[28] Other commentators suggest that the potential offender's calculation of the costs of crime also depends on the offender's attitude towards risk.[29]

Obstacles generated by criminal legislation

The dispersion of environmental administrative regulations makes it difficult to establish whether any given conduct is prohibited or whether it has exceeded the authorisation limits. Moreover, the fragmentation and dispersion of environmental laws and regulations, both administrative and criminal, hinders the ability of national legislators, judges, and prosecutors to have a holistic vision of the unlawful conducts and applicable sanctions.[30] This may explain the overlap between administrative and criminal offences and the existence of several crimes referring to the same kind of environmental harm.[31] This regulatory fragmentation can lead potential offenders to lack awareness of the prohibited violations and the penalties provided for in law,[32] which, in turn, could have a negative impact on the deterrent effect of the legislation. It is not surprising, therefore, that the European Commission insists on the need for Member States to have a coherent administrative and criminal environmental sanctioning system.[33]

---

26 Kleiman, 2009, p. 93; Paternoster, 2010, p. 783; Apel and Nagin, 2011, p. 426; Bernard et al., 2016, pp. 41–42 and following, p. 44, p. 53.

27 See Bernard et al., 2016, pp. 43 and following.

28 See Paternoster, 2010, pp. 784, 804; Apel and Nagin, 2011, p. 427.

29 See Becker, 1974, pp. 11 and following.

30 See Faure, 2017a, p. 141; Di Franceso Maesa, 2018, p. 203.

31 See Faure, 2017b, p. 269; Farmer et al., 2017, p. 323.

32 See Faure, 2017b, p. 271.

33 See European Commission, 2021a, pp. 4 and following.

In the EU, the existence of very different national environmental laws and regulations, particularly regarding infringements and penalties, across the Member States can make 'environmental penalty costs' a factor influencing competition in the EU internal market.[34] It is also noted that this disparity between state regulations across the EU Member States can contribute to areas of impunity at the European level which can be exploited by criminal organisations and which makes the prosecution of their actions more difficult.[35]

Some elements of the definition of environmental criminal offences are neither clearly described nor correctly outlined in the criminal law. For example, it is common for environmental criminal offences to apply indeterminate concepts to describe harmfulness, such as damaging 'the quality of water' or the 'balance of natural systems', or in a 'not insignificant amount'.[36] These terms lack sufficient clarity and certainty, making it difficult to affirm whether, in each specific case, the threshold of environmental harm required by the criminal law is present.[37] It will be for doctrine and jurisprudence to define these concepts through additional interpretations. Most worrying is that the vagueness of these concepts allows for arbitrary judgements. A particularly relevant manifestation of this can be seen in the lack of criteria for distinguishing between criminal and administrative offences[38] or in the use of usually vague terms (for example, 'essential', 'serious', 'insignificant', 'lasting', and so on). This is one of the recognised problems[39] when defining offences and penalties for environmental damage, as evidenced by the fact that the Council of the EU pointed out to the Member States '...the distinction between administrative and criminal sanction systems is not always very clear due to the absence or lack of clarity of legal definitions'.[40]

These above-mentioned challenges can be reduced by including in the definition of environmental offences the specific aspects to be taken into consideration when assessing whether a violation of environmental law is criminal. For example, when constructing an offence that punishes offenders for causing environmental harm, the penal precept would have to include, therefore, the level of destruction of the environment, the extent of the damage (spatial features and the elements of the environment affected), and whether the damage is irreversible. Moreover, this should be designed in a way that a distinction can be made between administrative and criminal offences depending on

34 See White, 2010, p. 373; Pereira, 2017, p. 155; Perilongo and Corn, 2017, p. 249; Di Franceso Maesa, 2018, pp. 205 and following.

35 See Europol 2022, p. 11; Colantoni et al., 2022, p. 56.

36 See critically, Gerstetter et al., 2016, p. 29; Pereira, 2017, pp. 151, 153; European Commission, 2021a, p. 2.

37 See Pereira, 2017, pp. 151 and following.

38 See Fuentes Osorio, 2021b, pp. 124 and following.

39 Not only restricted to the European level, see, for example Odeku and Gundani, 2017, p. 33.

40 Council of the European Union, 2019a, p. 13. See critically, Colas Turégano and Morelle Hungría, 2021, p. 30; Fuentes Osorio, 2021b, pp. 124 and following; European Commission, 2021a, p. 2.

the scale and seriousness of the environmental damage. Such considerations are what has led the NECD to require Member States to ensure that certain elements are taken into account when assessing whether harm or likely harm is substantial[41] or whether an amount is negligible or not for certain offences under the NECD.[42] For example, according to Article 3(6) NECD, these elements would be: '(a) the baseline condition of the affected environment; (b) whether the damage is long-lasting, medium-term or short-term; (c) the extent of the damage; (d) the reversibility of the damage'. Yet even when these factors are incorporated into the definition of national environmental criminal offences, it is observed that, although they may lead to more precision in the definition of offences, their practical implementation and application may still prove difficult. Indeed, the transposition of the NECD into national law will not be easy due to its complex drafting and length. In other words, the elements of the offences defined in the NECD make it easier to establish the existence and scale of environmental harm required for the commission of an offence in a specific case, but they always leave open questions. For example, how extensive is the surface area? And to what extent is the environmental damage permanent or long-lasting? In short, it may not be possible to fully satisfy the legal requirements for how severe environmental damage must be to amount to a criminal offence. In any case, the highest level of precision that can be obtained lies in the use of quantitative distinguishing criteria[43] between criminal and administrative offences.[44] The NECD assumes this last assertion and incorporates the basis on which quantitative criteria can be constructed: account should be taken of 'the extent to which a regulatory threshold, value or another mandatory parameter set out in Union or national law … or in an authorisation issued for the relevant activity is exceeded'.[45] This option is also not without its drawbacks. It is impossible to set an identical quantitative criterion in a criminal code or statute for all forms of environmental harm.[46] For this reason, it would be advisable for states to adopt sectoral environmental laws that contain both administrative and criminal offences.[47]

Not all criminal codes or statutes recognise the possibility that legal persons may be held criminally liable.[48] This refusal to penalise the unlawful behaviour of legal persons is a political decision that recognises their importance in national economies and aims to avoid imposing a criminal penalty (for example, a fine or a disqualification

41 NECD, Article 3(6).
42 NECD, Article 3(8).
43 The quantitative criteria specify numerically the criminally relevant harm in the penal precept. For example, the criminal law should indicate by what exact percentage (for example 10%) emissions into the atmosphere must exceed the allowed levels (depending on the substance) in order to qualify this pollution as a criminal offence.
44 So, Fuentes Osorio, 2021b, p. 164; Colas Turégano and Morelle Hungría, 2021, p. 30.
45 NECD, Article 3(7)(b).
46 For instance, it is not feasible to utilise an identical percentage of excess for both air pollution and noise pollution, given that the detrimental dynamics inherent to each phenomenon are markedly disparate.
47 See Morelle Hungría et al., 2023.
48 See Faure, 2017b, pp. 282 and following.

from the practice of business activities) that would endanger their 'survival'.[49] Yet this political decision means disregarding the potential for the criminal law to fulfil the goals of criminal justice (for example deterrence, retribution, symbolism) and to effectively punish one of the most harmful of the actual or potential environmental offenders.[50]

The absence of criminal liability for legal persons also means that the criminal response may be restricted to the natural persons linked to the corporation. The distribution of processes and activities between different individuals or departments within a corporation, its organisational complexity, and the cumulative nature of environmental harm make it difficult to identify the individuals who have breached the law and to assign criminal responsibility to them.[51] Thus, when the impossibility of holding legal persons criminally liable is coupled with difficulties in successfully prosecuting natural persons associated with legal persons, impunity for environmental crimes becomes more common.[52] Consequently, pragmatic reasons relating to the effectiveness of law enforcement and the effective safeguarding of the legal objects protected by the law strengthen the case for the criminal and autonomous sanctioning of legal persons.[53] Yet, even in countries that have opted for autonomous corporate criminal liability, there is still room for impunity where this is not specifically provided for environmental crimes (a system known as *numerus clausus*).[54] In order to overcome these challenges, it is recommended that states adopt a model of autonomous criminal liability for all crimes, including environmental crimes.[55] In this regard, the NECD requires that Member States '... ensure that legal persons can be held liable for criminal offences referred to in Articles 3 and 4 ...',[56] although specifying that these offences should be punishable by effective, proportionate and dissuasive penalties or measures, which may be of a criminal or non-criminal nature.[57]

The public administration as a legal person is usually excluded from the scope of criminal liability. This is recognised by the NECD, which states in the Preamble at (12) that '... With regard to offences and penalties defined in this Directive, the term "legal persons" should be understood as not including States or public bodies exercising State authority or public international organisations'.[58] Only natural persons, authorities, or civil servants involved and in the exercise of their duties can be held

49 See Nurse, 2022, p. 331.
50 See Odeku and Gundani, 2017, p. 31.
51 Known as 'organised irresponsibility', see Ortiz De Urbina, 2016, marg. 1439.
52 See Faure, 2017b, p. 285.
53 See Faure, 2017b, p. 285.
54 In Spain, for example, legal persons can be punished for crimes against natural resources but not for damage to flora and fauna. See critically, Fuentes Osorio and Fajardo Del Castillo, 2020, p. 27.
55 See, Faure, 2017b, p. 314.
56 NECD, Article 6(1). See also Preamble, 33.
57 NECD, Article 7(1). See also Preamble, 33, 37.
58 See also NECD, Article 2(a).

criminally liable, as long as there is a law or regulation prohibiting their intervention in certain contexts, which are normally classifiable as a specific offence of administrative corruption or as an aggravating circumstance of the environmental crime committed.[59] Nevertheless, as these public bodies are one of the main actors in the context of crimes against the environment, either as perpetrators or as collaborators, it would be advisable, from a perspective that seeks the effective prevention of environmental damage, to establish their criminal liability. The NECD rightly leaves the door open to this possibility: 'As this Directive establishes minimum rules, Member States can adopt more stringent rules, including rules on criminal liability for public bodies'.[60]

Another obstacle to the effective enforcement of criminal law and administrative regulations concerns the issue of 'administrative tolerance'.[61] This concept refers, at a legislative level, to cases where the public administration intentionally produces 'defective' regulations with loopholes or fails to update them. The following situations could be distinguished: the legalisation of forms of environmental damage or the establishment of exceptions in environmental legislation that contradict the purpose of protection;[62] the absence of transposition of European law;[63] the failure to update environmental regulations; and, finally, the absence of mechanisms to ensure the effective enforcement of environmental legislation in the process of being adopted.[64]

Finally, another obstacle commonly present in criminal legislation is that some penal codes do not admit the punishment of careless criminal behaviour towards the environment in situations in which it cannot be proved that the potentially liable person acted with the required *mens rea*. For instance, originally, in Spain, recklessness and negligence[65] was only admitted for crimes against natural resources.[66] Yet, damage to flora and fauna was excluded from criminal liability arising from acts committed

59 The NECD insists on this when it foresees the obligation for Member States to provide for a specific aggravating factor when the environmental crime is committed by a public official in the performance of his or her duties or when he or she has previously been convicted by final judgment of environmental offences: NECD, Article (8)(d)–(e).

60 NECD, Preamble, 12.

61 See Gerstetter et al., 2016, p. 30; South, 2016, p. 232; Fuentes Osorio, 2017a, pp. 198 and following; Fuentes Osorio and Fajardo Del Castillo, 2021, pp. 10 and following; Nurse, 2022, p. 330.

62 See, for example, the wolf (dis)protection in Spain and the exceptions to the rules in the Bern Convention and in the Habitat's Directive, (Council Directive 92/43/EEC of 21 May 1992 on the conservation of natural habitats and of wild fauna and flora), Fajardo Del Castillo, 2021, pp. 1 and following.

63 Criticising Spain for the lack of an effective enforcement system, see European Commission, 2022, p. 51.

64 With regard to the Aznalcóllar case, see Fuentes Osorio, 2017b, p. 487.

65 Article 331, Spanish Criminal Code (SCC), Organic Law 10/1995 of 23 November 1995.

66 Concerning harm against abiotic components of the ecosystem (water, soil, air).

by reckleness or negligence.[67] It was not until the adoption of Organic Law 1/2015 that finally criminal liability was extended for careless conduct related to this type of crime against the environment.

The prosecution of environmental crime by formal institutions

It must be stressed that, although there is still a long way to go, the growth of police and judicial activity in the field of environmental crime cannot be overlooked.[68] This increase in the likelihood of detection and conviction for environmental crimes should be seen as a positive achievement, since it implies a reduction in the so-called 'dark figure'[69] and in the impunity for ongoing attacks on the environment[70] However, it is true that this likelihood of detection and conviction, although generally higher in some EU Member States, overall remains low.[71] Therefore, there is still considerable room for improvement in the process of criminal prosecution and punishment of environmental crimes. In particular, there are numerous challenges that hinder the conviction of the perpetrators of environmental offences by the courts.

The first difficulty in the enforcement of environmental criminal law in specific cases lies in the fact that it is not possible to respond criminally to any damage that has been declared lawful by law or permissible by the public administration (for example through a license).[72] This is an inevitable consequence in a sanctioning system in which criminal law is accessory to administrative law, which defines permissible and therefore lawful environmental damage. Yet sometimes this accessory relationship hides a worrying reality. The requirement of prior administrative infringement before the imposition of criminal sanctions may not be fulfilled because the public administration may not be effectively enforcing environmental regulations and not detecting its infringements. This is another dimension of the so-called 'administrative tolerance', which has various implications. Firstly, it occurs when authorisations are granted or maintained even though only the formal conditions of a licence are

[67] Thus, for example, a person who recklessly kills an endangered animal would not be criminally liable.

[68] See on this continuous increase in the prosecution of environmental crimes in Spain, Fuentes Osorio and Fajardo Del Castillo 2020, pp. 46 and following. See also Redondo Almándoz 2022, pp. 5 and following.

[69] Varona, 2023, p. 62 emphasises, nevertheless, that environmental crimes continue to show a high number of 'dark figures', that is, many environmental crimes are underreported and undetected.

[70] See Fuentes Osorio, 2021a, pp. 175 and following.

[71] See European Commission, 2021a, p. 1, which notes that the risks of detection, prosecution and punishment for environmental crime are still low.

[72] Fuentes Osorio and Fajardo Del Castillo, 2021, p. 6 highlight, in their study on the reasons for acquittal in crimes against the environment in Spain from 2009 to 2019 (192 decisions for crimes against natural systems and 111 for crimes against fauna were analysed), that 'non-infringement of environmental regulations' was the third most common cause of acquittal in crimes against natural resources (appearing in 21.87% of the sentences).

met, but not the material ones (for example relating to the allowable environmental damage); or when the public administration decides to give an exceptional authorisation to validate conduct that does not comply with environmental regulations. When this happens, a formally valid licence can lead to a situation of criminal impunity[73] (that is, there is no administrative or criminal offence). The NECD, mindful of this problem, points out that '… [c]onduct will be unlawful even when carried out under an authorisation issued by a competent authority of a Member State if such authorisation has been obtained by fraud, corruption, extortion or coercion, or if such authorisation manifestly violates the relevant substantive legal requirements'.[74] Secondly, this interdependency between criminal law and administrative law is linked to a lack of control by the authorities over the degree of compliance with the authorisations granted for the exercise of harmful activities.[75]

The European Commission stresses the need for Member States to sanction obstruction of inspections and activities aimed at the enforcement of environmental laws.[76] Hence, this tolerance of environmental harm by administrative authorities is a reflection of the absence of monitoring and lack of appropriate sanctions for the illegal conduct detected.[77] This is a very worrying problem since it may favour the perception that it is possible to damage the environment without suffering criminal consequences; or may reinforce the impression that the environmental sanctioning system is unfair because only some offenders will be held responsible. This can lead to a loss of legitimacy of the environmental criminal justice system and consequently to a decrease in its preventative and deterrence role. The perception that '[t]here are "free riders" acting with impunity will undermine respect for both authorities and obligations';[78] and could reduce the stigmatising power of sanctions.[79]

Harmful behaviour condoned or tolerated by the public administration is often accompanied by incomplete information on regulatory compliance and enforcement. In this sense, Faure underlines in relation to environmental inspections that:

> … The major problem is that essential information to check effective compliance, such as the amount of classified installations that have to be inspected, the number of available inspectors, the number of violations and the result of those inspections, is lacking completely. Data collection in this respect is problematic at the Member State level. And

73 See Fuentes Osorio, 2021b, pp. 42 and following.
74 NECD, Article 3(1). See also, Preamble, 10.
75 An aspect highlighted by the European Commission, 2021b, p. 43 which '… distinguishes four forms of clandestine environmental infringements: Occasional unreported incidents; completely illegal and clandestine; apparently legal, but with a component of clandestine illegality; manifestly illegal, but tolerated or not addressed'.
76 European Commission, 2021a, p. 3. See also Colantoni et al., 2022, p. 55.
77 See García Ruiz 2017, pp. 289 and following; Faure, 2017b, p. 291; Fajardo Del Castillo, 2021, p. 31; Nurse, 2022, p. 336.
78 European Commission, 2021b, p. 49.
79 See Robinson, 2012, pp. 123, 167, 201 and following; Kennedy, 2016, p. 117.

even if Member States do collect this data, it is not adequately passed on to the European Commission.[80]

In this respect, it is striking that the NECD does not demand from Member States data on the control of authorisations as part of the minimum statistical information on the prosecution of environmental crime required by Article 22.

It should be noted that one of the most frequent grounds for acquittal in criminal trials is that the environmental damage in the particular case meets the threshold for an administrative offence but does not exceed the threshold required for a criminal offence.[81] Although this high number of acquittals may be due to the fact that the harm caused is minor, in some cases this can also be related to the ambiguity (or lack) of criteria to distinguish administrative and criminal offences. In a situation where it is unclear what types and levels of environmental damage must be proven under the criminal law, national courts may opt for the acquittal of the accused.

In some instances, it may not be possible to prove that the prosecuted conduct has endangered or damaged the environment to the degree required under the criminal law.[82] Some of the challenging legal questions concerning the prosecution of environmental crimes include proving the extent of environmental damage, the causal relationship between the infringing conduct and the harm to the environment, and other legal questions concerning the imputation of environmental harm on the defendant.[83] These questions are raised partly as a reflection of the fact that the environment is a dynamic and interactive system that does not conform with perfectly defined boundaries. So, if the environmental offence does not prescribe the scope of protection of an ecosystem, this element of the offence may be open to different interpretations and hence could make sentencing more difficult. For example, when measuring the environmental damage caused by an oil spill in a river, should the damage be assessed in terms of the affected area, the directly associated ecosystems, or the ecosystem linked to the whole river basin? Moreover, in the case of diffuse sources of pollution, the attribution of liability for environmental damage faces a fundamental problem as it is not always possible to place the blame on a single person or operator. This is often the result of the actions of a number of individuals or legal persons who, in some cases, act in ways that may in themselves be lawful. These difficulties in proving environmental

80 See Faure, 2017a, p. 144.

81 The research carried out by Fuentes Osorio and Fajardo Del Castillo (2021, p. 6) indicates that, in the case of Spain, this is the reason for acquittal in 71.87% of the decisions analysed for crimes against natural resources and in 93.44% of crimes against fauna. See above (n 60).

82 According to Fuentes Osorio and Fajardo Del Castillo (2021, p. 6), in Spain, evidentiary difficulties are mentioned as a cause for acquittal in 65.62% of the decisions in crimes against natural resources and in 14.75% of crimes against fauna. See above (n 60).

83 See White, 2010, p. 373.

harm and attributing liability to individual actors are amplified when the environmental crime affects several states[84] or involves large corporate networks.[85]

Two other scenarios are even more worrying. One of these scenarios is when there are evidentiary problems that have been generated by the attitude of perpetrators with great economic power who have mechanisms at their disposal to challenge the evidence or to delay (and even frustrate) the criminal proceedings.[86] Another potential scenario includes situations where evidence was insufficient or illegally taken. This may demonstrate that formal institutions have no real interest in pursuing justice for environmental harm, and may also reflect insufficient staff and technical and financial resources, or the lack of the necessary technical training by the authorities.[87] To tackle this problem, the competent authorities must prioritise the effective control of environmentally harmful activities and develop adequate and sufficient investigation tools[88] (which is now a requirement under the NECD[89]). There is no doubt that the complexity of environmental legislation and of the concrete cases prosecuted requires police,[90] forensic,[91] prosecutorial,[92] and judicial[93] specialisation. The NECD consequently insists on the need for Member States '[t]o take necessary measures to ensure that specialised regular training is provided to judges, prosecutors, police and judicial staff and to competent authorities' staff involved in criminal proceedings and investigations with regard to the objectives of this Directive'.[94]

84 See Di Francesco Maesa, 2018, pp. 209 and following.

85 See White, 2010, p. 372. See also in this volume, the chapter by Carolyn Abbot and Gary Lynch-Wood, Chapter 6 Transnational Environmental Crime Across Global Supply Chains – A Place for Due Diligence?.

86 See White, 2010, p. 373.

87 See Fajardo Del Castillo, 2016, p. 31; González Uriel 2017, pp. 160 and following; Fuentes Osorio and Fajardo Del Castillo, 2021, p. 6; Colas Turégano and Morelle Hungría, 2021, p. 29.

88 See critically, Fuentes Osorio, 2017a, p. 210; Farmer et al., 2017, p. 323; Fuentes Osorio and Fajardo Del Castillo, 2021, p. 13.

89 NECD, Preamble 53, Articles 13, 17 and 18.

90 See White, 2010, p. 377; Faure, 2017b, pp. 288 and following; Farmer et al., 2017, p. 324; Council of the European Union, 2019b, p. 8; European Commission, 2021a, p. 6, 2021b, p. 64; Colantoni et al., 2022, pp. 59 and following; Europol 2022, p. 40; Alfaro Moreno, 2023, pp. 44 and following. See also, Gerstetter et al., (2016, pp. 34 and following) who gives a list of 'green' police units in Europe.

91 See Farmer et al., 2017, pp. 324 and following; European Commission, 2021b, pp. 64, 142.

92 See Faure, 2017b, pp. 292 and following; Farmer et al., 2017, p. 323; European Commission, 2021b, pp. 64, 142.

93 See Gerstetter et al., 2016, pp. 34 and following; Faure, 2017b, pp. 297 and following; Farmer et al., 2017, p. 323; Greife and Maume, 2020, p. 352; European Commission, 2021a, p. 6, 2021b, p. 142; Colantoni et al., 2022, p. 59. Nurse, 2022, pp. 339 and following.

94 NECD, Article 18. See also Preamble, 32.

Another challenge arising from the prosecution of environmental crimes is the tendency of the authorities not to punish careless behaviour. As indicated above, the punishment of offences committed with recklessness or negligence requires that the criminal code or legislation expressly admits them for all offences or specifically for a certain group of offences. Once criminal liability for reckless or negligent environmental harm has been provided for in legislation, it is nevertheless possible to appreciate a refusal by the sentencing judge or jury to punish conduct in situations where the *mens rea* requirement cannot be proved. This resistance is expressed in two ways. Firstly, there may be no punishment by the courts for an offence committed with knowledge, despite the defendant's awareness of the (virtual) certainty or high likelihood that environmental damage would be caused by their action. Secondly, although the criminal law may allow for the punishment of conduct committed with recklessness or negligence, the judge does not consider that there is a breach of the duty of care in the specific case.[95]

Finally, insufficient coordination and cooperation (at strategic and operational levels) among the bodies responsible for the formal response (law enforcement agencies and judicial authorities) to this type of criminality at both national and international levels have been identified as factors that reduce the likelihood of conviction.[96] This is particularly evident in countries where environmental law enforcement is formally divided between different national and local authorities (for example in federal or decentralised states[97]), or in the context of organised crime[98] and transboundary environmental crime.[99] Gerstetter et al.[100] point out that this enforcement deficit may be due to the cost of international cooperation, the complexity of administrative regulations, the time required to request collaboration between different countries, and the additional workload for law enforcement officers in charge.[101] To address these difficulties, the NECD expressly requires increased cooperation between national and international authorities and European agencies.[102] There have also been calls for the creation of a central body at the national level to coordinate the cooperation between enforcement agencies and authorities.[103]

---

95 See on this problem in Spain, Fuentes Osorio and Fajardo Del Castillo, 2021, p. 7; Fuentes Osorio, 2017b, pp. 471 and following.

96 See White, 2010, p. 375; Gerstetter et al., 2016, p. 36; Farmer et al., 2017, pp. 328 and following; Pereira, 2017, p. 161; Di Francesco Maesa, 2018, p. 204; Colantoni et al., 2022, pp. 58 and following.

97 See Colantoni et al., 2022, p. 59 (who cites Belgium and Spain as examples).

98 On the situation of organised crime in the EU and its influence on environmental crime see FRONTEX 2021, pp. 54 and following.

99 See Di Francesco Maesa, 2018, p. 204; Colantoni et al., 2022, p. 56. See Frontex, (2021, p. 12) on the role of Eurojust in cross-border environmental crime.

100 Gerstetter et al., 2016, p. 36.

101 Gerstetter et al., 2016, p. 36.

102 NECD, Articles 19–21. See Colantoni et al., 2022, p. 67.

103 See European Commission, 2021b, p. 75.

IV. The probability of a severe criminal sanction

The deterrent effect of environmental criminal law also depends on the sanctions associated with environmental crimes. Thus, the punishment provided by law and the penalties actually imposed must be sufficiently severe.

The penalties for environmental crimes are not always proportionate to the seriousness of the offence and may not be sufficiently severe to generate the desired deterrent effect.[104] Firstly, this may be because there are certain environmental criminal offences which are not punishable by imprisonment or, where this penalty is provided for, it is of short duration. For example, in the Spanish environmental criminal justice system, the maximum prison sentence for the basic offence against natural resources currently does not exceed 24 months. For offences against flora and fauna, imprisonment is not always foreseen. When imprisonment is foreseen for those offences, it does not exceed 24 months and is not mandatory. Therefore, a fine may be applied as an alternative penalty,[105] which is not unusual because in some EU Member States it is normal practice for some domestic courts to choose between imprisonment or a fine when sentencing environmental offenders.[106] In contrast, other countries stipulate higher prison sentences for crimes against flora and fauna: up to five years in Poland, Germany, Estonia, Slovenia; six years in Sweden; seven years in France; and eight years in Slovakia.[107] In short, the provision of non-custodial penalties or lenient (e.g. less than two years) and non-mandatory prison sentences for serious environmental damage conveys the idea that environmental crime is an acceptable cost and that environmental protection is of lesser importance, ultimately contributing to a sense of impunity amongst environmental offenders.[108] In order to ensure that the criminal offences referred to in Articles 3 and 4 of NECD are subject to effective, proportionate and dissuasive criminal sanctions, the directive requires Member States to set a minimum maximum term of imprisonment for natural persons, depending on whether the offence causes the death of a person, the type of environmental offence, and so on.[109]

Besides this, in many EU national legal systems the maximum levels of criminal fines established in environmental criminal law are not particularly high or proportionate

[104] See Perilongo and Corn, 2017, p. 249; Nurse, 2022, p. 341; Greife and Maume, 2020, p. 352. However, it is also argued that '… there is no evidence that manipulating penalty levels necessarily leads to higher deterrent effects': Pereira, 2017, pp. 155 (also Varona, 2023, pp. 63 and following).

[105] See Fuentes Osorio, 2021a, pp. 177 and following.

[106] See Faure, 2017b, p. 310.

[107] See Gerstetter et al., 2016, pp. 32 and following.

[108] See critically, ENEC 2015, p. 9; Varona, 2023, pp. 63 and following.

[109] For example, NECD, Article 5(2) stresses that '(d) Criminal offences covered by Article 3(2), points (a) to (l), and points (p), (s) and (t), are punishable by a maximum term of imprisonment of at least five years; (e) criminal offences covered by Article 3(2), points (m), (n), (o), (q) and (r), are punishable by a maximum term of imprisonment of at least three years'.

to the actual or potential level of environmental damage. This may affect the deterrent effect of the criminal fine, especially when it is the main penalty provided for under the criminal law, as in the case of legal persons. Indeed, in order to have deterrent effects, a criminal fine must be sufficiently severe, that is it must be higher than the cost of compliance and the benefit obtained from the offence.[110] This has undoubtedly influenced the NECD to state that '[t]he maximum levels of fines provided for [legal persons] in this Directive for the criminal offences defined in it should apply at least to the most serious forms of such offences'.[111] Finally, another concern is that disqualification penalties tend to be of short duration[112] and may be too restrictive. For instance, a professional disqualification penalty does not automatically include hunting or fishing, since most hunters (and some fishermen) are not professional in the strict sense of the term, even if they do it in a usual and legal way (for example federated sport fishing). Although the NECD stresses the need for the Member States to impose disqualifying penalties such as a prohibition to pursue the activities that resulted in the criminal offence, it establishes them as accessory and non-compulsory penalties and does not stipulate that they must have a minimum duration.[113]

Notably, there is concern regarding the lack of severity of the criminal penalties applied in the EU Member States. The greater likelihood of conviction does not imply a greater likelihood that the accused will be sentenced to imprisonment, or to a heavy fine or severe disqualification order. The use of lenient penalties, which are disproportionate to the seriousness of the environmental crime, and which are not supplemented by additional penalties and measures such as confiscation of proceeds of crime or reparation of the damage to the environment,[114] may reduce the deterrent effect of environmental criminal law.[115] This is because the low level of penalties for environmental crimes can be perceived, from a rational economic perspective, as an acceptable cost of doing business.

In my previous research conducting an empirical analysis of sentences imposed in convictions against natural persons for crimes against natural resources, flora, and fauna in Spain during the years 2009–2019, which was published in 2021, I confirmed this inclination by domestic courts to impose light sentences.[116] Firstly, I observed that

110 See Kleiman, 2009, p. 50.
111 NECD, Preamble, 33.
112 For example, in Spain, basic disqualification sentences range from two years for crimes against natural resources to four years for crimes against flora and fauna, see SCC, Articles 325 and following.
113 See NECD, Preamble, 31, Articles 5(3)(b)–(f), and 7(2).
114 See White, 2017, pp. 129. The NECD underlines the importance of restoration, which is imposed as an accessory penalty; see NECD, Preamble, 31, 32, and Article 5(3)(a).
115 See critically, White, 2010, pp. 377 and following; Billiet and Rousseau, 2014, pp. 196 and following.
116 See Fuentes Osorio, 2021a, pp. 187 and following. I analysed 51 guilty judgments (with 86 convicted persons) for Articles 325 and following, and 31 guilty judgments (with 61

there was a propensity by Spanish courts to impose fines rather than imprisonment.[117] This is seen in wildlife offences where, given the choice between the two penalties, the courts tend to prefer fines[118] (only 11.47% of those convicted were sentenced to imprisonment).[119] This is not a problem exclusive to Spain.[120] Billiet and Rousseau[121] also point to the prevalence of fines in sentences for environmental crimes in the United States (US), the United Kingdom (UK), Belgium, Canada, and Australia,[122] as well as in Europe in general.[123] They suggested that imprisonment was more common in the US (30% of sentences) than in the EU (0.5–2.5% of sentences) in the years analysed by those authors.[124]

Secondly, my previous research also showed that the average length of custodial sentences in Spain was less than two years.[125] All of them could have been suspended since in Spain probation is possible for prison sentences of up to two years.[126] This last aspect is emphasised by several other studies. For example, Cochran et al. explain in their research on convictions for environmental crime in Florida (from 1994 to 2011) that environmental offenders are punished more leniently (compared to other offences), so that they '... were overall and substantially more likely to receive community-based sanctions (i.e., probation) than incarceration-based sanctions (i.e., jail, prison) ...'.[127] Moreover, Billiet and Rousseau[128] noted, in their study covering the years between 2003–07, with a particular focus on criminal prosecution of environmental legislation in Flanders (Belgium), that '... in first instance (appeal) 66 (76)% of the sentences are completely suspended and another 3 (5)% are partially suspended .... This seriously reduces the duration of the effective prison sentences ...'.[129]

convicted persons) for Articles 334SCC and following. The findings concern penalties imposed on natural persons, as there were hardly any convictions of legal persons.

117 This trend is present in other EU Member States. Faure (2017b, p. 310) insists on it: 'fines are in fact the most important sanctions that are applied in practice'.

118 This is consistent with the study by Redondo Almándo, 2022, p. 23.

119 Fuentes Osorio, 2021a, p. 189.

120 As evidenced by ENEC, 2015, p. 9.

121 'The empirical application summarizes evidence from several countries, but focuses on detailed data for criminal prosecution of environmental legislation in Flanders (Belgium) between 2003 and 2007': Billiet and Rousseau, 2014, p. 183.

122 See also White, 2017, p. 129.

123 Billiet and Rousseau, 2014, pp. 189 and following.

124 See note 121. Billiet and Rousseau, 2014, p. 190.

125 20.62 months for convictions under SCC, Article 325; 15.5 months under SCC, Article 334. See Fuentes Osorio, 2021a, p. 189.

126 In accordance with SCC, Articles 80 and following.

127 Cochran et al., 2018, p. 59.

128 See note 121.

129 Billiet and Rousseau, 2014, p. 193. See also, Perilongo and Corn, 2017, p. 251.

Thirdly, my previous research suggested that the average fine imposed by Spanish courts on natural persons was very low.[130] This lack of severity is particularly remarkable when taking into account the environmental damage caused and the fact that a fine is sometimes the only sanction imposed. These low average fines are consistent with the findings reported by Perilongo and Corn who, in their analysis of the country reports provided by the EU Forum of Judges for the Environment (EUFJE) on the protection of the environment through criminal law in several EU Member States including Belgium, the Czech Republic, Denmark, Estonia, Finland, France, Germany, Hungary, Italy, the Netherlands, Norway, Poland, Slovakia, and Sweden (as well as the UK), underline that '... criminal fines for natural persons generally amount to €5,000 and rarely exceed €10,000'.[131] Similarly, Poisel, in his study of the fines imposed by courts in New South Wales (Australia) from 2003 to 2012, critically highlights this: 'Although maximum penalties have increased over the last decade, the courts have continued to impose low fines, particularly when compared to the maximum penalty limits. The imposition of low penalties undermines the major consideration in sentencing – deterrence'.[132] Finally, the disqualification penalties also follow this trend.[133]

It should be noted that the fines imposed are not particularly high in relation to the economic wealth of the offender.[134] This makes the fine appear as an additional (and affordable) cost of doing business that, in the end may not be perceived as truly 'criminal'.[135] Therefore, adjusting the fine to the financial capacity of the convicted person would increase its deterrent effect[136] and bring us closer to a level of parity between subjects who have committed the same offences but who have different economic capabilities.[137]

In short, an effective fine must be dissuasive and both proportional to the seriousness of the environmental offence committed and the financial capacity of the offender. This balancing act by the sentencing judge seeks to avoid the so-called 'deterrence trap': that is, if the fine is not very severe, it may not be dissuasive (as it is an affordable cost), but if it exceeds the economic capacity of the convicted person, it may not be intimidating because it is known that it cannot be complied with.[138]

---

130 €3943.6 for convictions under SCC, Articles 325 and following and €3272.5 under SCC, Articles 334 and following. See Fuentes Osorio, 2021a, p. 193.

131 Perilongo and Corn, 2017, p. 251.

132 Poisel, 2013, p. 92.

133 16.46 months (convictions under SCC, Article 325); 36.27 months (SCC, Article 334). See Fuentes Osorio, 2021a, p. 192.

134 See Greife and Maume, 2020, p. 352.

135 See Poisel 2013, p. 92; Greife and Maume, 2020, p. 352; Nurse, 2022, p. 341.

136 See Faure, 2017b, p. 311.

137 See Kantorowicz-Reznichenko, 2015, pp. 482 and following; Fuentes Osorio, 2022, p. 207.

138 See Coffee, 1981, pp. 389 and following, 407; Nagin, 1998, p. 271; Fuentes Osorio, 2022, p. 206.

The NECD, mindful of this problem, requires the imposition of 'fines that are proportionate to the gravity of the conduct and to the individual, financial and other circumstances of the natural person concerned', as well as to '… the financial benefits generated from the offence'.[139] With regard to legal persons, the NECD also insists on fines being calculated on the basis of both of those standards. To this end, it provides that the maximum level of the fine shall not be less than a specified percentage of the total worldwide turnover of the legal person or a specific minimum maximum amount, both to be determined according to the type of offence.[140]

The perception by some domestic courts that environmental crime is a minor offence and that its perpetrators are not particularly 'dangerous' may explain their predisposition to impose lenient sentences.[141] Thus, Pereira points out that a Milieu Study on Sweden (2015) critically commented that Swedish judges '… are reluctant to impose severe sentences for environmental crimes as they are not considered as equally serious as other types of crimes, such as economic crimes or tax evasion'.[142] Cochran et al. highlight, based on the Formal Sentencing Guidelines that are applied in Florida, that it could be said that '… the state, arguably, "views" the typical environmental offender most similarly to a lowlevel drug or property offender'.[143] Finally, White argues that one of the reasons for the resistance to imposing serious penalties on legal persons is that '… corporate crime tends to be socially defined as less harmful'.[144] Conversely, this also explains why some courts impose more serious penalties when the environmental harm threatens the life or physical integrity of humans.[145]

The propensity to impose lenient sentences by some national courts may also be influenced by concerns about the social and economic consequences of the sanctions upon the offenders. Some courts may be reluctant to impose a severe sentence on a natural person for an environmental crime that may be considered 'minor', for fear of the negative repercussions (for the accused's family and in terms of employment opportunities, for example) that imprisonment may have on the offender. It may also be feared that the fine may endanger the economic survival of the legal person or affect third parties such as creditors, shareholders, employees, and clients – the so-called 'overspill effect'.[146] This may be a factor influencing the courts not to impose heavy fines, also known as the 'nullification effect'.[147]

---

139 See NECD, Article 5(3)(b).
140 See NECD, Article 7(3)(a)–(b).
141 See White, 2010, p. 376; Cochran et al., 2018, p. 60.
142 Pereira, 2017, p. 158. Milieu, 'National Report for Sweden, Evaluation Study on the Implementation of Directive 2008/99/EC on the Protection of the Environment through Criminal Law by Member States' (Milieu, 2015) ('National Report for Sweden').
143 Cochran et al., 2018, p. 61.
144 White, 2010, p. 371.
145 See Fuentes Osorio, 2021a, pp. 189 and following.
146 See Coffee, 1981, pp. 401 and following.
147 See Coffee 1981, pp. 405 and following; Nagin, 1998, p. 9; Fuentes Osorio, 2022, p. 202.

V. Conclusions

The main obstacles to making environmental criminal law an effective preventative instrument and mechanism for law enforcement are the following:

(1) Effective environmental protection requires changes in society and in risk management policies. Environmental damage is the consequence of an economic model of development that recognises the lawfulness of various types of environmental damage, some of which are very serious. States should prioritise environmental protection and develop viable environmental crime prevention strategies accordingly.
(2) The 'active' toleration of environmental crime by the public administration and national authorities is one of the most important problems related to the lack of compliance with and enforcement of environmental regulations. There is permissiveness of environmental harm through outdated laws, inadequate monitoring of risky environmental activities, and tolerance towards detected offences that are not always punished with effective sanctions.
(3) The legislative fragmentation and dispersion of environmental offences and the imprecision of the terms applied in their definition, particularly in the description of criminal environmental damage and regarding the distinction between criminal offences and administrative environmental infringements, are particularly notable problems.
(4) Sometimes environmental damage cannot be criminally sanctioned because of evidentiary problems. Issues such as the insufficient or wrongful taking of evidence may be attributed to a lack of expertise in environmental crime and a shortage of resources and technology by the enforcement authorities.
(5) An increase in the probability of conviction is not necessarily accompanied by an increase in the deterrent effect of environmental criminal law because of the lack of severity of the sanctions generally imposed by the courts in practice. The lack of severity of the penalties applied is evidenced by the relatively few custodial sentences imposed by domestic courts in practice (and in the short duration of these when imposed, as well as the fact they can generally be suspended), low levels of fines (both in terms of the overall amount and in that they are not tailored to the economic wealth of the perpetrator), as well as the very few and short-term disqualification sanctions.

It is recommended that further research investigates the deterrent effects of fines and other penalties typically applied in environmental criminal prosecutions, and how effectively environmental criminal law can be enforced through a range of penalties and measures aimed at deterring environmental offenders.[148]

[148] See also in this volume, the chapter by Sarah Wright and Victoria Colvin, Chapter 7 Enforceable Undertakings as an Alternative to Prosecution in Australian Environmental Law Enforcement.

References

Alfaro Moreno, J.A. (2023) 'Towards and understanding of consequences of the prioritisation of environmental crime in the European Union', *Cuadernos de la Guardia Civil*, 69, pp. 31–48.

Apel, R. and Nagin, D.S. (2011) 'General Deterrence: A Review of Recent Evidence' in J.Q. Wilson and J. Petersilia (eds) *Crime and Public Policy*, 4th edn, Oxford: Oxford University Press, pp. 411–36.

Barrett, K.L., Lynch, M.J., Long, M.A. and Stretesky, P.B. (2018) 'Monetary Penalties and Noncompliance with Environmental Laws: A Mediation Analysis', *American Journal of Criminal Justice*, 43, pp. 530–50.

Becker, G.S. (1974) 'Crime and Punishment: An Economic Approach' in G.S. Becker and W.M. Landes (eds) *Essays in the Economics of Crime and Punishment*, New York: Columbia University Press, pp. 1–54.

Bernard, T.J., Snipes, J.B. and Gerould, A.L. (2016) *Vold's Theoretical Criminology*, 7th edn, Oxford: Oxford University Press.

Billiet, C.M. and Rousseau, S. (2014) 'How real is the threat of imprisonment for environmental crime?', *European Journal of Law and Economics*, 37, pp. 183–98.

Cochran, J.C., Lynch, M.J., Toman, E.L. and Shields, R.T. (2018) 'Court Sentencing Patterns for Environmental Crimes: Is here a "Green" Gap in Punishment', *Journal of Quantitative Criminology*, 34, pp. 37–66.

Coffee, J.C. (1981) '"No Soul to damn: No Body to Kick": An unscandalized Inquiry into the Problem of Corporate Punishment', *Michigan Law Review*, 79(3), pp. 386–459.

Colantoni, L., Sarno, G.S. and Bianchi, M. (2022) *Fighting Environmental Crime in Europe*, Roma: Instituto Affari Internazionali.

Colas Turégano, A. and Morelle Hungría, E. (2021) 'El Derecho ambiental frente a los delitos ecológicos: la eficacia y eficiencia penal a debate', *Revista Electrónica de Ciencia Penal y Criminología*, 23(13), pp. 1–34.

Council of the European Union (2019a) *Informe final sobre la octava ronda de evaluaciones mutuas sobre la delincuencia medioambiental*, Doc. 14065/19 LIMITE, Brussels.

Council of the European Union (2019b) *Evaluation report on the eighth round of mutual evaluations 'The practical implementation and operation of European policies on preventing and combating environmental crime' - Report on Spain*, 6601/1/19 REV, Brussels.

Di Francesco Maesa, C. (2018) 'EPPO and Environmental Crime: May the EPPO ensure a more Effective Protection of the Environment in the EU?', *New Journal of European Criminal Law*, 9(2), pp. 191–215.

Enticott, G. (2011) 'Techniques of Neutralising Wildlife Crime in Rural England and Wales', *Journal of Rural Studies*, 27(2), pp. 200–208.

European Commission (2019) *The EU Environmental Implementation Review. Report – Spain*, Brussels.

European Commission (2021a) *Communication from the Commission to the European Parliament and the Council on stepping up the fight against environmental crime*, COM(2021) 814 final, Brussels.

European Commission (2021b) *Garantía del cumplimiento de la legislación medioambiental. La lucha contra los delitos medioambientales y las infracciones conexas*, Luxemburg: Publications Office of the European Union.

European Commission (2022) *The EU Environmental Implementation Review. Spain*, Brussels.

European Network Against Environmental Crime (ENEC) (2015) *Legal recommendations to eliminate illegal killing and taking of birds*, Madrid: SeoBirdlife.

Europol (2022) *Environmental Crime in the age of climate change. Threat assessment 2022*, Luxemburg: Publications Office of the European Union.

Fajardo Del Castillo, T. (2016) *Study on Wildlife Crime in Spain*, Strasbourg: European Parliament.

Fajardo Del Castillo, T. (2021) 'Wolf (Dis)Protection in Spain: Exceptions to the Rules in the Bern Convention and in The Habitats Directive as a Conservation and Management Tool', *Revista Catalana de Dret Ambiental*, XII(1), pp. 1–47.

Fajardo Del Castillo, T. and Campins Eritja, M. (2021), 'La CoP26 de Glasgow sobre el cambio climático: ¿Truco o Trato?', *Revista Catalana de Dret Ambiental*, XII(2), pp. 1–32.

Farmer, A., Faure, M. and Vagliansindi, G.M. (2017) 'Environmental Crime in Europe: State of Affairs and Future Perspectives' in A. Farmer, M. Faure and G.M. Vagliansindi (eds) *Environmental Crime in Europe*, Oxford: Hart Publishing, pp. 319–32.

Faure, M. (2017a) 'The Development of Environmental Criminal Law in the EU and its Member States', *RECIEL*, 26(2), pp. 139–46.

Faure, M. (2017b) 'The Evolution of Environmental Criminal Law in Europe: A Comparative Analysis' in A. Farmer, M. Faure and G.M. Vagliansindi (eds) *Environmental Crime in Europe*, Oxford: Hart Publishing, pp. 267–317.

FRONTEX (2021), *Environmental crime. Actions taken by EU justice and home affairs (JHA) agencies*, https://data.europa.eu/doi/10.2819/415719.

Fuentes Osorio, J.L. (2017a) 'Environmental Criminal Law in Spain' in A. Farmer, M. Faure and G.M. Vagliansindi (eds) *Environmental Crime in Europe*, Oxford: Hart Publishing, pp. 189–220.

Fuentes Osorio, J.L. (2017b) 'La "irresponsable" catástrofe ecológica de Aznalcóllar' in A. Medina Cuenca (ed) *Luces y sombras de la reforma penal y procesal penal en Iberoamérica. Libro homenaje al Prof. Dr. Ignacio F. Benítez Ortúzar*, La Habana: V-Lex, pp. 467–88.

Fuentes Osorio, J.L. (2021a) 'A Punch in the Face or a Slap on the Wrist? La exigua severidad de las condenas por delito medioambiental' in F. Miró Llinares and J.L. Fuentes Osorio (eds) *El derecho penal ante 'lo empírico'*, Madrid: Marcial Pons, pp. 173–96.

Fuentes Osorio, J.L. (2021b) *Delitos contra el medio ambiente*, Buenos Aires: Ad-Hoc.

Fuentes Osorio, J.L. (2022) 'Dolorosa, pero no letal. La cuantía de la multa según la capacidad económica de la persona jurídica', *InDret*, 2, pp. 203–29.

Fuentes Osorio, J.L. and Fajardo Del Castillo, T. (2020) 'Estudio sobre el carácter disuasorio, efectivo y proporcional de las sanciones penales impuestas en España en delitos contra el medio ambiente y su adecuación a la Directiva 2008/99/EC sobre protección del medio ambiente a través del derecho penal' in D. De la Bodega Zugasti (ed) *Estudio sobre el carácter disuasorio, efectivo y proporcional de las sanciones penales impuestas en España y Portugal en delitos contra el Medio Ambiente y su adecuación a la Directiva 2008/99/EC sobre protección del medio ambiente a través del derecho penal*, Madrid, Lisbon, pp. 7–97.

Fuentes Osorio, J.L. and Fajardo Del Castillo, T. (2021) 'Motivos de absolución en los delitos contra el medio ambiente: una comparación entre los delitos contra la fauna y contra los recursos naturales', *Revista Electrónica de Criminología*, 04(3), pp. 1–17.

García Ruiz, A. (2017) *Green Criminology. El ruido: un intruso en el Derecho penal medioambiental*, Madrid: Dykinson.

Gerstetter, C. et al. (2016) *Environmental crime and the EU. Synthesis of the Research Project 'European Union Action to Fight Environmental Crime'*, Berlin: EFFACE.

González Uriel, D. (2017) 'Dificultades en la sanción de los delitos contra el medio ambiente' in M. García Goldar and J. Ammerman Yebra (eds) *Propostas de modernización do dereito*. Santiago de Compostela, pp. 139–75.

Greife, M.J. and Maume, M.O. (2020) 'Do Companies Pay the Price for Environmental Crimes? Consequences of Criminal Penalties on Corporate Offenders', *Crime, Law and Social Change*, 73, pp. 337–56.

Kantorowicz-Reznichenko, E. (2015) 'Day-Fines: Should the Rich Pay More', *Review of Law & Economics*, 11(3), pp. 481–501.

Kennedy, D. M. (2016) *Disuasión y prevención del delito. Reconsiderando la expectativa de pena*, Madrid: Marcial Pons.

Kleiman, M.A. (2009) *When Brute Force Fails: How to Have Less Crime and Less Punishment*, Princeton: Princeton University Press.

Larrauri, E. (2015) *Introducción a la criminología y al sistema penal*, Barcelona: Trotta.

Leavitt, K., Wodahl, E.J. and Schweitzer, K. (2021) 'Citizen Willingness to Report Wildlife Crime', *Deviant Behavior*, 42(10), pp. 1256–72.

Morelle-Hungría, E., Bordehore, C., Fonfria, E.S. and Dobson, J.Y. (2023) 'Underwater Noise Pollution as an Ecological Crime: A Global Problem in the Anthropocene', *Kriminologie Das Online-Journal*, 5(4), pp. 348–63.

Nagin, D.S. (1998) 'Criminal deterrence Research at the Outset of the Twenty-First Century', *Crime and Justice*, 23, pp. 1–42.

Nurse, A. (2022) 'Contemporary Perspectives on Environmental Enforcement', *International Journal of Offender Therapy and Comparative Criminology*, 66(4), pp. 327–44.

Odeku, K.O. and Gundani, S.R. (2017) 'Accentuating Criminal sanctions for Environmental Degradation: Issues and Perspectives', *Environmental Economics*, 8(2), pp. 28–37.

Ortiz De Urbina Gimeno, I. (2016) 'Responsabilidad penal de las personas jurídicas (sección 1)' in I. Ayala Gómez and I. Ortiz de Urbina Gimeno (eds) *Memento penal y Económico de la Empresa*, Madrid: Francis Lefebvre, margs. 1300–1637.

Ost, F. (1996) *Naturaleza y Derecho*, Bilbao: Mensajero.

Pastor Muñoz, N. (2021) 'Erlaubtes Risiko und Gesetzlichkeitsprinzip im Strafrecht Zugleich ein Beitrag zur Bestimmung des Inhalts des erlaubten Risikos', *Goltdammer's Archiv für Strafrecht*, 168(1), pp. 16–33.

Paternoster, R. (2010) 'How much do we really know about Criminal Deterrence', *Journal of Criminal Law and Criminology*, 6(3), pp. 765–824.

Pereira, R. (2017) 'Towards Effective Implementation of the EU Environmental Crime Directive? The Case of Illegal Waste Management and Trafficking Offences', *RECIEL*, 26(2), pp. 147–62.

Perilongo, G.F. and Corn, E. (2017), 'The Ecocrime Directive and its Translation into Legal Practice EU Green Offences and their Impact at National level according to the Results of a Recent Survey', *New Journal of European Criminal Law*, 8(2), pp. 236–55.

Poisel, T. (2013) '(Environmental) Crime does not pay: The Effectiveness of the Criminal Prosecutions under Pollution Legislation in NSW', *LGLJ*, 18, pp. 77–92.

Redondo Almandoz, R. (2022) *Criminología verde: análisis criminológico de la delincuencia medioambiental en España*, Basque Country.

Robinson, P.H. (2012) *Principios distributivos del Derecho penal. A quién debe sancionarse y en qué medida*, Madrid: Marcial Pons.

South, N. (2016) 'Green Criminology and Brown Crime: Despoliation, Disposal and Demanufacturing in Global Resource Industries' in T. Wyatt (ed) *Hazardous Waste and Pollution*, Heidelberg: Springer International Publishing, pp. 1–25.

Varona, G. (2023) 'Victimización en delitos contra los ecosistemas y los animales: Percepción del daño y su reparación par parte de las personas internas en prisiones españolas', *Revista de victimología*, 15/2023, pp. 57–98.

White, R. (2010) 'Prosecution and Sentencing in Relation to Environmental Crime: Recent Socio-legal Developments', *Crime, Law and Social Change*, 53, pp. 365–81.
White, R. (2017), 'Reparative Justice, Environmental Crime and Penalties for the Powerful', *Crime, Law and Social Change*, 67, pp. 117–32.

7 Enforceable undertakings as an alternative to prosecution in Australian environmental law enforcement

Sarah Wright and Victoria Colvin

Introduction

Enforcement is critical in ensuring compliance with environmental laws.[1] Bates opined that '[t]he threat of criminal prosecution' constitutes 'the backbone of legal enforcement of environmental laws'.[2] As a higher-level sanction, theoretically, prosecution has a strong deterrent effect.[3] In practice, there has been some disillusionment with prosecution in a number of jurisdictions, including concerns regarding the 'trivialisation' of environmental offences through the level of fines courts have imposed[4] and the high costs involved for resource-poor regulators.[5] It is also recognised that prosecution is not appropriate for every breach[6] and that, in some jurisdictions, environmental

1 Brian J Preston, 'Principled Sentencing for Environmental Offences – Part 1: Purposes of Sentencing' (2007) 31 *Criminal Law Journal* 91, 91.

2 Gerry Bates, *Environmental Law in Australia* (LexisNexis, 11th edn, 2023), 742.

3 See Ian Ayres and John Braithwaite, *Responsive Regulation: Transcending the Deregulation Debate* (Oxford University Press, 1992), 35–6.

4 Stuart Bell, Donald McGillivray, Ole W Pedersen, Emma Lees, and Elen Stokes, *Environmental Law* (Oxford University Press, 10th edn, 2024), 229–30; Rob White, 'Ecocentrism and Criminal Proceedings for Offences against Environmental Laws' in Elizabeth Fisher and Brian Preston (eds), *An Environmental Court in Action: Function, Doctrine and Process* (Hart, 2022), 214; see also Richard B Macrory, *Regulatory Justice: Making Sanctions Effective, Final Report* (November 2006), 20, 22–3.

5 Macrory (n 4), 16; see also Rachel Pepper and Louise Gates, 'Sentencing for Environmental Offences: Tougher Penalties and Alternative Sentencing Options' (2012) 27(10) *Australian Environment Review* 357, 359.

6 Macrory (n 4), 7; NSW Environment Protection Authority, *Environment Protection Authority Prosecution Guidelines* (2022) 3–4 (*EPA Prosecution Guidelines*).

regulators had been 'too heavily reliant on criminal penalties'.[7] Accordingly, a wider range of instruments has been introduced to provide greater flexibility in enforcement responses.[8] In Australia, penalty notices with fixed fine amounts were introduced over three decades ago as an alternative to prosecution for minor environmental offences.[9] However, for those Australian jurisdictions lacking civil penalty systems, such as New South Wales (NSW),[10] this still left a dearth of alternatives to prosecution for matters too serious for a penalty notice. The subsequent introduction of Enforceable Undertakings (EUs) offered an intermediate sanction[11] which provided 'a new tool for regulators to facilitate an appropriate response to breaches of [environmental laws]'.[12]

EUs were 'invented in Australia' in the early 1990s as an enforcement tool in the trade practices area.[13] EUs are now available to many Australian regulators, including environmental regulators,[14] with similar mechanisms adopted in other jurisdictions, such as enforcement undertakings in the United Kingdom (UK).[15] An EU allows an alleged offender to offer proposed terms to a regulator that, if accepted, will generally settle

---

7 Elena Fasoli, 'Environmental Criminal Law in the United Kingdom' in Andrew Farmer, Michael Faure and Grazia Maria Vagliasindi (eds), *Environmental Crime in Europe* (Hart, 2017), 256; Macrory (n 4), 7.

8 See Macrory (n 4), 7. See, for example, the enforcement tools available in the Protection of the Environment Operation Act 1997 (NSW) (POEO Act).

9 For example, penalty notices were first introduced into NSW pollution law by the Environmental Offences and Penalties (Amendment) Act 1990 (NSW). See now, for example, POEO Act, Pt 8.3, div 3.

10 Civil penalties are available under some environmental statutes in the Australian states of South Australia, Tasmania, and Victoria and at the Commonwealth level. For a discussion, see: Brendan Grigg, 'Environmental Civil Penalties – An Australian Perspective' in LeRoy C Paddock, David L Markell and Nicholas S Bryner (eds), *Compliance and Enforcement of Environmental Law* (Cheltenham, UK and Northampton, MA: Edward Elgar Publishing, 2017), 141–53; Anna Reynolds, Tom Webb, Oscar Luke and Matt Floro, 'Civil Penalties in Federal Environmental Regulation' in Deniz Kayis, Eloise Gluer and Samuel Walpole, *The Law of Civil Penalties* (Federation Press, 2023), 243–60.

11 See Macrory (n 4), 63.

12 NSW, *Parliamentary Debates*, Legislative Council, 18 October 2017, 73 (Scot MacDonald).

13 Arie Freiberg, *Regulation in Australia* (Federation Press, 2017), 295; Richard Johnstone and Christine Parker, 'Enforceable Undertakings in Action – Report of a Roundtable Discussion with Australian Regulators', Working Paper, Griffith Law School (Griffith University and Melbourne Law School, University of Melbourne, February 2010), 4.

14 See Marina Nehme, 'Comparative Research into the Use of Enforceable Undertakings', Research Report, Centre for Law Markets and Regulation (UNSW Sydney, 2018).

15 See Regulatory Enforcement and Sanctions Act 2008 (UK); Ole W Pedersen, 'Environmental Enforcement Undertakings and Possible Implications: Responsive, Smarter or Rent Seeking?' (2013) 76(2) *Modern Law Review* 319.

an alleged breach[16] and avoid a prosecution.[17] EUs are voluntary for both parties and involve a negotiated outcome,[18] in comparison to the decision to prosecute which is 'imposed' by the prosecutor. Consequently, EUs are a form of 'contractually-based' enforcement[19] which, if breached, can be upheld through civil proceedings.[20]

In recent years, EUs have become available as an enforcement tool to an increasing number of Australian environmental regulators, particularly in NSW, Australia's most populous state. Pederson argued in the UK context that 'there is reason to assume that the use of enforcement undertakings have in part displaced the use of criminal prosecutions'.[21] Similarly, the utilisation of EUs by NSW environmental regulators has somewhat displaced prosecutions, particularly for more serious matters that might have been prosecuted in the NSW Land and Environment Court (NSWLEC),[22] a specialist, superior court of record. Concerns were raised in the UK that EUs 'may not provide a sufficient deterrent effect', being viewed as 'less punitive' and 'more lenient' than prosecution, and that a reduction in prosecutions in preference for EUs may diminish the perception of environmental crimes as being 'morally wrong'.[23] The (over)use of EUs rather than litigation has been criticised in other legal areas.[24] Nevertheless, EUs have been lauded as a beneficial enforcement tool for environmental regulators. EUs are considered 'a quicker, more cost-effective alternative

16 See Penny Armytage, Jane Brockington, and Jane van Reyk, 'Independent Inquiry into the Environment Protection Authority', Report of the Environment Protection Authority Inquiry Ministerial Advisory Committee, State of Victoria (16 May 2016), 241.

17 It is noted that in two circumstances NSW environmental regulators have used prosecution in tandem with an EU: see Natural Resources Access Regulator, 'Maules Creek Coal Judgment Strengthened by Enforceable Undertaking' (Media Release, 25 November 2021), <https://www.nrar.nsw.gov.au/news/maules-creek-coal-judgment-strengthened-by-enforceable-undertaking>; NSW Environment Protection Authority, 'Sydney Water to Pay Over $865K After Huge Sewage Overflow' (Media Release, 11 July 2023), <https://www.epa.nsw.gov.au/news/media-releases/2023/epa-media230711-sydney-water-to-pay-over-$865k-after-huge-sewage-overflow>.

18 See, for example, NSW Environment Protection Authority, *Guidelines on Enforceable Undertakings* (2017), 1–3, 8 (*EPA EU Guidelines*).

19 Ole W Pedersen, 'Revisiting the Role of Negotiation and Trivialization in Environmental Law Enforcement' (2019) 46(1) *Journal of Law and Society* 29, 31; see also Freiberg (n 13), 296.

20 See, for example, POEO Act, s 253A.

21 Pedersen, 'Revisiting the Role of Negotiation and Trivialization in Environmental Law Enforcement' (n 19), 31; see also Bell et al (n 4), 233.

22 EUs are more likely to be used as an alternative to NSWLEC prosecutions rather than local court prosecutions given the size of financial commitments involved: Sarah Wright, 'Re-examining the Role of Enforceable Undertakings as an Enforcement Mechanism in Environmental Law', Conference Paper, Frontiers in Environmental Law Colloquium (26 February 2021).

23 Bell et al (n 4), 236.

24 *Royal Commission into Misconduct in the Banking, Superannuation and Financial Services Industry, Final Report* (February 2019), Vol 1, 433.

to litigation'[25] and are praised by regulators as achieving better and more innovative outcomes for the environment and community than prosecution.[26]

This chapter considers the use of EUs in practice by the three key NSW environmental regulators: the NSW Environment Protection Authority (EPA), the (former) Department of Planning and Environment (DPE)[27] and the Natural Resources Access Regulator (NRAR). Their use is considered across four areas: pollution and waste management by the EPA; planning laws by the DPE; biodiversity conservation and native vegetation clearing laws by the DPE; and water management by the NRAR. Comparisons are also made with these regulators' use of prosecution. Data for this study on EUs and prosecutions has been drawn from the regulators' public registers available on their websites, the EPA's annual reports and NSWLEC decisions. The EU documents were available on the regulators' websites. The study period is the five financial years from 2018–19 to 2022–23. While the EPA has made use of EUs since 2007, the DPE and NRAR were given EU powers shortly before the study period and first utilised EUs within that period. Accordingly, as EUs have recently received increasing attention from a broader range of environmental regulators in Australia, it is a pertinent time to examine their use as an alternative to prosecution. NSW provides an apt jurisdiction for analysis given the availability of EUs to multiple environmental regulators and the jurisdiction's treatment of environmental crimes as serious offences. This is reflected in the maximum fines for environmental offences (of up to AU$5 million during the study period),[28] the availability of imprisonment

25 NSW, *Parliamentary Debates*, Legislative Assembly, 13 September 2005, 17643 (Bob Debus, Minister for the Environment).

26 NSW Department of Planning, Industry and Environment, *Prosecution Guidelines* (2021), 6 (*DPE Prosecution Guidelines*); Natural Resources Access Regulator, 'Regulator Secures Third Significant Agreement with Mining Company Over Water' (Media Release, 2 August 2023), <https://www.nrar.nsw.gov.au/news/tahmoor-coal-media-release>, citing Lisa Stockley, Director, Investigations and Enforcement, NRAR.

27 On 1 January 2024 the DPE was replaced and its functions were moved into two new departments. Planning laws are now managed by the NSW Department of Planning, Housing and Infrastructure. 'Environment and heritage' laws are now managed by the NSW Department of Climate Change, Energy, the Environment and Water.

28 See, for example, POEO Act, ss 119, 123; Environmental Planning and Assessment Act 1979 (NSW) (EP&A Act), ss 9.52–9.54; Water Management Act 2000 (NSW) (WM Act), s 363B; Local Land Services Act 2013 (NSW) (LSS Act), s 60N; Biodiversity Conservation Act 2016 (NSW) (BC Act), s 13.1. Maximum monetary penalties under the POEO Act were increased to up to AU$10 million after the study period (on 3 April 2024): see s 119. It is noted that the maximum penalties available for NSW environmental offences are considered to indicate that these are serious offences in the context of Australian environmental law. However, it is also noted that these maximum penalties may be lower than those considered appropriate for serious offences in other jurisdictions: see, for example, Directive (EU) 2024/1203 of the European Parliament and of the Council, which provides for maximum penalties of '5% of the total worldwide turnover of the legal person' or EUR 40 million (Art 7(3)(a)).

for certain serious offences,[29] and the specialist NSWLEC which deals with more serious environmental offences. There is also a trend of increasing monetary penalties in NSWLEC prosecutions,[30] although imprisonment is rarely imposed.[31] Furthermore, the regulators studied have the power to prosecute (and enter EUs) themselves; they do not refer potential prosecutions to a generalist public prosecutor.[32] This allows for direct examination of how regulators are utilising EUs compared to prosecution.

This chapter begins by explaining the enforcement responsibilities and EU powers of the regulators studied. It then examines the factors considered in deciding whether to prosecute or enter an EU. Next, it considers the content and key objectives of EUs, before examining the use of EUs in practice across the different regulatory areas, including in comparison to prosecution. The chapter aims to consider the uptake in the use of EUs by Australian regulatory agencies and elucidate some of the benefits and outcomes achievable through EUs, as well as examining some disadvantages of EUs as an enforcement instrument.

Environmental regulators, offences and EUs

This section examines the enforcement responsibilities of the Australian regulatory agencies mentioned above: the EPA, the DPE, and the NRAR. It also canvasses key offences and EU powers.[33]

Multiple NSW environmental laws, enforced by different regulators, may apply to the same activity. The state's 'primary environmental regulator' is the EPA,[34] whose responsibilities mainly cover pollution and waste management.[35] The main legislation, the Protection of the Environment Operations Act 1997 (NSW) (POEO Act), aims to protect the environment and human health.[36] The EPA is the lead regulator for serious

29 See, for example, POEO Act, ss 115–116, 144AA(2), 144AB; WM Act, ss 60A, 60C, 91I, 91K, 363B; BC Act, ss 2.1–2.5, 2.14.

30 See *Georges River Council v SAF Developments Pty Ltd* [2023] NSWLEC 50, [125].

31 Bates (n 2), 782; Sarah Wright, 'Cracking Down on Waste Crimes: A Strengthened Legislative and Enforcement Response' (2021) 167 (Nov/Dec) *Precedent* 26, 29.

32 See POEO Act, s 217; Natural Resources Access Regulator Act 2017 (NSW), s 12; BC Act, s 13.3; Criminal Procedure Act 1986 (NSW), s 14.

33 This chapter focuses solely on state government regulators. While local councils also play an important role in enforcing some NSW environmental laws, they cannot enter into EUs; although it is noted that the Secretary of the DPE can accept an EU on a local council's behalf under planning law: EP&A Act, s 9.5.

34 NSW Environment Protection Authority, *Our Organisation* (Web Page), <https://www.epa.nsw.gov.au/about-us/our-organisation>.

35 See NSW Environment Protection Authority, *Acts Administered by the EPA* (Web Page), <https://www.epa.nsw.gov.au/licensing-and-regulation/legislation-and-compliance/acts-administered-by-the-epa>.

36 POEO Act, s 3.

breaches[37] and conducts all enforcement for licenced activities.[38] More serious offences for which the EPA regularly takes enforcement action include water pollution,[39] breach of licence conditions,[40] and waste dumping.[41]

Developments and infrastructure are assessed, approved, and controlled through planning laws, primarily the Environmental Planning and Assessment Act 1979 (NSW) (EP&A Act). The DPE[42] undertook enforcement action for major projects.[43] These included projects over a specified capital investment value, identified project sites, and large infrastructure projects such as rail and ports.[44] A common alleged offence for major projects is a breach of consent conditions.

The DPE also had enforcement responsibilities regarding 'environment and heritage' laws, including:

- The Biodiversity Conservation Act 2016 (NSW) (BC Act) which aims to conserve biodiversity[45] and protect threatened species and ecological communities, as well as other native flora and fauna. Examples of offences include harming animals or picking plants that are threatened species or otherwise protected,[46] or knowingly damaging habitat of threatened species.[47]
- Part 5A of the Local Land Services Act 2013 (NSW) (LSS Act), under which the main offence is unlawful clearing of native vegetation in a rural regulated area.[48]

---

37 *EPA Prosecution Guidelines* (n 6), 6.

38 POEO Act, ss 6, 217, 218.

39 POEO Act, s 120(1).

40 POEO Act, s 64(1).

41 POEO Act, s 143(1).

42 The DPE has undergone various changes to its name and areas of responsibility (in addition to planning) in recent years. For ease of reference, the department and its former predecessor entities will be referred to as DPE throughout this chapter, unless specifically identified. See also n 27 regarding subsequent changes to DPE after the study period.

43 NSW Department of Planning, Industry and Environment, *Enforceable Undertakings Guidelines* (2020), 1 (*DPE EU Guidelines*). Major projects include projects within the categories of State Significant Development and State Significant Infrastructure. Major projects are approved at the state level by either by the Minister for Planning or the Independent Planning Commission. For a discussion of these projects, see Rosemary Lyster, Zada Lipman, Ed Couzens, Susan O'Neill, and Jeff Smith, *Environmental and Planning Law in New South Wales* (Federation Press, 2021), 152–68.

44 See EP&A Act, ss 4.36, 5.12; State Environmental Planning Policy (Planning Systems) 2021 (NSW), ss 2.6, 2.13, 2.14, Schs 1–4.

45 BC Act, s 1.3.

46 BC Act, ss 2.1(1), 2.2(1).

47 BC Act, s 2.4(1).

48 LSS Act, s 60N(1).

- The National Parks and Wildlife Act 1974 (NSW) (NP&W Act), which protects national parks, other reserves, and Aboriginal cultural heritage.[49]

'Environment and heritage' laws were managed by a different group than planning laws within DPE and are treated separately within this chapter given the different nature of these laws and historical changes to government entities within (and after)[50] the study period. Prior to 1 July 2019, biodiversity and native vegetation laws were the responsibility of the NSW Office of Environment and Heritage (OEH) which sat within the DPE cluster and was abolished on that date.[51] For ease of reference, the regulator will be referred to as DPE, which incorporates OEH and former emanations of DPE as a department.

The NRAR commenced operation in April 2018[52] with a sole focus on water management compliance and enforcement.[53] The Water Management Act 2000 (NSW) (WM Act) aims to ensure sustainable water use and sharing of water between different users and purposes,[54] including agricultural irrigation, industrial and other commercial uses, and environmental purposes. Water access and use, as well as water management works (such as dams and bores), are regulated through licences and approvals. WM Act offences include illegal construction and use of water management works[55] and 'water theft' offences, such as taking water without an access licence[56] or a sufficient water allocation.[57]

EPA, DPE and NRAR enforcement tools include notices, orders and directions, civil enforcement (with remedies such as injunctions), penalty notices (an administrative sanction whereby the regulator imposes a fixed fine amount), EUs, and prosecution.[58] Civil enforcement is rarely used given the breadth of notice powers available

---

49 The inclusion of Aboriginal cultural heritage within the National Parks and Wildlife Act 1974 (NSW) (NP&W Act) is considered 'offensive' and inappropriate: NSW Office of Environment and Heritage, *A Proposed New Legal Framework: Aboriginal Cultural Heritage in NSW* (2017), vii. NSW has been working towards proposed standalone Aboriginal cultural heritage legislation for a number of years.

50 On 1 January 2024 (after the study period) the DPE was replaced and its planning and 'environment and heritage' functions are now split and separately undertaken by two new departments: see n 27.

51 Administrative Arrangements (Administrative Changes—Public Service Agencies) Order 2019 (NSW), cls 2, 12.

52 NSW Department of Industry, *Annual Report 2017–2018* (2018), 1.

53 Natural Resources Access Regulator Act 2017 (NSW), s 10.

54 WM Act, s 3.

55 WM Act, ss 91B–91D.

56 WM Act, s 60A.

57 WM Act, s 60C.

58 See NSW Environment Protection Authority, *Environment Protection Authority Regulatory Policy* (2021), 32–4 (*EPA Regulatory Policy*); NSW Department of Planning and Environment, *Compliance Policy* (2020), 11–14 (*DPE Compliance Policy*); NSW Office of Environment and Heritage, *Compliance Policy: Office of Environment and*

to regulators,[59] such as clean-up notices utilised by the EPA shortly after an incident. Court proceedings to seek a civil penalty are not available as an enforcement option in NSW,[60] nor can a regulator impose variable monetary penalties, which are available in the UK.[61] Accordingly, EUs offer the only alternative to prosecution for 'serious' breaches,[62] with penalty notices utilised in minor matters.

Table 7.1 below sets out current key legislation permitting the regulators studied to enter EUs and when that power was introduced. The first NSW environmental regulator given EU powers was the EPA in 2006 under the POEO Act. It was more than a decade later that EUs were introduced in areas beyond pollution and waste management. However, EUs are not available for current offences under the NP&W Act, such as damage to national parks.[63] This is a significant omission given their inclusion in the other main environmental and planning statutes.

Regulators can enter into EUs with individuals and organisations, such as corporations, state-owned corporations, and government bodies. In this chapter, the regulated party who enters an EU is called an EU 'entrant'.

Deciding whether to prosecute or accept an EU

Environmental regulators identify deterrence of the alleged offender and broader regulated community and achieving compliance as 'key aims of ... enforcement action'.[64] They also emphasise the use of a proportionate enforcement response.[65] Regulators have a range of enforcement tools of increasing severity, often represented within an

Heritage (2018), 9–12, 16–17 (*OEH Compliance Policy*); Natural Resources Access Regulator, *Natural Resources Access Regulator Regulatory Policy* (2021), 7, 9 (*NRAR Regulatory Policy*).

59 See Bates (n 2), 737.

60 See Reynolds et al (n 10), 259.

61 See, for example, Fasoli (n 7), 256–7.

62 *EPA EU Guidelines* (n 18), 1; *DPE EU Guidelines* (n 43), 2; Natural Resources Access Regulator, *Enforceable Undertakings Guideline* (INT20/216270 ed, undated) (*NRAR EU Guidelines*), 1.

63 As discussed below, EUs are available under s 13.27 of the BC Act for offences under the NP&W Act that were repealed and replaced by offences in the BC Act (as well as offences under the repealed Native Vegetation Act 2003 (NSW) (NV Act) which Pt 5A of the LSS Act replaced): see Biodiversity Conservation (Savings and Transitional) Regulation 2017 (NSW), cl 59A. This provision took effect from 10 August 2018.

64 Natural Resources Access Regulator, *Prosecution Guidelines* (2018), 4 (*NRAR Prosecution Guidelines*); see also *DPE Prosecution Guidelines* (n 26), 3; *EPA Prosecution Guidelines* (n 6), 3–4.

65 *DPE Prosecution Guidelines* (n 26), 3; *NRAR Prosecution Guidelines* (n 64), 4; *EPA Regulatory Policy* (n 58), 12, 14.

Table 7.1 NSW environmental regulators and key legislation providing for EUs

Regulator	Current key legislation/ EU power	Date EUs available from
EPA	• Protection of the Environment Operations Act 1997 (NSW) s 253A	1/5/2006
	• Protection from Harmful Radiation Act 1990 (NSW) s 24A	1/7/2013
	• Contaminated Land Management Act 1997 (NSW) s 96A	1/1/2015
	• Pesticides Act 1999 (NSW) s 110	1/12/2015
DPE	• Biodiversity Conservation Act 2016 (NSW) s 13.27	25/8/2017
	• Local Land Services Act 2013 (NSW) (Pt 5A - native vegetation clearing in rural areas) s 60ZM/ BC Act s 13.27	25/8/2017
	• Environmental Planning and Assessment Act 1979 (NSW) s 9.5	1/3/2018
NRAR	• Water Management Act 2000 (NSW) s 336E	27/06/2018

Note: This list is not exhaustive, but lists key legislation only. It is noted that the EU provision in s 253A of the POEO Act extends to a number of other pieces of legislation: see s 213.
Source: Authors.

enforcement pyramid[66] based on Ayres and Braithwaite's theory of responsive regulation.[67] The EPA, DPE and NRAR recognise criminal penalties and EUs as higher-level sanctions, with EUs sitting below criminal penalties in the enforcement pyramid.[68] In determining the appropriate enforcement response, these regulators consider their prosecution guidelines,[69] EU guidelines[70] and other relevant compliance or regulatory policies.[71] These guidelines and policies assist with decision making in terms of enforcement action but 'are not legally binding'.[72] This section examines factors considered in determining whether to prosecute or enter an EU. Despite OEH's abolition

66 *DPE Compliance Policy* (n 58) 12; *NRAR Regulatory Policy* (n 58), 9. See also the enforcement pyramid in the NSW Environment Protection Authority, *Environment Protection Authority Compliance Policy* (2013), 5 (*EPA Compliance Policy*), replaced by the *EPA Regulatory Policy* (n 58).

67 Ayres and Braithwaite (n 3), 35.

68 *DPE Compliance Policy* (n 58), 12; *NRAR Regulatory Policy* (n 58), 9; *EPA Compliance Policy* (n 66), 5.

69 *EPA Prosecution Guidelines* (n 6); *DPE Prosecution Guidelines* (n 26); *NRAR Prosecution Guidelines* (n 64).

70 *EPA EU Guidelines* (n 18); *DPE EU Guidelines* (n 43); NSW Office of Environment and Heritage, *Guidelines for Enforceable Undertakings* (2018) (*OEH EU Guidelines*); *NRAR EU Guidelines* (n 62).

71 *EPA Regulatory Policy* (n 58); *DPE Compliance Policy* (n 58); *OEH Compliance Policy* (n 58); *NRAR Regulatory Policy* (n 58).

72 See, for example, *EPA Prosecution Guidelines* (n 6), 2.

in 2019 and DPE assuming OEH's enforcement functions regarding biodiversity, native vegetation, and the NP&W Act, some OEH guidelines still seem to be applied when enforcing these laws and are referred to where relevant.

A necessary precursor to prosecution is that the 'evidence establishes a prima facie case'[73] and 'there are reasonable prospects of success'.[74] However, even if an offence could be established, commencing a prosecution is discretionary and hence not automatic and 'may not always be the appropriate response'.[75] Nor do regulators have the resources to prosecute every breach.[76] Prosecution is only appropriate if it is in 'the public interest',[77] which involves considering a range of factors such as: seriousness of the offence; actual or potential harm including to (depending on the offence) the environment, heritage, human health, or the community; whether the offence is prevalent; the alleged offender's 'degree of culpability', level of cooperation in the investigation and prior record of enforcement actions; the likely sentencing outcome in a prosecution; 'the availability and efficacy of any alternatives to prosecution'; the anticipated time and cost involved in proceedings; and 'any precedent which may be set by instituting or by not instituting proceedings'.[78]

Some prosecution guidelines make greater reference to EUs than others. The NRAR's prosecution guidelines simply indicate that the full range of enforcement responses should be considered regarding an alleged breach, including EUs.[79] The EPA's prosecution guidelines indicate 'the EPA may consider whether an enforceable undertaking is a more appropriate regulatory response versus a potential prosecution' by considering the factors in the EPA's EU guidelines.[80] The DPE's prosecution guidelines go further by essentially identifying EUs as 'an alternative but comparably strong regulatory response' to prosecution,[81] even though EUs sit below prosecution in the DPE's enforcement pyramid[82] and other regulators recognise EUs as 'a less serious response than prosecution'.[83] The DPE's prosecution guidelines also state that EUs 'are frequently able to achieve a greater benefit for the community than could be gained

73 *EPA Prosecution Guidelines* (n 6), 3; *DPE Prosecution Guidelines* (n 26), 3–4; *NRAR Prosecution Guidelines* (n 64), 5.
74 *DPE Prosecution Guidelines* (n 26), 4; *EPA Prosecution Guidelines* (n 6), 3; *NRAR Prosecution Guidelines* (n 64), 5.
75 *EPA Prosecution Guidelines* (n 6), 3–4; *DPE Prosecution Guidelines* (n 26), 3; *NRAR Prosecution Guidelines* (n 64), 3–4.
76 *EPA Prosecution Guidelines* (n 6), 3; *DPE Prosecution Guidelines* (n 26), 4; *NRAR Prosecution Guidelines* (n 64), 4.
77 *EPA Prosecution Guidelines* (n 6), 3; *DPE Prosecution Guidelines* (n 26), 3–4; *NRAR Prosecution Guidelines* (n 64), 5.
78 *EPA Prosecution Guidelines* (n 6), 4–5; *DPE Prosecution Guidelines* (n 26), 5; *NRAR Prosecution Guidelines* (n 64), 5.
79 *NRAR Prosecution Guidelines* (n 64), 3.
80 *EPA Prosecution Guidelines* (n 6), 16.
81 *DPE Prosecution Guidelines* (n 26), 6.
82 *DPE Compliance Policy* (n 58), 12.
83 *EPA EU Guidelines* (n 18), 1.

through prosecution alone'.[84] However, 'creative' sentencing orders[85] are available in many environmental prosecutions in NSW via alternative sentencing orders (ASOs).[86] Examples of ASOs include orders requiring the defendant to:

- remediate any environmental harm caused;
- undertake action to prevent a recurrence, an audit, or training;
- pay clean-up or investigation costs;
- pay monetary benefits gained through the offence;
- publicise the offence, its environmental consequences, and court orders made, such as through a notice in a newspaper (referred to as 'publication orders'); and
- make a payment towards an environmental project, the Environmental Trust, or to an organisation 'for general environmental purposes'.[87] Such projects and payments, referred to as 'environmental service orders', are additional to any remediation of harm caused by the offence. Essentially, part or all of the money that would otherwise be paid as a fine to consolidated government revenue may instead be directed to be paid towards an environmental project or to an organisation for environmental purposes.[88]

Many types of undertakings within environmental EUs, such as remediation, measures to prevent future incidents, payments towards projects for the benefit of the environment, and requirements to publish a notice about the incident and EU in a newspaper, could also be achieved through ASOs in prosecutions.[89] For instance, payments towards environmental projects can replace a fine in prosecutions[90] and, as discussed below, form a key financial component of EUs. However, while a number of ASOs have been utilised in EPA prosecutions and prosecutions under the NP&W Act by the former OEH (and its predecessors), the fuller suite of ASOs has been used to a lesser extent in DPE planning and NRAR prosecutions. For instance, at the time of writing, only publication orders had been used in DPE planning matters, with monetary penalties imposed through a fine rather than payments directed towards environmental projects. Accordingly, while innovative outcomes are available through prosecution

---

84 *DPE Prosecution Guidelines* (n 26), 6.

85 Carolyn Abbot, *Enforcing Pollution Control Regulation* (Hart, 2009), 179.

86 POEO Act ss 243–250A; EP&A Act, s 9.56; WM Act, ss 353–353G; BC Act, ss 13.18–13.25; LSS Act, s 60ZM. For a discussion of ASOs, see Sarah Wright, 'Re-examining the Approach to Alternative Sentencing Orders in New South Wales Pollution Law' (2018) 35 *Environmental and Planning Law Journal* 606. It is noted the WM Act refers to ASOs as additional orders (to a fine or imprisonment), whereas other legislation, such as the POEO Act, refers to ASOs as additional or alternative orders (to a fine or imprisonment): see POEO Act, s 244; WM Act, s 353A(2); *Budvalt Pty Ltd v Barnes, Chief Regulatory Officer, Natural Resources Access Regulator* [2022] NSWCCA 9, [52]–[72].

87 See POEO Act, ss 243–250A.

88 Wright, 'Re-examining the Approach to Alternative Sentencing Orders' (n 86), 616; POEO Act, s 250(1)(e).

89 Wright, 'Re-examining the Role of Enforceable Undertakings…' (n 22).

90 See, for example, POEO Act, s 250(1)(e).

and EUs, it is through EUs that some regulators are more fully exploring 'creative' outcomes. Nevertheless, the prosecution guidelines implicitly recognise there will be cases where, although an EU could achieve beneficial outcomes, the circumstances of the offence and public expectations may dictate prosecution is necessary.[91]

The EPA, DPE and NRAR also consider their EU guidelines in determining if an EU is appropriate.[92] EUs are considered an appropriate alternative to prosecution for 'serious' breaches[93] where the entrant takes responsibility for what occurred, cooperates with the regulator, and offers a 'genuine' response through the proposed EU terms.[94] The DPE and NRAR indicate EUs are appropriate where they can provide 'the best solution' or outcome.[95] The regulators' EU guidelines contain a range of factors to consider in determining whether an EU is appropriate in a particular case. These are broadly similar to the factors relevant to prosecution, such as the nature of the alleged breach, extent of harm, compliance history, and response and attitude to the incident.[96] The considerations in EU guidelines are sometimes framed as factors that 'weigh in favour of an [EU] being considered an appropriate response', such as the incident being accidental or limited environmental harm.[97] Some favourable factors, such as promptly offering an EU and the prospect of a fast resolution,[98] reflect perceived benefits of EUs, namely they are 'a quicker, more cost-effective alternative to litigation'.[99]

Whether an EU is an appropriate enforcement response also depends on the proposed terms and outcomes a proffered EU seeks to achieve.[100] These are discussed in the following section.

---

91 See, for example, *DPE Prosecution Guidelines* (n 26), 5; *NRAR Prosecution Guidelines* (n 64), 5.

92 *EPA EU Guidelines* (n 18); *DPE EU Guidelines* (n 43); *OEH EU Guidelines* (n 70); *NRAR EU Guidelines* (n 62).

93 *EPA EU Guidelines* (n 18), 1; *DPE EU Guidelines* (n 43), 2; *NRAR EU Guidelines* (n 62), 1.

94 *EPA EU Guidelines* (n 18), 1–3; *OEH EU Guidelines* (n 70), 2; *NRAR EU Guidelines* (n 62), 1.

95 *DPE EU Guidelines* (n 43), 2; *OEH EU Guidelines* (n 70), 2; *NRAR EU Guidelines* (n 62), 1.

96 *EPA EU Guidelines* (n 18), 3–4; *DPE EU Guidelines* (n 43), 2; *OEH EU Guidelines* (n 70), 7; *NRAR EU Guidelines* (n 62), 1–2; *EPA Prosecution Guidelines* (n 6), 4–5; *DPE Prosecution Guidelines* (n 26), 5; *NRAR Prosecution Guidelines* (n 64), 5.

97 *EPA EU Guidelines* (n 18), 3–4; *OEH EU Guidelines* (n 70), 7.

98 Ibid.

99 NSW, *Parliamentary Debates*, Legislative Assembly, 13 September 2005, 17643 (Bob Debus, Minister for the Environment); *DPE EU Guidelines* (n 43), 2; *NRAR EU Guidelines* (n 62), 1.

100 *EPA EU Guidelines* (n 18), 4–7, 11–13; *DPE EU Guidelines* (n 43), 5–6, 10–11; *OEH EU Guidelines* (n 70), 2–4, 8–9; *NRAR EU Guidelines* (n 62), 2–3.

Content and key objectives of EUs

EU content varies based on the circumstances and between environmental regulators given differences in legislation, offences, and EU guidelines. Nevertheless, EUs generally have three main sections:[101] (1) a background section summarising matters such as the EU entrant and their operations, the incident, and measures already taken by the entrant in response to it, and an acknowledgement of an alleged breach; (2) the undertakings offered (discussed further below); and (3) a series of acknowledgements, such as that the regulator 'will make [the EU] publicly available'.[102]

EUs are 'designed to achieve improved environmental outcomes'.[103] The EPA's EU Guidelines set out key objectives for EUs, with examples of types of terms that may satisfy these objectives and also standard conditions.[104] The EPA's main three key objectives are to: 'drive improvements in [the EU entrant's] environmental performance'; 'deliver benefits to the local environment and/or community'; and 'drive improvements in environmental performance industry-wide'.[105] The OEH EU guidelines relating to biodiversity and native vegetation matters also list key principles EUs are expected to cover.[106] The DPE planning and NRAR EU guidelines contain more generalised lists of EU content, with some further guidance provided in templates.[107] For example, the DPE planning EU guidelines identify that undertakings should include the 'remedies offered and the process to audit or verify their implementation' and 'future actions to prevent recurrence and improve compliance programs'.[108] Similar factors are listed by the NRAR and in the OEH guidelines (in addition to its key principles for EUs).[109] While, as noted, there are differences in terminology and content between regulators and individual EUs, some of the key undertakings within environmental EUs cover:

- *Remediation or rectification of the incident.* For example, where native vegetation has allegedly been illegally cleared, carrying out restoration or remediation of the area.[110] Remediation undertakings are rarer in some areas, such as for pollution incidents which have usually already been cleaned up.

---

101 See, for example, *DPE EU Guidelines* (n 43), 10–11; *OEH EU Guidelines* (n 70), 8–9.

102 *DPE EU Guidelines* (n 43), 5, 11; *OEH EU Guidelines* (n 70), 4, 9; *EPA EU Guidelines* (n 18), 12; *NRAR EU Guidelines* (n 62), 3.

103 *EPA EU Guidelines* (n 18), 1; see also *DPE EU Guidelines* (n 43), 2; *OEH EU Guidelines* (n 70), 1–2.

104 *EPA EU Guidelines* (n 18), 4–7, 12–13.

105 Ibid, 4–6; Nehme (n 14), 18–19.

106 *OEH EU Guidelines* (n 70), 2.

107 *DPE EU Guidelines* (n 43), 5–6, 10–11; *NRAR EU Guidelines* (n 62), 2–3.

108 *DPE EU Guidelines* (n 43), 5.

109 *NRAR EU Guidelines* (n 62), 3; *OEH EU Guidelines* (n 70), 3.

110 *OEH EU Guidelines* (n 70), 2.

- *Improved environmental performance.* This is aimed at measures which 'address the alleged breach' and prevent a recurrence.[111] Examples include installing new equipment, carrying out works, improving procedures, training staff, improving a compliance programme, and conducting and implementing an audit.[112]
- *Funding or providing environmental and community benefits.* Examples include funding a project for the benefit of the local environment or community impacted by the alleged breach (such as restoration of a creek), making a payment to an environmental organisation (such as one that cares for native animals) and 'making a public and genuine apology' to impacted communities.[113] Environmental and community projects and payments provide an additional benefit; they are not aimed at remediation of the actual incident.[114] They are sometimes referred to as 'financial contributions'[115] and represent a key component of environmental EUs in practice. In determining the 'appropriate amount' to be paid towards a project for the benefit of the environment or community, regulators such as the EPA consider factors including 'the likely penalty' in a prosecution and the actual or potential environmental harm.[116]
- *Improvements to environmental performance industry-wide by sharing lessons learnt.*[117] Examples include sharing research or EU outcomes through industry forums and journal articles[118] and 'funding of education and awareness initiatives'.[119] Only the EPA and OEH EU guidelines for biodiversity and native vegetation matters identify this category as a potential undertaking, with it being a key EPA EU objective.[120] OEH identified 'positive behaviour change in the regulated community' as a key principle.[121] However, OEH identified either an individual compliance programme or broader industry education as examples of meeting this principle[122] and undertakings aimed at industry-wide performance improvements were not observed in these EUs during the study period.

Additionally, related undertakings within EUs seek to ensure the EU commitments are realised through provisions regarding monitoring, auditing, and reporting on EU

111 *EPA EU Guidelines* (n 18), 4; *DPE EU Guidelines* (n 43), 5; *OEH EU Guidelines* (n 70), 2–3; *NRAR EU Guidelines* (n 62), 3.
112 *EPA EU Guidelines* (n 18), 4–5; *DPE EU Guidelines* (n 43), 10; *OEH EU Guidelines* (n 70), 2.
113 *EPA EU Guidelines* (n 18), 5; *OEH EU Guidelines* (n 70), 2.
114 Wright, 'Re-examining the Role of Enforceable Undertakings…' (n 22).
115 See, for example, *DPE EU Guidelines* (n 43), 6. In addition to statements in guidelines, in some EUs environmental projects appear under a heading such as 'financial', such as some EUs entered into by the EPA.
116 *EPA EU Guidelines* (n 18), 5, 11; see also *DPE EU Guidelines* (n 43), 6.
117 *EPA EU Guidelines* (n 18), 5; see also *OEH EU Guidelines* (n 70), 2.
118 *EPA EU Guidelines* (n 18), 5; *OEH EU Guidelines* (n 70), 2.
119 *OEH EU Guidelines* (n 70), 2.
120 *EPA EU Guidelines* (n 18), 5–6; *OEH EU Guidelines* (n 70), 2.
121 *OEH EU Guidelines* (n 70), 2.
122 Ibid.

compliance.[123] Terms regarding recovery of the regulator's investigation, legal and/or monitoring costs may also be included.[124] The EPA and NRAR EUs regularly provide for cost recovery, particularly investigation and legal costs. In comparison, only one DPE EU in the study period provided for cost recovery, despite the DPE (and OEH) guidelines identifying cost recovery as a potential EU term.[125]

As EUs are meant to be public documents, the regulators' EU guidelines identify that the regulator will publish the EU on their website and may publicise it through additional means, for example, in their media releases.[126] However, a notable omission from the regulators' EU guidelines is whether EUs should require the EU entrant to publicise details of the alleged breach and EU terms, such as in a newspaper, industry magazine, or on social media, which will be referred to in this chapter as 'publication notices'.[127] Such notices are equivalent to publication orders – an ASO regularly imposed in NSWLEC prosecutions.[128] While publication orders can have a 'name and shame' effect, the courts have particularly recognised their value in educating the broader regulated community.[129] Given that environmental regulators' guidelines identify deterring the regulated community as a 'key aim of … enforcement action'[130] and the EPA and OEH EU guidelines identify improved performance of the regulated community as a key EU objective or principle,[131] it is surprising that EU guidelines do not set expectations regarding publication notice requirements for EU entrants. While regulators may issue media releases on their websites for finalised EUs, publication notices can have a wider reach in terms of the regulated community.[132] It is noted that a number of EPA EUs did require EU entrants to place publication notices

123 See, for example, *EPA EU Guidelines* (n 18), 6–7.

124 Ibid, 12; *DPE EU Guidelines* (n 43), 5, 10; *OEH EU Guidelines* (n 70), 4, 8; *NRAR EU Guidelines* (n 62), 3.

125 *DPE EU Guidelines* (n 43), 5, 10; *OEH EU Guidelines* (n 70), 4, 8.

126 *EPA EU Guidelines* (n 18), 7–8, 12; *DPE EU Guidelines* (n 43), 8, 11; *OEH EU Guidelines* (n 70), 5, 9; *NRAR EU Guidelines* (n 62), 4. Information regarding EUs entered into under the POEO Act must be included on the EPA's public register: see Protection of the Environment Operations (General) Regulation 2022 (NSW), cl 156(e). The DPE and NRAR voluntarily include EUs on their public registers: see also Natural Resources Access Regulator Act 2017 (NSW), s 12A; Natural Resources Access Regulator Regulation 2023 (NSW), cl 5(g), (h).

127 Wright, 'Re-examining the Role of Enforceable Undertakings…' (n 22).

128 See, for example, POEO Act, s 250(1)(a), (b); Wright, 'Re-examining the Approach to Alternative Sentencing Orders' (n 86), 627.

129 See, for example, *Environment Protection Authority v Hughes* [2019] NSWLEC 108, [182]–[183]; *Harris v Harrison* [2014] NSWCCA 84, [128]; Wright, 'Re-examining the Approach to Alternative Sentencing Orders' (n 86), 626–7.

130 *NRAR Prosecution Guidelines* (n 64), 4; see also *EPA Prosecution Guidelines* (n 6), 3–4; *DPE Prosecution Guidelines* (n 26), 3.

131 *EPA EU Guidelines* (n 18), 5–6; *OEH EU Guidelines* (n 70), 2.

132 See *Environment Protection Authority v Incitec Ltd* [2003] NSWLEC 381, [60]–[61]; *Environment Protection Authority v Visy Pulp and Paper Pty Ltd* [2024] NSWLEC 55, [129]–[131].

in newspapers, industry magazines or journals, or social media. However, in the study period, only one DPE EU (under planning law) and one NRAR EU included publication notice requirements. Furthermore, while the EPA and NRAR regularly publish media releases themselves after entry into EUs, few media releases could be located by the authors for DPE EUs. Consequently, some regulators arguably are not fully harnessing publicity of EUs to deter and educate the broader regulated community despite, as discussed below, some sizeable financial commitments being agreed to under EUs.

The use of EUs in practice

This section considers the use of EUs in practice by the EPA, DPE and NRAR and examines some benefits and pitfalls of EUs, including in comparison to prosecution. It first compares the use of EUs to prosecution by these regulators. It then examines the use of EUs across the different regulatory areas studied.

Comparison of the use of EUs versus prosecution

Table 7.2 below sets out the number of entrants that entered EUs with the environmental regulators regarding alleged breaches during the study period[133] versus the number of defendants successfully prosecuted in the NSWLEC.[134] Data was not available regarding the number of: (i) EUs proposed but rejected by the regulator (or not otherwise finalised); or (ii) prosecutions commenced but subsequently withdrawn due to the prosecutor and offender agreeing to settle the matter through an EU. Accordingly, the data focused on finalised EUs and successfully completed prosecutions. The EPA completed significantly more enforcement actions through prosecutions and EUs than the DPE and NRAR. It also completed more prosecutions (62.3%) than EUs (37.7%). In comparison, the DPE and NRAR used similar numbers of prosecutions to EUs, although the DPE used more EUs than prosecutions later in the study period. It is noted that some DPE prosecutions finalised during the study period may have been commenced prior to the relevant EU power being introduced, although the power had been introduced and was available at the time the proceedings were determined. Furthermore, EUs were not available as an enforcement tool for three defendants prosecuted by the DPE under the NP&W Act.[135] The NRAR was established shortly

---

133 Some EUs had more than one entrant. The statistics are reported by number of entrants, not the number of EUs, to allow for equivalence with the number of defendants in prosecutions.

134 It is noted that while prosecutions can also be instituted in the local court, these are generally more minor matters. EUs are more likely to be used as an alternative to NSWLEC prosecutions given the size of financial commitments involved: Wright, 'Re-examining the Role of Enforceable Undertakings…' (n 22).

135 See the note to Table 7.2. There were two NP&W Act matters (one individual, one local council) in the 2018–19 financial year for which EUs were not available. There was one NP&W Act matter in the 2020–21 financial year against an individual for which an EU was not available.

before the study period, which likely explains a lack of finalised prosecutions, and to some extent finalisation of EUs, until later in the study period given the time gap between alleged incidents and finalisation of EUs and prosecutions. Some prosecution outcomes may also have been delayed due to the Covid-19 pandemic.

When the types of EU entrants and defendants in prosecutions are examined, some different patterns emerge: see Table 7.3. For organisations (including companies and some public bodies, see Table 7.3), the total number of EU entrants (44) versus defendants prosecuted (46) across all environmental regulators was virtually equivalent. However, the EPA used more prosecutions than EUs for organisations: 55.7% versus 44.3%. The NRAR and also the DPE in planning matters used EUs more than prosecutions for organisations. Overall, individuals were more likely to be prosecuted (68.4%) than enter an EU (31.6%). However, when specific regulators are examined, there are stark differences in EU use for individuals compared to organisations. The EPA and NRAR used EUs almost exclusively for organisations, with very limited use for individuals.[136] Indeed, the two individuals who entered EUs with the EPA did so in their capacity as directors of a corporation that entered an EU in order to ensure the EU covered any 'potential offences' by both the company and its directors. However, the EU only expressly identified alleged offences by the company.[137] In planning matters, the DPE's enforcement actions through EUs (and prosecutions) were solely for organisations (all corporations), which is to be expected given the entities undertaking major projects. Notably, there was greater use of EUs for individuals than organisations in the DPE biodiversity and native vegetation matters than other areas. Six of these EUs were entered into by one or more individuals (nine individuals total), two by corporations, and one by a local council. The greater use of EUs against individuals for alleged biodiversity and native vegetation offences is consistent with the type of defendants in NSWLEC prosecutions in this area, where the majority of defendants have been individuals rather than organisations.

EUs have therefore replaced prosecutions in a significant proportion of matters, particularly for organisations for which overall nearly half had alleged breaches dealt with through EUs. However, individuals are more likely to be prosecuted and thereby subject to the associated stigma and a criminal conviction. The higher use of EUs for organisations may be due to the significant financial commitments that can be attached to EUs.[138]

While regulators emphasise the beneficial nature of EUs, utilising an EU rather than prosecution has some ramifications in subsequent prosecutions. As an administrative enforcement measure, an EU does not result in a criminal conviction, nor establish guilt of an offence. The EU entrant usually merely acknowledges the regulator has

136 See also Wright, 'Re-examining the Role of Enforceable Undertakings…' (n 22).

137 *Undertaking by Southern Oil Collection Pty Ltd to the Environment Protection Authority Given for the Purposes of Section 253A of the Protection of the Environment Operations Act 1997 (NSW)* (Enforceable Undertaking, 10 September 2020), 4.

138 Wright, 'Re-examining the Role of Enforceable Undertakings…' (n 22).

Table 7.2 Number of EU entrants versus number of defendants in successful prosecutions completed in the NSWLEC during the study period

Financial year	EPA: EU[a]	EPA: P[b]	DPE: Planning:[c] EU[a]	DPE: Planning: P[b]	DPE: BNV[d] EU[a]	DPE: BNV[d] P[b]	NRAR: EU[a]	NRAR: P[b]	Total: EU[a]	Total: P[b]
2018–19	4	9	–[e]	1	1	6	–	–	5	16
2019–20	7	11	–	–	2	3	1[e]	–	10	14
2020–21	11	10	–	2	2	1	–	2	13	15
2021–22	3	10	4	1	5	1	6	3	18	15
2022–23	4	8	2	–	2	–	2	4	10	12
Five-year total	29	48	6	4	12	11	9	9	56	72

Notes: [a] EU = EUs by number of EU entrants.

[b] P = NSWLEC prosecutions by the number of defendants. Defendants subsequently prosecuted or those who entered an EU for further incidents were counted on each separate occasion.

[c] DPE Planning matters excludes EUs entered into by the DPE on behalf of local councils

[d] DPE BNV category includes biodiversity, native vegetation and NP&W Act matters. EUs are not available for current offences under the NP&W but are available for NP&W Act offences repealed and replaced by the BC Act (that is, biodiversity offences).

[e] Excludes one EU related to the settlement of legal proceedings regarding an order or direction, rather than an alleged breach.

Source: Data to create this table has been drawn from the public registers of the environmental regulators available on their websites, NSWLEC decisions available via the NSW Caselaw website, and the EPA's annual reports. It is noted that some data has been drawn from data sets previously prepared by one of the authors, Sarah Wright, which were based on data from the public registers, case law, and the EPA's annual reports.

Table 7.3 Types of EU entrants versus types of defendant in successful prosecutions completed in the NSWLEC during the study period

EU entrant or defendant category	EPA: EU[a]	EPA: P[b]	DPE: Planning:[c] EU[a]	DPE: Planning: P[b]	DPE: BNV[d] EU[a]	DPE: BNV[d] P[b]	NRAR EU[a]	NRAR P[b]	Total EU[a]	Total P[b]
Individuals	2	14	-	-	9	7	1	5	12	26
Organisations - Total	27	34	6[e]	4	3	4	8[e]	4	44	46
• Corporation	18	24	6[e]	4	2	3	8[e]	4	34	35
• State owned corporation	5	7	-	-	-	-	-	-	5	7
• Other organisation	-	1	-	-	-	-	-	-	0	1
• State government entity	-	2	-	-	-	-	-	-	0	2
• Local Council	4	-	-	-	1	1	-	-	5	1
Total	29	48	6	4	12	11	9	9	56	72

Notes: [a] EU = EUs by number of EU entrants.
[b] P = NSWLEC prosecutions by the number of defendants. Defendants subsequently prosecuted or those who entered an EU for further incidents were counted on each separate occasion.
[c] DPE Planning matters excludes EUs entered into by the DPE on behalf of local councils.
[d] DPE BNV category includes biodiversity, native vegetation and NP&W Act matters. EUs are not available for current offences under the NP&W but are available for NP&W Act offences repealed and replaced by the BC Act (that is, biodiversity offences).
[e] Excludes one EU related to the settlement of legal proceedings regarding an order or direction, rather than an alleged breach.
Source: Data to create this table has been drawn from the public registers of the environmental regulators available on their websites, NSWLEC decisions available via the NSW Caselaw website, and the EPA's annual reports. It is noted that some data has been drawn from data sets previously prepared by one of the authors, Sarah Wright, which were based on data from the public registers, case law, and the EPA's annual reports.

alleged a breach occurred, rather than admitting one occurred, despite undertakings often involving hefty financial commitments. The NSWLEC has declined to take EUs into account as an aggravating factor in subsequent prosecutions, stating that 'because [EUs] are not criminal convictions they are irrelevant for the purposes of [the relevant sentencing consideration]'.[139] Similarly, the NSWLEC refused to take EUs into account regarding whether specific deterrence is required, noting that an EU 'is not evidence of a criminal breach'.[140] Accordingly, while regulators view EUs as a strong and beneficial alternative to prosecution for serious matters,[141] they are weak in terms of being 'invisible' enforcement instruments to the court in any subsequent sentencing proceedings.

Environmental regulators have, however, secured some significant financial commitments through EUs, particularly through projects and payments for the benefit of the environment and community. As discussed further below, in a number of regulatory areas, the highest project payment in an EU exceeded the highest total monetary penalty imposed by the NSWLEC for offences in the same regulatory area. The maximum penalties for environmental offences vary between legislation. During the study period, for more serious offences, maximum monetary penalties were generally around AU$1 million to AU$5 million for corporations and AU$250 000 to AU$1 million for individuals, with offences requiring proof of mens rea at the higher end of that scale.[142] The sentence imposed in an individual case is determined by considering the relevant objective circumstances of the offence, subjective circumstances of the offender, purposes of sentencing, and other relevant sentencing principles.[143] The sentencing considerations are set out in legislation[144] and case law. Unlike other jurisdictions, such as the UK, NSW does not have sentencing guidelines for environmental offences to guide sentencers on the monetary penalty to be imposed.[145] While

---

139 *Environment Protection Authority v Sydney Water Corporation* [2019] NSWLEC 100, [298]; see Crimes (Sentencing Procedure) Act 1999 (NSW), s 21A(2)(d); cf *Environment Protection Authority v Bartter Enterprises Pty Ltd [No 4]* [2021] NSWLEC 45, [87]–[88].

140 *Environment Protection Authority v Sydney Water Corporation* [2020] NSWLEC 153, [93].

141 See, for example, *DPE Prosecution Guidelines* (n 26), 6.

142 See, for example, POEO Act, ss 64(1), 119, 123, 142A(1), 143(1); EP&A Act, ss 9.52–9.54; WM Act, s 363B; LSS Act, s 60N; BC Act, s 13.1. Maximum monetary penalties under the POEO Act were increased to up to AU$10 million after the study period (on 3 April 2024): see s 119.

143 For a discussion of sentencing considerations in a NSW context, see, for example, Brian J Preston, 'Principled Sentencing for Environmental Offences' in LeRoy Paddock, Du Qun, Louis J Kotzé, David L Markell, Kenneth J Markowitz, and Durwood Zaelke (eds), *Compliance and Enforcement in Environmental Law: Towards More Effective Implementation* (Cheltenham, UK and Northampton, MA: Edward Elgar Publishing, 2011), 313–66.

144 Crimes (Sentencing Procedure) Act 1999 (NSW) and see, for example, POEO Act, s 241.

145 See Sentencing Council (UK), *Definitive Guidelines for Environmental Offences* (2014).

the monetary penalties in NSWLEC sentencing decisions have increased in recent years,[146] NSW has not seen the level of fines imposed in some UK cases achieved as a result of unlimited fine amounts, the introduction of sentencing guidelines, and consideration of a corporation's size and profits.[147] The highest total monetary penalty imposed in a NSWLEC prosecution across all regulators studied was AU$1.05 million.[148] In comparison, the highest value of environmental projects and payments achieved under EUs by those regulators was nearly AU$2.9 million.[149] The value of financial contributions under some EUs perhaps dispels some concerns regarding EUs being viewed as a more lenient enforcement option than prosecution.[150] However, the deterrent effect of both prosecution and EUs may be questioned when these monetary amounts are compared to the annual profits of large corporations.[151]

Notably, not all EUs identify the alleged actual or potential environmental harm caused by an incident. This is perhaps not surprising regarding the EPA's EUs because, in contrast to the DPE and NRAR EU guidelines,[152] the EPA's EU guidelines do not identify environmental harm as a matter to be addressed within EUs.[153] Environmental harm is a key factor in determining the seriousness of the incident and is relevant in ensuring a proportionate outcome in prosecutions in terms of the type and level of penalty and the nature and financial value of undertakings within an EU, including EU project values.[154] While the regulator is likely aware of the level of harm, it is preferable that details of the environmental harm are addressed within an EU so the public can also assess the appropriateness of the enforcement response and measures agreed

146 See *Georges River Council v SAF Developments Pty Ltd* [2023] NSWLEC 50, [125].

147 See Bell et al (n 4), 230–3, who note a £90 million fine imposed against Southern Water in 2021 in the UK. There are no sentencing guidelines in place for environmental offences in NSW.

148 *Environment Protection Authority v Clarence Colliery Pty Ltd* [2017] NSWLEC 82. This was a joint prosecution by the EPA under the POEO Act and the OEH under the NP&W Act.

149 *Enforceable Undertaking Given Under Section 336E of the Water Management Act 2000 (NSW) to the Natural Resources Access Regulator by Illawarra Coal Holdings Pty Ltd* (Enforceable Undertaking, 30 June 2023), [4.3].

150 See Bell et al (n 4), 236, including fn 76.

151 See Macrory (n 4), 21.

152 *DPE EU Guidelines* (n 43), 5; *OEH EU Guidelines* (n 70), 3; *NRAR EU Guidelines* (n 62), 2.

153 Wright, 'Re-examining the Role of Enforceable Undertakings…' (n 22).

154 Ibid; Sarah Wright, 'The Use of Enforceable Undertakings as an Enforcement Mechanism: Ensuring Transparency, Accountability, Certainty and Environmental Outcomes', Conference Paper, Australasian Environmental Law Enforcement and Regulators Network and the International Network for Environmental Compliance and Enforcement Conference (12 March 2020); *Camilleri's Stock Feeds Pty Ltd v Environment Protection Authority* (1993) 32 NSWLR 683, 701.

to.[155] This provides greater transparency and accountability, which are key concerns regarding EUs as an enforcement instrument because they are privately negotiated.[156]

The following sections examine the use of EUs in the different areas studied. The content and outcomes sought to be achieved by EUs in practice are examined, including some comparison with the outcomes of prosecutions.

EUs in pollution law

The EPA was the first NSW environmental regulator given access to EUs.[157] To date, it has entered into over 60 EUs. The 25 EUs entered into during the study period (by 29 entrants) all related to the POEO Act or regulations. The most frequently alleged breaches were water pollution,[158] breach of licence conditions,[159] land pollution,[160] and waste offences.[161]

In some respects, the EPA's EUs have a comparatively wider range of provisions than other EUs. Like other NSW environmental regulators, the EPA's EUs contain undertakings such as those requiring actions to prevent a recurrence and improve environmental performance, payments for projects for the benefit of the environment and community, and measures to report on EU compliance. However, unlike DPE and NRAR EUs, the EPA's EUs often contain publication notice requirements for entrants to place notices in newspapers (and sometimes also on social media). Some EPA EUs contain provisions aimed at improving industry-wide performance (a key EPA EU objective),[162] such as providing workshops or training to industry bodies. Such undertakings rarely feature in other regulators' EUs. EPA EUs also regularly provide for cost recovery.

An EU entered into by Ampol Refineries (NSW) Pty Ltd (Ampol) shortly after the study period is an example of an alternative enforcement mechanism used in a high-profile incident widely reported by the media.[163] Floodwaters caused by heavy rains

---

155 Wright, 'Re-examining the Role of Enforceable Undertakings…' (n 22).

156 Bell et al (n 4), 236.

157 Wright has examined the use of EUs by the EPA since their inception: Wright, 'The Use of Enforceable Undertakings as an Enforcement Mechanism…' (n 154); Wright, 'Re-examining the Role of Enforceable Undertakings…' (n 22).

158 POEO Act, s 120(1).

159 POEO Act, s 64(1).

160 POEO Act, s 142A(1).

161 This included offences such as 'waste dumping', unlawful use of land as a waste facility, or providing false or misleading information about waste: POEO Act, ss 143(1), 144(1), 144AA.

162 *EPA EU Guidelines* (n 18), 5–6.

163 See, for example, Madeline Achenza, 'Petrol Leaking Onto Roads in Sydney Suburb of Kurnell After Pump Failure', *The Australian* (7 April 2022), <https://www.theaustralian.com.au/breaking-news/petrol-spilling-onto-roads-in-sydney-suburb-of-kurnell-after-pump-failure/news-story/881cd1e3342486313c25d7bc5bf347a5>; Max Aldred, 'Stinky

inundated a wastewater treatment plant at an Ampol fuel transfer terminal, resulting in approximately 9200 litres of hydrocarbon entering the floodwaters, which then migrated to wetlands, creeks, residences, and recreational spaces.[164] People in the area 'reported … nausea, headache[s], scratchy throat[s] and eye irritation' and 'serious actual, likely and potential harm to [local] ecological communities' resulted.[165] Although an 'extreme weather event' triggered the incident, 'Ampol acknowledge[d] that improvements to its operations and plant may have reduced the volume of hydrocarbon that escaped'.[166]

The alleged breaches in the EU related to water pollution, land pollution, and the duty to notify a pollution incident.[167] Prior to the EU, Ampol had undertaken clean-up, remediation, and measures to prevent a recurrence.[168] Accordingly, the crux of the EU was a AU$700 000 payment to fund environmental and community projects.[169] Despite the significant financial commitment, Ampol did not actually acknowledge a breach occurred, but rather acknowledged the EPA's concerns that a breach may have occurred. This is common practice within EUs, particularly given that the EU guidelines do not require admission of a breach, but rather provide that 'at an absolute minimum' the regulator's concerns regarding an alleged breach must be acknowledged.[170]

During the study period, the EPA utilised five EUs and successfully completed five NSWLEC prosecutions (involving ten charges) regarding alleged offences by Sydney Water Corporation (SWC), a state-owned corporation.[171] This allowed some comparison of the outcomes achieved through each mechanism. SWC holds multiple POEO Act licences regarding sewage treatment and reticulation systems across its large network. All five EUs related to sewage overflows from sewer mains and pipes due to corrosion or other pipe failures. SWC took remedial action when all incidents occurred. Some alleged discharges reached waterways, including a beach. Some

---

Black Substance Bubbles Up Out of the Sink of a Suburban Home - After Diesel Waste Spill in Sydney', *Daily Mail Australia* (7 April 2022), <https://www.dailymail.co.uk/news/article-10694785/Ampol-Kurnell-spill-Video-black-substance-bubbling-drain.html>; Sarah Keoghan, '"Do We Sell Now?": Kurnell Residents Report Health Issues After Fuel Spill', *Sydney Morning Herald* (17 April 2022), <https://www.smh.com.au/national/nsw/do-we-sell-now-kurnell-residents-report-health-issues-after-fuel-spill-20220413-p5ad5p.html>.

164 *Enforceable Undertaking to the NSW Environment Protection Authority Given for the Purpose of Section 253A of the Protection of the Environment Operations Act 1997 by Ampol Refineries (NSW) Pty Ltd* (Enforceable Undertaking, 21 August 2023) (*Ampol EU*), 2–3.

165 Ibid, [2.8]–[2.9].

166 Ibid, [2.11].

167 Ibid, [4.1]; POEO Act, ss 120(1), 142A(1), 152(1).

168 *Ampol EU* (n 164), [2.10], [6.1].

169 Ibid, [7.1] and Sch 1.

170 *EPA EU Guidelines* (n 18), 12.

171 Sydney Water Act 1994 (NSW), s 4; State Owned Corporations Act 1989 (NSW), s 20A(1), Sch 5.

incidents impacted local residents, recreational water users, and a golf course. The alleged offences were mainly breaches of licence conditions, water pollution, and/or land pollution.[172] The EUs contained similar key components, including payments towards environmental and community projects, publication notices, and payment towards the EPA's investigation, legal and/or monitoring costs. Some also contained undertakings regarding improving environmental performance and industry-wide performance.

Projects for the benefit of the environment and community constituted a key component of SWC EUs, with funding commitments ranging between AU$347 100 and AU$1 million. Similarly, sentencing orders in SWC prosecutions – which mainly related to water pollution and licence breaches – also focused on delivering benefits to the environment and community. Overall, 73.5% of the total monetary penalties in SWC prosecutions were diverted to environmental projects and payments, rather than imposed as fines. Other sentencing orders also achieved similar outcomes to EUs, namely publication orders and payment of legal and investigation costs. However, during the study period, the range of financial contributions by SWC to projects under EUs was higher than the monetary penalties in SWC prosecutions (including both fines and environmental payments). Total monetary penalties in prosecutions ranged between AU$145 000 and AU$269 500, much less than the highest EU project value of AU$1 million. One SWC EU used to resolve three alleged breaches included a payment of AU$500 000 to fund environmental and community projects.[173] In comparison, a prosecution against SWC in which it pleaded guilty to three separate charges relating to the same incident as the EU resulted in total monetary penalties of AU$365 625, with half diverted to the Environmental Trust (this prosecution was finalised after the EU and just outside the study period).[174] These figures highlight the large financial commitments and beneficial outcomes being achieved through EUs.

EUs in planning law for major projects

Of the six DPE planning EUs relating to alleged breaches, five were regarding alleged breaches of development consent conditions under the EP&A Act relating to matters such as biodiversity rehabilitation, subsidence impacts from coal mining, traffic requirements, and conditions protecting Aboriginal cultural heritage. Five EUs contained payments towards environmental and/or community projects. The highest

172 One EU referred only to concerns that an overflow 'may have constituted offences against the POEO Act and caused a pollution incident', with no specific alleged offences cited: *Undertaking by Sydney Water Corporation to the Environment Protection Authority Given for the Purposes of Section 253A of the Protection of the Environment Operations Act 1997 (NSW)* (Enforceable Undertaking, 30 March 2023), [2.2].

173 *Undertaking to the NSW Environment Protection Authority Given for the Purpose of Section 253A of the Protection of the Environment Operations Act 1997 by Sydney Water Corporation* (Enforceable Undertaking, 14 February 2023), [5.2]–[5.4].

174 *Environment Protection Authority v Sydney Water Corporation* [2023] NSWLEC 68, [190].

project value of AU$150 000 in an EU in the planning area was far less than those in the other regulatory areas studied of AU$1 million or more. It was also below the highest total fine imposed in a DPE planning prosecution of AU$250 000,[175] whereas in other areas, some values of environmental or community benefit projects within EUs exceeded the highest monetary penalty in prosecutions. Nevertheless, the DPE utilised EUs to achieve environmental and community outcomes through such payments.[176] For instance, an EU was used to address an alleged breach of development consent conditions relating to traffic requirements for an outdoor music festival which resulted in 'significant traffic delays [for] the wider local community including school children'.[177] Under the EU, the company donated AU$100 000 to ten local schools ($10 000 each) to 'support and improve learning outcomes for their students'.[178] While one media outlet referred to the donation as 'a whopping $100 000',[179] the local mayor was reported as stating that amount 'was "a drop in the ocean" for the organisation as a whole'.[180]

Beyond payments for environmental and community projects, most planning EUs contained few other substantive undertakings. For instance, one EU contained remediation requirements[181] and another contained requirements for a report regarding environmental monitoring.[182] One EU relating to the accidental felling of an Aboriginal scar tree required the EU entrant to undertake 'remedial actions' by fund-

---

175 *Secretary, Department of Planning and Environment v Sell & Parker Pty Ltd* [2022] NSWLEC 60, [466].

176 See, for example, Department of Planning and Environment, 'Action Taken Against Splendour Organisers' (Media Release, 20 December 2022), <https://www.planning.nsw.gov.au/news/action-taken-against-splendour-organisers>.

177 *Enforceable Undertaking Given Under Section 9.5 of the Environmental Planning and Assessment Act 1979 (NSW) to the Secretary, Department of Planning and Environment by Billinudgel Property Pty Ltd* (Enforceable Undertaking, 15 December 2022), 1.

178 Ibid, 2.

179 Savannah Meacham, 'Splendour in the Grass Fined $100,000 for Traffic Queues', *9News* (20 December 2022), <https://www.9news.com.au/national/splendour-in-the-grass-organisers-fined-100-thousand-dollars-over-traffic-management-issues/5122bad7-a175-49fa-a065-ea6b024b91d0>. It is noted that while the article referred to the amount as a 'fine', it does not constitute a fine.

180 James Lemon, 'Splendour in the Grass Host Fined $100,000 Over Traffic Chaos', *Sydney Morning Herald* (20 December 2022), <https://www.smh.com.au/national/nsw/splendour-in-the-grass-host-fined-100-000-over-traffic-chaos-20221220-p5c7u3.html>, citing Byron Shire Mayor, Michael Lyon. It is noted that while the article referred to the amount as a 'fine', it does not constitute a fine.

181 *Enforceable Undertaking Given Under Section 9.5 of the Environmental Planning and Assessment Act 1979 (NSW) to the Secretary, Department of Planning and Environment by Centennial Airly Pty Ltd* (Enforceable Undertaking, 26 May 2022), 4–5.

182 *Enforceable Undertaking Given Under Section 9.5 of the Environmental Planning and Assessment Act 1979 (NSW) to the Secretary, Department of Planning and Environment by Mawland Quarantine Station Pty Ltd* (Enforceable Undertaking, 13 February 2023), 2.

ing the preservation of the culturally scarred part of the tree and works for a memorial area for the tree.[183] The entrant also agreed to undertake staff training, review relevant policies and procedures, and complete related reports and audits to demonstrate compliance with the EU.[184] However, the EU contained no additional community benefit payment beyond the 'remedial actions'.

EUs in biodiversity and native vegetation clearing matters

The nine EUs related to alleged offences under native vegetation clearing legislation or alleged biodiversity offences all involved the clearing of native vegetation. Six EUs related to alleged unlawful clearing of native vegetation in a rural area[185] with one of those also alleging an offence of damaging the habitat of a threatened ecological community.[186] The other EUs contained alleged offences related to picking protected native plants[187] or picking plants that are threatened species or part of a threatened ecological community.[188] All but one EU involved alleged clearing on property owned by the EU entrant/s.[189] EUs in this area provided little or, in three cases, no context as to why the clearing occurred. While it was evident that some EUs related to clearing for crops, commercial harvesting of trees, road upgrade works, and clean-up after bushfires, the vast majority of EUs provided no context as to why the alleged clearing occurred and what (if any) financial gain resulted. For instance, one EU involving the alleged clearing of 1282 hectares of native vegetation stated that clearing occurred using machinery and indicated '[c]learing and conversion to cropping' had occurred.[190] There was no other explanation of the incident, although the alleged environmental harm was discussed. The EU contained a sizeable commitment involving entry into a separate Conservation Agreement over 636 hectares of land and a AU$1.01 million payment to the DPE. The lack of detail within EUs in the biodiversity and native vegetation clearing area makes it difficult for the public to assess whether an EU and the specific undertakings given were an appropriate regulatory response.

The crux of the EUs in this area was usually financial commitments aimed at 'restitution … to benefit the environment and the community', reflecting a key goal of

---

183 *Enforceable Undertaking by PCL Constructors Pacific Rim Pty Ltd to the Department of Planning and Environment for the purposes of Section 9.5 of the Environmental Planning and Assessment Act 1979 (NSW)* (Enforceable Undertaking, 3 June 2022), 4–5.

184 Ibid, 5–6.

185 These offences were under the LSS Act, s 60N and/or repealed NV Act, s 12.

186 BC Act, s 2.4(1).

187 NP&W Act, s 117 (now repealed).

188 Ibid, s 118A(2)(b) (now repealed); BC Act, s 2.2(1)(a).

189 As indicated by the Enforceable Undertakings Register under the BC Act (available at: https://www.environment.nsw.gov.au/policy-and-law/public-registers/enforceable-undertakings) and the EUs available within that register.

190 *Undertaking Given Under Section 13.27 of the Biodiversity Conservation Act 2016 to the Secretary, Department of Planning and Environment by [entrant redacted from public register]* (Enforceable Undertaking, 17 June 2022), 2.

EUs in this area.[191] These took the form of payments towards an environmental project or programme, a payment to the DPE, a payment to the DPE in combination with a Conservation Agreement, or management of an area of vegetation. Some EUs simply required remediation/revegetation of the allegedly cleared area. Six EUs contained substantial financial commitments in terms of making 'restitution … to benefit the environment and the community'. This involved payments ranging between AU$100 000 and AU$1.01 million, with two of those EUs also requiring entry into a Conservation Agreement[192] over substantial areas of the EU entrant's land. In comparison, to date, the highest penalty imposed in a biodiversity or native vegetation clearing prosecution is AU$405 000.[193]

In terms of where EU payments were directed, two EUs specified a particular project or programme. For instance, one EU payment to the DPE identified that the money would be directed to the DPE's Saving Our Species programme to be applied to projects for threatened species whose habitat had been damaged by the alleged breach.[194] However, four of the EUs simply stated that the payments (between AU$100 000 and AU$1.01 million) were to be made to the DPE, without identifying how the DPE was to apply that money for the benefit of the environment or community. While nothing untoward is being alleged, for transparency and accountability purposes, EUs should identify how monetary payments are to be applied, rather than simply providing for payment to a regulator.[195] Namely, a specific environmental or community benefit project or programme should be identified in the EU. One benefit of prosecutions over EUs is that the court provides oversight regarding the terms of any ASOs proposed by the parties, such as a proposed payment towards an environmental project, to ensure they are drafted with specificity.

EUs in water management

The nine NRAR EUs involved alleged breaches related to water use in activities such as mining, farming, and irrigation. Alleged breaches included taking or using water without a licence or approval,[196] contravening an approval condition (such as exceeding an annual extraction limit),[197] taking water with no (or an insufficient) water allocation[198] or constructing or using a water supply work without approval.[199]

---

191 *OEH EU Guidelines* (n 70), 2, 8. The quoted wording reflects headings within EUs.

192 See BC Act, ss 5.20–5.26.

193 *Chief Executive of the Office of Environment and Heritage v Turnbull* [2023] NSWLEC 137, [92].

194 *Undertaking Given Under Section 13.27 of the Biodiversity Conservation Act 2016 to the Secretary, Department of Planning, Industry and Environment by Atilol Holdings Pty Ltd* (Enforceable Undertaking, 21 March 2022), 2–3.

195 See Australian Law Reform Commission, *Principled Regulation: Federal Civil and Administrative Penalties in Australia*, Report 95 (December 2002), 600–601.

196 WM Act, ss 60A, 91A.

197 WM Act, s 91G.

198 WM Act, s 60C.

199 WM Act, s 91B.

Key undertakings within NRAR EUs focused on measures to bring EU entrants into compliance and prevent future breaches. These included preventing alleged unlawful surface water capture, redressing alleged unlawful water management works, obtaining relevant licences or approvals, ensuring water was taken in accordance with allocations, and installing updated metering equipment to monitor compliance. Environmental and community projects or payments, reporting on compliance with the EU, and payment of the NRAR's investigation, legal and/or monitoring costs were also common terms. Six NRAR EUs featured undertakings unique to this area, requiring payment of a specified sum for the value of water allegedly unlawfully taken, to purchase and forfeit water allocations, or to pay a charge of two or more times the value of the water allegedly taken. These undertakings reflect the nature of WM Act offences, which support the statute's aims of sustainable use and sharing of water, and are similar in nature to other NRAR powers available outside of EUs.[200] Such undertakings indicate that a key focus of NRAR EUs was on restitution or recouping any potential benefit from allegedly taking water unlawfully either through purchasing and forfeiting water allocations or providing monetary compensation.

The NRAR achieved some significant financial commitments within EUs, including a record environmental project amount of nearly AU$2.9 million from a coal mining company for allegedly taking surface water without the required licence during a five-year period.[201] The funds were to be targeted towards 'waterways or wetlands restoration and management'.[202] The project is required to 'protect the cultural value of waterways in the local area and will involve and require consultation with the local Aboriginal community'.[203] The NRAR stated the EU was a 'landmark agreement'.[204] Emphasis was placed on the large financial commitment that 'far outweighed any court imposed penalty NRAR had been able to secure'.[205] In contrast, the largest total monetary penalty in an NRAR NSWLEC prosecution to date is AU$353 750.[206] The NRAR also highlighted the outcomes and benefits achieved for the community,

200 WM Act, ss 3, 60G; Natural Resources Access Regulator Act 2017 (NSW), cl 11(1)(e), Sch 2, cl 1(a).

201 *Enforceable Undertaking Given Under Section 336E of the Water Management Act 2000 (NSW) to the Natural Resources Access Regulator by Illawarra Coal Holdings Pty Ltd* (Enforceable Undertaking, 30 June 2023), 1–2.

202 Ibid, 4.

203 Ibid, 4–5.

204 Natural Resources Access Regulator, 'Millions for Environmental Project in Landmark Agreement with Coal Mine' (Media Release, 11 July 2023), <https://www.nrar.nsw.gov.au/news/millions-to-be-spent-on-community-project-in-landmark-agreement-with-coal-mine>.

205 Kate McIlwain, 'Dendrobium Mine Ordered to Fund $3 Million Project for Taking Water Without a Licence', *Illawarra Mercury* (11 July 2023), <https://www.illawarramercury.com.au/story/8265269/illawarra-mine-ordered-to-fund-3-million-project-for-taking-water-without-a-licence/?cs=300>, citing Grant Barnes, Chief Regulatory Officer, NRAR.

206 *Barnes, Chief Regulatory Officer, Natural Resources Access Regulator v Henry Payson Pty Ltd* [2023] NSWLEC 5, [319].

improvement of environmental practices, and establishment of a dialogue with the local Aboriginal community in formulating an appropriate project given the alleged potential impacts on that community arising from the alleged water take.[207]

Conclusion

EUs have somewhat displaced prosecutions for alleged breaches of NSW environmental and planning laws, particularly for organisations. The NSW experience demonstrates that EUs can include a wide range of 'innovative outcomes'[208] addressing matters such as remediation and rectification of the issues or behaviour that led to the alleged offence to prevent a recurrence, as well as providing additional beneficial outcomes through environmental and community projects. While ASOs in NSW environmental prosecutions also allow for innovative responses, some regulators appear to be favouring EUs to implement more innovative outcomes. EUs are also considered beneficial as they can provide a quicker and cheaper response than prosecution.[209] Notably, a number of EUs have involved significant financial commitments of a greater magnitude than penalties imposed in prosecutions in the same area.

EUs will not be an appropriate enforcement response in all cases, either because the regulator considers the proposed terms inadequate, or because the circumstances may dictate that prosecution is the appropriate response in the public interest. Nevertheless, this study has shown that EUs are increasingly widely used in NSW environmental law enforcement, including for serious matters. However, as a newer regulatory instrument, further research is required into the operation and effectiveness of EUs in practice in environmental law. Despite their benefits, their long-term effect on matters such as deterrence and compliance outcomes is under-examined.

---

207 McIlwain (n 205), citing Grant Barnes, Chief Regulatory Officer, NRAR.

208 *DPE EU Guidelines* (n 43), 2.

209 NSW, *Parliamentary Debates*, Legislative Assembly, 13 September 2005, 17643 (Bob Debus, Minister for the Environment).

PART II

Green criminology and multi-disciplinary approaches to environmental crime

8 The global illegal wildlife trade crisis

Angus Nurse

1. Introduction

Wildlife trafficking is generally recognised as an international phenomenon and a key issue in transnational crime discourse. Depending on which measures and monitoring mechanisms are invoked, wildlife crime routinely scores highly in classifications of high-value international trafficking measures, jockeying for position behind drugs, human trafficking, and weapons. In particular, the estimated global value of wildlife trafficking regularly places it in the top four of illicit commerce areas globally, where the value of the black market 'is thought to be between USD 10 and USD 20 billion'.[1] Wildlife crime's position in the global crime league table is determined in part by whether the definition of 'wildlife' is taken to include the illegal trades in animals, plants, timber, and fisheries products, as well as the extent to which national trafficking activities are included alongside transnational ones. Existing evidence and prior research also show the involvement of organised criminals in wildlife crime, particularly in wildlife trafficking, where the legal and illegal trade often have a symbiotic relationship.[2] Organised crime groups who branch into wildlife crime make use of their existing networks and transit infrastructure, taking advantage of global markets, continued demand for wildlife products, and a comparatively weak enforcement regime relative to that in place for other serious global trafficking commodities such as drugs and weapons.

---

1 Tanya Wyatt, *Wildlife Trafficking*, 1st edn (Palgrave Macmillan, 2013), 9.

2 See, for example, Liana Wyler and Pervaze Sheikh, 'International Illegal Trade in Wildlife: Threats and US Policy' (2013), available at: https://sgp.fas.org/crs/misc/RL34395.pdf; and Claudia McMurry, 'Illegal Trade in Wildlife and World Environment Day' (2008), available at https://2001-2009.state.gov/g/oes/rls/rm/106259.htm. Studies in wildlife crime use different definitions of wildlife and different methodologies and, therefore, present different findings depending on the study methodology.

Wildlife trafficking is considered within environmental crime and environmental law scholarship and within criminology, law enforcement, and political science scholarship. Wildlife crime can most obviously be considered within debates on the protection and exploitation of natural resources, from the perspective of crime, deviance, and law enforcement. But it can also invoke environmental security concerns given that the destruction of natural habitats often occurs where wildlife trafficking takes place. Research into wildlife trafficking considers the nature and scope of wildlife crime, the behaviour of wildlife offenders, the public policy and enforcement response to wildlife crime, and the effectiveness of sanctions and measures to address wildlife crime. Accordingly, wildlife crime research is covered by several different disciplines, including law, criminology (and policing studies), sociology, and politics. Given that wildlife trafficking is recognised as an environmental security concern and that the relationship between states where wildlife trafficking takes place is of a cross-border nature, research in the international law and international relations fields may also be applicable. UN resolutions such as the General Assembly Resolution 73/343 on tackling illicit trafficking in wildlife crime, for example, note that the illicit trade in small arms and light weapons could be linked to illicit trafficking in wildlife, which may pose a serious threat to national and regional stability in some parts of Africa. The resolution calls on Member States to make illicit trafficking in protected species of wild fauna and flora a serious crime, in accordance with their national legislation. While criminology has historically been quiet, if not silent, in respect of crimes against non-human animals and the environment more generally, there is a strong, emerging body of criminological research, scholarship, and policy developments on wildlife trafficking. This is particularly the case within green criminology, which is primarily concerned with the nature of harms against the non-human natural environment. Yet in many respects, wildlife trafficking aligns closely with the criminological gaze, incorporating discussion of organised crime, corruption, transnational crime, the behaviour of offenders, and the failures of governance and enforcement mechanisms. As a result, wildlife trafficking is a developing area of criminological scholarship and a core concern of green criminology.

Despite legal protection in conservation law and through international and domestic law measures that regulate the trade in wildlife, illegal trafficking in wildlife remains a persistent challenge. Much of the criminological literature on transnational environmental crimes is concerned with the illegal wildlife trade (IWT), particularly that involving rare and endangered animals considered threatened by trade. This chapter explores the global wildlife trade crisis, adopting a broad definition of wildlife to include flora and fauna and deploying a green criminological approach to consider wildlife crime not just from the perspective of crime as defined by the criminal law, but also to examine wildlife crime from the perspective of the environmental harm caused by the IWT. This chapter also examines the need for policy and enforcement approaches that extend beyond standard retributive justice approaches into those that also consider crime prevention and reparation for the harms of wildlife crime.[3]

2. Wildlife trade and law

Wildlife trafficking is situated within a broad conception of illegal activities affecting non-human animals and non-human nature living in the wild. While various conceptions of such illegality exist, Nurse and Wyatt proposed a holistic definition of 'wildlife crime' that 'includes a broad range of harmful acts that encompasses direct and indirect acts or omissions and that indicate failure to comply with legal obligations or comply with legislation, irrespective of whether the legislation or its associated sanction is distinctly criminal in nature'.[4] This classification is in contrast with the general definition of environmental crime proposed by Situ and Emmons, which defined environmental crime primarily as those acts defined as such by the criminal law and subject to criminal sanctions.[5] Thus, according to this definition, the nature of environmental crime is broadly negative in its wording, relating to the prohibitive acts commonly defined in criminal law (although omissions may also be covered), the nature of the generally punitive sanction, and retributive punishment notions of fines and prison as the typical responses from the criminal justice system.[6] The more expansive definition of wildlife crime, which this chapter also adopts, reflects the reality that legislation governing IWT is more regulatory than criminal in nature, something that emerges consistently in the scholarly and policy research literature, particularly in the literature that is critical of the law's relative failure to address wildlife trafficking. Thus, the law regulating wildlife trade is arguably separate from laws that aim to conserve wildlife and/or protect it for the common good by strictly preventing trade from taking place. Instead, wildlife trade is a regulated activity, with policy arguably concerned with managing the trade along sustainable lines, whereas the criminal activity that is synonymous with wildlife trafficking raises questions about the efficacy of the law to effectively deal with criminal activity.

The global trade in wildlife occupies a potentially paradoxical position in law. International law and standards such as the World Charter for Nature 1982, a soft law instrument that recommends principles for states to apply,[7] and the Convention on Biological Biodiversity 1992 (CBD),[8] provide frameworks for the general protection of wildlife, establishing the fundamental basis for protecting natural resources (includ-

3 See also Anna Di Ronco and Nigel South's Chapter 9 Environmental Harms, Ecocidal Trends and Restorative Responses: Some Interdisciplinary Directions in this volume.
4 Angus Nurse and Tanya Wyatt, *Wildlife Criminology* (Bristol University Press, 2020), 7–8.
5 Yingyi Situ and David Emmons, *Environmental Crime* (Sage, 2000).
6 Jeremy Horder, *Ashworth's Principles of Criminal Law*, 8th edn (Oxford University Press, 2016).
7 World Charter for Nature 1982, UNGA Res 37/7, Part 1 General Principles.
8 Convention on Biological Diversity 1992, Article 1. See further https://www.cbd.int/.

ing wildlife) from anthropocentric exploitation. Principle 1 of the World Charter for Nature, for example, specifies that nature should be respected, and its essential processes shall not be impaired. Principle 2 specifies that population levels of all life forms, both wild and domesticated, should be 'at least sufficient for their survival' and requires that habitats should be protected to ensure the survival of wildlife. However, Principle 4 indicates that ecosystems and organisms that are used by humans should be managed in a way that achieves 'optimum sustainable productivity', identifying that the use of wildlife as an exploitable natural resource is generally permissible subject to certain restrictions. Similar sustainability principles are also contained within the CBD, Article 1 of which states:

> The objectives of this Convention, to be pursued in accordance with its relevant provisions, are the conservation of biological diversity, the sustainable use of its components and the fair and equitable sharing of the benefits arising out of the utilization of genetic resources, including by appropriate access to genetic resources and by appropriate transfer of relevant technologies, taking into account all rights over those resources and to technologies, and by appropriate funding.[9]

Thus, both international instruments provide for continued exploitation of wildlife as a natural resource, albeit within the confines of an ideological, anthropocentric approach consistent with the principles of maintaining sustainable wildlife populations and not allowing species to be driven to extinction. The implementation of these sustainability principles and the precise nature of wildlife protection are primarily left to national law to determine.[10] Thus, states may determine how best to protect and utilise their biodiversity, subject to complying with their obligations under the international agreements to which they are a party. Accordingly, the starting point for international law on wildlife protection is not one of outright prohibition, preventing any exploitation or use of wildlife as an exploitable natural resource. Instead, wildlife law seeks to achieve several, sometimes conflicting, objectives. These objectives generally operate according to four key themes:

- Control – killing and management of wildlife so it does not interfere unduly with human interests.
- Exploitation – use of wildlife as a valuable natural asset.
- Protection – prohibition of acts that harm individual flora and fauna beyond a permitted level.
- Conservation – Implementing the public good and wildlife trust doctrines by applying legal protection to animals regarded as being in the common ownership of (or held in trust by) humanity.[11]

---

9 Ibid.

10 Angus Nurse, *Policing Wildlife* (Palgrave Macmillan, 2015).

11 Ibid ; Keith Vincent, 'Reforming wildlife law: proposals by the Law Commission for England and Wales' (2014) 3(2) *IJCJSD* 67–80, available at: https://www.crimejustice-journal.com/article/view/726.

Thus, while wildlife is generally protected by conservation law, that protection is often limited rather than absolute. For example, certain wildlife might be deemed 'pests' that can be killed to protect food, farming, and livestock interests. 'Pest' classifications can be general, such as the United Kingdom's (UK's) historic use of open general licences to allow the killing of designated wildlife species such as crows and rooks in order to protect crops or to conserve other wildlife. They can also be specific, such as the removal of protection under the Endangered Species Act of 1973 for grey wolves in certain parts of the US to allow the animals to be killed to protect farming and ranching interests. Exploitation of wildlife can also include sporting and shooting interests, which can be of vital economic benefit to those states reliant on wildlife tourism and the revenues from sport and trophy hunting. Several African states, for example, have large sport and trophy hunting industries that legitimise the killing of otherwise protected wildlife. These industries are closely regulated although research identifies some links between legal and illegal activity.[12]

A specific crime of 'wildlife trafficking' arguably does not exist in international law, although international treaties such as the 1973 Convention on International Trade in Endangered Species of Wild Fauna and Flora (CITES) (discussed further below), the Convention on the Conservation of Migratory Species of Wild Animals (the Bonn Convention) and the International Whaling Convention 1948 articulate the nature of trafficking as the illegal taking and trading in wildlife, its parts, or derivatives contrary to the protections and prohibitions defined in law. In addition, policy measures such as the EU wildlife trade regulations, a set of EU laws implemented uniformly in all EU countries to enforce the provisions of CITES, combine with other EU policies that are designed to ensure that wildlife products only enter the EU market if they are of legal and sustainable origin.[13] Thus, there are legal provisions in place to regulate the trade in wildlife, and the levels of criminalisation for wildlife trafficking vary depending on the country and how it has framed international perspectives within its domestic law. For example, EU Member States are required to criminalise illegal

12 Angus Nurse, *Animal Harm. Perspectives on Why People Harm and Kill Animals* (Ashgate, 2013).

13 EU Wildlife Trade regulations include Council Regulation (EC) No 338/97 on the protection of species of wild fauna and flora by regulating trade therein (the Basic Regulation), complemented by its implementing regulations (Commission Regulation (EC) No 865/2006of 4 May 2006 laying down detailed rules concerning the implementation of Council Regulation (EC) No 338/97 on the protection of species of wild fauna and flora by regulating trade therein; Commission Implementing Regulation (EU) No 792/2012 of 23 August 2012 laying down rules for the design of permits, certificates and other documents provided for in Council Regulation (EC) No 338/97 on the protection of species of wild fauna and flora by regulating trade therein and amending Commission Regulation (EC) No 865/2006; and their subsequent amendments; and Commission Implementing Regulation (EU) 2019/1587 of 24 September 2019 prohibiting the introduction into the Union of specimens of certain species of wild fauna and flora in accordance with Council Regulation (EC) No 338/97 on the protection of species of wild fauna and flora by regulating trade therein).

wildlife trade in accordance with the EU Environmental Crime Directive.[14] CITES requires state parties to implement a sanctions regime, although research indicates that this requirement has not been effectively implemented by all states.[15]

As the key international law instrument intended to regulate the trade in wildlife, strictly restricting trade in certain species while regulating the trade in others, breaches of CITES would likely amount to wildlife trafficking and should be subject to sanctions under domestic legislation that implements CITES, if not under other domestic wildlife protection legislation. CITES regulates the international trade in wildlife through a process of classification, protecting over 38 700 endangered species from over-exploitation, comprising about 5950 species of animals and 32 800 species of plants. CITES was brought into force in 1975 and part of its function is to monitor the amount of international trade and IWT activity. This is reported to the CITES Secretariat in Geneva by member countries, each of which has its own CITES management authority.

CITES works through a series of Appendices, a listing system classifying different levels of protection afforded to wildlife and that is an integral part of international policy on transnational crime.[16] Appendix I largely prohibits trade for species considered to be highly endangered (with limited exceptions); Appendix II lists species considered less threatened by trade but for which trade must be controlled, specifying limitations on which species may be traded; Appendix III relates to species not currently threatened by trade but where there is some form of concern about the species population.

Although CITES is legally binding on state parties, it is generally not self-executing. This means that it cannot be fully implemented until specific domestic legislative measures have been adopted for that purpose. It is therefore essential that parties to CITES (that is states that have ratified the Convention) enact legislation allowing them to implement and enforce all aspects of the Convention. The core objective of CITES is to regulate trade by calling on states to enact legislation designed to protect wildlife from international trade. However, as the United Nations Office on Drugs and Crime (UNODC) notes in its *World Wildlife Crime Report 2020: Trafficking in Protected Species*, CITES is not an international wildlife trafficking treaty. The UNODC comments that:

> CITES is limited to regulating international trade, so the illegal harvesting of wildlife, such as the poaching of protected species, does not fall within its scope if the product is not transported internationally.[17]

---

14 See also Ludwig Krämer's Chapter 5 Biodiversity Crime in this volume.

15 Tanya Wyatt, *Is CITES Protecting Wildlife?* (Routledge, 2021).

16 Ibid.

17 UNODC, *World Wildlife Crime Report: Trafficking in Protected Species* (United Nations Office on Drugs and Crime, 2020), 9.

Therefore, domestic markets for wildlife are also beyond the scope of CITES and are subject to national law. Moreover, there are millions of species that are not listed by CITES that may be illegally harvested (that is in contravention of national law) and traded internationally. The UNODC notes that this 'is frequently the case in timber and fish trafficking'.[18] Accordingly, while CITES sets the international framework for regulating wildlife trade, its implementation via domestic legislation is essential to addressing wildlife trafficking. This is usually achieved via the creation of a domestic monitoring and sanctioning regime, but the manner in which this is implemented varies from country to country, and domestic regimes are not always effective in combatting wildlife trafficking.

2.1 Defining wildlife trafficking

Wildlife faces threats from a range of human activities, both legal and illegal. The International Union for the Conservation of Nature (IUCN) identified that thousands of species are potentially threatened with extinction due to human pressures.[19] Some of these pressures are more general, such as habitat destruction, commercial development that displaces wildlife or encroaches on its territory, and climate change. Other threats are more direct, including hunting, wildlife trafficking, illegal predator control, and the collecting of wild birds' eggs, which has the potential to drive rarer species to extinction. As will be discussed below, trafficking in particular has been the subject of policy and international law and enforcement initiatives aimed at tackling wildlife trafficking as a transnational crime problem.

Wildlife is generally defined as 'the native fauna and flora of a state and is arguably commonly understood to mean animals that live in a wild state outside human control'.[20] Some definitions exclude fish, plants, non-native fauna and flora, for example, introduced species (often described as 'invasive' species) and those that have escaped into the wild (even where escaped populations have become established in the wild) from legal definitions of wildlife. Wildlife laws often contain prohibited methods of killing or taking wildlife, such as prohibitions on using snares, poison, or taking or harming or disturbing wildlife during the breeding season. Accordingly, wildlife law creates a range of offences or prohibitions whilst arguably allowing continued exploitation of wildlife.

Definitions of wildlife crime are socially constructed such that legislative definitions of wildlife vary across jurisdictions and in academic discourse. According to one definition, for an act to be a wildlife crime it must be proscribed as such by legislation; an act committed against or involving wildlife, for example wild birds, reptiles, fish, mammals, plants, or trees which form part of a country's natural environment or species that migrate to a range state; and involve an offender (individual, corporate,

---

18 Ibid.

19 IUCN, *The IUCN Red List of Threatened Species* (IUCN, 2015), available at: www.iucnredlist.org.

20 Nurse and Wyatt (n 3), 3.

or public official) who commits a proscribed unlawful act or commits a breach of obligations towards wildlife.[21] Typically a wildlife crime must also be subject to some form of criminal sanction such as a fine or prison sentence which is designed primarily as a punitive measure, embodying principles of retributive justice and deterrence.[22] However, the more expansive definition adopted across green criminological scholarship often includes regulatory offences which are not criminalised, that is those breaches of the law which may not attract a criminal sanction or be strictly defined as crimes, but which nevertheless attract some form of penalty or enforcement activity. In accordance with green criminological principles, this definition is concerned less with whether an act is specifically defined as a crime, and more with the harm that is caused to wildlife (broadly defined to include non-human animals (including fish), trees, and plants) and to the environment more generally.

These elements clarify that wildlife crime is a social construction as it relates to the violation of *existing* laws. Accordingly, laws can be changed, which can reconfigure what is considered to be a crime according to contemporary and jurisdiction-specific conceptions. Most jurisdictions, however, have some form of regulation on the taking and sale of wildlife, classifying different conduct (taking, possession, or sale) in wildlife trade as either an administrative or criminal offence. Thus, illegal taking of wildlife in contravention of regulations would generally be classed as a form of wildlife trafficking, while the terms smuggling and trafficking are often used interchangeably. While a universally agreed definition of trafficking has yet to be established, there is generally common acceptance that wildlife trafficking may be defined as:

> any environment-related crime that involves the illegal trade, smuggling, poaching, capture or collection of endangered species, protected wildlife (including animals and plants that are subject to harvest quotas and regulated by permits), derivatives or products thereof.[23]

As this definition implies, for trafficking to take place 'wildlife is first poached, collected or harvested', with poaching being the act of killing the non-human animal for its subsequent use or exploitation.[24] 'Harvesting' refers to the routine killing of non-human animals or plants in order to supply both the legal and illegal markets, although wildlife is sometimes taken alive to facilitate smuggling to its final destination.[25] Harvesting is also the term used in timber trafficking, where 'trees are harvested, both legally and illegally, to be used for building houses and furniture, for fuel, etc'.[26] Wildlife may also be killed for parts or derivatives such as horns, tusks (ivory),

---

21 Nurse and Wyatt (n 3), 7.

22 Jacob Öberg, 'The Definition of Criminal Sanctions in the EU' (2013) 3(3) *European Criminal Law Review* 1–27.

23 WWF and Dalberg, *Fighting Illicit Wildlife Trafficking* (2012), 9, available at: https://www.worldwildlife.org/publications/fighting-illicit-wildlife-trafficking-a-consultation-with-governments.

24 Wyatt, *Wildlife Trafficking*, (n 1), 3.

25 Ibid.

26 Ibid.

skins, or internal organs that might be used as traditional medicine products. The collection or harvesting of wildlife is thus only the first stage of trafficking. As Wyatt notes: 'Once taken, either alive or dead, the wildlife is then transported towards the market or final buyer. This may be directly to a market, or for wildlife that is used to make products, to a processing place'.[27]

In some cases, and indeed in much of wildlife trafficking, the transportation can involve transnational activity, as in the case of the transport of parrots to exotic pet shops or of ivory or tropical timber to processing and retail markets in the Global North (although it should be noted that major consumer markets for wildlife and wildlife parts also exist in China and parts of Southeast Asia). Where this is the case, wildlife products may be transported covertly in order to avoid border controls and import duties. Alternatively, action may be taken to 'mis-label the species, so documentation shows one species that is allowed to be traded when in fact the actual wildlife is another similar species. In these and other instances with fraudulent documentation, what is actually illegal then gets transferred into the legal sphere'.[28]

As the preceding discussion suggests, wildlife trafficking involves several different processes and actors. First, consumers are the main drivers of the illegal wildlife trade and are the end users of wildlife and wildlife-related products, parts, and derivatives whose needs wildlife trafficking aims to satisfy. Consumer demand is arguably the top of the pyramid of wildlife trade, driving all activities further down in the chain and frequently creating a situation in which legal and illegal markets operate within a symbiotic relationship (as the discussion of wildlife crime networks below indicates). Suppliers are primarily driven by economic needs or interests 'ranging from small-scale subsistence needs for some to major high-profit business for others'.[29] While retailers may make large profits from the end retail value of wildlife products (such as the high value placed on ivory and rhino horn), the hunters and collectors of wildlife (including plants and timber) who occupy the bottom and first stage of the supply chain can involve comparatively poor actors, although it should be noted that professional hunters are also involved in wildlife trafficking. Professional hunters and middlemen play a key role, as middlemen are connected to trafficking networks and transnational or global markets. Felbab-Brown notes that 'both middlemen and top traffickers can also establish networks of corruption, such as customs officials, and cultivate political patrons'.[30] This can include the use of diplomats or payments to officials to organise and facilitate transit and falsified permits.

Other actors, such as private game reserves and wildlife parks, conservation officials, and logging companies, may also be involved in trafficking activities. The nature of trafficking is such that it often involves dedicated effort to subvert or ignore wildlife legislation, and any legislative or policy response needs to address the deliberate

27 Ibid, 4.
28 Ibid, 4.
29 Vanda Felbab-Brown, *The Extinction Market* (OUP, 2017), 89.
30 Ibid, 93.

criminal and non-compliant behaviour involved and the various harms resulting from wildlife trafficking.

3. Green criminological and socio-legal approaches

Green criminology provides for interdisciplinary and multidisciplinary engagement with environmental crimes and wider environmental harms. Green criminology applies a broad 'green' perspective to environmental harms, ecological justice, and the study of environmental laws and criminality, which includes crimes affecting the environment and non-human animals. Green criminological perspectives are critical of criminology's relative silence on the harms caused to ecosystems and the non-human natural environment, and the lack of both scholarly and law enforcement attention to trafficking in wild animals and plants despite it being one of the most serious global crime problems.[31] A green criminological perspective, and particularly an ecological justice or species justice one, contends that justice systems need to adapt to consider the needs of nature and non-human animals.[32] Law enforcement and policy perspectives also need to be developed to provide for the protection of wild animals and plants as well as timber in order to address illegal activity that impacts negatively on the non-human natural environment.[33] Within the ecological justice and species justice perspectives of green criminology, there is a contention that justice systems need to do more than just consider anthropocentric notions of criminal justice; they should also consider, for example, the position of the environment and non-human animals as victims of crime and how justice systems can provide protection and redress for the environment and other non-human species. This involves direct consideration of repairing environmental harm and not just retributive punishment. Green criminology also takes a zemiological approach, considering activities such as wildlife trafficking in the context of the social harm caused. Green criminological scholarship has thus paid direct attention to theoretical questions of whether and how justice systems deal with crimes against animals and the environment more generally; it has begun to conceptualise policy perspectives that can provide contemporary ecological justice alongside mainstream criminal justice. Moving beyond mainstream criminology's focus on individual offenders and mainly anthropocentric conceptions of victimology, green criminology also explores state failure in environmental protection and corporate environmental offending and environmentally harmful business practices.[34]

---

31 Michael Lynch and Paul Stretesky, *Exploring Green Criminology: Toward a Green Criminological Revolution* (Ashgate, 2014).

32 See Ragnhild Sollund's Chapter 10 A Green Criminology Perspective on Animal Rights in this volume.

33 See further, Ted Benton, 'Rights and justice on a shared planet' (1998) 2(2) *Theoretical Criminology* 149–75; Piers Beirne, *Confronting Animal Abuse: Law, Criminology, and Human Animal Relationships* (Rowman & Littlefield, 2009).

34 Angus Nurse, 'Green criminology: shining a critical lens on environmental harm' (2017) Palgrave Commun 3, 10, available at: https://doi.org/10.1057/s41599-017-0007-2.

Wildlife crime's specialised nature and distinct legislation require specialised knowledge and training that fall outside of mainstream policing and incorporate a range of approaches. Broadly, there are four enforcement models adopted for wildlife law enforcement:

1. Enforcement by mainstream statutory police agencies including customs authorities.
2. Enforcement by a specialist regulatory agency (for example the Environmental Protection Agency, Fish & Wildlife Service).
3. Enforcement by conservation bodies, natural resource, and parks agencies.
4. Enforcement by NGOs (and enforcement by non-governmental organisations (NGOs) in cooperation with law enforcement agencies).

The models are not mutually exclusive, but for those agencies that do not specialise in environmental enforcement, this raises issues concerning the adequacy of law, policy, and training needs. Prior research identifies that wildlife crime problems are predominantly dealt with by state environmental departments or regulatory agencies rather than criminal justice bodies and are marginalised in mainstream criminal justice discourse.[35]

Wildlife law's public policy response is significantly influenced by NGOs. Indeed, green criminologist Rob White suggests that third parties such as NGOs often play a significant role in investigating and exposing environmental harm and offending and have become necessary for effective environmental law enforcement.[36] In wildlife protection, NGOs are integral to practical enforcement and policy development, where they act as policy advisers, researchers, field investigators, expert witnesses at court, scientific advisers, casework managers, and, in some cases, as prosecutors.[37]

4. Wildlife trafficking research

Historically, wildlife crime was under-represented in both mainstream criminological discourse and within green criminology, with much of the research in these areas being carried out by international organisations such as Interpol and NGOs such as Global Witness and the Environmental Investigations Agency (EIA), as well as scholars working in the fields of forestry conservation and policy and sustainable development. However, there has arguably been a substantial increase in attention by scholars and policy-makers aimed at the trade in wildlife and wildlife parts and derivatives, representing a growing area of scholarship and policy debate. From

[35] Nurse (n 10).

[36] Rob White, 'NGO Engagement in Environmental Law Enforcement: Critical Reflections' (2012) 4(1) *Australasian Policing: A Journal of Professional Practice and Research* 7–11.

[37] Note that this is generally possible in countries that allow prosecution by individuals and NGOs, such as the UK.

a green criminology perspective, wildlife trafficking aligns closely with the criminological gaze in respect of the focus on identifiable 'criminal' actors in respect of organised crime groups who have increasingly become involved in wildlife crime.[38] The links with other forms of crime such as drugs, human trafficking, and the illicit trade in weapons allow for comparison of trade routes, methods of operation, and the operation of neutralisation techniques. These are the justifications used by offenders to understate the harmful nature of their behaviour and deny its criminal characteristics.[39] Neutralisation techniques include offenders claiming wildlife trafficking as a victimless crime, or who may condemn their condemners (for example those seeking to prosecute them) and challenge the motivation for pursuing wildlife crime rather than 'real' crime.[40] This may be particularly effective where enforcers are those outside of mainstream law enforcement activity and can be demonised by certain sectors of society as NGOs exercising a public relations (PR) activity that allows them to raise money or anti-wildlife crime campaigns targeting offenders from an ideological position.[41]

Wildlife trade research encompasses a wide range of scholarship dealing with wildlife in a broad sense. As indicated earlier, a considerable amount of research is concerned with the trafficking of endangered species, particularly charismatic megafauna and species threatened by illegal trade. Species such as rhinos, elephants, and tigers arguably dominate the research landscape given the nature of global bans or restrictions on trade in ivory and rhino horn imposed because of decisions taken by CITES. These are also species considered important in policy terms and because research has identified that the trade in wildlife and derivatives has the capacity to render certain species extinct. Thus, previous research has identified and considered species-related issues such as the scale of the illegal trade in wildlife, the impact of the illegal wildlife trade on the sustainability of wildlife populations, the security threats wildlife populations face from armed conflicts and natural disasters, and issues relating to the harmful impacts of wildlife tourism on wildlife populations. Such species-centred research has identified a range of emerging threats such as that faced by the pangolin, now considered to be one of the species most threatened by trade, as well as those faced by less charismatic species such as the illegal trade in shark fins and the commodification of vulture brains.[42]

---

38 Tanya Wyatt, Daan van Uhm and Angus Nurse, 'Differentiating criminal networks in the illegal wildlife trade: organized, corporate and disorganized crime' (2020) 23 *Trends Organ Crim* 350–66.

39 Gresham Sykes and David Matza, 'Techniques of Neutralization: a theory of delinquency' (1957) 22 *American Sociological Review* 664–73.

40 Nurse (n 12).

41 Angus Nurse, 'Privatising the green police: the role of NGOs in wildlife law enforcement' (2013) 59 *Crime Law Soc Change* 305–18.

42 Angus Nurse, 'Vulture brains and muthi markets, Johannesburg, South Africa' in Adam Lynes, Craig Kelly and James Tredwell (eds), *50 Dark Destinations: Crime and Contemporary Tourism* (Policy Press, 2023).

Species-related research enables an understanding of the dimensions of contemporary wildlife crime problems, while other forms of wildlife crime research have clarified the nature of wildlife trafficking's processes and behaviours. Wyatt's research into wildlife trafficking provided an in-depth deconstruction of how wildlife crime occurs and the various actors and stages involved in wildlife trafficking.[43] This study illuminates that a range of different actors are involved in wildlife trafficking, from those involved on the ground who are sometimes themselves marginalised by the trade as procurers and trappers, through to the middlemen involved in transporting wildlife, and the retailers ultimately selling wildlife and derivatives or parts thereof. Thus, policy and enforcement approaches need to consider the different motivations and justifications for those involved in wildlife trafficking and tailor the enforcement response accordingly. Research has identified that a range of wildlife offenders exist, not just those who might be considered rational choice offenders dealing with wildlife purely for profit, but also those whose engagement with illegal wildlife activities might be linked to otherwise law-abiding employment.[44] In the context of Global South countries, where sensibilities towards wildlife may well differ from Global North perspectives, and food and security imperatives may also be motivations, participation in aspects of wildlife trafficking might reflect a subsistence necessity. This is particularly the case in those contexts in which the benefits of income raised through activities such as sports tourism or trophy hunting may fail to reach the indigenous peoples and local communities most affected by wildlife.

Prior research has also examined the involvement of organised crime in wildlife trafficking. Research evidence exists of the diversification of the criminal activities carried out by organised crime groups to include wildlife crime, sometimes using supply routes developed for other forms of illicit commerce to facilitate wildlife trafficking. Crucially, previous research has identified a range of organised crime and corporate groups involved in wildlife trafficking. Zimmerman identified three categories of organised crime groups as being involved in wildlife trafficking, namely:

1. Low level – groups of farmers who sell species illegally in order to supplement their incomes.
2. Mid level – mafia-style groups that purchase species from peasants to sell at a large profit.
3. High level – major international smuggling rings that are also involved in other illegal trades and utilise the same smuggling routes, using violence and intimidation to facilitate their trade.[45]

---

43 Wyatt (n 1).
44 Nurse (n 12).
45 Mara E Zimmerman, 'The Black Market for Wildlife: Combatting Transnational Organized Crime in the Illegal Wildlife Trade' (2003) 36 *Vanderbilt Journal of Transnational Law* 1668.

South and Wyatt's 2011 research drew comparisons between wildlife trafficking and the illegal drugs trade, adding to discussions of the different types of organised groups involved in wildlife trafficking. In brief, these are:

1. Trading charities – collectors and Traditional Chinese Medicine (TCM) practitioners are involved because of an ideological attachment to TCM and a belief in the medicinal properties of animal products.
2. Mutual Societies – traffickers and traders whose lifestyles revolve around their work and who effectively deal to order in wildlife.
3. Business sideliners – legal entrepreneurs who view drugs or wildlife as lucrative sidelines to their main – often legal – business.
4. Criminal diversifiers – traditional criminals who identify profitable opportunities in either drugs or wildlife trafficking and exploit these as an adjunct to their main business.
5. Opportunistic irregulars – street-level operatives who deal in wildlife whenever the opportunity arises.[46]

South and Wyatt's identified categories suggest that the overlap between drugs and wildlife trade sometimes occurs outside of the large-scale organised wildlife trafficking context and is not confined to transnational crime. While profit is a significant motive in IWT, it sometimes occurs as a secondary motive or is the product of opportunity rather than specific intent to illegally trade in wildlife. Historically, the concepts of a 'criminal network' or 'serious organised crime' were amorphous, with the terminology used interchangeably and describing all crime that is structured rather than solely reflecting crime that fits within normative definitions of 'organised' crime. More recently, Wyatt, van Uhm, and Nurse (2020, note 47 below) further identified variations in organised crime groups, classifying these as: (1) organised crime groups, (2) corporate crime groups, and (3) disorganised criminal networks. These categories further highlight the reality of criminal networks as being more diverse, which reflects the fact that, with globalisation and expanding markets, a range of criminal networks have become involved in different stages of IWT. Wyatt et al.'s conception of organised crime groups, corporate crime groups, and disorganised criminal networks, as well as collaborations between such groups (in addition to independent individuals that also function in this market), are an endemic part of the global wildlife trade. Each of these criminal groups or networks is distinctive in terms of levels of organisation, the degree to which they act opportunistically, have links to other crimes, and employ corruption. However, current research consistently suggests that corruption is a key facilitator and integral part of laundering processes involved in organised crime. In wildlife trafficking, fraud or corruption is manifested in different forms: evidence exists of officials accepting bribes during border crossings, the making of false claims of captive breeding to subvert permit and documentation requirements, and the involvement of government officials in the smuggling process, sometimes involving

[46] Nigel South and Tanya Wyatt, 'Comparing Illicit Trades in Wildlife and Drugs: An Exploratory Study' (2011) 32 *Deviant Behavior* 552–5.

fraudulent permits. Wyatt et al. note that 'organized crime groups are highly organized, sometimes act opportunistically, often if not always have links to other crimes (particularly other illicit markets), and rely on corruption as a tool to perpetrate their illegal activities'.[47] In contrast, corporate crime groups operating in wildlife trafficking are also highly organised and sometimes act opportunistically, but they are less likely to be linked to other crimes and are less reliant on corruption to facilitate their activities. The disorganised criminal networks are the least organised, the most likely to act opportunistically, can sometimes be linked to other crimes (but not necessarily), and have the lowest levels of corruption as a tool of perpetration.[48]

Much research is targeted at the causes and scope of wildlife crime, law enforcement approaches, and the criminality involved. Wellsmith's research, for example, looked at the lack of preventative techniques and sentencing practices in wildlife crime, while other research has looked in depth at how wildlife laws are enforced.[49] But less research has been targeted at addressing the end user aspect of wildlife trafficking. Given the enduring nature of demand for wildlife crime products, Schneider's research, published in 2008, suggested applying a consumer market reduction approach to tackling wildlife crime, recognising that the legality of trading in wildlife products is arguably an externality as far as markets are concerned.[50] Thus, consumers do not pay the true costs of their products, and the market is often concerned with supply and demand and not with monitoring the legality of products. The essence of the market reduction approach consists of identifying 'hot' products and conducting market-based analysis of these products to identify who is involved in their criminal exploitation, followed by subsequent analysis of the reasons for their involvement in the illegal activity and then targeted enforcement. Thus, in wildlife trafficking, a detailed understanding of the reasons why rhino horn and ivory continue to be traded despite known prohibitions and the potential for sanctions is useful to identify what might work as a deterrent with traders. Besides those users that exist on the supply side 'such as local subsistence users, commercial hunters and forest concessionaires, a diverse group of users exist on the demand side … [t]hese include consumptive end-users in markets and restaurants, and non-consumptive users such as tourists'.[51] In the case of plants, timber, and lesser derivatives such as wildlife-derived clothing (for example shawls, coats) or food (for example shark fin soup, tiger wine), the end consumers are not traditionally the subject of law enforcement attention, but unless the end consumers

---

47 Tanya Wyatt, Daan van Uhm and Angus Nurse, 'Differentiating criminal networks in the illegal wildlife trade: organized, corporate and disorganized crime' (2020) 23 *Trends Organ Crim* 350–66.

48 Ibid. The disorganised crime network is less structured, does not employ violence as a tool, and is often not territorial, highly organised or monopolistic and these networks are more fleeting and less stable than a group.

49 Melanie Wellsmith, 'Wildlife crime: The problems of enforcement' (2011) 17(2) *European Journal on Criminal Policy and Research* 125–48; Nurse (n 10).

50 Jacqueline Schneider, 'Reducing the illicit trade in endangered wildlife: The market reduction approach' (2008) 24(3) *Journal of Contemporary Criminal Justice* 274–95.

51 Nurse (n 10), 137.

and the nature of the market are also addressed, wildlife trafficking is likely to persist as a means of satisfying consumer demand. Accordingly, there is a need for further research to consider how best to influence consumer behaviour to eliminate the consumption of illegal wildlife products through effective demand reduction strategies. Policy-makers also need to consider approaches that might strengthen the effectiveness of law enforcement and deterrence, for example, by raising awareness of the legal protections against wildlife trade and any penalties that may be applicable under national laws for the sale and consumption of illegal wildlife products.

Common market-based strategies to prevent the illegal trade in wildlife products include the following:[52]

- imposing taxes or other levies to raise consumer prices or reduce producer profitability;
- lowering tax rates on (sustainable) substitute products; and
- increasing the profitability of sustainably-harvested production through subsidies, value-adding, certification, and labelling.

In respect of timber trafficking, for example, market-based approaches have been attempted that aim to address the demand for, and supply of, timber products by targeting prices and markets for timber products such as sustainably-harvested resources. Potentially, synthetic products might be introduced into markets to ease pressure on wild products, although this policy response might be seen as controversial. These mechanisms arguably lend themselves readily to timber products where a large legal market operates, and consumers may be influenced by price and ethical considerations. Thus, certification schemes and price manipulation through taxes or incentives may impact consumer behaviour positively, thus reducing demand for illegal products. However, market-based instruments rely on clearly established property rights, although the idea of assigning rights and ownership is potentially a contested area in many source countries for wildlife products. The cooperation of governments is also needed to apply financial and economic instruments to the wildlife trade. Therefore, certification measures and trade regulation (both international and domestic) provide a means through which social crime prevention might be attempted by addressing consumer and retailer behaviour. Arguably, the focus on producers as criminal actors could be shifted or expanded to also encompass the retailer who sells illegally sourced timber products and the consumer who purchases and ultimately possesses these products. Some market-based approaches already exist, such as the 2023 EU Regulation on deforestation-free products (Regulation (EU) 2023/1115 of the European Parliament and of the Council of 31 May 2023) which repeals the EU Timber Regulation (Regulation (EU) 995/2010 of the European Parliament and of the Council of 20 October 2010).[53] This approach and the regulations may be complemented by

---

52 UNODC, *Wildlife and Forest Analytic Toolkit* (UNODC, 2012), 346.

53 Regulation (EU) 2023/1115 of the European Parliament and of the Council of 31 May 2023 on the making available on the Union market and the export from the Union of

the application of criminal sanctions such as those concerning illegal trade in forest commodities in EU Environmental Crime Directive 2024/203, Article 3(2) (p).[54] There are questions concerning the extent to which market-based incentives are effective in reducing illegal activity in source countries and how they compare with command-and-control approaches, with some research suggesting that market-based initiatives may reduce imports by consumer countries but may not reduce illegal activity in source countries.[55] This is a potential area for further research.

5. Future trends for wildlife crime research

This chapter has suggested that, historically, wildlife trafficking research has focused primarily on charismatic megafauna and has considered only certain aspects of the trafficking landscape (for example animals, timber trafficking). Future research needs to extend into those under-explored areas such as plant trafficking, which is arguably under-explored in wildlife crime and wildlife trafficking scholarship. The marginalisation of plant crime in criminological discourse can, in part, be explained by the concept of 'plant blindness' in the context of current sustainability debates.[56] The illegal trade in plants arguably lacks the immediacy and media-friendly nature of trafficking in charismatic megafauna. Plant trafficking also operates in the context of a large legal trade in rare and ornamental plants, one in which there are recognised collecting societies operating within a relatively closed subculture. However, several studies 'have revealed that the trade in wild-sourced orchids, mostly undeclared and undocumented, may in fact be much greater than currently estimated.'[57] Research into specific markets, including China, has identified widespread trade in illegally taken orchids both in the context of transnational trade and in domestic markets. One study that aimed to quantify the illegal trade in China recorded more than 400

certain commodities and products associated with deforestation and forest degradation and repealing Regulation (EU) No 995/2010.

54 Article 3(2)(p) creates offences of 'placing or making available on the Union market or the export from the Union market of relevant commodities or relevant products, in breach of the prohibition set out in Article 3 of Regulation (EU) 2023/1115, except where such conduct concerns a negligible quantity'. It requires that Member States should ensure that such conduct constitutes a criminal offence where it is unlawful and committed intentionally, or with at least serious negligence (see Article 3 (4)).

55 Ragnar Jonsson, Alexandru Giurca, Mauro Masiero, Ed Pepke, Davide Pettenella, Jeffrey Prestemon, and Georg Winkel, *Assessment of the EU Timber Regulation and FLEGT Action Plan* (European Forest Institute 2015).

56 James Wandersee and Elisabeth Schussler, 'Towards a theory of plant blindness' (2001) 47(1) *Plant Science Bulletin* 2–9.

57 Shreya Dasgupta, 'Wild orchid trade in China is huge, overlooked and "devastating", study finds', *Mongabay* (2019), available at: https://news.mongabay.com/2019/08/wild-orchid-trade-in-china-is-huge-overlooked-and-devastating-study-finds/.

species of wild-caught orchids, involving 1.2 million individual plants worth potentially more than $14.6 million being traded at markets in southern China.[58]

Recent research has also illuminated the extent and nature of online trading in wildlife. The role of the internet in facilitating IWT has been the subject of research by conservation and criminological researchers, as well as NGOs and enforcement agencies. Internet-facilitated crime represents a hybrid of online and offline activities, with 'connections easily made in cyberspace between vendors and specialist collectors of rare and threatened species'.[59] Analysis carried out as part of the FloraGuard project to assess aspects of the online trade in wild plants identified a number of online markets active in the illegal sale of live plant specimens and derivative plants. Trading through social media networks and the possibility of trade via the 'dark web' also make this a challenging area for research. Perhaps unsurprisingly the FloraGuard research identified that 'plants are barely considered in mainstream policing' and addressing online plant trafficking highlighted problems common to other aspects of wildlife crime, including: the notion that plant crimes are victimless crimes; low levels of enforcement; lack of resources (both financial and manpower); lack of training for enforcement officers.[60] The result is that plant crimes (in the UK for example) are not treated as a priority and the low levels of enforcement risk becoming self-perpetuating.

Research into the contemporary nature of wildlife trafficking has considered the extent to which the online environment either facilitates the illegal trade or creates new forms of wildlife trade. The International Fund for Animal Welfare (IFAW) conducted research into the scale and nature of the online illegal wildlife trade over several months. In an intensive one-week analysis of wildlife offered for sale online in the UK, IFAW indicated that it had found over 9000 wild animal products and specimens and live wild animals for sale, predominantly from species protected by law.[61] The evidence indicates that despite legal protection for wildlife, the largely unmonitored online environment allows for the sale of protected species, with limited law enforcement activity in place to address this problem.[62]

---

58 Stephan W Gale, Pankaj Kumar, Amy Hinsley, Mang Lung Cheuk, Jiangyun Gao, Hong Liu, Zhi-Long Liu, and Sophie J Williams, 'Quantifying the trade in wild-collected ornamental orchids in South China: Diversity, volume and value gradients underscore the primacy of supply' (2019) 238 *Biological Conservation* 108204, available at: https://doi.org/10.1016/j.biocon.2019.108204.

59 D Whitehead, CR Cowell, A Lavorgna, SE Middleton, 'Countering plant crime online: Cross-disciplinary collaboration in the FloraGuard study' (2021) 1 *Forensic Science International: Animals and Environments* 100007.

60 Anita Lavorgna and Maurizio Sajeva, 'Studying Illegal Online Trades in Plants: Market Characteristics, Organisational and Behavioural Aspects, and Policing Challenges' (2021) 27 *Eur J Crim Policy Res* 451–70.

61 IFAW, *Caught in the Web: Wildlife Trade on the Internet* (2005), available at: https://d1jyxxz9imt9yb.cloudfront.net/resource/685/attachment/original/Report_2005_Caught_in_the_web_UK.pdf.

62 Further research in relation to online IWT, which shows coordinated action between NGOs and law enforcement agencies, is forthcoming. See, for example, UNITE, a

Research into the effectiveness of crime prevention mechanisms also represents a frontier for wildlife trade scholarship. This could include the use of artificial intelligence (AI) and other technological advances to address wildlife crime issues.[63] Green criminologists have identified the relative lack of preventative techniques applied to wildlife trafficking with the result that policy is often reactive, dealing with wildlife crime incidents through a 'detection, apprehension, and sanctioning' approach.[64] However, the nature of wildlife trafficking, which is inherently destructive for both the wildlife involved and the environment on which it depends, arguably requires a preventative approach that takes advantage of the preventative measures employed in other areas of crime. Situational crime prevention (for example the use of drones or 'target hardening' measures such as those interventions designed to make it more difficult to commit an offence) should be stepped up to prevent trafficking in endangered species, including measures to reduce the desirability (and availability) of rhino horn or elephant tusks. For example, the dehorning of rhinos has been attempted as a situational crime prevention technique. By safely removing the horn of the rhino, the crime of taking and possessing a rhino horn becomes more difficult to commit.[65] Such situational preventative measures should also be used in respect of less 'charismatic' species. Future protection of wildlife requires not only robust legislation that protects wildlife but also an effective enforcement regime containing preventative mechanisms for dealing with wildlife criminality alongside punitive measures and sanctions aimed at reducing repeat wildlife offences.[66]

6. Conclusions

As this chapter illustrates, despite international and domestic laws designed to address the illegal trade in wildlife, wildlife trafficking remains a persistent problem. Within wildlife trade and wildlife crime discourse, there is potential inconsistency between narratives that call for increased and improved levels of enforcement, stiffer penalties, and the classification of wildlife trafficking as a serious crime dealt with via retributive justice, and those perspectives, particularly green criminological ones, that focus instead on repairing the harm caused by wildlife trafficking, including the use of restorative principles and reparation for indigenous peoples, local communities, and the wider ecosystem. One approach risks being primarily reactive and situating itself

European project aimed at tackling environmental crime, at https://www.uniteproject.eu/.

63 See Stefano Porfido and Alberto Quintavalla's Chapter 12 Artificial Intelligence and Environmental Crime in this volume.

64 Melanie Wellsmith, 'The applicability of crime prevention to problems of environmental harm' in Rob White (ed), *Global Environmental Harm* (Willan, 2013).

65 Eleanor Jane Milner-Gulland, 'How many to dehorn? A model for decision-making by rhino managers' (1999) 2 *Animal Conservation* 137–47.

66 See, for example, Directive (EU) 2024/1203 of the European Parliament and of the Council of 11 April 2024 on the protection of the environment through criminal law and replacing Directives 2008/99/EC and 2009/123/EC.

in the punishment of individual offenders, whereas the other seeks to address and repair the harm to wildlife and ecosystems. However, irrespective of which approach is adopted, the aim is similar: to address the negative impacts of wildlife trafficking on the animals and plants targeted, the habitats and natural environment that are affected by the illegal removal of wildlife, and the indigenous and local communities affected by wildlife trafficking and that are sometimes dependent on wildlife for sustenance. Accordingly, policy and enforcement approaches also need to consider the wider social and economic harm caused to Global South countries for whom wildlife is a key economic resource, where failure to effectively combat wildlife crime impacts negatively on source countries both in terms of loss of natural resources and loss of revenues from wildlife-dependent industries (for example tourism).

To effectively address the specific characteristics of the wildlife trafficking problem, arguably an approach beyond international trade regulation is required. Policy responses need to consider the various motivations of the different actors who become involved in IWT, as well as the actions of consumers who continue to drive the trade, and the issue of corruption in the context of wildlife crime enforcement. This chapter contends that addressing the illegal trade in wildlife requires a more holistic approach situated within preventative and restorative principles rather than a primarily retributive justice approach.

9 Environmental harms, ecocidal trends and restorative responses: some interdisciplinary directions

Anna Di Ronco and Nigel South

1. Introduction

Just over 60 years ago, Rachel Carson (1962 [1965]) published her classic study *Silent Spring*, drawing attention to what she saw as worrying signs of the degradation of the natural environment and the threat of the extinction of species. Carson was a pioneering ecologist and biologist who aimed to set out the evidence that could support calls for serious intervention and action to preserve the environment at a time when science, economies, and society were changing rapidly at an 'impetuous and heedless pace' that was at odds with the 'deliberate pace of nature' (Carson, 1962 [1965], p. 24). Although it was obvious that there would be necessary lessons to learn about the impact of the increasing use of chemical pesticides and fertilisers in intensive agriculture, Carson faced considerable criticism, opposition, and negative responses, generated by the pesticide and chemical companies as well as other (male!) scientists. Others in the conservation field, however – as well as President Kennedy – all agreed that Carson's arguments and warnings were too powerful to be ignored. Perhaps figures like Kennedy could see the significance of Carson's (1962 [1965], p. 25) warning that: 'Along with the possibility of the extinction of mankind by nuclear war, the central problem of our age has … become the contamination of man's total environment with … substances of incredible potential for harm.' Today, the world is still facing serious threats of harm, contamination, and extinction. In this chapter – taking our starting point from the work of a biologist – we draw upon an interdisciplinary body of work to describe some of the environmental crimes and ecocidal trends that have not diminished but have gathered pace since the mid-twentieth century, largely because they have not been taken seriously or have strategically been ignored by states and corporations alike. Despite the numerous international environmental treaties in force regionally and globally, they are frequently weak in scope, enforcement, and effectiveness because states tend to be reluctant to limit their sovereignty. In this chapter, in the case of biodiversity protection, we can only make reference to the Convention on International Trade in Endangered Species of Wild Fauna and Flora

(CITES) but there are many other agreements, such as the Framework Convention on Biological Diversity, that could be more fully employed in practice and analysed here (see also Angus Nurse's Chapter 8 The Global Illegal Wildlife Trade Crisis, in this volume). We then focus on Environmental Restorative Justice (ERJ), addressing its origins, aims, uses and challenges. By drawing upon recent interdisciplinary ERJ projects that explore new, imaginative ways of hearing the voices of the more-than-human and have them represented in RJ circles, we show the transformative potential of ERJ and call for greater support for restorative responses to the harms done to the planet and to us all on a daily basis.

2. 'Silent Spring' over 60 years on: birds still fading from the skies

The heading to this section is taken from an article by the environmental and wildlife journalist Sharon Guynup (2022) which reflected on the impact of Carson's book as a landmark chronicle of 'the damage – and looming consequences – of human "contamination of air, earth, rivers, and sea with dangerous and even lethal materials", which she called "elixirs of death"'. Guynup quotes from the justly famous 'parable' or 'fable for tomorrow' (Carson, 1962 [1965], p. 21) with which Carson opens Chapter 1, describing the transformation of 'a town in the heart of America' from one 'where all life seemed to live in harmony with its surroundings' into a community living under a 'shadow of death' and where nature seemed affected by 'a strange stillness' and a silent spring arrived: 'On the mornings that had once throbbed with the dawn chorus of robins, catbirds, doves, jays, wrens, and scores of other bird voices there was now no sound; only silence lay over the fields and woods and marsh' (Carson, 1962 [1965], p. 22).

The cause – Carson's 'elixirs of death' – was the 'lethal materials' in 'sprays, dusts and aerosols … applied almost universally to farms, gardens, forests and homes' (Carson, 1962 [1965], p. 25), examples being pesticides such as DDT that humans had developed to exert control over nature. Carson suggested such products should 'not be called "insecticides" but "biocides"' and used this term to convey alarm and warn about the widespread nature of the damage to the earth that would come from the escalating use of toxic materials in agriculture, industry, and everyday life.

The changing nature of such terminology is interesting and provides a lexicological insight into how levels of alarm have been raised but also normalised in the decades since Carson's warning. Slowly, but with developing urgency since the 1970s, environmentalists, critical criminologists, socio-legal scholars, and others have begun to use the term 'ecocide' (Higgins, Short and South, 2013) to describe the destruction of plant and animal life and, in the 1980s, the Venezuelan writer Rosa del Olmo coined the term 'eco-bio-genocide' (del Olmo, 1987; South, 2023) – both terms conveying the sense of disaster and finality signposting the road to extinction – for species and the planet. Rather chillingly, however, the word 'biocide' has actually become just a conventional, normalised term used in the chemical and landscape management industries, and defined by the British Health and Safety Executive as follows: 'Biocidal products are used to protect people and animals, preserve goods, stop pests like insects or rodents and control viruses, bacteria and fungi through a chemical or biological action. Common examples are disinfectants, wood preservatives and insect repellents'.[1]

Considering the message that Carson wanted to convey – and the many subsequent critiques of our over-reliance on the chemical management of nature (for example European Environment Agency, 2023) – there may be some irony or oddity in the claim that such products are to be used to '*protect* people and animals' (emphasis added). The question is whether any immediate benefits outweigh the cumulative impacts of biocides, which may mean they could end up doing more harm than good.

Carson's work – alongside that of other pioneers in the 1960s (Rome, 2003) – stimulated various important initiatives, assisted, as mentioned above, by the forward-looking administration of President Kennedy. This was a key moment in the political science record of the twentieth century. Indeed, although we focus here on developments related to justice and law, a full account would also highlight the roles of environmental politics and environmental economics in influencing environmental criminal law and policies.

As Rome (2003, p. 532) reports:

> In the White House, Kennedy's top domestic priority was a growth-boosting tax cut. But he took a few important steps to address the issue of environmental quality. … In 1962 he held a White House Conference on Conservation [and] [a]fter the publication of *Silent Spring*, … instructed his advisers to report on the use of pesticides. He also appointed an activist secretary of the interior, Stewart L. Udall, who energetically promoted the cause of environmental protection … and argued that the nation's deteriorating environment was a sign of the 'disorder of our post-war priorities.

The 1963 book authored by Udall, *The Quiet Crisis*, contrasted the priorities given to the economy versus the environment, suggesting that for all the 'wealth and power' of modern America, it was becoming 'a land of vanishing beauty, … and of an overall environment that is diminished daily by pollution and noise and blight' (Udall, 1963, p. viii). Awareness of a 'silent spring' and of the 'quiet crisis' led to some response and remediation, yet Udall's words could easily have been written today and, of course, resonated then and now around the world.

On the international stage, one of the most significant responses to these warnings was the signing of the Convention on International Trade in Endangered Species of Wild Fauna and Flora (CITES).[2] Launched in Washington DC in March 1973, CITES was an expression of a new conservationism, with the declared aim to 'ensure that no

1 See https://www.hse.gov.uk/biocides/introduction.htm.
2 See https://cites.org/eng/disc/what.php.

species of wild fauna and flora becomes or remains subject to unsustainable exploitation because of international trade' (JNCC, 2019).

Despite a subsequent history of both celebration and critique of CITES (Wyatt, 2021; Goergen, 2022), it is important to note that its introduction occurred at a time when environmental awareness was still weak and calls for action were relatively scarce. As the CITES website[3] notes: 'when the ideas for CITES were first formed, in the 1960s, international discussion of the regulation of wildlife trade for conservation purposes was something relatively new'. Since then, the CITES strategic vision has been subject to regular revision and updates. This has partly been accomplished through the mechanism of its Conferences of the Parties (COPs) which, while remaining anthropocentric, adopted the first Strategic Vision at its 11th meeting in 2000. Most recently, at its 18th meeting, it agreed a new Strategic Vision for 2021–30, taking into account the 2030 Agenda for Sustainable Development.

Nonetheless, one question regarding the aims and hopes of CITES was – and is – whether the promise of protection of non-human species – *in the sense of preservation of species sustainability* – simply provides an enabling system for legitimate exploitation, abuse, and excessive use of non-human species?

According to the CITES mission description: 'Thousands of species are internationally traded and used by people in their daily lives for food, housing, health care, ecotourism, cosmetics or fashion' (CITES, 2021).[4] This occurs with the aim of ensuring 'that international trade in wild animals and plants is legal, sustainable and traceable, and does not threaten the survival of the species …'.[5] On this point, it is worth noting what the CITES website suggests, in relation to the UN Sustainable Development Goals (SDGs) that: 'The main challenge for CITES, within the broader framework of the SDGs, is to make species conservation and the promotion of prosperity mutually supportive'.[6] This is, unsurprisingly, a source of tension given that economic growth as a foundation of 'prosperity' tends to be highly – and ecocidally – dependent on the opposite of conservation, i.e. extraction, exploitation, increasing production and expanding consumption (Stretesky, Long, and Lynch, 2013; Brisman and South, 2014). Such tensions are not unfamiliar in the field of environmental policy. For example, the imperatives of international organisations such as the World Trade Organization (for example economic growth) and the United Nations Environment Programme (UNEP) (for example sustainability and environmental protection) are in direct conflict yet present to the world a message of 'joined up' cooperation (South, 2016).

3 Ibid.
4 See https://cites.org/eng/news/experts_advise_trade_levels_conservation_status_of_CITES-listed_animals.
5 Ibid.
6 See https://sustainabledevelopment.un.org/index.php?page=view&type=30022&nr=650&menu=3170.

To some extent, Udall's 'quiet crisis' remains background noise for most; many of its symptoms are hidden, kept invisible, or denied. As Monbiot (2019) argues:

> What we see is not the economy. What we see is the tiny fragment of economic life we are supposed to see: the products and services we buy. The rest – the mines, plantations, factories and dumps required to deliver and remove them – are kept as far from our minds as possible. Given the scale of global extraction and waste disposal, it is a remarkable feat of perception management.

This 'way of seeing' – or *not seeing* – hides the numerous invisible harms and crimes (Berger, 1972; Davies, Francis, and Wyatt, 2014; South, 2014a) degrading the environment and is a product of a 'world-view' dominated by the Global North, its embedded interests, and its epistemologies (Franko Aas, 2012; de Sousa Santos, 2014; Goyes and South, 2019). The result is that the impacts of climate change and responsibility for its causes are massively differentiated and unequal (South, 2012) – and this is very starkly apparent in the case of communities that live close to nature. These are peoples who have done the least to contribute to climate change and yet are most at risk of losing their lands and indeed their future as sustainable populations – the Indigenous populations of the world.

Addressing this distortion of perception and priorities has been central to efforts made over recent decades to draw attention to the importance of global warming and related climate change. Many causes of these threats have been detailed in the scientific literature (Intergovernmental Panel on Climate Change (IPCC), 2022) but there has been an odd disconnect between such explanations and one major source of contributory environmental harms. As a major report from the United Nations Office on Drugs and Crime (UNDOC) and the World Wide Fund for Nature (WWF) (2022, p. 5) put it: 'As pressure grows to respond to the climate crisis, so too does the recognition that this response needs to be multidimensional, including by stepping up the efforts to protect biodiversity.' One element of these efforts, according to the report, is to take environmental *crime* far more seriously – an argument that was, in fact, already made a decade earlier by the International Criminal Police Organization (Interpol) and UNEP with regard to CITES (Nelleman and Interpol, 2012, p. 6): 'To become effective, voluntary trade programmes and the effective implementation of CITES, must be combined with an international law enforcement investigative and operational effort in collaboration with domestic police and investigative task forces in each country'. In their report, the UNODC and WWF (2022, p. 5) point out that 'environmental crime impedes the transition to a more resilient and climate neutral society' but a focus on this has been 'largely absent from the climate agenda', perhaps because 'most activities contributing to climate change are caused by lawful behaviour' (however 'lawful but awful' (Passas, 2005) they may be) and in light of the fact that the 'predominant international response has been to use incentives rather than enforcement' (UNODC and WWF, 2022, p. 5).

This needs to change to respond to the ecocidal trends facing the planet and to provide justice-based restorative responses. As Higgins, Short, and South (2013, p. 262) argued, what is required is a law of ecocide that, first, responds to 'human-caused environmental damage and degradation (whether committed during or outside of war-time), as a crime of strict liability (in other words, without intent)';[7] and, second, puts in place forms of restorative justice that build on a duty of remedy for harm caused and address 'the needs of the beleaguered party to restore that which has been harmed rather than simply fixating on the punishment of the perpetrator' (Higgins, Short and South, 2013, p. 255).

2.1 Ecocidal trends and climate change denial

For such important bodies as the UNODC and WWF to link 'climate' and 'crime' together so explicitly is significant. It is not, however, a link that has been ignored elsewhere. For example, in his book, *Carbon Criminals, Climate Crimes*, the critical criminologist Ronald Kramer (2020) recounts two factors that propelled his research interest in climate change. As a criminologist concerned with the crimes of the powerful, he was not surprised by links being made between climate change and the operations of corporations and states, but he was surprised by the gravity of the climate crisis and also by one other notable feature appearing in his reading: 'how often those who commented on climate change used the word "crime" in discussing the topic' (Kramer, 2020, p. 2; see also Stephan Sina's Chapter 11 Climate Change and Criminal Justice, in this volume). Among the most famous of these statements is that by the former executive director of Greenpeace UK, John Sauven, after the disappointing outcome of the 2009 Copenhagen conference on climate change: 'The city of Copenhagen is a *crime scene* tonight, with the *guilty* men and women fleeing to the airport' (quoted in Vidal, Stratton and Goldenberg, 2009). Kramer also quotes the question posed by Donald Brown, professor in environmental ethics, science and law at Pennsylvania State University, who asked whether 'climate science disinformation is a crime against humanity?' and who observed that, while '[w]e may not have a word for this type of crime yet, … the international community should find a way of classifying extraordinarily irresponsible scientific claims that could lead to mass suffering as some type of crime against humanity' (Brown, 2010).

One key theme of Kramer's book – and some other similar excellent studies such as Harvey's (2021) *The Climate Emergency* – is (again) the tension or incompatibility between capitalism and sustainability. As Kramer (2020, p. 46) notes, capitalism is based on 'a high carbon system' (Urry, 2011), and also fixated on *growth* (Ruggiero and South, 2013, p. 269). These two – carbon (for example dependence on oil) and growth (for example obsession with GDP) – make the possibility of *sustainability* an oxymoron: the capitalist thrust towards growth at all costs leads to the unsustainable use of planetary resources that will take us beyond a tipping point (Rockström et al,

7 More recent work on the development of a definition of ecocide for the purpose of drafting an instrument of international law (Stop Ecocide International, 2021), has suggested that 'For the purpose of [the Rome Statute], "ecocide" means unlawful or wanton acts committed with knowledge that there is a substantial likelihood of severe and either widespread or long-term damage to the environment being caused by those acts.'

2009). This argument has been made across many relevant scholarly disciplines but is well illustrated in the 2019 UNEP report, *Global Resources Outlook*, submitted to the International Resources Panel, which examined the pace of resource extraction and consumption from the 1970s onwards:

> The extraction and processing of materials, fuels and food contribute half of total global greenhouse gas emissions and over 90 per cent of biodiversity loss and water stress. Resource extraction has more than tripled since 1970, including a fivefold increase in the use of non-metallic minerals and a 45 per cent increase in fossil fuel use. By 2060, global material use could double to 190 billion tonnes (from 92 billion), while greenhouse gas emissions could increase by 43 per cent.

Regardless of such evidence, however, forms of denial (Thiel and South, 2022) or what McGoey (2012) calls 'strategic ignorance', are powerful shapers of resistant human behaviour, 'business-as-usual' economic activity, and timid government policies. An example is provided by the United States (US) oil and gas multinational company Exxon, which, from the 1970s, had access to research that accurately predicted the impact of its activities on climate change but not only decided to ignore such predictions but also publicly dismiss all claims that associated climate change with the burning of fossil fuels (see, for example Milman, 2023).

Even when the climate change challenge is acknowledged, it is treated as what Britzman (1998) calls 'difficult knowledge'. So although (at least in some countries and surveyed populations) there is increasing awareness of, and anxiety about, climate change, there is still resistance to proposals that would affect *quality of life*. As Bryan (2022, p. 331; drawing on Britzman, 1998) puts it, 'socially traumatic knowledge' comes up against defences that enable 'us to negate, resist, ignore or not know certain truths about ourselves and the world'. Furthermore, the impacts of changes to our planet, as well as unwelcome reminders of climate instability signalling future disasters conveyed via news, science, and entertainment media, are not just to be counted in physical but also in psychological terms. This is an area of interdisciplinary research that needs further work, as Bryan (2022, p. 331) observes: 'Because research on the affective dimensions of climate change is very much in its infancy, our understanding of the complex ways in which various climate-related emotions such as grief, anxiety etc. manifest across geographies, cultures, and demographics remains limited, as does our understanding of the long-term effects of ecological grief' (Adams, 2021).

Of course, the additional global social trauma of the Covid-19 pandemic has added layers of complexity to the task of responding to 'difficult knowledge'. Some have argued that a 'convergence of crises' (Lam, South, and Brisman, 2022) should be acting as a stimulus to action (Hook and Wisniewska, 2020, pp. 34–5), such as that urged by the UNODC, which has noted that: 'Habitat loss and wildlife exploitation – including its illegal trade – are making it easier for diseases to pass from other species to humans ... Wildlife crime sets in motion a vicious circle jeopardizing our health, security and development' and must be tackled to prevent the next pandemic (UNODC, 2020). At the same time, others have claimed that the risks associated with both the Covid-19 pandemic and climate change have been exaggerated or are examples of manufactured hoaxes (Rutjens, van der Linden, and van der Lee, 2021; Dobson, 2022). Enormous global challenges inevitably provoke serious and continuing debate, but it is problematic if such debate is circular and does not move forward and yield concrete action.

2.2 COP 27 and 'loss and damage' fund proposals

One such action may – eventually – follow from the conclusion of the 2022 Climate Change Conference which led to proposals for a new fund for 'loss and damage' resulting from climate change.[8] This could provide an advance on current mechanisms for climate change mitigation, but the necessary resources for implementation are not yet available. The proposition is based on the assumption that economically poor countries will reduce their CO_2 emissions if rich countries provide money and technology in exchange, and these discussions have allowed nations of the Global South to take a lead in negotiations about the relevant levels of contributions to be made by nations of the Global North.

The path to a global agreement on common environmental standards, including compensation for environmental and climate-related damage, will be difficult to achieve, but such proposals could dovetail with calls for the introduction of a law of ecocide. For example, Killean (2021) considers the idea of '"greening" the Rome Statute' to explore whether reparations administered within the International Criminal Court (ICC) to respond to mass violence and human rights violations could also address environmental harms and damages. According to Killean (2021, p. 323), such an environmental reparation framework within the ICC could be enabled '(i) by introducing the concept of "eco-sensitivity" to reparations designed to respond to other anthropocentric harms; (ii) by awarding reparations that explicitly recognise the harm caused by environmental destruction when possible; and (iii) by exploring the possibilities of an environmental approach towards "transformative reparations".' Such directions lead us to our next section.

3. Environmental restorative justice

Restorative Justice (or RJ) offers some hope about ways forward but also signals the promise of breaking away from the constraints of 'northern' epistemologies and disciplinary silos, owing much to models of justice, respect, and arbitration in 'southern' knowledge systems, and working across borders of knowledge and practice in the fields of law, therapy, theatre, art, and so on (see for example Pali et al, 2022; Pointer and Pali, 2022). Indeed, the roots of RJ can be traced to 'southern' Indigenous dispute resolution traditions which are focused on repairing harm, healing damaged relationships, fostering awareness of the rules, promoting community inclusion and cohesion,

---

8 See https://www.carbonbrief.org/cop27-key-outcomes-agreed-at-the-un-climate-talks-in-sharm-el-sheikh/.

and reintegrating offenders. In the past decades, these traditions have informed efforts to reform the criminal justice system in Western countries, as a way to deal with its perceived ineffectiveness in deterring crime and addressing harms to victims. In many varied forms, RJ is now employed all around the world and has recently also been used to address environmental harms (Wijdekop, 2019; Pali and Aertsen, 2021; Pali, Forsyth, and Tepper, 2022; Widowaty, Astuti, and Adrian, 2022; Haluska, 2023) – in both administrative/civil and criminal cases. What generally goes under the label of 'Environmental Restorative Justice' (ERJ) grounds its roots in many Indigenous cultures and cosmologies, which hold the central belief that humans and nature are fundamentally interconnected and interdependent. It therefore opposes the typically Western, anthropocentric view that nature belongs to human domination and is a commodity for human consumption and exploitation (Goyes et al, 2021; Haluska, 2023). ERJ embraces this ecocentric perspective and promotes the establishment of safe spaces where broadly defined victims and offenders voluntarily come together and engage in meaningful dialogue involving deep listening, participation, knowledge exchange, and efforts directed at healing and repairing harms, and at restoring communities, relationships, institutions, and ecosystems damaged by human action or inaction.

Some countries have institutionalised ERJ and have introduced it into their legal and criminal justice systems. For example, in the past two decades, specialist environment courts were established in both Australia and New Zealand, which have experimented with using restorative justice conferences and sentencing (Forsyth et al, 2021; Hamilton, 2021; Haluska, 2023). Recent proposals suggested expanding the remit of ERJ beyond enforcement procedures to all stages of regulatory processes (Forsyth et al, 2021), and to the preparatory phases of constructing major, 'strategic' harm-bearing infrastructures often riddled with conflict between state-corporations and the local community (Di Ronco and Chiaramonte, 2022). In the latter cases, it should not be forgotten that, even if public participation is standard practice in public infrastructure projects, it is often difficult for affected communities and activists to access information and effectively participate in decision-making processes (Brisman, 2013; South, 2014b). This is especially the case when their knowledge is intentionally undermined and mystified by corporations and state actors alike, and the actions of activists heavily policed and criminalised (Goyes, 2016; Di Ronco and Chiaramonte, 2022; Di Ronco, 2023). The participation of affected populations and the public more generally is, however, crucial to reduce conflict and minimise harms related to developments such as 'megaprojects'.

Outside these recent developments, it is worth clarifying that ERJ is mainly focused on repairing *past harms*. By addressing past harms, however, ERJ also has an eye on the *future*: it seeks to avoid reccurrence of harms and also contributes to (re)constructing relations within the community – and between the community and nature – which enable it to build capacity to prevent future harms (Forsyth, Pali, and Tepper, 2022). Indeed, as Forsyth et al (2022, p. 6) argue, the key idea is that restorative approaches to environmental harms 'can support an agenda of reconnecting humans with the environment in ways that recognise our essential interdependence and seek to put limits on extractivist ideologies'. While some communities may spontaneously embrace and embody ecocentric perspectives and practice RJ (however locally named) to repair environmental harms after they happen (see, for example Komatsubara, 2021; Papadopoulos, de la Bellacasa, and Tacchetti, 2023), others may need a little help: people's 'seed of environmental philosophy in their inner world' (Komatsubara, 2022,: p. 382) could organically be stimulated by restorative practitioners, artists, and researchers during their interactions – a point to which we shall return later. For Haluska (2023), in the long run, a renewed connection with nature linked to the systematic use of ERJ may also lead to enhanced support for the introduction and better enforcement of rights of nature laws (see, for example Stone, 1972; Darpö, 2021), not only due to public demand but also following pressure put on governments by corporations (which have far more political capital with which to lobby policymakers and shape governmental decisions).

In essence, recent literature cites ERJ as the ideal approach to dealing with cases of environmental harm, particularly in the face of extremely low reporting, prosecution, and sentencing regarding environmental crimes (Pali and Aertsen, 2021), and the well-known incapability of fines – the usual sanction used against environmental offences – to lead to repair of environmental harm and devastation (Wijdekop, 2019).[9] Nonetheless, ERJ also poses some important challenges that cannot be ignored. While the relevant literature discusses many of these challenges (see for example, Forsyth, Pali and Tepper, 2022; White, 2022), we focus here on only two – the issues of participation and representation in ERJ circles and conferences. We believe these two challenges to be crucial and worthy of our attention for different reasons: while the lack of participation can obstruct access to ERJ and frustrate its long-term aim to activate a renewed connection with nature, the effective representation of all (broadly defined) victims – including the more-than-human – through interdisciplinary collaborations and projects, offers much hope for the future of ERJ, and hence also for the conservation of all living forms on our planet.

Starting with the issue of participation, ERJ requires that all affected parties directly and willingly participate in the RJ process, including multinational corporations, which are often the source of environmental and ecological devastation through their actions or inaction and neglect. Earlier in this chapter we discussed the conflict between the capitalist mantra of growth and progress-at-all-costs (see also Varona, 2021), on the one hand, and sustainability and the need to protect the environment, on the other. Prioritising the former often leads to the strategic denial of harms or to resistance to what may be deemed 'difficult knowledge' (see above). ERJ can help

---

9 The importance of ecological restoration is also recognised in international legal scholarship, which sees it not only as essential to the survival of the planet (and of life on it) but also to the avoidance of global conflicts over ecosystem services and benefits, and to the achievement of social and environmental justice for current and future generations (see, for example Telesetsky, Cliquet, and Akhtar-Khavari, 2016). It should be noted here that such scholarship tends to be 'intentionally focused on ecological restoration ultimately benefitting human beings' (ibid, p. 39).

overcome state and corporate denial in specific practical cases, encouraging acknowledgement of the harms caused and the need to take responsibility for these, ultimately leading to action to repair such harms.

Ensuring that corporations become active participants in RJ circles is, however, not an easy task, most notably as it necessarily requires them to *acknowledge* the harms that they have caused, affecting human and non-human animals, plants, the environment, and entire ecosystems. Acknowledging harms goes hand in hand with taking responsibility for them. However, more often than not, corporations deny such responsibility, as in the case of the operations of the fossil fuel giant Shell in the Niger delta. In this area regular oil spills have contaminated the water stream, killing fish, increasing human mortality rates, and damaging local communities' livelihoods based on farming and fishing (South, 2015), leading to a number of transnational lawsuits filed against Shell in both Dutch and English courts.[10] Recently, nearly 14 000 affected people took Shell to court asking the company to clean up water pollution and to provide compensation for the loss of livelihood and the damages caused to communal properties (Laville, 2023). As Laville (2023) reports however: 'The company says it bears no responsibility for the clandestine siphoning off of oil from its pipelines by organised gangs, which it says causes many of the spills'. Many neutralisation techniques have so far been used by the oil giant, including denial of responsibility, which, in this specific case, involved blaming others for the spills, whether they are organised crime networks (as in the quote above) or Shell's own local subsidiaries. In essence, after 80 years of extremely profitable operations, Shell is leaving the Niger delta without addressing the environmental pollution and damages it has caused.

The second challenge we want to address here focuses on the representation of the 'more-than-human' in ERJ circles and conferences. Indeed, ERJ also poses questions about how to make sure that the voices of all parties – including the harmed more-than-human – are effectively heard during ERJ processes (Pali and Aertsen, 2021; Forsyth, Pali and Tepper, 2022). This challenge is significant given the ontological impossibility of humans *knowing* what it means to be a river, a mountain, a non-human animal, or a plant.

In some cases, such as in New Zealand, Colombia, Ecuador, India, and Uganda (Pali and Aertsen, 2021; Haluska, 2023), more-than-human entities have been given the status of legal subjects to be protected, which can be upheld in court. But even in such cases, the challenge is not overcome. In practice, the issue is resolved through a fiction: non-human subjects are represented by humans – mainly by 'guardians' or custodians with local knowledge and a distinctive (often spiritual) place attachment, such as Indigenous Peoples, local communities, and also environmental activists (Forsyth et al, 2021). In fact, as the interdisciplinary projects discussed below illustrate, every one of us could potentially become a guardian. As the artist, activist, and researcher

---

10 See, for example https://www.business-humanrights.org/en/latest-news/nigeria-shell-settles-lawsuit-in-the-netherlands-for-15-million-over-oil-spillages-in-niger-delta/.

Maria Lucia Cruz Correia (2021, p. 168) cogently put it: 'To be a guardian of nature means to hold a cosmological view of people as part of nature, not separate from nor above it, to abide to an ethic of reciprocity and to have a sacred regard for all living species as kin. As Māori people share in the Whanganui's declaration of identity, "I am the river, the river is me"'.

Many innovative, interdisciplinary projects have investigated and tested new ways to 'be with' nature and encourage their participants to hear the voices of, for example, rivers, non-human animals, and plants, and become their guardians. Such interdisciplinary projects have often involved the arts, social sciences, and law, among others – all disciplines that meet in the terrain of imagination (Pali et al, 2022) through the skilful mediation of the arts. Art, in particular, provides a 'space in between' (Pali et al, 2022 p. 395) that facilitates connections, accountability, and repair, and opens up new ways of imagining our relationship with Earth and its species and ecosystems.

For example, the recent performative, participatory, and immersive art project *Voice of Nature: The Trial* by artist Correia (2021) used the example of ecocide in Ecuador to explore ways for participants to develop an empathetic, ecocentric perspective that allows them to become guardians of nature. As the leading artist argued, the project is an 'artistic speculative model to become a guardian of nature – a legal representative of a non-human entity' (Correia, 2021, p. 168); such a model invites participants to decolonise themselves and open up to a new type of relationship with the environment, one that enables them to hear the voices of the more-than-human and care for them through legal and extra-legal struggles.

Hosted in the Old Court of Ghent (Belgium), *Voice of Nature: The Trial* built on previous experiences of mock trials that tested how an international crime of ecocide would work in practice. This performative 'restorative trial' experimented with using RJ to repair harms to nature (obviously, only when harms are acknowledged by those who have caused them, and pending their willing participation) and, crucially, also attempted to hear the voice of nature and legally recognise its rights (see Pali et al, 2022, p. 387). Noteworthy earlier examples include the famous mock trial hosted in 2011 by the UK Supreme Court on the initiative of lawyer and activist Polly Higgins, and the follow-up sentencing event a year later in our own institution – the University of Essex – which also involved guardians representing birds and other natural life.[11]

Another creative, interdisciplinary attempt to represent more-than-human voices was imagined and developed within the project *Walking-with-Zenne*, which started at the beginning of 2021 and involved a group of researchers, artists, locals, and interested people (Pali et al, 2022). The project focused on engaging – 'being with' – the Belgian river Zenne, a river that has been polluted, diverted, harmed, and taken for granted throughout the centuries (Pali et al, 2022). Participants attempted to 'be with' Zenne through walking – a mundane yet powerful act that engages all senses (see, for

11 See https://www1.essex.ac.uk/news/event.aspx?e_id=4036.

example O'Neill and Roberts, 2019; McClanahan and South, 2020), invites an attitude of respect, and enables the establishment of a connection between walkers, the river, and 'her' (Zenne is indeed a 'she', see Pali et al, 2022) surrounding environment. The project also involved the use of a number of artistic wooden objects or 'props' which assisted participants – practically or symbolically – in the practices of observing, listening, and collecting while 'mapping the river' – her relationships, harms, repair and resistance attempts and processes, etc. For example, to hear the voice of the river during an RJ circle, the project involved the use of an underwater microphone connected to a listening antenna (one of the artistic props). Through such symbolic prompts, Zenne could speak for herself, with her own voice, and be collectively listened to within the RJ circle. At the end of the walk and immersive experience, enriched by new ideas and imaginaries, and cherishing a new connection with Zenne, participants co-created a 'guardian of nature contract': they embraced an ecocentric perspective that envisages humans as part of nature – not above it – and took responsibility to protect and care for the river and her future conservation and thriving.

What these recent interdisciplinary ERJ projects demonstrate is that positive, empathetic, caring, ecocentric attitudes towards nature could reside in (at least some) people and emerge from them while they are immersed in damaged or endangered environments, or while confronted with sensory, affective, and emotional clues and information on ecocide and harms to nature (on this point, see also Di Ronco, 2023). Such an attitude – which very much features people who mobilise for eco-justice – is a necessary prerequisite to actions aimed at repairing present and preventing future harms, and to discussions challenging our current ecocidal lifestyle that relies so much on extraction, exploitation, and dominance of nature. Finding ways to facilitate the emergence and activation of such attitudes – through interdisciplinary projects and beyond – seems crucial to the survival of our planet.

4. Concluding thoughts

Following the interdisciplinary direction taken in green criminology, in this chapter we have drawn upon an interdisciplinary body of work to describe some environmental crimes and ecocidal trends which have gathered pace over roughly the past 70 years. We have also discussed the largely insufficient steps taken so far to protect the environment at the local, national, and international levels, and found encouragement only when addressing the practice and ethos of ERJ. As explained above, while ERJ is mostly focused on repairing past harms, it also activates a process of capacity building within affected communities that enables them to (re)construct relations – both within them and with nature – and prevent future harms. More generally, as the interdisciplinary projects mentioned above have demonstrated, many among us have in their 'inner worlds', the 'seeds' (Komatsubara, 2022) of ecocentric cosmologies, which – if allowed to germinate and grow – could enable people to become allies or guardians of nature, helping them to engage in empathic attempts to understand the interests, needs, and pain of nature and defend it legally or through activist practices.

Finding ways to facilitate such germination – through ERJ, interdisciplinary projects and beyond – seems to us urgent and essential to the survival of life on our planet.

References

Adams, M. (2021) 'Critical psychologies and climate change', *Current Opinion in Psychology*, 42, pp. 13–18.

Berger, J. (1972) *Ways of Seeing*. London: Penguin.

Brisman, A. (2013) 'The violence of silence: Some reflections on access to information, public participation in decision-making, and access to justice in matters concerning the environment', *Crime, Law and Social Change*, 59, pp. 291–303.

Brisman, A. and South, N. (2014) *Green cultural criminology: Constructions of environmental harm, consumerism, and resistance to ecocide*. Abingdon: Routledge.

Britzman, D. (1998) *Lost subjects, contested objects: toward a psychoanalytic inquiry of learning*. Albany, NY: State University of New York Press.

Brown, D. (2010) 'Is climate science disinformation a crime against humanity?', *The Guardian*, 1 November 2010. Available at: https://www.theguardian.com/environment/cif-green/2010/nov/01/climate-science-disinformation-crime (Accessed: 16 March 2023).

Bryan, A. (2022) 'Pedagogy of the implicated: Advancing a social ecology of responsibility framework to promote deeper understanding of the climate crisis', *Pedagogy, Culture & Society*, 30(3), pp. 329–48.

Carson, R. (1965) *Silent Spring*. Reprint, Harmondsworth: Penguin [originally published 1962, Boston: Houghton Mifflin].

Correia, M. (2021) 'Voice of nature: The trial. An artistic response for environmental justice', *The International Journal of Restorative Justice*, 4(1), pp. 166–71.

Darpö, J. (2021) 'Can Nature Get it Right?', European Parliament, Directorate-General for Internal Policies, PE 689.328- March 2021. Available at: https://www.europarl.europa.eu/RegData/etudes/STUD/2021/689328/IPOL_STU(2021)689328_EN.pdf (Accessed: 18 July 2023).

Davies, P., Francis, P., and Wyatt, T. (eds) (2014) *Invisible crimes and social harms*. Basingstoke: Palgrave.

Del Olmo, R. (1987) 'Aerobiology and the war on drugs', *Crime and Social Justice*, 30, pp. 28–44.

De Sousa Santos, B. (2014) *Epistemologies of the South: Justice against epistemicide*. Boulder: Paradigm.

Di Ronco, A. (2023) *Policing environmental protest: Power and resistance in pandemic times*. Bristol: Bristol University Press.

Di Ronco, A. and Chiaramonte, X. (2022) 'Harm to knowledge: Criminalising environmental movements speaking up against megaprojects' in Pali, B., Forsyth, M., and Tepper, F. (eds) *The Palgrave handbook of environmental restorative justice*. Cham: Palgrave, pp. 421–47.

Dobson, G. (2022) 'Wired to doubt: Why people fear vaccines and climate change and mistrust science', *Frontiers in Medicine*, 8, doi:10.3389/fmed.2021.809395.

European Environment Agency (2023) *How pesticides impact human health and ecosystems in Europe*, EEA Briefing no. 06/2023. Available at: https://www.eea.europa.eu/publications/how-pesticides-impact-human-health (Accessed: 14 March 2025).

Forsyth, M., Cleland, D., Tepper, F., Hollingworth, D., Soares, M., Nairn, A., and Wilkinson, C. (2021) 'A future agenda for environmental restorative justice', *The International Journal of Restorative Justice*, 4(1), pp. 17–40.

Forsyth, M., Pali, B., and Tepper, F. (2022) 'Environmental restorative justice: An introduction and an invitation' in Pali, B., Forsyth, M., and Tepper, F. (eds) *The Palgrave handbook of environmental restorative justice*. Cham: Palgrave, pp. 1–24.

Franko Aas, K. (2012) '"The Earth is one but the world is not": Criminological theory and its geopolitical divisions', *Theoretical Criminology*, 16(1), pp. 5–20.

Goergen, R. (2022) 'The problem with CITES, the convention to protect endangered wildlife', *Geographical*, 28 April 2022. Available at: https://geographical.co.uk/wildlife/the-problem-with-the-cites-endangered-wildlife-convention (Accessed: 14 March 2025).

Goyes, D. (2016) 'Green activist criminology and the epistemologies of the South', *Critical Criminology*, 24, pp. 503–18.

Goyes, D. and South, N. (2019) 'Between "conservation" and "development": The construction of 'protected nature' and the environmental disenfranchisement of indigenous communities', *International Journal for Crime, Justice and Social Democracy*, 8(3), pp. 89–104.

Goyes, D., Abaibira, M., Baicué, P., Cuchimba, A., Ñeñetofe, D., Sollund, R., South, N., and Wyatt, T. (2021) 'Southern green cultural criminology and environmental crime prevention: representations of nature within four Colombian Indigenous communities', *Critical Criminology*, 29, pp. 469–85.

Guynup, S. (2022) 'Rachel Carson's "Silent Spring" 60 years on: Birds still fading from the skies', *Mongabay*, 23 May 2022. Available at: https://news.mongabay.com/2022/05/rachel-carsons-silent-spring-60-years-on-birds-still-fading-from-the-skies/ (Accessed: 16 March 2023).

Haluska, A. (2023) 'Restorative justice and the rights of nature: Using indigenous legal traditions to influence cultural change and promote environmental protection', *Mitchell Hamline Law Review*, 49(1), 91. Available at: https://open.mitchellhamline.edu/cgi/viewcontent.cgi?article=1309&context=mhlr (Accessed: 8 March 2023).

Hamilton, M. (2021) 'Restorative justice conferencing in Australia and New Zealand: Application and potential in an environmental and Aboriginal cultural heritage protection context', *The International Journal of Restorative Justice*, 4(1), pp. 81–97.

Harvey, M. (2021) *Climate emergency*. Bingley: Emerald.

Higgins, P., Short, D., and South, N. (2013) 'Protecting the planet: A proposal for a law of ecocide', *Crime, Law and Social Change*, 59(3), pp. 251–66.

Hook, L. and Wisniewska, A. (2020) 'Saving the planet after saving ourselves', *The I*, 21 April 2020, pp. 34–5.

IPCC (2022) *Climate change 2022: Impacts, adaptation and vulnerability*. Available at: https://www.ipcc.ch/report/ar6/wg2/ (Accessed: 16 March 2023).

Joint Nature Conservation Committee (JNCC) (2019) *Convention on International Trade in Endangered Species of Wild Fauna and Flora (CITES)*, Convention summary. Available at: https://jncc.gov.uk/our-work/convention-on-international-trade-in-endangered-species-of-wild-fauna-and-flora-cites/. (Accessed: 14 March 2025).

Killean, R. (2021) 'From ecocide to eco-sensitivity: "Greening" reparations at the International Criminal Court', *The International Journal of Human Rights*, 25(2), pp. 323–47.

Komatsubara, O. (2021) 'Imagining a community that includes non-human beings: The 1990s Moyainaoshi movement in Minamata, Japan', *The International Journal of Restorative Justice*, 4(1), pp. 123–40.

Komatsubara, O. (2022) 'Exploring environmental restorative philosophy for victims: The pollution and life-world in Minamata, Japan' in Pali, B., Forsyth, M., and Tepper, F. (eds) *The Palgrave handbook of environmental restorative justice*. Cham: Palgrave, pp. 361–84.

Kramer, R. (2020) *Carbon criminals, climate crimes*. New Brunswick: Rutgers University Press.

Lam, A., South, N., and Brisman, A. (2022) 'A convergence of crises: COVID-19, climate change and bunkerization', *Crime, Media, Culture*, pp. 1–18. doi:17416590221120581.

Laville, S. (2023) 'Nearly 14000 Nigerians take Shell to court over devastating impact of pollution', *The Guardian*, 2 February 2023. Available at: https://www.theguardian.com/world/2023/feb/02/nearly-14000-nigerians-take-shell-to-court-over-devastating-impact-of-pollution (Accessed: 15 March 2023).

McClanahan, B. and South, N. (2020) '"All knowledge begins with the senses": Toward a sensory criminology', *British Journal of Criminology*, 60(1), pp. 3–23.

McGoey, L. (2012) 'The logic of strategic ignorance', *The British Journal of Sociology*, 63(3), pp. 533–76.

Milman, O. (2023) 'Revealed: Exxon made "breathtakingly" accurate climate predictions in 1970s and 80s', *The Guardian*, 12 January 2023. Available at: https://www.theguardian.com/business/2023/jan/12/exxon-climate-change-global-warming-research (Accessed: 16 March 2023).

Monbiot, G. (2019) 'Britain's dirty secret: The burning tyres choking India', *The Guardian*, 30 January 2019. Available at: https://www.theguardian.com/commentisfree/2019/jan/30/worse-than-plastic-burning-tyres-india-george-monbiot (Accessed: 14 March 2025).

Nelleman, C. and Interpol. (2012) *Green carbon, black trade: Illegal logging, tax fraud and laundering in the worlds tropical forests*. Available at: https://www.grida.no/publications/126 (Accessed: 16 March 2023).

O'Neill, M. and Roberts, B. (2019) *Walking methods: Research on the move*. London: Routledge.

Pali, B. and Aertsen, I. (2021) 'Inhabiting a vulnerable and wounded earth: Restoring response-ability', *The International Journal of Restorative Justice*, 4(1), pp. 3–16.

Pali, B., Cruz Correia, M.C., Calmet, M., Jones, V., Vranken, L., Mendes, M., Nowak, E. and Požlep, M. (2022) 'The art of repair: bridging artistic and restorative responses to environmental harm and ecocide' in Pali, B., Forsyth, M., and Tepper, F. (eds.) *The Palgrave handbook of environmental restorative justice*. Cham: Palgrave, pp. 385–419.

Pali, B., Forsyth, M., and Tepper, F. (2022) *The Palgrave handbook of environmental restorative justice*. Cham: Palgrave.

Papadopoulos, D., de la Bellacasa, M., and Tacchetti, M. (2023) *Ecological reparation: Repair, remediation and resurgence in social and environmental conflict*. Bristol: Bristol University Press.

Passas, N. (2005) 'Lawful but awful: "Legal corporate crimes"', *Journal of Socio-Economics*, 34(6), pp. 771–86.

Pointer, L. and Pali, B. (2022) 'Editorial: Advancing restorative justice through art', *International Journal of Restorative Justice*, 5(3), pp. 315–22.

Rockström, J et al. (2009) 'Planetary boundaries: Exploring the safe operating space for humanity', *Ecology and Society*, 14(2), p. 32.

Rome, A. (2003) '"Give Earth a chance": The environmental movement and the sixties', *The Journal of American History*, 90(2), pp. 525–54.

Ruggiero, V. and South, N. (2013) 'Green Criminology and crimes of the economy: Theory, research and praxis', *Critical Criminology*, 21, pp. 359–73.

Rutjens, B.T., van der Linden, S., and van der Lee, R. (2021) 'Science skepticism in times of COVID-19', *Group Processes & Intergroup Relations*, 24(2), pp. 276–83.

South, N. (2012) 'Climate change, environmental (in)security, conflict and crime' in Farrall, S., French, D., and Ahmed, T. (eds) *Climate change: Legal and criminological implications*. Oxford: Hart, pp. 97–111.

South, N (2014a) 'Foreword: seeing the invisible' in Davies, P., Francis, P., and Wyatt, T. (eds) *Invisible Crimes and Social Harms*. London: Palgrave, pp. vii–viii.

South, N. (2014b) 'Green criminology, environmental crime prevention and the gaps between law, legitimacy and justice', *Journal of Criminal Investigation and Criminology* (*Revija za Kriminalistiko in Kriminologijo*), 65(4) pp. 373–81.

South, N. (2015). 'Green criminology, brown crime and problems of despoiling, disposal and de-manufacturing in global resource industries' in Wyatt, T. (ed) *Hazardous Waste and Pollution: Detecting and Preventing Green Crimes*. London: Springer.

South, N. (2016) 'Free trade agreements, private courts and environmental exploitation: Disconnected policies, denials and moral disengagement', *International Journal for Crime, Justice and Social Democracy*, 5(4), pp. 45–59.

South, N. (2023) 'Revisiting Rosa: Eco-bio-genocide, drug wars and Southern green criminology' in Goyes, D. (ed) *Green crime in the Global South: Essays on Southern green criminology*. Bingley: Emerald.

Stone, C. (1972) 'Should trees have standing? Towards legal rights for natural objects', *Southern California Law Review*, 45, pp. 450–501.

Stop Ecocide International (2021) *Legal definition of ecocide: an historic moment*. Available at: https://www.stopecocide.earth/legal-definition. (Accessed: 12 March 2024).

Stretesky, P., Long, M., and Lynch, M. (2013) *The treadmill of crime: Political economy and green criminology*. Abingdon: Routledge.

Telesetsky, A., Cliquet, A., and Akhtar-Khavari, A. (2016) *Ecological restoration in international environmental law*. London and New York: Routledge.

Thiel, D. and South, N. (2022) 'Criminal ignorance, environmental harms and processes of denial' in Gross, M. and McGoey, L. (eds) *Routledge international handbook of ignorance studies*. Abingdon: Routledge, pp. 334–44.

Udall, S. (1963) *The quiet crisis*. New York: Holt, Rinehart and Winston.

UNODC (2020) *Wildlife crime and Covid 19*. Available at: https://www.unodc.org/unodc/en/environment-climate/covid-19.html (Accessed: 17 March 2025).

UNODC and WWF (2022) *Crimes that affect the environment and climate change*. Available at: https://www.worldwildlife.org/publications/crimes-that-affect-the-environment-and-climate-change (Accessed: 14 March 2025).

Urry, J. (2011) *Climate change and society*. Cambridge: Polity Press.

Varona, G. (2021) 'Why an atmosphere of transhumanism undermines green restorative justice concepts and tenets', *The International Journal of Restorative Justice*, 4(1), pp. 41–59.

Vidal, J., Stratton, A., and Goldenberg, S. (2009) 'Low targets, goals dropped: Copenhagen ends in failure', *The Guardian*, 19 December 2009. Available at: https://www.theguardian.com/environment/2009/dec/18/copenhagen-deal. (Accessed: 16 March 2023).

White, R. (2022) 'Restorative justice, repairing the harm and environmental outcomes' in Pali, B., Forsyth, M., and Tepper, F. (eds) *The Palgrave handbook of environmental restorative justice*. Cham: Palgrave, pp. 27–50.

Widowaty, Y., Astuti, L., and Adrian, M. (2022) 'Towards a restorative justice system for environmental waste pollution in Indonesia', *Environmental Engineering & Management Journal*, 21(11), pp. 1877–87.

Wijdekop, F. (2019) *Restorative justice responses to environmental harm*. Amsterdam: IUCN.

Wyatt, T. (2021) *Is CITES protecting wildlife? Assessing implementation and compliance*. Abingdon: Routledge.

10 A green criminology perspective on animal rights

Ragnhild Sollund

Introduction

In this chapter, I will present the ways in which the rights of animals and nature are regarded within the growing field of criminology commonly referred to as green criminology (Beirne and South, 2007) or eco-global criminology (White, 2012), and show why such perspectives are crucial in the present nature crisis and in view of the increasing knowledge we have obtained about the abilities of non-human animals. Part of the analysis will focus on how the perception of animal rights within green criminology differs from the ways in which animals and their rights have been perceived generally and traditionally in criminology. Additionally, I will analyse how the anthropocentrism that characterises how animals are regarded therein also characterises the international nature conventions implemented in order to protect endangered animal species from extinction, such as the Convention on International Trade in Endangered Species of Wild Fauna and Flora (CITES) and the Council of Europe Bern Convention which mainly aims to protect wildlife and their habitats in Europe. My main focus is on animals who are born free, so-called wildlife,[1] and animals who are close descendants of animals who were born free and therefore are not adapted to a life in captivity. This does not imply that I do not regard animals who are usually kept under human dominion as 'nature', or as less of an animal than those who are born free and not meriting attention, but since my concern herein is with animal rights in nature conventions, my focus remains with those who are usually defined within the concept of wildlife. I will start by briefly sketching out important perspectives in the field of green criminology and how they relate to animal rights.

---

1 Both 'animal' and 'wildlife' are anthropocentric words that create a difference between the human animal and all other animals who, between species and individuals, differ more than, for example a human and a chimpanzee, who are placed on each end of the artificial human-animal dichotomy. 'Wildlife' is a mass term that fails to incorporate individual intrinsic value and interest. For simplicity, and with regret, I use both 'animal' and wildlife herein.

Green criminology and species (in)justice[2]

Mainstream criminology has traditionally focused on crimes – that is, in breach of the law – offenders, crime prevention, and the consequences of punishment, such as imprisonment and deterrence, whether for the individual offender or for the general public. Green criminology is rooted in critical criminology (Sollund, 2015), a field that is conscious of the crimes of the powerful, the need to engage with social movements (Ellefsen, 2016; Goyes, 2018) and often employs Marxist critiques of capitalism (for example Lynch and Stretesky, 2016). Rather than only focusing on what is criminalised, green criminology acknowledges that many environmental harms committed around the world are not criminalised, yet may be equally, or even more, harmful, for example, global warming causing ecocide (White, 2018a). For instance, during the wildfires in Australia in 2020, more than three billion animals were killed, injured or displaced: 'In total, 143 million mammals, 2.46 billion reptiles, 180 million birds, and 51 million frogs were harmed' (WWF, 2020). Despite such disastrous results, legally speaking, the actions that together contribute to climate change are harms rather than crimes.

In addition, often environmental crimes, including animal abuse and wildlife crimes, result in administrative sanctions such as fines. When concerning corporate environmental crimes, such administrative sanctions often lack a deterrent effect because they are simply a cost that corporations will pass on to consumers (Faure et al., 2016; Ruggiero and South, 2010). Green criminologists therefore sought to engage also with harms that are leniently criminalised or not criminalised because of the weakness of environmental law (Lynch and Stretesky, 2016; Ruggiero and South, 2010). However, generally, criminologists have only focused on a very small range of harmful human behaviour that, given the critical effects of humans' environmentally harmful acts, has proven too limited. A harms perspective is therefore central to green criminological study (South, 2008; White, 2013; Sollund, 2019), with a critical victimology that includes non-human victims of harm (for example Nurse and Wyatt, 2021; Spencer and Fitzgerald, 2013; Sollund, 2016; White, 2018b).

As a prolongation of this, much attention in green criminology is paid to the human-inflicted suffering of animals, particularly those suffering from what has been defined as wildlife crime (Nurse and Wyatt, 2021), for example wildlife trafficking (for example Wyatt, 2013, van Uhm, 2016; Sollund, 2019). Harms involved in hunting and trafficking, for example, are breaches of animal rights and species justice (Beirne, 2007; White, 2013; Sollund, 2013). Species justice implies ensuring the wellbeing both of species as a whole and of individual animals, who should be shielded from abuse, degradation, displacement, and torture (White, 2013). Species justice relates to two other important analytical foci in green criminology: *environmental justice*, where the main focus is on differences between human populations and their access to environmental

2 Parts of this section are adapted from Sollund, R. (2023).

rights;[3] and *ecological justice*, where the main focus is on 'the environment' as such, and the aim to conserve and protect ecological wellbeing, for example of forests, is seen as intrinsically worthwhile (White, 2013).

Traditionally, while animal abuse in most countries is a criminalised harm (Beirne, 2009), where some sort of legislation against animal cruelty exists, generally, animals' status as property (Francione 2008) overrules their intrinsic value and interests, and their use value reduces their legal protection (for example Sollund, 2021). Even when the judicial system recognises that a crime against an animal has been committed, the punishment is usually lenient, if punished at all. Much harm is done to animals in the name of, for example, entertainment in circuses, zoos, and aquaparks, hobby hunting, and for science (for example Sollund, 2021). While animals who are protected under animal welfare legislation should enjoy protection, there exists a hierarchy between species that determines whether or not harms and crimes against them will be punished and to what extent. For example, some species are regarded as 'iconic' or 'charismatic', like elephants, while others are regarded as 'meat', such as pigs. Naming and regarding some species as 'charismatic' and others not, is, however, also an aspect of speciesism, through which the value of the species is judged by the likes or dislikes of humans, rather than by, for example, the importance a species has for its ecosystem. Moreover, it should be noted that much environmental harm is legal, for example in many countries male chickens are ground alive in factory farms (Sollund, 2021). In comparison, the live grinding of unwanted puppies would create outrage and likely entail harsh punishment in the Western world,[4] since a dog in the West is regarded as having greater value than a chick.

While there exists animal welfare legislation supposedly aiming at creating a normative foundation for the good treatment of animals, there are plenty of exceptions in which the harms inflicted on animals are not acknowledged as such, for example in the slaughter process, which is regulated yet harmful, of course (Joy, 2020; Gålmark 2008; Sollund, 2021), or is simply ignored. For example, to be killed by the use of carbon dioxide is extremely painful, but its use is regulated in slaughter regulations (Sollund, 2021).

Wildlife has even less protection since it is regarded as a 'mass', which serves to undermine individual protection (Sollund, 2019). After all, most free-born animals can be legally hunted and shot, just as animals referred to as 'livestock' are bred to be killed and 'lab rats' are bred to be used in experiments and then 'sacrificed'. There are rules meant to protect animals who are exploited from *unnecessary* harm, whether in the food sector, laboratories, or in the woods, such as through the Norwegian wildlife law,

---

[3] See the European Commission about the Aarhus declaration with regards to the legal framework for access to environmental justice in United Nations Economic Commission for Europe (UNECE) states.

[4] In several other countries, for example China and South Korea, dogs (and cats) are regarded as food and are treated in ways that are regarded as appalling in most Western countries, such as during the dog meat festival in Yulin.

which regulates hunting, for example what kind of weapons may be used for which species, time of year, and so on but such legislation may have more of a symbolic than protective effect, although different standards apply across different countries (Francione, 2008; Beirne, 2009; Ellefsen, 2009; Sollund, 2021). One such symbolic effect is the function of creating a general perception in society that animals are protected from harm and that humans treat them well. This, again, reinforces and prolongs the harms that are caused to animals and serves as a false justification. This is because such legislation is primarily implemented to protect anthropocentric interests, rather than to protect animals from human-inflicted suffering. The reason for this lack of recognition of the harms that humans cause to animals is the overarching ideologies of modern society that are created by humans for their own good.

Anthropocentrism and speciesism

Anthropocentrism largely directs human interaction with the natural world and, generally, ecosystems and their inhabitants are regarded as resources for human exploitation, determined by the Aristotelian view that there exists a hierarchy of species placing the human animal on the top, and all other species below (Sollund, 2008). Speciesism is thus the other wheel in the governing anthropocentrism that penetrates the human-animal relationship. Speciesism is humans' discrimination, degradation, and oppression of non-human animal species based on them being non-human, and is analogous to other 'isms' such as racism and sexism. Speciesism is both ideology and practice (Nibert, 2002), and the two are mutually reinforcing one another. This ideology entails both a structural, systemic, and systematic discrimination of animals other than humans, which is deeply engrained in cultural ideas and practices (Cazaux, 1999; Sollund 2008), such as meat eating or carnism (Gålmark 2008) and hunting (Lynch et al., 2015; Sollund, 2017; 2021). That animals are used is regarded as part and parcel of daily practice; it is doxa, that is, it is taken for granted (Bourdieu 2020; Sollund 2012).

Another important vehicle in speciesism that upholds the abusive character of the human-animal relationship is denial (Sollund, 2008; Vetlesen, 2015). Denial is a mechanism by which humans can reject emotions that could guide their actions in another direction; they can reject the empathy that would otherwise be produced through witnessing and causing suffering (Cohen, 2001). Denial is supported by physical, mental, and social distance, in addition to the aforementioned illusion that animals are protected from harm (Sollund, 2008). Factors that are important in causing animal abuse can be summed up as the three Ds, standing for difference, distance, and denial (Sollund 2008; 2023).

This stands in contrast to species justice, but also to ecocentrism and biocentrism, which are eco-philosophical orientations that acknowledge the intrinsic value of each of the components of ecosystems and their mutual interdependency (Næss, 1984; Halsey and White, 1998). With roots in Indigenous populations' relationships to nature, for example, rivers in several jurisdictions, such as Colombia, New Zealand,

and Australia have been attributed with legal personhood rights (O'Donnell and Macpherson, 2019), and lawyers in the United States (US) are working to achieve legal personhood rights for non-humans (Lynch, 2023; Wise, 2018).

Animal rights: what should they be?

While the struggle for non-human animal rights is ongoing, it is timely to consider what such rights should consist of, and why. Many animals have the same sensory capacities as – or better than – humans, and are highly intelligent, such as octopuses (Godfrey-Smith, 2016), many bird species (Pepperberg, 1999; Martinho-Truswell, 2022) and cetaceans (King and Jensen, 2022). Like humans, many species are social beings who interact with their family groups and flocks, whether parrots, dolphins, or wolves (as examples of wildlife groups), or sheep and cows (as examples of 'domesticated' animal species). Just as it would be cruel to separate a human mother from her offspring, it would be cruel to separate a chimpanzee, a wolf, a cow, or a crow from theirs. In spite of this, such separations take place all the time, for example when calves are taken away from their mothers to be slaughtered, when chimpanzee babies are taken from their mothers (who may often be killed) to be part of the international wildlife trade – whether for the pet trade or for the pharmaceutical industry – or when family groups of wolves are slaughtered by means of shotgun fire from helicopters, as is the case in Norway. One right could therefore be to not be forcefully and/or violently separated from offspring before the separation process animals go through has come to a natural end, and the right to not have to witness the theriocide (Beirne, 2014) of your family members. In that regard, it deserves mentioning that, for example, in the case of wolves, offspring will naturally continue to hang around with their parents for years, helping out with new pups.

The most essential right is, however, the right to live and not be subjected to human-orchestrated, violent premature death. This right was also established in the 1978 United Nations Educational, Scientific and Cultural Organization (UNESCO) declaration of animal rights (Wordpress, 1978) as the first animal right. This is not a universal declaration of animal rights like the United Nations human rights declaration, but was presented by a non-governmental organisation (NGO) at the UNESCO meeting and can be regarded as a draft of what animal rights could consist of, were they to be acknowledged. Other important rights proposed in this declaration are that animals should be entitled to respect and have the right to fulfil their natural lifespans; rights that are incompatible with the governing ideology of speciesism. In addition, no animal should be subject to ill-treatment or cruel acts and should have the right to liberty in their natural environment as well as the right to procreate.

Animal welfare organisations argue for the five freedoms (ASPCA, undated). These are particularly relevant for animals who are captives. They are: *freedom from hunger and thirst; freedom from discomfort; freedom from pain, injury, or disease; freedom to express normal behavior; and freedom from fear and distress.* While the five freedoms should be guaranteed to all animals who are held in captivity, with the pace of the anthropogenic destruction of the world and, consequently, of the natural habitats of many species, ways in which humans could assist wildlife in enjoying these freedoms deserve consideration and expansion, for example by providing animals with food and water and shelter from storms and heat, as well as in the form of rescue programmes such as wildlife rehabilitation centres where animals who are victims of trafficking crimes, war, and wildlife fires can be rehabilitated. While NGOs (for example War Paws, undated) that do such work exist, this should also be the responsibility of states that are participatory agents in such harmful acts. The right to a clean natural environment would imply the accomplishment of species justice and eco-justice and resonate with environmental rights, as these are envisioned for humans.

Where to draw the line – and should a line be drawn?[5]

A question that frequently comes up in the discussion of animal rights is which species precisely should be entitled to rights (for example Regan, 2004). The Nonhuman right project (NrHP)[6] run court cases for particular individual elephants and chimpanzees who are regarded as meriting the status of legal persons rather than 'things' due to their capacity for autonomy; ability to act voluntarily; and ability to control one's behaviour according to one's preferences and goals (Wise, 2018). While a large number of species share these abilities, the choice of these particular individuals and species may again be contingent on a form of speciesism through which some species are regarded as more deserving of rights than others. The case for non-human animal rights would perhaps not have the same potential impact and success were it to concentrate on pigs, who are among the most intelligent animals on Earth and whose flesh is on dinner tables in many countries. The use value humans place on animals counteracts the recognition of rights of the animals who are used.

Regan (2004) argues that rights should be accorded to different species depending on their degree of sentience and (self-)awareness. Various pieces of animal welfare legislation, be it national, as in the United Kingdom (UK) and Norway, or international, as in European Union (EU) legislation,[7] have made a point of animal sentience. Primordially, according to Regan, primates should thus be accorded rights. However, the mirror test that is supposed to indicate an individual's self-awareness has proven that a wide range of species are capable of recognising the spot that is painted on their body and will try to remove it after having seen it in the mirror, which is considered an indication of self-awareness. Animals who have performed well include dolphins (Morrison and Reiss, 2018) and elephants (Plotnik et al., 2006), as one would expect due to their intelligence. A recent study showed, however, that the cleaner fish *Labroides dimidiatus* also passed the self-recognition mirror test (Kohda et al., 2023).

5 This part of the chapter is adapted from a work for Oxford University Press (Sollund et al., 2024).

6 The NhRP is a civil rights organisation in the US that dedicates its work to securing rights for non-human animals. See https://www.nonhumanrights.org/about-us/.

7 https://eur-lex.europa.eu/EN/legal-content/glossary/animal-welfare.html.

They were able to recognise their own face in a photograph. While most people perhaps do not find it surprising that species like great apes, dolphins, and elephants can perform well in such tests, the fact that the cleaner fish also accomplished this should be a call for caution.

Tool use is another sign of intelligence, and to document the ability to use tools, experiments have been carried out among, for example different species of birds, such as parrots and bullfinches, crows, and apes (Audet et al., 2016). That birds and apes are intelligent tool users who can also save tools for future use is well established (Ackerman, 2017; Mulcahy and Call, 2006). Crows and corvids are generally known to be very intelligent – capable of making and using their own tools (St Clair et al., 2016), which are part of cultural transmissions (Rutz et al., 2018). They recognise human faces and alert each other to those who are kind and those who display unfriendly behaviour towards them (Marzluff et al., 2010; Sollund, 2021). Some researchers believe crows are as intelligent as apes (Balakhonov and Rose, 2017). According to Balakhonov and Rose (2017), the results of their study show that crows, like primates, evolved a high working memory capacity that reflects the result of convergent evolution of higher cognitive abilities in both species.

An example of animal intelligence and creativity in a very different species, which also an argument for why animal rights should extend to species that are not yet included in the NhRP project, is the geometric perfection of the decoration the puffer fish creates to attract a partner, as documented by BBC Earth (undated). Another example demonstrates planning and cooperation among clownfish, as they were filmed finding, and together moving, half a coconut shell towards the anemone on which they lived, to provide the matriarch with a place to lay her eggs (BBC Earth, undated).

Bumblebees are also proven to have culture and can learn to use tools through cultural transmission (Bridges et al., 2022). Bumblebees have been taught to pull a string to get a snack, and they also learnt by watching other bumblebees doing it (Chittka, 2017). Chittka describes how bumblebees could solve a string-pulling puzzle and learnt by individual trial-and-error learning (Chittka, 2017).

The intention, with these examples, is to emphasise that any hierarchisation of species based on the assumed similarity to the human species is itself speciesist. As long as we lack knowledge about the capabilities of most non-human species, particularly since we continue to use our own species as the yardstick, one should aim at avoiding exploitative and abusive anthropocentric practices. Essentially, therefore, humans should grow respect for difference rather than similarity, as in the gender equality[8] debate.

---

8 This could be seen in relation to whether rights should be given based on similarity or difference. For example, women should, due to their biological function of carrying and delivering children, have additional rights. To grant fathers the same paternal rights as mothers have in relation to maternal rights in the name of gender equality jeopardises the rights of the mother when paternity leave is expanded at the cost of

Taking the above into consideration, how do nature conventions such as CITES and the Bern Convention succeed in protecting free-born animals? To explore this, in the next section I will use Norway[9] as an example.

Norway's implementation of CITES and the Bern Convention

Norway has been a party to CITES since 1976 and joined the Bern Convention in 1986. CITES regulates trade in endangered species. It aims to prevent species of wild animals and plants from going extinct due to trade through an appendix system and through the monitoring trade via the state parties' submissions of annual trade reports. It is, nonetheless, established that many countries fail to submit the annual trade reports, and therefore the trade numbers that appear in the trade database are unreliable (Wyatt, 2021). Much of the illegal trade is also under-reported because of enforcement agents' lack of priority or capacity (Sollund and Runhovde, 2020) and because many species have never been listed on CITES (see also Nurse's Chapter 8 The Global Illegal Wildlife Trade Crisis, in this volume).

Critique has been raised of CITES for being anthropocentric. For example, a main driver of CITES, as stated in the preamble, is to protect endangered wildlife species so they can continue to be of use to humans, whether as resources or for their aesthetic value, rather than offering individuals of (other) animal species genuine protection (Goyes and Sollund, 2016; Sollund, 2019). When species are moved between appendices, this is not done out of concern for individuals within a species that are subject to trade, but out of considerations for the conservation of a species as a whole. Norway is among the world's top ten countries when it comes to legal wildlife trade (Andersson et al., 2021). Norwegians import, for example, trophies, fashion products, traditional Asian medicinal products, and live reptiles and parrots (Sollund, 2019; Sollund, 2025).

Norway had a ban against the trade in live reptiles until 2017, whereupon a list of 19 species that could be legally imported and traded was introduced (Sollund, 2025). While rules are in place, for example animals who have been abducted from nature are banned, the rules can be easily circumvented (Sollund, 2025). Twelve of the reptile species are CITES-listed and require CITES permits, which are extended from the CITES national management authority, the Norwegian Environment Agency (NEA) (Mattilsynet, 2023). As a general rule, if a live animal is seized they will be killed by the veterinarians of the Food Safety Authority who thereby execute the decision of the NEA (Sollund, 2021). This way of implementing and enforcing CITES is consequently

maternity leave, as in Norway. Just as the human male should not be the yardstick for women or other genders, neither should the human be what other species are measured against.

9 I have carried out empirical research concerning the implementation and enforcement of these two conventions in Norway for 13 years and since 2019 under the CRIMEANTHROP project, funded by the Research Council Norway. See https://www.jus.uio.no/ikrs/english/research/projects/crimeanthrop/.

paradoxical in that animals who should be protected due to the risk of extinction of their species are killed as an enforcement measure (Sollund, 2019). This is a breach of CITES recommendations, stating that confiscated animals should be rehomed in sanctuaries or returned to the country of origin.[10]

In addition, Norway fails to comply with regard to the hunting and trade of whales. The International Whaling Commission (IWC, undated) decided, in 1982, to introduce a moratorium on commercial hunting of all whale species (Rueness et al., 2022). The Minke whale was then listed in Appendix I of CITES. Norway objected to the moratorium and has continued its annual hunts of Minke whales, with the quota for 2023 set at 1000 individuals, an increase of 84 individuals since 2022 (Regjeringen, 2023). The Norwegian Government regards Minke whales as exploitable meat resources rather than highly intelligent animals with intrinsic value.

The Bern Convention[11] is more of a genuine nature conservation convention than CITES, which aims to protect wildlife and their natural habitats, but also protects through an appendix system listing species according to their vulnerability to extinction. Norway's implementation of the Bern Convention is also subject to much dispute and conflict in the country (for example Skogen et al., 2017; Sollund and Goyes, 2021). The annual culling of wolves, and also the killing of other large endangered species for which Norway holds a specific responsibility according to the Bern Convention, is done, allegedly, to reduce social conflict and the human-wildlife conflict entailed by the reccurrence of these species after Norway joined the Bern Convention in 1986. Norwegian farmers had become accustomed to releasing their sheep into the wild without surveillance and wanted to proceed this way. In addition, hunters do not want the wolves to take the animals they hunt, particularly elks, even though what wolves take in comparison to the hunters is very limited. For example, one wolf family group may take 120 elks per year (Zimmerman, 2023); in 2023 there were nine wolf family groups in Norway (Rovdata, 2023), meaning altogether, they may take around 1000 elks. The hunters, in comparison, killed 27 500 elks and 49 300 deer in the 2022–23 season, according to Statistics Norway (2023). The wolf, wolverine, lynx, and brown bear are species that are held at minimum levels, not based on scientific evidence of the numbers required to uphold healthy populations, but on political, populistic decisions made in Parliament (Sollund and Goyes, 2021).

The numbers of endangered carnivores are kept at minimal levels. For example, in the case of the wolf in 2023, there were only 43–4 family groups found in Norway, while 46–8 family groups were found partly in Norway and partly in Sweden (Rovdata, 2023) This is the result of increased culling. For example, Norway has a zone system through which the Norwegian wolves should enjoy particular protection in 5% of Norwegian territory, but in recent years family groups of wolves are also hunted

10 CITES (2022). Conf. 17.8 (Rev. CoP19). Disposal of illegally traded and confiscated specimens of CITES-listed species. Accessed on 1 September 2023 from https://cites.org/sites/default/files/documents/COP/19/resolution/E-Res-17-08-R19.pdf.

11 https://www.coe.int/en/web/bern-convention.

in the protected zones. Hunters use helicopters from which they fire automatic shotguns. Appendix IV of the Bern Convention explicitly forbids the use of aircraft and also automatic and semi-automatic weapons that can hold more than two rounds of ammunition in hunts, so this represents a significant breach of the convention.[12] The annual winter hunts can proceed for days, as members of the family groups are killed one by one, with the panic and suffering this implies (Sollund, 2023). The Norwegian large carnivore killing has been the subject of various legal proceedings, and complaints have been raised several times to the Bern Convention, where the secretariat so far has failed to criticise Norway, despite its evident failure to comply with the convention (Trouwborst et al., 2017).

Conclusion

The perspectives of green criminology are essential in the analysis of harms committed against the natural environment and the non-human beings who are part of it, since a legal perspective alone is too limited to encapsulate all serious types of environmental and animal harm. As stated previously (Sollund, 2016; 2017), the methods by which the Norwegian authorities kill animals of endangered species that are protected under the Norwegian Nature Diversity Act (*Naturmangfoldoven*)(2009) are no more 'humane'[13] when the authorities orchestrate the killing than when an individual hunter does this, but if the killing is done without a licence, it is strictly illegal and may entail prison sentences (Sollund, 2016; 2017). A legal perspective would not encompass the harm that takes place when the authorities decide to kill, although the legality of such acts is disputed, which is why a green criminological harm and justice perspective is necessary to properly analyse such harms. Despite the harm inherent in the culling of wolf family groups, consecutive Norwegian governments have gone to great lengths to defend their killing practices of animals, including endangered species. Yet it is crucial to thoroughly examine their motivations and actions because we are living in a global biodiversity crisis, through which our world has lost 69% of all wildlife since the 1970s (WWF, 2022). To claim that the killing of non-human animal species is legal, therefore, becomes an invalid argument, in view of the protection they should be entitled to and in view of species – and eco-justice.

Similarly, the paradoxical killing of confiscated animals in Norway clearly illustrates the deficiencies of a legal approach when animals of endangered species are killed to

12 Annex IV of the Convention on the Conservation of European Wildlife and Natural Habitats of the Council of Europe, (Bern Convention, CETS 104), 1979. Accessed on 1 September 2023 from https://rm.coe.int/168097eb58.

13 'Humane' is, again, an anthropocentric term that erroneously ascribes human action as being less cruel, more compassionate, and empathic than the actions of, for example, a large carnivore who attacks and kills their prey. However, there is no reason to claim that the industrial, systemic killing of animals causes less suffering, or in any way should cause less harm, than that caused by, for example a lion or a wolf. Rather, such systems of mass destruction can be regarded as particularly cruel.

enforce a law aiming to protect wildlife from extinction through trade. It is an anthropocentric approach that underlines the objectification of the trafficking victims; they are regarded as 'specimens', not individuals with intrinsic value and interests. CITES is also fundamentally anthropocentric through its rationale, which encourages and prolongs the trade in innocent animals as though they are objects and have no interests of their own. Therefore, CITES should be reformed and converted into a convention that truly has the wellbeing of nature and those who belong to nature as its primary goal (Sollund, 2022).

Animals who are now killed in their natural habitats, where they should enjoy the right to live in harmony with their family groups, or as solitary individuals for those for whom this is natural, such as lynx, brown bears, and wolverines, should receive genuine protection. Whether solitary animals or social animals, they should be left in peace with their offspring, which should be a fundamental right for all wildlife, just as it should be for human animals. Animals who are domesticated and captive, such as pigs, cows, and hens should be allowed the minimum of the five freedoms and thus be allowed to live according to their natural needs and capabilities.

Humans are rather slow in acknowledging the capabilities of other species and generally mistrust and underestimate the direct human actions towards them. In view of recent discoveries, a better step to ensure multispecies justice would be to anticipate that all animal species – ranging from insects, fish, shellfish, vertebrates and to invertebrates – are, or may be, sentient and therefore we should be careful not to cause harm. To that end, we should generally adopt a hands-off approach unless our interference is needed to assist animals, as during war and natural catastrophes. Nature is better off unmanaged by humans, since humans mainly disturb and destroy the delicate balance of ecosystems through, for example, deforestation, hunting, and culling of wildlife, including both endangered and non-endangered species.

References

Ackerman, J. (2017) *The genius of birds*. Penguin.

American Society for the Prevention of Cruelty to Animals (ASPCA) (undated). *Five Freedoms*, https://www.aspca.org/sites/default/files/upload/images/aspca_asv_five_freedoms_final1.ashx_.pdf Accessed on 1 April 2025).

Andersson, A. A., Tilley, H. B., Lau, W., Dudgeon, D., Bonebrake, T. C., and Dingle, C. (2021) 'CITES and beyond: Illuminating 20 years of global, legal wildlife trade', *Global Ecology and Conservation*, *26*, e01455.

Audet, J. N., Ducatez, S., and Lefebvre, L. (2016) 'Bajan birds pull strings: two wild Antillean species enter the select club of string-pullers', *PLoS One*, 11(8), e0156112.

Balakhonov, D., and Rose, J. (2017) 'Crows rival monkeys in cognitive capacity', *Scientific Reports*, 7(1), 1–8.

BBC Earth (undated) 'Puffer Fish Constructs A Masterpiece of Love', https://www.youtube.com/watch?v=rzv37FuS8hI (Accessed 1 April 2025).

BBC Earth, *Blue Planet II* (undated) 'Amazing Clownfish Teamwork', https://www.youtube.com/watch?v=rn6R4ncd2OU (Accessed 1 April 2025).

Beirne, P. (2007) 'Animal rights, animal abuse and green criminology' in Beirne, P., and South, N. (eds) *Issues in green criminology*. Devon Willan.

Beirne, P. (2009) *Confronting animal abuse: Law, criminology, and human-animal relationships*. Rowman & Littlefield Publishers.

Beirne, P. (2014) 'Theriocide: naming animal killing', *International Journal for Crime, Justice and Social Democracy*, 3(2), 50–67.

Beirne, P., and South, N. (eds) (2007) *Issues in green criminology*. Devon Willan.

Bourdieu, P. (2020) 'Outline of a Theory of Practice' in Seidman, S. and Alexander, J. C. (eds) *The New Social Theory Reader*. Routledge, pp. 80–6.

Bridges, A. D., MaBouDi, H., Procenko, O., Lockwood, C., Mohammed, Y., Kowalewska, A., Romero González, J. C., Woodgate, J. L., and Chittka, L. (2022) 'The establishment and transmission of novel foraging techniques indicates a capacity for culture in bumblebees (Bombus terrestris)'. *bioRxiv*, 2022-10.

Cazaux, G. (1999) Beauty and the beast: Animal abuse from a non-speciesist criminological perspective', *Crime, Law and Social Change*, 31(2), 105–25.

Chittka, L. (2017) Bee cognition', *Current Biology*, 27(19), R1049–R1053.

Cohen, S. (2001) *States of Denial. Knowing about Atrocities and Suffering*. Polity.

Ellefsen, R. (2009) Ny dyrevelferdslov: Beskyttes dyr eller næring? Interessekonflikt og motstridende syn på dyrs status i lovprosessen forut for dyrelferdsloven. M.A.Thesis in sociology of law, Dep. of criminology and sociology of law, University of Oslo.

Ellefsen, R. (2013) *Med lov til å pine: Om bruk og beskyttelse av dyr*. Fritt forlag/Inspirator forlag.

Ellefsen, R. (2016) 'Judicial opportunities and the death of SHAC: Legal repression along a cycle of contention', *Social Movement Studies*, 15(5), 441–56.

Faure, M., Philipsen, N., Fajardo del Castillo, T., Farmer, A., Gerstetter, C., Germani, A. R., Hoare, A., Mitsilegas, V., Sollund, R., Sina, S., Stefes, C., Vagliasindi, G. M., and Veening, W., (2016). *EFFACE [European Action to Fight Environmental Crime]. Conclusions and recommendations*, https://www.efface.eu/sites/default/files/publications/EFFACE_Conclusions_recommendations/index.pdf (Accessed 1 April 2025).

Francione, G. L. (2008) *Animals as persons: Essays on the abolition of animal exploitation*. Columbia University Press.

Godfrey-Smith, P. (2016) *Other minds: The octopus, the sea, and the deep origins of consciousness*. Farrar, Straus and Giroux.

Goyes, D. (2018) '"Tactics Rebounding" in the Colombian defence of seed freedom', *International Journal for Crime, Justice and Social Democracy*, 7(1), 91–107.

Goyes, D. R., and Sollund, R. (2016) 'Contesting and contextualising CITES: Wildlife trafficking in Colombia and Brazil', *International Journal for Crime, Justice and Social Democracy*, 5(4), 87–102.

Gålmark, L. (2008) 'Aristotle revisited: Anthro-androcentrism and meat normativity' in Sollund, R. (ed) *Global Harms*. New York: Nova Science Publishers.

Halsey, M., and White, R. (1998) 'Crime, ecophilosophy and environmental harm', *Theoretical Criminology*, 2(3), 345–71.

IWC (n.d.). IWC | International Whaling Commission.

King, S. L., & Jensen, F. H. (2022). Rise of the machines: Integrating technology with playback experiments to study cetacean social cognition in the wild. *Methods in Ecology and Evolution*, *14*(8), 1873–1886. https://doi.org/10.1111/2041-210x.13935.

O'Donnell, E., and Macpherson, E. (2019) 'Voice, power and legitimacy: the role of the legal person in river management in New Zealand, Chile and Australia', *Australasian Journal of Water Resources*, 23(1), 35–44.

Lynch, M. J. (2023) 'Writs of Habeas Corpus for Nonhuman Primates in the United States and the Nonhuman Rights Project: Legal Processes and Arguments Used to Secure Nonhuman Animal Rights', *International Journal for Crime, Justice and Social Democracy*, 12(3), 15–26.

Lynch, M. J., Long, M. A., and Stretesky, P. B. (2015) 'Anthropogenic development drives species to be endangered: Capitalism and the decline of species' in Sollund, R. (ed) *Green Harms and Crimes*. Palgrave Macmillan, London, pp. 117–46.

Lynch, M. J., and Stretesky, P. B. (2016) *Exploring Green Criminology: Toward a Green Criminological Revolution*. Routledge.

Martinho-Trushwell, A. (2022) *The Parrot in the Mirror*. Oxford University Press.

Marzluff, J. M., Walls, J., Cornell, H. N., Withey, J. C., and Craig, D. P. (2010) 'Lasting recognition of threatening people by wild American crows', *Animal Behaviour*, 79(3), 699–707.

Mattilsynet (2023) 'Eksotiske reptiler som er tillatt i Norge', *Mattilsynet*, 22 March 2023, https://www.mattilsynet.no/dyr/kjaeledyr/reptiler-og-eksotiske-dyr/eksotiske-pattedyr-reptiler-og-amfibier/eksotiske-reptiler-som-er-tillatt-i-norge (Accessed 1 April).

Morrison, R., and Reiss, D. (2018) 'Precocious development of self-awareness in dolphins', *PLoS One*, 13(1), e0189813.

Mulcahy, N. J., and Call, J. (2006) 'Apes save tools for future use', *Science*, 312(5776), 1038–40.

Næss, A. (1984) 'A defence of the deep ecology movement', *Environmental Ethics*, 6(3), 265–70.

Naturmangfoldloven [Lov om naturens mangfold] [The Nature Diversity Act] (2009) https://lovdata.no/dokument/NL/lov/2009-06-19-100.

Nibert, D. (2002) *Animal Rights/Human Rights: Entanglements of Oppression and Liberation*. Rowman & Littlefield Publishers.

Nonhuman Rights Project (undated). https://www.nonhumanrights.org/about-us/.

Nurse, A., and Wyatt, T. (2020) *Wildlife Criminology*. Bristol University Press.

Pepperberg, I. M. (1999) *The Alex Studies: Cognitive and Communicative Abilities of Grey Parrots*. Harvard University Press.

Plotnik, J. M., De Waal, F. B., and Reiss, D. (2006) 'Self-recognition in an Asian elephant', *Proceedings of the National Academy of Sciences*, 103(45), 17053–7.

Regan, T. (2004a) *Empty Cages: Facing the Challenge of Animal Rights*. Rowman & Littlefield.

Regan, T. (2004b) *The Case for Animal Rights*. University of California Press.

Regjeringen (2023) 'Høyere vågehvalkvote i 2023', Press Release, 27 March 2023, https://www.regjeringen.no/no/aktuelt/hoyere-vagehvalkvote-i-2023/id2967259/ (Accessed 1 April 2025).

Rovdata (2023) *Ulv i norge pr. 31. Mars 2023 foreløpige konklusjoner fra bestandsovervåking vinteren 2022-2023*, https://rovdata.no/Portals/Rovdata/Dokumenter/Rapporter/Forel%C3%B8pige%20ulverapporter/Ulv-Norsk%20StatusRap%204-pr_%2031%20mars%202023-PW%20m_fl_-2023_05_11_1.pdf?ver=Ad5B6zpCNeiCVxYenv7q5w%3d%3d (Accessed 1 April 2025).

Rueness, E. K., Nilsen, E. B., Kvie, K. S., de Boer, H., Eldegard, K., Hindar, K., Hole L. R., Järnegren, J., Kauserud, K., Måren, I., Nielsen, A., Thorstad, E. B., and Velle, G. (2022) *Compilation of knowledge on the global population of common minke whale (Balaenoptera acutorostrata)*. Scientific Opinion of the panel of Alien Organisms and Trade in Endangered Species of the Norwegian Scientific for Food and Enviroment.

Ruggiero, V., and South, N. (2010) 'Green criminology and dirty collar crime', *Critical Criminology*, 18(4), 251–62.

Rutz, C., Hunt, G. R., and St Clair, J. J. (2018) 'Corvid technologies: how do new caledonian crows get their tool designs?', *Current Biology*, 28(18), R1109–R1111.

Skogen, K., Krange, O., and Figari, H. (2017) *Wolf Conflicts: a Sociological Study* (1). Berghahn Books.

Sollund, R. (2008) 'Causes for speciesism: Difference, distance and denial' in Sollund, R. (ed) *Global Harms. Ecological Crime and Speciesism*. New York: Nova, pp. 109–30.

Sollund, R. (2012) 'Speciesism as Doxic Practice Versus Valuing Difference and Plurality' in Ellefsen, R., Sollund, R., and Larsen, G. (eds) *Eco-global Crimes: Contemporary Problems and Future Challenges*. Rune, UK: Ashgate Publishing Ltd, pp. 91–113.

Sollund, R. (2013) 'Animal abuse, animal rights and species justice', presented at a presidential panel at the American Society of Criminology 69th Annual Meeting, Atlanta.

Sollund, R. (2015) *Green Harms and Crimes: Critical Criminology in a Changing World*. Critical Criminological Perspectives. Palgrave Macmillan.

Sollund, R. (2016) 'The animal other: Legal and illegal theriocide' in Hall, M., Wyatt, T., South, N., Nurse, A., Potter, G., and Maher, J. (eds) *Greening Criminology in the 21st Century*. Routledge, pp. 93–113.

Sollund, R. (2017) 'Perceptions and law enforcement of illegal and legal wolf killing in Norway: organized crime or folk crime?', *Palgrave Communications*, 3(1), 1–9.

Sollund, R. A. (2019) *The Crimes of Wildlife Trafficking: Issues of Justice, Legality and Morality*. Routledge.

Sollund, R. (2021) 'The development of the enforcement of CITES in Norway: Discretionary omissions and theriocides', *Revista Catalana de Dret Ambiental*, 12(1), 1–34.

Sollund, R. (2022) 'Wildlife Trade and Law Enforcement: A Proposal for a Remodeling of CITES Incorporating Species Justice, Ecojustice, and Environmental Justice', *International Journal of Offender Therapy and Comparative Criminology*, 66(9), 1017–35.

Sollund, R. (2023) 'The dark side of nature conventions. A call to end anthropogenic destruction', *Criminology and Criminal Justice* OnlineFirst, 10.1177/17488958231181309.

Sollund, R. (2024) 'Speciesism and the Non-human' in Pontell H. N. (ed) *Oxford Research Encyclopedia of Criminology and Criminal Justice*. Oxford: Oxford University press. 10.1093/acrefore/9780190264079.013.748.

Sollund, R. (2025) *Wildlife Trade and Animal Victimization: Parallel Harms and Crimes*. Routledge.

Sollund, R., and Goyes, D. R. (2021) 'State-organized crime and the killing of wolves in Norway', *Trends in Organized Crime*, 24(4), 467–84.

Sollund, R. and Runhodve, S. R., 'Responses to Wildlife Crime in Post-Colonial Times. Who Fares Best?', *British Journal of Criminology*, 60(4), 1014–33.

South, N. (2008) 'Nature, difference and the rejection of harm: Expanding the agenda for green criminology' in Sollund, R. (ed) *Global harms. Ecological crime and Speciesism*. New York: Nova, pp. 187–201.

Spencer, D. C., and Fitzgerald, A. (2013) 'Three ecologies, transversality and victimization: The case of the British Petroleum oil spill'. *Crime, Law and Social Change*, 59(2), 209–23.

St Clair, J. J., Klump, B. C., van der Wal, J. E., Sugasawa, S., and Rutz, C. (2016) 'Strong between-site variation in New Caledonian crows' use of hook-tool-making materials', *Biological Journal of the Linnean Society*, 118(2), 226–32.

Statistics Norway (2025) Jegerne felte færre dyr under elg og hjortejakta. Jegerne felte færre dyr under elg- og hjortejakta – SSB Accessed on 1 April 2025.

Trouwborst, A., Fleurke, F. M., and Linnell, J. D. (2017) 'Norway's wolf policy and the Bern convention on European wildlife: Avoiding the "manifestly absurd"', *Journal of International Wildlife Law & Policy*, 20(2), 155–67.

Van Uhm, D. (2016). *Uncovering the illegal wildlife trade: In the world of poachers, smugglers and traders*. Springer.

Vetlesen, A. J. (2015) *The Denial of Nature: Environmental Philosophy in the Era of Global Capitalism*. Routledge.

War Paws (undated) 'Helping the forgotten animals of war and Rescuing animals during wildfires', – United States | IFAW.

White, R. (2012) 'The foundations of eco-global criminology' in Ellifsen, R., Sollund, R., and Larsen, G. (eds) *Eco-global Crimes, Contemporary Problems and Future Challenges*. London: Ashgate, pp. 15–31.

White, R. (2013) *Environmental Harm: An Eco-justice Perspective*. Policy Press.

White, R. (2018a) 'Climate change and criminology' in White, R. *Climate Change Criminology*. Bristol University Press, pp. 1–18.

White, R. (2018b) 'Green victimology and non-human victims', *International Review of Victimology*, 24(2), 239–55.

Wise, S. M. (2018) 'The struggle for the legal rights of animals begins-the experience of the nonhuman rights project in New York and Connecticut' *Animal Law Review*, 25, 367.

World Wildlife Foundation (WWF) (2020) '3 billion animals harmed by Australia's fires', https://www.worldwildlife.org/stories/3-billion-animals-harmed-by-australia-s-fires (Accessed 5 July 2023).

World Wildlife Foundation (WWF) (2022) '69% average decline in wildlife populations since 1970, says new WWF report', Press Release, 13 October 2022, https://www.worldwildlife.org/press-releases/69-average-decline-in-wildlife-populations-since-1970-says-new-wwf-report (Accessed 5 July 2023).

Wyatt, T. (2013) *Wildlife Trafficking: A Deconstruction of the Crime, the Victims and the Offenders*. Palgrave Macmillan.

Wyatt, T. (2021) *Is CITES Protecting Wildlife?: Assessing Implementation and Compliance*. Routledge.

Zimmermann, B. (2023) '*Ulv i Store norske leksikon* på', https://snl.no/ulv (Accessed 6 July 2023).

PART III

Pushing the boundaries of legal and socio-legal research: new and emerging themes in environmental criminal law

11 Climate change and criminal justice

Stephan Sina

1. Introduction

For some time now, the fight against climate change has been high on the political agenda worldwide. The Paris Agreement (PA)[1] brought new momentum by providing, for the first time, a precise reference point: to hold the global average temperature increase well below 2° Celsius above pre-industrial levels, while pursuing efforts to stay below 1.5° Celsius. In order to achieve this collective target, parties have to submit Nationally Determined Contributions (NDC).[2] The European Union (EU) and its Member States fulfil this obligation jointly.[3]

At the EU level, the mitigation targets submitted, including achieving climate neutrality[4] by 2050, are fixed in the European Climate Law[5] and have been specified in

1 UNTS Vol. 54113, 1.

2 PA, Arts 4.2, 4.9.

3 See Submission by Spain and the European Commission on behalf of the European Union and its Member States, *The update of the nationally determined contribution of the European Union and its Member States*, 16 October 2023, https://unfccc.int/sites/default/files/NDC/2023-10/ES-2023-10-17%20EU%20submission%20NDC%20update.pdf (accessed 15 August 2024).

4 Climate neutrality means the balance between GHG emissions and removals (by sinks), thus reducing emissions to net zero; see Regulation (EU) 2021/1119 of 30 June 2021 establishing the framework for achieving climate neutrality (European Climate Law) [2021] OJ L 243/1, Art. 2(1).

5 Regulation (EU) 2021/1119 of 30 June 2021 establishing the framework for achieving climate neutrality (European Climate Law) [2021] OJ L 243/1.

EU legislation according to the 'European Green Deal'[6] and the 'Fit for 55 Package'[7] announced in 2019 and 2021, respectively. Some of the key reforms include tightening up the EU Emissions Trading System (ETS 1) and the EU Effort Sharing Regulation covering 'non-ETS' areas, and the introduction of a new Emission Trading System specifically for buildings and the transport sector (ETS 2).[8]

At the national level, an increasing number of framework climate change laws serving as governance systems for national climate policy have been introduced following the groundbreaking United Kingdom (UK) Climate Change Act in 2008.[9] Specific national legislation is needed both to implement the requirements of the above-mentioned EU legislation and to achieve the national mitigation targets.

In this context, landmark climate litigation cases have forced governments to strengthen their mitigation efforts: in the Netherlands, the *Urgenda* case of the Supreme Court in 2019;[10] in Germany, the decision in *Neubauer et al.* of the Federal Constitutional Court in 2021[11] and in France, the decision *Commune de Grande-Synthe* of the *Conseil Constitutionel* in 2021.[12] In the *KlimaSeniorinnen* case in 2024, the European Court of Human Rights (ECtHR) found that Switzerland had failed to comply with its positive obligations under the European Convention on Human Rights (ECHR) concerning

---

6 Communication from the Commission to the European Parliament, the European Council, the Council, the European Economic and Social Committee and the Committee of the Regions, the European Green Deal, COM(2019) 640 final.

7 Communication from the Commission to the European Parliament, the European Council, the Council, the European Economic and Social Committee and the Committee of the Regions 'Fit for 55': delivering the EU's 2030 Climate Target on the way to climate neutrality, COM(2021) 550 final.

8 See Directive (EU) 2023/959 of 10 May 2023 amending Directive 2003/87/EC establishing a system for greenhouse gas emission allowance trading within the Union and Decision (EU) 2015/1814 concerning the establishment and operation of a market stability reserve for the Union greenhouse gas emission trading system, [2023] OJ L 130/134; Regulation (EU) 2023/857 of 19 April 2023 amending Regulation (EU) 2018/842 on binding annual greenhouse gas emission reductions by Member States from 2021 to 2030 contributing to climate action to meet commitments under the Paris Agreement, and Regulation (EU) 2018/1999, [2023] OJ L 111/1.

9 See, for example Ecologic Institute, 'Climate Framework Laws Info-Matrix'. Ecologic Institute, Berlin 2023, https://www.ecologic.eu/19320 (accessed 1 August 2024).

10 *Urgenda Foundation v. State of the Netherlands* NL:HR:2019:2007, http://climatecasechart.com/non-us-case/urgenda-foundation-v-kingdom-of-the-netherlands/ (accessed 1 August 2024).

11 *Neubauer, et al. v. Germany* (24 March 2021) 1 BvR 2656/18 and others, http://climatecasechart.com/non-us-case/neubauer-et-al-v-germany/ (accessed 1 August 2024).

12 *Commune de Grande-Synthe v. France* case no. 427301, Decision of 1 July 2021, http://climatecasechart.com/non-us-case/commune-de-grande-synthe-v-france/ (accessed 1 August 2024).

climate change.[13] Litigation has also been launched against companies, either to force them to greater mitigation efforts (for example *Milieudefensie et al. v. Royal Dutch Shell plc*)[14] or to obtain damage payments for climate damage (for example *Luciano Lliuya v. RWE*).[15]

With all these ongoing efforts, it is surprising that criminal law does not play a substantial role in current discussions on mitigating climate change, although promoting action to step up efforts against environmental crime has been included in the European Green Deal.[16] Cases of civil disobedience by climate activists in several countries[17] and discussions on the introduction of 'ecocide' in the Statute of the International Criminal Court[18] are arguably exceptions to the minor role of criminal law in debates on climate change.

The aim of this chapter is to analyse why this is so and whether this could or should be changed. It will start with a discussion of the role of criminal law in enforcing mitigation obligations in section 2; and then briefly consider in section 3 how far other crimes play a role in the context of mitigation obligations. The chapter then proceeds with general considerations about a potential autonomous role of criminal law in contributing to mitigation efforts in section 4. Section 5 presents the concluding remarks.

It should be noted that the analysis in this chapter will be restricted to the role of criminal law in the context of climate change mitigation, that is measures to limit or prevent anthropogenic greenhouse gas (GHG) emissions and enhance activities that remove these gases from the atmosphere, for example through sinks such as forests.[19]

---

13 *KlimaSeniorinnen v. Switzerland* (ECtHR) (Application No. 53600/20), https://climatecasechart.com/non-us-case/union-of-swiss-senior-women-for-climate-protection-v-swiss-federal-council-and-others/ (accessed 1 August 2024).

14 *Milieudefensie et al. v. Royal Dutch Shell plc* NL:RBDHA:2021:5337, http://climatecasechart.com/non-us-case/milieudefensie-et-al-v-royal-dutch-shell-plc/ (accessed 1 August 2024).

15 *Luciano Lliuya v. RWE AG*, case No. 2 O 285/15 Essen Regional Court, https://climatecasechart.com/non-us-case/lliuya-v-rwe-ag/ (accessed 1 August 2024).

16 See European Green Deal, n. 6, p. 23.

17 See the brief discussion in section 3 below.

18 See further Thomas Obel Hansen's Chapter 4 Towards a New Agenda for Ecocide Norms Adoption and Enforcement, in this volume.

19 See https://www.ipcc.ch/working-group/wg3/ (accessed 15 August 2024) and the definition of mitigation in IPCC (V. Möller, R. van Diemen, J.B.R. Matthews, C. Méndez, S. Semenov, J.S. Fuglestvedt, A. Reisinger (eds)) (2022) 'Annex II: Glossary' in IPCC (H.-O. Pörtner, D.C. Roberts, M. Tignor, E.S. Poloczanska, K. Mintenbeck, A. Alegría, M. Craig, S. Langsdorf, S. Löschke, V. Möller, A. Okem, B. Rama (eds)) *Climate Change 2022: Impacts, Adaptation and Vulnerability. Contribution of Working Group II to the Sixth Assessment Report of the Intergovernmental Panel on Climate Change*, Cambridge University Press, Cambridge, UK and New York, NY, USA, 2022, pp. 2897–2930: 'A human intervention to reduce emissions or enhance the sinks of greenhouse gases'.

It will not address adaptation to climate change, that is the process of adjustment to actual or expected climate and its effects, in order to moderate harm or exploit beneficial opportunities.[20] It will be suggested that such a 'climate criminal law' aimed at mitigation challenges the underlying features of criminal law.

2. Criminal enforcement of mitigation obligations

a. The current state of criminal enforcement of mitigation obligations

As mentioned in the introduction, many laws must be implemented at the EU level and by the Member States to achieve their mitigation targets. This includes a wide range of instruments, ranging from market-based instruments such as the EU ETS to regulations, carbon taxes, or state aids. Non-compliance can, to the extent that a regulatory element is involved,[21] lead to sanctions. As far as EU legislation is concerned, Member States are traditionally free to choose the instruments to implement EU directives, that is the enforcement mechanism.[22] According to the case law of the Court of Justice of the European Union (CJEU), however, sanctions for violating implementing legislation have to be 'effective, dissuasive and proportionate'.[23] 'Effective' and 'dissuasive' mean that the Member States must endeavour to attain and implement the objectives of the violated provisions, for which a preventive effect on the individual and the general public is to be expected.[24] 'Proportionate' requires an appropriate sanction in terms of the objective pursued and the gravity of the offence. Where there is a choice between several appropriate penalties, recourse must be had to the least onerous.[25]

Such sanctions could include criminal sanctions. Yet, according to the case law and the criminal legal doctrine that criminal law should have a subsidiary role and be only used as a last resort (*ultima ratio*),[26] the choice of criminal sanctions would only be proportionate if other sanctions are not deemed sufficiently effective and dissuasive. This corresponds to the trend in the EU Member States towards a toolbox approach

---

20 See the definition of adaptation in IPCC (2022), n. 19.

21 Cf. Frisch, W., 'Strafrecht und Klimaschutz. Möglichkeiten und Grenzen eines Beitrags des Strafrechts zum Klimaschutz nach Maßgabe internationaler Klimaübereinkünfte' (2015) 162 *Goltdammer's Archiv für Strafrecht* 427, 428–9.

22 Faure, M., 'European Environmental Criminal Law: Do we really need it?' (2004) 13(1) *European Energy and Environmental Law Review* 18, 19–20.

23 See *Commission v. Greece (Greek Maize)* (C-68/88) EU:C:1989:339, 21 September 1989, [23]–[25].

24 Satzger, H., *Internationales und Europäisches Strafrecht*, 10th edn, Nomos, 2022, § 9 para. 27; see also Klip, A., *European Criminal Law*, 4th edn, Intersentia, 2021, pp. 81, 87–88.

25 Satzger, ibid; Klip, ibid, pp. 86–87.

26 See Faure (2004), n. 22.

which suggests a more limited role for criminal penalties and a greater role for alternative sanctions such as administrative fines.[27]

Notwithstanding these general considerations, there are more and more instances where specific sanctions or criminal penalties are prescribed. Two examples shall be given. First, Article 16 of the EU Emissions Trading System Directive[28] provides for a differentiated penalty system. While paragraph 1 refers to the general requirement of effective, dissuasive and proportionate penalties, paragraph 2 requires a 'naming and shaming' penalty, that is the publication of the names of the operators, aircraft operators, and shipping companies that have not surrendered sufficient emission allowances. Paragraph 3 prescribes an excess emissions penalty of €100[29] for each ton of carbon dioxide equivalent emitted by the installation for which the operator, aircraft operator, or shipping company has not surrendered allowances, which does not release the operator from their obligation to purchase and surrender a number of allowances equal to the amount of the excess emissions. Contrary to a view in the literature that describes this specific penalty as a sanction *sui generis* with partially criminal character, the German Federal Administrative Court (BVerwG) considers it a mere preventative coercion instrument to enforce the duty to surrender emission allowances.[30] Finally, as measures of last resort, paragraphs 5 and 11a enable the imposition of an operating ban on aircraft operators and the issuance of an expulsion order or a flag state detention order against shipping companies.

Second, the Environmental Crime Directive (ECD)[31] requires Member States to provide criminal sanctions for certain unlawful conduct, especially if it causes death or serious injury to individuals, or conduct posing at least a considerable risk of substantial damage to the environment, or conduct considered otherwise to be particularly harmful to the environment.[32] Although Recital 4 seems to indicate the belief that only criminal sanctions are sufficient to achieve compliance with EU laws for the protection of the environment, other provisions make it clear that criminalization is

---

27 See Faure, M., 'The Development of Environmental Criminal Law in the EU and its Member States' (2017) 26 *Review of European Community & International Environmental Law* 139, 141–5; see further in the Australian law context, Sarah Wright and Victoria Colvin's Chapter 7 Enforcement Undertakings as an Alternative to Prosecution in Australian Environmental Law Enforcement, in this volume.

28 Directive 2003/87/EC of 12 October 2003 establishing a scheme for greenhouse gas emission allowance within the Community [2003] OJ L 275/32, last amended by Directive (EU) 2023/959 of 10 May 2023 [2023] OJ L 130/134.

29 According to Directive 2003/87/EC, Art. 4, para. 4, this value refers to the EUR price level of 2012 and must be increased in accordance with the European index of consumer prices.

30 BVerwG, decision of 20 February 2014, 7 C 6.12, para. 23 with overview of the literature in para. 22.

31 Directive (EU) 2024/1203 of 11 April 2024 on the protection of the environment through criminal law and replacing Directives 2008/99/EC and 2009/123/EC [2024] OJ L 2024/1203 of 30 April 2024 (Environmental Crime Directive (ECD)).

32 See ECD, Recital 9.

restricted to serious infringements committed intentionally or at least with serious negligence.[33]

The ECD mentions climate change in Recital 23. However, only two criminal offences are clearly connected to mitigation. The first is under Article 3(2)(t) of the ECD regarding the production, placing on the market, import, export, use, or release of fluorinated GHGs, whether alone or as mixtures, as referred to in Article 2(a) of Regulation (EU) 2024/573, or the production, placing on the market, import, export or use of products and equipment, and parts thereof, containing fluorinated GHGs or whose functioning relies upon those gases as referred to in Article 2(b) of that Regulation, or the putting into operation of such products and equipment. These 'F-gases' are powerful GHGs which were developed to substitute ozone-depleting substances. For this reason, they shall be reduced and ultimately banned according to the Kigali Amendment[34] to the Montreal Protocol on Substances that Deplete the Ozone Layer[35] and the aforementioned EU Regulation 2024/573.[36]

The second criminal offence related to mitigation is under Article 3(2)(p) of the ECD regarding the placing or making available on the Union market or the export from the Union market of relevant commodities or relevant products, in breach of the prohibition set out in Article 3 of Regulation (EU) 2023/1115, except where such conduct concerns a negligible quantity. According to Article 1(1) of Regulation 2023/1115, the regulatory aim is to minimize the EU's contribution to deforestation and forest degradation worldwide, and to reduce the EU's contribution to GHG emissions and global biodiversity loss. According to Recital 3 of the Regulation, deforestation and forest degradation contribute to the global climate crisis in multiple ways, especially by increasing GHG emissions and permanently removing carbon sink capacities. Deforestation alone accounts for 11% of GHG emissions globally.[37] Article 25 of

---

33 See ECD, Recitals 5, 8, and 73, Art. 3(1) and, regarding the predecessor of the ECD, Directive 2008/99/EC, Vagliasindi, G.M., 'The EU Environmental Directive' in Farmer, A., M. Faure and G.M. Vagliasindi (eds), *Environmental Crime in Europe*, 82 Modern Studies in Environmental Law, Hart, 2017, p. 31, pp. 46–7; Satzger, H., 'Umwelt- und Klimastrafrecht in Europa – die mögliche Rolle des Strafrechts angesichts des "Green Deal" der Europäischen Union' in Engelhart, M., H. Kudlich and B. Vogel (eds), *Digitalisierung, Globalisierung und Risikoprävention. Festschrift für Ulrich Sieber*, Vol. 2, Duncker & Humblot, 2021, p. 1267, p. 1271.

34 Amendment to the Montreal Protocol on Substances that Deplete the Ozone Layer, Kigali, 15 October 2016, in force since 1 January 2019, https://treaties.un.org/Pages/ViewDetails.aspx?src=IND&mtdsg_no=XXVII-2-f&chapter=27&clang=_en (accessed 15 August 2024).

35 See Dupuy, P.-M. and J.E. Viñuales, *International Environmental Law*, 2nd edn, Cambridge University Press, 2018, pp. 168–9.

36 Regulation (EU) 2024/573 of 7 February 2024 on fluorinated greenhouse gases, amending Directive (EU) 2019/1937 and repealing Regulation (EU) No 517/2014 [2024] OJ L 2024/573.

37 Regulation (EU) 2023/1115 of 31 May 2023 on the making available on the Union market and the export from the Union of certain commodities and products associated

Regulation 2023/1115 provides penalties that include, inter alia, fines, confiscations of products and revenues, and temporary exclusion from public procurement processes and from access to public funding. According to the Explanatory Memorandum of the Commission's ECD proposal, however, '[t]he underlying pattern of timber-related infringements are of such serious nature that authorities must have the means of criminal enforcement to tackle them'.[38]

Aside from those offences, there are no criminal offences covered by the ECD clearly connected to mitigation. It is worth noting that Article 3(2)(s) of the ECD classifies as an offence the production, placing on the market, import, export, use, or release of ozone-depleting substances, whether alone or as mixtures, as referred to in Article 2(a) of Regulation (EU) 2024/590, or the production, placing on the market, import, export or use of products and equipment, and parts thereof, containing ozone-depleting substances or whose functioning relies upon those substances as referred to in Article 2(b) of that Regulation.[39] Despite its limited scope, the wider purpose of this provision is to protect the atmosphere. Yet only to the extent that ozone-depleting substances are also GHGs, that criminal offence also contributes to climate mitigation.[40] In addition, some of the environmental offences of the ECD may also cover non-permissible GHG emissions. For example, the unlawful disposal of waste according to Article 3(2)(f) of the ECD includes infringements of the Landfill Directive[41] which, inter alia, aims at preventing methane emissions from non-permissible landfills.[42] Furthermore, Article 3(2)(f)(ii) of the ECD requires, as far as non-hazardous waste is concerned, that specified conduct (e.g. the collection, transport or treatment [...] of waste) that causes or is likely to cause death or serious injury to any person or substantial damage to the quality of air, soil, or water, or substantial damage to an ecosystem, animals or plants is treated as a criminal offence.[43] However, this suggests that the negative greenhouse effects alone caused by this waste offence are not sufficient for a criminal penalty.

---

with deforestation and forest degradation and repealing Regulation (EU) No 995/2010 [2023] OJ L 150/233.

38 Proposal for a Directive of the European Parliament and of the Council on the protection of the environment through criminal law and replacing Directive 2008/99/EC, COM(2021) 851 final of 15 December 2021, https://eur-lex.europa.eu/legal-content/EN/TXT/?uri=CELEX:52021PC0851 (accessed 15 August 2024), p. 6.

39 Regulation (EU) 2024/590 of 7 February 2024 on substances that deplete the ozone layer, and repealing Regulation (EC) No 1005/2009 [2024] OJ L 2024/590.

40 See from an international law perspective Dupuy and Viñuales (2018), n. 35, pp. 167–8.

41 Directive 1999/31/EC of 26 April 1999 on the landfill of waste [1999] OJ L 182/1, last amended by Directive (EU) 2018/850 of 14 June 2018 [2018] OJ L 150/100.

42 According to Article 1, the objective of the directive is '[...] to prevent or reduce as far as possible negative effects on the environment, in particular the pollution of surface water, groundwater, soil and air, and on the global environment, *including the greenhouse effect*, as well as any resulting risk to human health, from landfilling of waste, during the whole life-cycle of the landfill' (emphasis by the author).

43 See ECD, Art. 3(2)(f)(i).

Thus, as a rule, EU law currently does not display an intention to oblige Member States to introduce criminal sanctions for the infringement of climate mitigation obligations. This does not, as clarified by Article 3(5) of the ECD, prevent Member States from imposing such penalties independently. While it is outside the scope of this chapter to analyse the Member States′ sanctioning systems in this respect, a few remarks shall be made. As mentioned before, in the last few decades, many Member States have introduced a toolbox approach, providing for other remedies as alternatives to criminal penalties.[44] Thus, in Germany, the regular sanction provided for infringements of mitigation laws is an administrative fine (*Geldbuße*), which is the default penalty for administrative penal offences (*Ordnungswidrigkeiten*).[45] Only exceptionally are penal sanctions provided for as well.[46] In the Netherlands, on the other hand, such infringements may be prosecuted either as criminal or as administrative offences, depending on a number of factors such as the severity of the offence.[47]

b. More criminal enforcement of mitigation obligations?

In light of the above analysis, a question arises as to whether the criminal law should be used to a wider extent for the enforcement of climate mitigation laws.

From an EU perspective, the decisive point is whether the current sanctions in national laws transposing EU directives on mitigation are sufficiently effective, proportionate, and dissuasive to ensure compliance. If this is not the case, criminal penalties would be necessary, provided the offences are serious ones. As mentioned before, there is a presumption that the use of criminal law or criminal penalties contributes to better enforcement.[48]

The EU′s focus on criminal law as a means of enforcement of EU environmental law has been criticized by criminal lawyers in the Member States. According to them, the

44 See Faure (2017), n. 27, and Faure, M., 'The Evolution of Environmental Criminal Law in Europe: A Comparative Analysis' in Farmer, Faure and Vagliasindi (2017), n. 33, pp. 267, 298–304.

45 See, for example section 32 of the Greenhouse Gas Emission Allowance Trading Act (TEHG) of 21 July 2011 (*Federal Law Gazette* I, p. 1475), as last amended by the Act of 10 August 2021 (*Federal Law Gazette* I, p. 3436); section 22 of the Fuel Emission Allowance Trading Act (BEHG) of 12 December 2019 (*Federal Law Gazette* I, p. 2728), as last amended by the Act of 22 December 2023 (*Federal Law Gazette* I, no. 412).

46 For example in section 8 of the Timber Trade Security Act (HolzSiG) of 11 July 2011 (*Federal Law Gazette I*, p. 1345), as last amended by the Act of 10 August 2021 (*Federal Law Gazette I*, p. 3436).

47 Cf. Lopik, S. and S. Stax, 'Klimaatverandering en strafrecht: een verkenning' (2020) 3 *Boom Strafblad (BSb)*, 116, 120–3. Generally, on the relationship between criminal and administrative law in the Netherlands, see Faure, M. and K. Svatikova, 'Criminal or Administrative Law to Protect the Environment? Evidence from Western Europe' (2012) 24 *Journal of Environmental Law* 253, 272–5.

48 See ECD, Recital 4 and Klip (2021), n. 24, p. 291.

issue of using criminal law is mainly one of criminal policy.[49] According to German criminal law doctrine, the decisive question is whether conduct is worthy of punishment (*Strafwürdigkeit*) and needs punishment (*Strafbedürftigkeit*).[50] According to the prevailing opinion, the purpose of criminal law is to protect legal goods (*Rechtsgüter*).[51] Thus, criminalization of certain conduct presupposes the existence of a legal good that needs protection against such conduct. In this regard, proponents of a normative approach to the concept of legal good[52] recognize that the traditional concept of the protection of legal goods needs to be extended, for example to the life of future generations with respect to climate and resources.[53] Indeed, some of the earliest attempts in criminal legal theory and practice to argue in favour of the climate or the atmosphere as a new legal good requiring protection,[54] have noted that this would correspond to the prevailing ecological-anthropocentric concept of legal good. Moreover, they have pointed to Article 20a of the German Basic Law (GG) according to which the state shall protect the natural foundations of life and the interests of future generations.[55] However, the existence of such a legal good is not sufficient to criminalize certain conduct. The severity of the injury, which depends on the value of the protected legal good and the nature of the infringing act (*Handlungsunrecht*) are also considered

---

49 See, for example European Criminal Policy Initiative, 'The Manifesto of European Criminal Policy in 2011' (2011) 1 *European Criminal Law Review (EuCLR)* 83, 86. From a German perspective, Kloepfer, M. and M. Heger, *Umweltstrafrecht*, 3rd edn, C.H.Beck, 2014, para. 28; Satzger (2022), n. 24, § 9 para. 63. But see the different view of Vogel, J. and J. Eisele, 'Art. 83 AEUV' in Grabitz, E., M. Hilf and M. Nettesheim (eds), *Das Recht der Europäischen Union: EUV/AEUV*, 82th supplementary delivery, Mayy 2024, paras 19–21, 75; see also Klip (2021), n. 24, pp. 292–294.

50 See, for example Kloepfer and Heger (2014), n. 49; Deckert, A., 'Zum Strafwürdigkeitsbegriff im Kontext legislativer Kriminalisierungsentscheidungen im Verfassungsstaat' (2013) 8 *Zeitschrift für Internationale Strafrechtsdogmatik (ZIS)* 266–75; German Federal Constitutional Court (BVerfG), judgment of 25 February 1975, 1 BvF 1 et al., BVerfGE 39, 1, 8.

51 See, for example Kloepfer and Heger (2014), n. 49, para. 35; Roxin, C. and L. Greco, *Strafrecht Allgemeiner Teil*, Vol. I, 5th edn, Beck, 2020, § 2 para. 7. Opposed to this view is the German Federal Constitutional Court; see judgment of 26 February 2008, 2 BvR 392/07, BVerfGE 120, 224, 241–242.

52 This approach does not regard legal goods as all legal interests protected by the legislature (positivist approach) but as a concept that tells the legislature what it may punish and what it shall leave without punishment. See Ouwerkerk, J.W., 'Old Wine in a New Bottle: Shaping the Foundations of EU Criminal Law through the Concept of Legal Interests (Rechtsgüter)' (2021) 27 *European Law Journal* 426, 432–3.

53 See, for example Roxin and Greco (2020), n. 51, § 2 paras 57–9.

54 Frisch (2015), n. 21, p. 435; Satzger, H. and N. von Maltitz, 'Das Klimastrafrecht – ein Rechtsbegriff der Zukunft' (2021) 133(1) *Zeitschrift für die gesamte Strafrechtswissenschaft (ZStW)* 1, 8–13; see also Schmidt, F.-L., 'Der „Klimanotstand" als rechtfertigender Notstand?' (2023) *Klimarecht (KlimR)* 16, 17–18.

55 Schmidt (2023), ibid, p. 18; Higher Regional Court Schleswig-Holstein, judgment of 9 August 2023 – 1 ORs 4 Ss 7/23, para. 27.

relevant.[56] According to another view, it is the principle that criminal sanctions shall be applied as a last resort, which corresponds to the proportionality principle, that determines whether certain conduct requires either a criminal or an administrative (penal) sanction.[57] Thus, there is consensus that some kind of evaluation of effectiveness, deterrent effect, and proportionality ultimately determines the question of the type of punishment.

As a starting point, there can hardly be any doubt that the protection of the climate or the atmosphere is of supreme importance, being the basis of Earth's ecosystems and its environmental media such as water, air, flora, and fauna.[58] Much more difficult is to establish the extent to which, if any, conduct threatening the climate should be criminalized. According both to the ECD and Member States' criminal laws, criminal penalties demonstrate a major social disapproval of certain conduct.[59] However, individual GHG emissions contribute to climate change only to a small extent. It is their summation which leads to global warming, which makes it difficult to attribute criminal responsibility to individual emitters.[60] In addition, most GHG emissions are still considered socially acceptable and thus allowed in industrial societies.[61] In order to avoid contradictions in the legal system, national criminal laws can only penalize what is forbidden by other, typically administrative (environmental) laws. This is the so-called administrative law dependence of environmental criminal law, following the German concept of *Verwaltungsakzessorietät*.[62] Thus, as far as the environment or the climate is concerned, criminal law basically has a complementary function.[63]

However, to the extent that there are mitigation laws enforceable by (administrative) sanctions, neither the problem of attribution nor that of the administrative law dependence of environmental criminal law is at stake, so that criminal penalties could be provided to complement administrative penal sanctions. The decisive question is whether the use of criminal penalties in such cases could be considered proportionate.

---

56 Cf. Deckert (2013), n. 50, pp. 270–71; Jescheck, H.-H. and T. Weigend, *Lehrbuch des Strafrechts. Allgemeiner Teil*, 5th edn, Duncker & Humblot, 1996, p. 51.

57 See, for example BVerfG, judgment of 26 February 2008, n. 51; order of 9 March 1994, 2 BvL 43 et al., BVerfGE 90, 145, 172–3; Deckert (2013), n. 50, pp. 268, 274–5; Roxin and Greco (2020), n. 51, § 2 para. 62.

58 Frisch (2015), n. 21, p. 435; Satzger and von Maltitz (2021), n. 54, p. 12.

59 See ECD, Recital 4; COM(2021) 851 final, n. 38, p. 6; Satzger (2022), n. 24, § 8 para. 9; for Germany see BVerfG, order of 16 July 1969, 2 BvL 2/69, BVerfGE 27, 18, 29, 33; order of 9 November 1976, 2 BvL 1/76, BVerfGE 43, 101, 105.

60 Lopik and Stax (2020), n. 47, p. 118; Satzger and von Maltitz (2021), n. 54, p. 4.

61 Frisch (2015), n. 21, pp. 433–4; Lopik and Stax (2020), n. 47; Satzger and von Maltitz (2021), n. 54, p. 6.

62 See, for example Faure, M., The Development of Environmental Criminal Law in the EU and its Member States, (2017) 26 Review of European Community & International Environmental Law, 139, 141–145.

63 Frisch (2015), n. 21, p. 437; Satzger and von Maltitz (2021), n. 54, pp. 6–8; implicitly also Lopik and Stax (2020), n. 47, pp. 120–25.

This would first require that other sanctions, in particular administrative (penal) sanctions, are not effective and dissuasive enough to secure the enforcement of climate laws. Such an examination should be based on relevant data.[64] If data demonstrates that other sanctions are insufficient, penal sanctions could be prescribed provided that their use would be more effective and dissuasive, as well as appropriate for the relevant conduct. The effectiveness and dissuasiveness of criminal penalties is a complex issue, depending on many factors including the resources and expertise at all levels of the enforcement chain and the cooperation between all competent authorities.[65] From the experience with environmental criminal law in Germany, a certain level of effectiveness and dissuasiveness can generally be attributed to criminal law, although the deterrent effects of criminal law are difficult to measure.[66]

Finally, the use of criminal law to enforce mitigation obligations must be appropriate. As noted before, according to the ECD's approach, the criminalization of serious breaches of environmental law is proportionate according to the principle of proportionality as set out in Article 5(4) of the Treaty on European Union (TEU).[67] Such an approach corresponds to findings in the literature comparing environmental criminal law with administrative penal law that suggest that administrative fines may be more efficient for minor violations, whereas criminal sanctions are more appropriate for the most serious cases.[68] Moreover, generally exempting mitigation laws from criminal sanctions would not only be asymmetric compared to other fields of environmental law but also hardly compatible with the importance of the goal of protecting the Earth's atmosphere from growing GHG emissions.[69]

---

64 See Faure, M., 'Effective, Proportional and Dissuasive Penalties in the Implementation of the Environmental Crime and Ship-source Pollution Directives: Questions and Challenges' (2010) *European Energy and Environmental Law Review* 256, 259, and 278. Regarding harmonization of criminal sanctions according to the Treaty on the Functioning of the Euiropean Union (TFEU), Art. 83(2), the German Federal Constitutional Court requires that it must be demonstrably established that a serious enforcement deficit exists and can only be eliminated by the threat of punishment, see judgment of 30 June 2009, 2 BvE 2/08 et al., BVerfGE 123, 267, 410–12. But see the criticism by Vogel and Eisele (2024), n. 49, paras 74–5.

65 See, for example Farmer, A., M. Faure and G.M. Vagliasindi, 'Environmental Crime in Europe: State of Affairs and Future Perspectives' in Farmer, Faure and Vagliasindi (2017), n. 33, p. 319, pp. 325–7. The need for improvements in the enforcement chain has been acknowledged by ECD, Arts 17–22. See further Juan Fuentes Osorio's Chapter 6 The Effectiveness of Environmental Criminal Law Enforcement, in this volume.

66 Frisch (2015), n. 21, p. 432; Saliger, F., *Umweltstrafrecht*, 2nd edn, Vahlen, 2020, para. 62; Sina, S., 'Environmental Criminal Law in Germany' in Farmer, Faure and Vagliasindi (2017), n. 33, pp. 95, 113.

67 See also COM(2021) 851, n. 38, pp. 3–4.

68 Faure and Svatikova (2012), n. 47, pp. 285–7. See also Hall, M., 'Criminal Law and Climate Change' in *Volume I: Climate Change Law. Elgar Encyclopedia of Environmental Law*, Cheltenham, UK and Northampton, MA, Edward Elgar Publishing, 2016, pp. 103, 107, 112.

69 Frisch (2015), n. 21, p. 440.

Thus, there is a strong argument that serious breaches of mitigation obligations should be criminalized.[70] However, it is not easy to identify which breaches of mitigation provisions are to be considered serious. Endangering or injuring people, animals, or plants, as traditionally required by environmental law, cannot be used as standards applicable for violations of GHG emissions obligations since the impacts of climate change can hardly be attributed to the violator of mitigation obligations, at least not in criminal law.[71] One criterion to establish a serious breach of a mitigation provision could be the different levels of harmfulness of the different GHGs. For example, breaches of mitigation obligations concerning F-gases could always be considered serious, while violations of mitigation obligations related to methane, and even more so to carbon dioxide, only under further conditions.[72] Another criterion could be the total levels of GHG emissions by a company or operator.[73] Moreover, emitting GHGs without a permit, where required, could be criminalized, as is the case in the Netherlands and also (albeit indirectly) in Germany.[74] Not only GHG emissions but also substantial removals of carbon sink capacities could qualify as a serious breach of a mitigation obligation, as in the case of Article 3(2)(p) of the ECD regarding deforestation-related infringements.[75] Finally, the way the wrongful act is committed

---

70 See Frisch (2015), n. 21, pp. 440–41.

71 Cf. Satzger and von Maltitz (2021), n. 54, p. 5, with reference to the civil litigation case *Luciano Lliuya v. RWE*, n. 15. According to Satzger, an abstract endangerment offence would be possible, but only in relation to an endangerment of the climate itself; Satzger, H., 'Umwelt- und Klimastrafrecht in Europa – die mögliche Rolle des Strafrechts angesichts des "Green Deal" der Europäischen Union' in Engelhart, M., H. Kudlich and B. Vogel (eds), Digitalisierung, Globalisierung und Risikoprävention. Festschrift für Ulrich Sieber, Vol. 2, Duncker & Humblot, 2021, pp. 1267–1271.

72 See Annexes I to III of Regulation (EU) 2024/573, n. 36, and the corresponding Recital 2: 'Fluorinated greenhouse gases are human-made chemicals that are very strong greenhouse gases, which are often several thousand times stronger than carbon dioxide (CO2)'; Recital 2 of Regulation (EU) 2024/1787 of 13 June 2024 on the reduction of methane emissions in the energy sector [2024] OJ L 2024/1787: '… according to IPCC, while methane has 29.8 times greater global warming potential than CO2 on a 100-year timescale, it is 82.5 times more potent on a 20-year timescale'.

73 Frisch (2015), n. 21, p. 436.

74 See Lopik and Stax (2020), n. 47, p. 120. In Germany, TEHG, n. 45, section 32(3) no. 1 provides only an administrative penalty, and section 327(2)(1) of the Criminal Code, n. 93, only covers installations that need a permit according to the Federal Immission Control Act, not a permit according to TEHG, section 4(1). However, since the latter permits are regularly included in the former ones, emitting GHG without a permit commonly means that the conditions laid down in section 327(2)(1) of the Criminal Code are satisfied.

75 See also United Nations Office on Drugs and Crime (UNODC)/World Wide Fund for Nature (WWF), *Crimes that Affect the Environment and Climate Change*, pp. 10–16 with a rather general list of 'crimes affecting the environment and climate change response', https://www.unodc.org/res/environment-climate/resources_html/Crimes_that_Affect_the_Environment_and_Climate_Change.pdf (accessed 15 August 2024).

could be a deciding factor for criminalization, for example whether it is committed intentionally, with serious negligence,[76] or repeatedly.[77]

Overall, care must be taken to ensure that there are no significant discrepancies with the basic tenets of other environmental criminal laws. Frisch, for example, criticizes the sanctions provided by the EU Emissions Trading System Directive and transposed into German law as inadequate.[78] Again, however, it is not so simple: according to the CJEU, the application of an excess penalty of €100 for each ton of carbon dioxide equivalent emitted by the installation for which the operator has not surrendered allowances in Article 16(3) of the EU Emissions Trading System Directive is subject to a strict liability standard,[79] which means that it applies regardless of fault considerations as generally required by criminal law. Providing a criminal penalty for the violation of this ETS obligation would require evidence not only that the current types and levels of penalties are not sufficiently effective and dissuasive to enforce the obligation to surrender allowances, but that a criminal penalty would better conform to these criteria.

Finally, as the BVerfG has established in the case *Neubauer et al.*, the more climate change progresses, the more drastic measures to combat it need to be.[80] Accordingly, with progressing climate change and in view of the climate neutrality targets of the EU and an increasing number of countries, not only will there be tighter regulatory control of GHG emissions,[81] but violations of mitigation obligations are likely to be treated as serious offences so that criminal law will arguably play a greater role in the enforcement of mitigation obligations.[82]

3. Other crimes in the context of mitigation obligations

In addition to the criminal enforcement of mitigation obligations, there are other criminal offences that take place in the context of mitigation obligations. For example, the EU Emission Trading System has been targeted by criminal activities such as

76 Cf. ECD, Art. 3(1).

77 In the Netherlands, this is used as a criterion for applying criminal law instead of administrative law; see Lopik and Stax (2020), n. 47, p. 120.

78 Frisch (2015), n. 21, p. 440.

79 See *Billerud v. Naturvårdsverket* (C-203/12) EU:C:2013:664, judgment of 17 October 2013, [25]–[27], [38]–[39].

80 BVerfG, order of 24 March 2021, 1 BvR 2656/18 et al., BVerfGE 157, 30, paras 118–120, 185–186. For more details see Bodle, R. and S. Sina, 'The German Federal Constitutional Court's Decision on the Climate Change Act' (2022) 16 *Carbon & Climate Law Review* 18, 20–22.

81 See Frisch (2015), n. 21, pp. 433, 438–9; Lopik and Stax (2020), n. 47, p. 124.

82 Lopik and Stax (2020), n. 47, pp. 123, 125.

Value Added Tax (VAT) fraud and allowance theft.[83] Such offences are mainly financial crimes.

Financial crimes are economic crimes, towards which environmental crimes are often counted.[84] For example, in the Netherlands, when criminal law is used, most of the environmental laws are enforced through the Economic Offences Act (*Wet op de economische delicten*, WED).[85] However, meanwhile, 'the two areas tend to be better recognized as separate domains'.[86] In recent years, financial environmental crime is considered a specific category of financial fraud leading to environmental damage.[87] Thus, Interpol spoke of the criminal activities targeting the EU ETS as 'carbon trading crime as a new and emerging type of environmental and financial crime'.[88]

Whether certain fraudulent conduct formally belongs to environmental crimes arguably depends on whether it is included in the body of rules recognized as environmental criminal law. For example, Article 3(26)(c) of Regulation (EU) 2024/1157[89] defines that 'illegal shipment' includes shipment of waste effected with consent obtained from the competent authorities concerned through falsification, misrepresentation or fraud.[90] Therefore, under German criminal law, the widespread practice of document fraud[91] or similar conduct constitutes an environmental crime according to section 18(1)(1) of the German Waste Shipment Act.[92] Similar definitions, albeit not restricted to waste legislation, are included in Article 3(1), sub-paragraph 3 of the ECD and section 330d (1)(5) of the German Criminal Code.[93] According to German criminal law doctrine, these cases of abuse of rights are treated as exceptions to the principle of

---

83 See the detailed analysis by Nield, K. and R. Pereira, 'Financial Crimes in the European Carbon Markets' in Weishaar, S.E. (ed), *Research Handbook on Emissions Trading*, Cheltenham, UK and Northampton, MA, Edward Elgar Publuishing, 2016, pp. 195, 199 and following.

84 See, for example for Germany, Saliger (2020), n. 66, paras 13–17; for the Netherlands, see Lopik and Stax (2020), n. 47, p. 120.

85 See Lopik and Stax (2020), n. 47, p. 120; Faure and Svatikova (2012), n. 47, pp. 172–3.

86 Colantoni, L., G.S. Sarno and M. Bianchi, *Fighting Environmental Crime in Europe. An assessment of trends, players and actions*, 2022, p. 75, https://www.iai.it/sites/default/files/ambitus_report.pdf (accessed 15 August 2024).

87 Ibid.

88 Interpol, *Guide to Carbon Trading Crime*, June 2013, https://www.interpol.int/content/download/5172/file/Guide%20to%20Carbon%20Trading%20Crime.pdf (accessed 15 August 2024). From an EU perspective Eurojust, *Economic crimes*, https://www.eurojust.europa.eu/crime-types-and-cases/crime-types/economic-crimes (accessed 15 August 2024).

89 Regulation (EU) 2024/1157 of 11 April 2024 on shipments of waste [2024] OJ L 2024/1157.

90 The shipment of waste is an offence under ECD, Art. 3(g).

91 Cf. Colantoni, Sarno and Bianchi (2022), n. 86, p. 77.

92 Abfallverbringungsgesetz (AbfVerbrG) of 19 July 2007 (*Federal Law Gazette I*, p. 1462), as last amended by Act of 2 March 2023 (*Federal Law Gazette I*, no. 56).

93 Strafgesetzbuch (StGB) of 13 November 1998 (*Federal Law Gazette I*, p. 3322), as last amended by the Act of 24 June 2024 (*Federal Law Gazette I*, no. 213).

administrative law dependence in environmental criminal law.[94] On the other hand, criminal investigations in Germany as part of the 'Dieselgate' cases focused on classical fraud and financial criminal provisions instead of environmental offences. The manipulation of exhaust emission values of diesel vehicles by several manufacturers is presumably not covered by criminal liability for air pollution according to section 325 of the German Criminal Code.[95] This is because manipulations during the manufacturing process are not covered by the term 'air pollution when operating a facility' in paragraph 1 of section 325, while the release of harmful substances in a significant amount into the air in breach of duties under administrative law according to paragraph 2 of that provision does not apply to emissions from facilities including vehicles.[96]

From the perspective of whether to criminalize mitigation-related conduct, however, the fluid borderline between financial and environmental crimes is not relevant. Such fraudulent conduct is a serious offence and thus clearly criminal conduct regardless of whether it belongs to criminal mitigation law, financial criminal law, or classical criminal law. Indeed, prison sentences for environmental crimes are usually limited to cases of fraud or serious environmental harm.[97] When deciding whether to apply administrative or criminal law to breaches of ETS obligations in the Netherlands, fraud is considered an aggravating circumstance and always leads to the application of criminal law.[98]

In any case, an extension of mitigation legislation increases the potential for criminal activities to circumvent or abuse the relevant laws.[99] Recent examples include tax fraud in other areas such as illegal logging, document fraud in order to hide illegal trade in F-gases, fraud related to the composition of sustainable biofuels to fulfill the requirements of the Renewable Energy Directive,[100] climate-related investor

---

94 Saliger (2020), n. 66, para. 101.

95 According to Spapens, Member States having responsibility for setting adequate penalties and for enforcement under the relevant EU emissions regulations resulted in insufficient penalties and sloppy investigations in most of the Member States concerned. See Spapens, T., 'The "Dieselgate" Scandal: a criminological perspective' in Spapens, T., R. White, and D. van Uhm (eds), *Green Crimes and Dirty Money*, Routledge, 2016, pp. 91, 98–9 with reference to the report of the European Parliament's Commission of Enquiry of March 2017.

96 Saliger (2020), n. 66, para. 413a.

97 Faure (2010), n. 64, p. 266. See also the aggravating circumstances in ECD, Art. 8(a), (c), (d), and (h) and the qualified criminal offences in ECD, Art. 3(3).

98 Lopik and Stax (2020), n. 47, p. 120. In ECD, Art. 8(c).

99 Colantoni, Sarno and Bianchi (2022), n. 86, pp. 75–6.

100 Directive (EU) 2018/2001 of 11 December 2018 on the promotion of the use of energy from renewable sources (recast) [2018] OJ L 328/82, last amended by Directive (EU) 2023/2413 of 18 October 2023 amending Directive (EU) 2018/2001, Regulation (EU) 2018/1999 and Directive 98/70/EC as regards the promotion of energy from renewable sources, and repealing Council Directive (EU) 2015/652 [2023] OJ L 2023/2413.

deception, fraud regarding the amount of livestock, or illegal solar panel and battery waste trafficking.[101]

A completely different kind of criminal conduct in the context of mitigation represents the cases of civil disobedience by which climate activists aim at raising public awareness of the 'climate crisis'. In contrast to the financial crimes discussed above, these are basically classical crimes such as coercion, property damage, or trespassing, with the particularity that a state of climate emergency is invoked as justifying the action.[102] The outcome of such cases is not only determined by criminal law but also by principles of constitutional law, as shown by a recent judgment in Germany where a district court acquitted an activist by referring to the case *Neubauer et al.* of the BVerfG.[103] Although this judgment was overruled by the court of appeal,[104] the chances of success of such a 'climate emergency' defence may grow with progressing climate change[105] to the same extent that criminal law will arguably play a greater role in contributing to mitigation efforts.

4. Autonomous climate criminal law

Beyond the enforcement or abuse of mitigation laws, one could think of an autonomous role of criminal law in contributing to climate change mitigation. This could be in line with a trend in the Member States to abandon the absolute administrative dependence of criminal law in favour of an autonomous protection of the environment through criminal law.[106]

However, criminalizing climate-harmful conduct beyond what is already forbidden by administrative laws would raise some serious challenges. First, a general criminalization of climate-harmful conduct, such as emitting GHGs, would be difficult to formulate in a way compatible with the principle of legal certainty (*lex certa*).[107] Second, it is extremely difficult to establish individual and corporate responsibility for the deterioration of the global climate according to the principles of attribution and causation (for example the *conditio sine qua non* principle).[108] While using models

---

101 See Colantoni, Sarno and Bianchi (2022), n. 86, p. 76; Lopik and Stax (2020), n. 47, pp. 119, 124; UNODC/WWF, n. 75, p. 27.

102 See from a German perspective, for example, Schmidt (2023), n. 54, pp. 16–20.

103 District Court Flensburg, decision of 7 November 2022 – 440 Cs 107 Js 7252/22. See also Roxin and Greco (2020), n. 51, § 22 paras 130–33, who propose an exclusion of criminal liability due to minor culpability under certain conditions.

104 Higher Regional Court Schleswig-Holstein, judgment of 9 August 2023 – 1 ORs 4 Ss 7/23; see also the criticism by Schmidt (2023), n. 54, pp. 16–20.

105 Satzger and von Maltitz (2021), n. 54, pp. 31–2.

106 For the latter see Faure (2017), n. 27, pp. 141–2.

107 Frisch (2015), n. 21, p. 436; Lopik and Stax (2020), n. 47, p. 118.

108 Lopik and Stax (2020) n. 47, p. 118; Satzger and von Maltitz (2021), n. 54, pp. 4–5.

like the cost-benefit integrated assessment models (IAMs)[109] may contribute to establishing civil liability in litigation cases as the ones mentioned in the introduction, the threshold to establish criminal liability is higher and requires that personal responsibility for a certain outcome is clearly established.[110]

Third, a general criminalization of climate-harmful conduct would be hardly compatible with the fact that most GHG emissions are still permissible, sometimes even expressly, for example by permits. A general criminal prohibition would thus undermine the principle of the unity of the domestic legal order,[111] which is the main pillar of the principle of the administrative law dependence of environmental criminal law. It might also disregard the fact that criminal law demonstrates a higher degree of social disapproval of certain conduct.[112]

An interesting approach to overcoming those challenges has recently been proposed by Satzger and von Maltitz.[113] They consider any increase in the average global GHG concentration, that is the bringing about of climate change as such, as a relevant result of a 'climate offence' *de lege ferenda*.[114] Thus, such a criminal offence would not be designed as an endangerment crime (*Gefährdungsdelikt*) but as a crime dependent on an outcome (*Erfolgsdelikt*). The relevant conduct would be to bring about any impact on the atmosphere either through positive emissions or via interventions in carbon sinks. However, such conduct should only be regarded as damaging the atmosphere if it is not compensated by measures such as afforestation or carbon dioxide removal (CDR), so an overall balance of positive and negative emissions is needed to establish 'climate damage'. While any uncompensated positive emission or intervention in sinks is clearly a *conditio sine qua non* for the increase in the average global GHG concentration, only 'post-industrial' conduct should be attributed to individuals and companies. In addition, a *de minimis* rule should ensure that minor cases, such as lighting a lighter, are excluded as well, although this threshold may vary depending on the state of climate change.

Such a proposal would thus be able to address the problem of attribution and lay the foundations for the design of a 'climate criminal offence' that conforms with the principle of legal certainty. With regard to the main challenge described above, that is that the bulk of climate-damaging conduct is still socially accepted and legally allowed, Satzger and von Maltitz argue that social acceptance of climate-damaging conduct is already changing, as evidenced by framework climate change laws in several countries that aim at climate neutrality.[115] Ultimately, climate neutrality will require that

---

109 See UNODC/WWF, n. 75, p. 24.
110 See Satzger and von Maltitz (2021), n. 54, pp. 4–5.
111 Frisch (2015), n. 21, pp. 436–7; Lopik and Stax (2020), n. 47, p. 118; see also Satzger and von Maltitz (2021), n. 54, pp. 6–7.
112 See ECD, Recital 4; COM(2021) 851 final, n. 38.
113 Satzger and von Maltitz (2021), n. 54, pp. 8–34.
114 For the following see Satzger and von Maltitz (2021), n. 54, 13–18.
115 Satzger and von Maltitz (2021), n. 54, pp. 19–20.

any uncompensated GHG emission is forbidden, thus leading to a reversal of the current legal situation where GHG emissions are generally permitted and only forbidden in certain express cases. In such a situation, it is arguable that the criminal law will be indispensable to secure the status of climate neutrality.[116]

A problematic consequence of designing a 'climate criminal offence' linked to an increase in the average global GHG concentration would be, however, that any state could prosecute foreign perpetrators for any uncompensated GHG emissions committed abroad.[117] This is so because the airspace above the land mass of a state where global warming takes place, the troposphere,[118] belongs to that state's territory,[119] with the result that any increase in the average global GHG concentration also takes place in that territory. According to Satzger and von Maltitz, such a consequence could create serious conflicts of jurisdiction and undermine state sovereignty. Moreover, it would hardly be compatible with key principles of climate justice such as the principle of common but differentiated responsibility.[120] In their view, this is one of the problems that needs to be addressed by criminal law theory and practice.[121]

The approach by Satzger and von Maltitz is an interesting proposal for an autonomous climate criminal law that goes one step further than the trend described in section 2 above, suggesting that, with progressing climate change, violations of mitigation obligations will be perceived as more serious offences and thus increasingly be treated as criminal offences. As noted by those authors themselves, their proposal would need further testing and elaboration.[122] Such efforts should also take into account the developments at the European and international levels towards climate neutrality and the long-term goal of negative emissions.[123]

5. Conclusion

An assessment of the current state of criminal enforcement of climate change mitigation obligations reveals that, except for a few provisions in the ECD, European law

116 Cf. Satzger and von Maltitz (2021), n. 54, pp. 23–5.
117 For the following see Satzger and von Maltitz (2021), n. 54, pp. 25–30.
118 See Dupuy and Viñuales (2018), n. 35, p. 172. Satzger and von Maltitz, n. 54, p. 27, also mention the stratosphere which Dupuy and Viñuales ((2018), n. 35, p. 159) connect with the protection of the ozone layer.
119 See Hobe, S., *Space law*, Nomos, C.H. Beck, Hart, 2019, p. 15, according to whom outer space starts at least 110km above sea level. The troposphere and the stratosphere are the two layers closest to the Earth's surface: up to 12km and approximately between 12 and 50km altitude, see Dupuy and Viñuales (2018), n. 35, pp. 147–8.
120 See UN Framework Convention on Climate Change (UNFCCC), 9 May 1992, 1771 UNTS 107, Art. 3.1; PA, Art. 2.2.
121 See Satzger and von Maltitz (2021), n. 54, p. 30.
122 See Satzger and von Maltitz (2021), n. 54, pp. 18, 33–4.
123 See PA, Arts 4.1, 5.1; European Climate Law, Art. 2(1).

does not display an intention to oblige Member States to introduce criminal offences or penalties for the infringement of mitigation obligations. Nor does there appears to be evidence that the criminal laws of the Member States penalize such infringements to a significant extent, as demonstrated by the example of Germany discussed in this chapter, although the example of the Netherlands shows evidence to the contrary. This is not surprising since criminal penalties demonstrate a higher level of social disapproval of certain conduct, while most GHG emissions are still considered socially acceptable and thus allowed in industrial societies. On the other hand, criminal law has a complementary function that enables it to penalize what is forbidden by other (typically administrative) laws, including those protecting the climate. Generally exempting mitigation obligations from criminal sanctions would not only be asymmetric compared to other fields of environmental law, but also hardly compatible with the importance of the goal of protecting the Earth's atmosphere from growing GHG emissions. Thus, there is a strong argument that serious breaches of mitigation laws should be criminalized, while minor violations can be left to alternative sanctions such as administrative (penal) law. However, it is not easy to identify which breaches of mitigation obligations are to be considered serious since individual GHG emissions contribute to climate change only to a small extent. Notwithstanding the necessity of further research in this area, some of the criteria that could be applied include the different levels of harmfulness of the different GHGs emitted, the emitted amount, emitting GHG without a permit where one is required, and the way the wrongful act is committed. In addition, substantial removals of carbon sinks could also qualify as serious breaches of mitigation obligations. With progressing climate change, it can be expected that not only more types and levels of GHG emissions will be prohibited, but also that violations of mitigation laws will be perceived as more serious offences so that criminal law will play a greater role.

In addition to existing and potential new criminal offences for the violation of mitigation obligations, there are other criminal offences that take place in the context of mitigation obligations. Most of these are financial crimes, for example tax or document fraud related to mitigation instruments. Whether these can be regarded as discrete forms of environmental crime is debatable. In any case, such fraudulent activities are serious offences and thus clearly criminal conduct. With the increase in mitigation commitments under national and international laws, the potential for criminal activities to circumvent or abuse the relevant laws will increase. Equally, civil disobedience by climate activists is likely to be regarded as criminal conduct in most countries, with the particularity that a state of climate emergency may be invoked as justifying the action.

Finally, one could think about the role of an autonomous criminal law in contributing to mitigation. Currently, criminalizing climate-harmful conduct beyond what is already unlawful under administrative laws would hardly be compatible with the fact that most GHG emissions are still permitted, and that it is extremely difficult to establish individual or corporate criminal responsibility for the deterioration of the global climate according to the principles of attribution. In the longer term, however, it is anticipated that the quest for climate neutrality will ultimately require that any uncompensated GHG emission is regarded as unlawful. According to an interesting new approach suggested by Satzger and von Maltitz, criminal law will then be indispensable to secure the status of climate neutrality. One of the controversial aspects of this approach that would need further elaboration is how far a state could prosecute foreign perpetrators for any uncompensated GHG emissions committed abroad, which could create conflicts of jurisdiction and undermine state sovereignty as well as key principles of climate justice such as common but differentiated responsibilities.

To sum up, the role of criminal law in climate justice is likely to grow from its currently modest role of primarily securing compliance with mitigation administrative law obligations, to potentially a more autonomous role in light of the increase in global warming and the quest for climate neutrality. In accompanying this process, legal scholarship and practice will have to intensively scrutinize the challenges of using criminal law for climate change mitigation. This process is still at the beginning,[124] and in addition to the aspects addressed in this chapter, many fundamental issues require further research, such as the role of criminal law in penalizing violations of obligations to adapt to climate change, or the implications for transnational judicial cooperation of an emerging 'climate criminal law'.

124 See the recent compilation by Satzger, H. and N. von Maltitz (eds), *Klimastrafrecht. Die Rolle von Verbots- und Sanktionsnormen im Klimaschutz*, 3 *Schriften zum Klimaschutzrecht*, Nomos, 2024.

12 Artificial Intelligence and environmental crime

Stefano Porfido and Alberto Quintavalla

1. Introduction

Numerous technological advances have had an impact on criminal law. The criminal justice system is fundamentally reliant on the collection of accurate information for evidentiary purposes, both in the course of investigations and at trial. This is obvious from the effects of technological advancements in fingerprinting, DNA testing, the use of surveillance cameras, and more recently, GPS tracking, satellite data collection, online data extraction, the employment of sensors, and the digitalisation of biometric parameters. Furthermore, recent developments in the digitalisation of trials have enabled parties such as victims and offenders to participate in hearings via online platforms. These technological breakthroughs have fundamentally shaped the criminal justice system. For instance, the expansion of investigative powers has led to calls for the fundamental guarantees of the legal rights of defendants to be strengthened to ensure that trials are fair.

In the criminal justice system, artificial intelligence (AI) can certainly be as impactful as other technological advancements.[1] It can influence political choices and produce considerable legal consequences. The manifold prospective benefits of AI can prompt legislators and law enforcement bodies to develop a different, and perhaps more effective, approach to many forms of illegal conduct. This chapter examines the applications of AI in the context of environmental crime, which has become a particularly important topic in recent years due to the simultaneous emergence and increasing relevance of the criminalisation of environmental harms and the use of AI in environmental governance at the national and supranational level.[2] However, the interplay

---

1 See, for example A.G. Ferguson, 'Big Data and Predictive Reasonable Suspicion' (2015) 163 *University of Pennsylvania Law Review* 327.

2 For a recent and multidisciplinary research handbook on environmental crimes, see S.L. Smith and I. Sahramäki (eds), *Research Handbook on Environmental Crimes and Criminal Enforcement* (Cheltenham, UK and Northampton, MA: Edward Elgar

between AI and the criminalisation of environmental harms has had little influence on the law thus far, as exemplified by recent changes in the European Union (EU) legal framework. The EU has introduced the new Environmental Crimes Directive (ECD),[3] which is aimed at enhancing environmental protection by addressing the shortcomings of previous legislation. In addition, the EU has positioned itself as a leader in AI regulation by adopting the Artificial Intelligence Act (AIA).[4] Despite their significance, these instruments provide few insights into the role that AI could play in bolstering or undermining environmental protection through criminalisation and more effective law enforcement. For instance, while the AIA does refer to the impact of AI on environmental sustainability[5] and has environmental crimes among prohibited AI practices,[6] it does not address, to a considerable extent, the interplay between AI and environmental crime. The ECD is likewise silent on these connections and does not even mention AI directly. Instead, it refers to technologies in general and acknowledges their role in the perpetration of crimes[7] as well as their importance as resources that enable national authorities to combat environmental crime.[8]

This chapter evaluates the synergies and tensions that could arise from the use of detective and predictive AI capabilities to address environmental crimes. Specifically, we look at the actual or potential impacts of AI on the enforcement of (criminal) environmental law, and we pay attention to the broader role that such technology might play in influencing sovereign decisions about criminalisation. To that end, the analysis is premised on a broad definition of 'environmental crime', which accounts for both legalistic definitions and socio-legal perspectives from green criminological scholarship.[9] This approach helps us to distinguish between behaviours that have been

---

Publishing 2024). For the use of AI for environmental governance, see, for example M. Tironi and L. Di Rivera, 'Artificial Intelligence in the New Forms of Environmental Governance in the Chilean State: Towards an Eco-Algorithmic Governance' (2023) 74 *Technology in Society* 102264.

3 Directive (EU) 2024/1203 of the European Parliament and of the Council of 11 April 2024 on the protection of the environment through criminal law and replacing Directives 2008/99/EC and 2009/123/EC (Environmental Crimes Directive) (2024 ECD).

4 Regulation (EU) 2024/1689 of the European Parliament and of the Council of 13 June 2024 laying down harmonised rules on artificial intelligence and amending Regulations (EC) No 300/2008, (EU) No 167/2013, (EU) No 168/2013, (EU) 2018/858, (EU) 2018/1139 and (EU) 2019/2144 and Directives 2014/90/EU, (EU) 2016/797 and (EU) 2020/1828 (Artificial Intelligence Act) (AIA).

5 See, for instance, provisions under AIA, Articles 1, 46, 59, and 95.

6 AIA, Article 5(1)(h)(iii), and Annex II.

7 See, for example 2024 ECD, Recital 16.

8 See, for example 2024 ECD, Article 17.

9 See, for example M.J. Lynch et al., *Green Criminology: Crime, Justice, and the Environment* (University of California Press 2017); R. White, *Theorising Green Criminology: Selected Essays* (Routledge 2021).

formally categorised as 'criminal' and harms that, although they may be very serious, are currently outside the province of the criminal law.[10]

Our decision to embrace a comprehensive notion of environmental crime and to go beyond the strict legal definitions of crime has to do with the capacity of AI to generate representations of phenomena of potential criminal relevance, such as harm-relevant insights, more quickly and accurately than humans. AI technology converts rich troves of data into actual information which is accessible and comprehensible to all relevant actors (for example decision-makers and enforcement authorities).[11] AI could thus facilitate the identification of indicators and patterns of activity that are relevant to criminal law or point to likely illegal conduct. Illegal activities and, more broadly, environmental harms may become easier to detect, which in turn would strengthen law enforcement and provide a strong incentive for corporate compliance. At the same time, the use of AI for environmental protection could also generate significant tensions. We argue that these tensions are primarily linked to issues of control over AI: its misuse could undermine efforts to combat crime and unlawful conduct and could ultimately affect decision-making about the criminalisation of environmental offences.

The remainder of this chapter is structured as follows. Section 2 briefly outlines the potential of AI in environmental crime prevention and control; thereafter, it distinguishes AI impacts according to different categories of environmental harm. This analysis is necessary for an evaluation of the influence of AI on different types of environmental crimes. Section 3 examines the potential implications of AI for environmental crimes. Section 4 investigates several issues that are associated with AI which can aggravate the consequences of environmental crimes. Section 5 concludes.

2. The advent of artificial intelligence in crime: increased surveillance and enhanced crime prediction

AI has begun to play an essential role in our daily lives in the last decade. This trend is bound to persist and will pervade most – if not all – aspects of life. The impact of AI technology is not limited to improvements in business performance – it will also change the way in which humans relate to crime. In particular, criminologists and legal academics are increasingly paying attention to AI crime.[12] For instance, research

---

10 Yet it should be noted that this chapter considers the role of AI in addressing environmental harms in terms of enforcement-related issues and criminalisation processes. Therefore, it does not touch on any of the doctrinal and procedural issues that characterise specific domestic legal systems.

11 A.M. Rahmani et al., 'Artificial intelligence approaches and mechanisms for big data analytics: a systematic study' (2021) 7 *PeerJ Computer Science* e488.

12 T.C. King et al., 'Artificial intelligence crime: an interdisciplinary analysis of foreseeable threats and solutions' (2019) 26 *Science and Engineering Ethics* 89; M.R.

has been conducted on the potential malicious uses of AI systems[13] as well as on their offensive and defensive applications in specific settings.[14] As a general matter, this scholarship has shown that the definition of 'AI' is key to understanding the influence that such systems can exert on crime. Some scholars tend to focus on computational criminology,[15] others study digital criminology,[16] and others still are interested in data-era criminology.[17] Their findings are helpful in untangling the implications of specific AI features, but they do not typically adopt a comprehensive and integrated approach to the interface between AI and crime, which would be key for the emergence of a new sub-field of criminal law.

Given the aims of this chapter, we adopt a definition of AI technology that is as broad as possible: here, the term 'artificial intelligence' denotes automated technologies that perform activities which would otherwise call for human intelligence.[18] This definition is broad enough to capture all of the concrete applications of AI technology in criminal justice, such as visual recognition and natural language processing. In the enforcement of environmental criminal law, AI systems are used, among other things, to classify data, to detect anomalies in environmental indices,[19] and to identify the areas which illegal loggers and poachers are most likely to target.[20]

The wide range of functions that AI technology can discharge does affect criminal (environmental) law in a more general way, too. Two themes have emerged consistently

McGuire and T.J. Holt (eds), *The Routledge Handbook of Technology, Crime and Justice* (Routledge 2017).

13 M. Brundage et al., *The malicious use of artificial intelligence* (Future of Humanity Institute 2018) <https://dataspace.princeton.edu/handle/88435/dsp01th83m203g?mode=full> (accessed 8 August 2024).

14 See, for example R. Broadhurst et al., *Artificial Intelligence and Crime: A Report for the Korean Institute of Criminology* (ANU Cybercrime Observatory 2018).

15 M.L. Williams and P. Burnap, 'Cyberhate on social media in the aftermath of Woolwich: a case study in computational criminology and Big Data' (2016) 56 *British Journal of Criminology* 211.

16 A. Powell, G. Stratton and R. Cameron, *Digital Criminology* (Routledge 2018).

17 J. Chan and L. Bennett Moses, 'Making sense of Big Data for security' (2017) 57 *British Journal of Criminology* 299; G.J.D. Smith, L. Bennett Moses and J. Chan, 'The challenges of doing criminology in the Big Data era: towards a digital and data-driven approach' (2017) 57 *British Journal of Criminology* 259.

18 S. Russell and P. Norvig, *Artificial Intelligence: A Modern Approach* (Pearson 2016). For a more systematic attempt to devise a definition of AI, see M. Scherer, 'Regulating Artificial Intelligence Systems: Risks, Challenges, Competencies, and Strategies' (2015) 29 Harvard JLT 353, 360.

19 See, for example Y. Himeur et al., 'Using artificial intelligence and data fusion for environmental monitoring: A review and future perspectives' (2022) 86–87 *Information Fusion* 44.

20 See, for example USC Center for Artificial Intelligence in Society, *Conservation & Sustainability* (2022) <https://www.cais.usc.edu/projects/conservation-sustainability/> (accessed 8 August 2024).

in the literature, namely increased surveillance and, relatedly, a sharper focus on crime prediction and prevention. For instance, AI can be employed to identify and differentiate emotions as well as suspicious behaviours.[21] Advances in AI-enabled automatic video analytics and data storage have significantly increased the surveillance capabilities typically held by state enforcement agencies.[22] It is in this context that several commentators have alerted us to the human-rights concerns that such surveillance raises.[23] These concerns have been confirmed by case law from, inter alia, the European Court of Human Rights (ECtHR).[24]

These developments have not occurred in a vacuum. The emergence of novel interconnections between systems can facilitate surveillance and enable the authorities to expand it. For instance, AI systems can be combined with new sensors. This combination improves surveillance capabilities and may allow larger areas to be monitored. That citizens (and corporations) are more likely to be subject to the control of public authorities through AI systems could also make it easier for the latter to regulate the behaviour of the former. For instance, in smart cities the use of certain types of architectural features coupled with the possibilities offered by AI systems may impel citizens to adopt behaviours that the authorities deem desirable, as well as eliminate or reduce crime.[25] For instance, the use of advanced metering technology, which collects granular data on consumption patterns, may prompt users to refrain from wasteful uses of water.[26]

Finally, AI systems can enable the prediction of criminal conduct and thus facilitate targeted preventative interventions. By using AI systems, public authorities can reduce their outlays on monitoring and enforcement and focus on thwarting criminal conduct before it occurs. For instance, in the United States (US), AI systems have been used to determine the eligibility of detainees for bail. The use of statistical data and AI makes it possible for the authorities to reduce offending by basing detention decisions on empirically robust correlations rather than the intuitions of judges and law

---

21 L. Podoletz, 'We Have to Talk about Emotional AI and Crime' (2023) 38 *AI & Society* 1067.

22 J. Stanley, *The Dawn of Robot Surveillance* (American Civil Liberties Union 2019); X. Wu and X. Zhang, 'Automated inference on criminality using face images' (2016) *arXiv preprint arXiv:1611.04135* 4038.

23 See, for example E. Selinger and W. Hartzog, 'The Inconsentability of Facial Surveillance' (2020) 66 *Loyola Law Review* 101; F. Palmiotto and N.M. González, 'Facial recognition technology, democracy and human rights' (2023) 50 *Computer Law & Security Review* 105857.

24 See, for example *S and Marper v the United Kingdom* (App nos 30562/04 and 30566/04) (ECtHR, 4 December 2008); *Gaughran v the United Kingdom* (App no 45245/15) (ECtHR, 13 February 2020).

25 K. Yeung, '"Hypernudge": Big Data as a mode of regulation by design' (2017) 20(1) *Information, Communication & Society* 118.

26 A. Quintavalla, 'Water law and municipal water in an era of technological development' in V. Casado Pérez and R. Larson (eds), *A Research Agenda for Water Law* (Cheltenham, UK and Northampton, MA: Edward Elgar Publishing 2023), 185.

enforcement officials.[27] These improvements magnify the deterrent effect of the law by reducing the expected likelihood of pre-trial release for those who contemplate engaging in illegal conduct persistently. Moreover, the higher accuracy of these bail decisions frees up law-enforcement resources that would otherwise have to be allocated to monitoring individuals who are on bail, enabling those resources to be directed at preventative efforts.

These developments may call for a thorough reconceptualisation of *all* criminal law, not just environmental criminal law. Such a monumental endeavour is obviously far beyond the scope of the present contribution. What we propose to do here is to develop a taxonomy of environmental crimes that is conducive to an analysis of both the positive and the negative influence of AI on environmental crime. Indeed, as we will show later, the ramifications of AI will be palpable far beyond the relatively small set of strictly defined environmental crimes. Before we present our taxonomy, however, we must dispose of several definitional matters, which is the task to which we now turn.

'Environmental crime' is an umbrella term. It is vague because it covers a wide and heterogeneous array of conduct and accounts for several factors, including temporal and spatial contingencies, societal values, the peculiarities of domestic legal orders and, ultimately, the vantage point from which one observes these phenomena. Here, we adopt a notion of 'environmental crime' that encompasses not only traditional legalistic perspectives but also social scientific notions from the field of green criminological studies, which focus on non-criminalised harms.[28] From a legalistic standpoint, environmental crime entails actions that breach a penal statute. Traditionally, criminal law in the environmental sector evolved as part of the effort to enhance the enforcement of administrative measures.[29] More recently, criminal law has taken on a more autonomous role in addressing environmentally degrading activities. Most Western criminal law systems nowadays include not only pure regulatory offences but also qualified criminal ones. The latter are designed to sanction unlawful actions more severely when they pose abstract or concrete risks of environmental harm and when they actually cause such harm.[30] To a certain degree, national laws recognise

27 M. Kaufmann, S. Egbert, and M. Leese, 'Predictive policing and the politics of patterns' (2018) 59 *British Journal of Criminology* 674.

28 See, in this volume, Anna Di Ronco and Nigel South's Chapter 9 Environmental Harms, Ecocide Trends and Restorative Responses: Some Interdisciplinary Perspectives, and Ragnhild Sollund's Chapter 10 A Green Criminology Perspective on Animal Rights.

29 See, for example M Faure, 'The Development of Environmental Criminal Law in the EU and Its Member States' (2017) 26 *Review of European, Comparative & International Environmental Law* 139.

30 The 2024 ECD moves in this direction as Article 3(3) requires that Member States shall ensure that criminal offences relating to conduct listed in paragraph 2 constitute qualified criminal offences if such conduct causes (a) the destruction of, or widespread and substantial damage which is either irreversible or long-lasting to, an ecosystem of considerable size or environmental value or a habitat within a protected site, or (b) widespread and substantial damage which is either irreversible or long-lasting to the quality of air, soil, or water.

independent environmental crimes that penalise harm to the environment even in the absence of regulatory infractions.[31] The distinction between criminal, civil, and administrative violations, the choice between abstract and concrete endangerment and actual harm, and the degree to which criminal law relies on administrative regulations are context-specific and value-driven issues. Decisions about these issues rest with national legislatures and reflect adherence, to a certain degree, to anthropocentric or ecocentric views.[32]

Conversely, scholars in the green criminological tradition generally go beyond the legal definitions that conform to a state's criminal law or law in general.[33] By adopting a social harm approach, green criminological notions of environmental crimes also account for 'lawful but awful'[34] activities, that is to say, detrimental legal uses of natural resources – and modes of managing them – that affect people and the environment in different ways, including physically, economically, and culturally.[35] This sociological viewpoint is grounded in the belief that crimes and legal labels are social constructs that are shaped by vested interests[36] which reflect the inherently space- and time-dependent political process of negotiations among social systems.[37] Under this perspective, environmental crime might be conceived as:

---

31 See, for example, arson to forests is a felony crime under Article 423-bis of the Italian Criminal Law Code.

32 For a comprehensive analysis on definitory and justificatory grounds of environmental crime, see S.L. Smith, 'Issues in Defining and Punishing Environmental Crimes: An Introduction' in S.L. Smith and I. Sahramäki (eds), *Research Handbook on Environmental Crimes and Criminal Enforcement* (Cheltenham, UK and Northampton, MA: Edward Elgar Publishing 2024) and R. Pereira, *Environmental Criminal Liability and Enforcement in European and International Law* (Brill 2015).

33 M. Hall, *Exploring Green Crime: Introducing the Legal, Social and Criminological Contexts of Environmental Harm* (Bloomsbury Publishing 2017), 58 and following; L. Bisschop, *Governance of the Illegal Trade in E-Waste and Tropical Timber: Case Studies on Transnational Environmental Crime* (Routledge 2016), 32; C. Gibbs et al., 'Introducing Conservation Criminology: towards interdisciplinary scholarship on environmental crimes and risks' (2010) 50 *British Journal of Criminology* 124, 125; R. White, *Crimes Against Nature: Environmental Criminology and Ecological Justice* (Routledge 2013), 88 and following.

34 N. Passas, 'Lawful but Awful: "Legal Corporate Crimes" (2005) 34 *The Journal of Socio-Economics* 771.

35 On the social harm approach, see P. Hillyard et al. *Beyond Criminology: Taking Harm Seriously* (Pluto Press 2004); P. Davies, P. Leighton, and T. Wyatt (eds), *The Palgrave Handbook of Social Harm* (Springer Nature 2021).

36 R. Quinney, *The Social Reality of Crime* (Transaction Publishers 1970), 15–16; H.S. Becker, *Outsiders: Studies in the Sociology of Deviance* (Free Press 1963), 9.

37 M.J. Lynch, P.B. Stretesky, and M.A. Long, *Defining Crime: A Critique of the Concept and Its Implication* (Palgrave Macmillan 2015), 112; E.H. Sutherland, 'White-Collar Criminality' (1940) 5 *American Sociological Review* 1.

> any intentional or negligent activity or manipulation [by an individual or a corporation] that entails avoidable and unnecessary, immediately noticeable or indiscernible (only noticeable over time) environmental harm to biotic [faunal/floral] or a-biotic [natural resource contamination] natural resources, resulting in immediately noticeable or indiscernible (only noticeable over time) natural resources trauma of any magnitude, which might transfer regional and national boundaries and is serious enough to warrant state intervention.[38]

By including this broader definition, we are able to highlight the potential impacts of AI on environmental crime, ranging from law enforcement aspects to the dynamics of criminalisation. With the definitions outlined above, we are now in a position to articulate our taxonomy: we categorise environmental crimes into three categories based on degrees of legal formalisation. These categories are as follows: i) formal environmental crimes, ii) environmental harms that result from formal crimes other than those that have been labelled 'environmental', and iii) environmental harms that are not formally criminal and whose perpetration is therefore either fully lawful or unlawful but only within the scope of administrative or tort law. It is important to note here that these categories are not mutually exclusive – environment-related crimes, whether formally criminalised or not, often overlap in specific contexts. For instance, it has been estimated that unauthorised mining activities generate between 12 and 48 billion US dollars annually.[39] Those activities entail formally illegal conduct, such as the use of and trade in prohibited toxic chemicals, which might be related to other crimes, such as labour exploitation, sexual abuse, and migrant smuggling.[40] The overlap between these crimes and industrial extractive activities makes it difficult to delineate unlawfulness and criminality precisely.[41] The purpose of our taxonomy is thus not to establish clear boundaries between different types of crimes – its constituent categories are not 'boxes' but 'interlocking circles' – but to discriminate between different forms of environmental harm so that we can analyse the influence of AI on each more clearly. In this context, we turn to describing the benefits of AI in section 3, and then to the tensions to which AI may give rise in section 4.

38 This definition is provided by Bisschop (n. 33), 33, who was inspired by definitions provided by F.J.W. Herbig and S.J. Joubert, 'Criminological Semantics Criminology - Vision or Vagary?' (2006) 19(3) *Acta Criminologica: African Journal of Criminology & Victimology* 88, and N. Passas, 'Globalization, Criminogenic Asymmetries and Economic Crime' (1999) 1(4) *European Journal of Law Reform* 399.

39 Interpol, *Illegal mining and associated crimes. A Law Enforcement Perspective on One of the Most Lucrative Crimes* (2022), 7.

40 Ibid, 16. See also Y. Zabyelina and D. van Uhm, *Illegal Mining: Organized Crime, Corruption, and Ecocide in a Resource-Scarce World* (Springer Nature 2020).

41 On this issue, see Y. Zabyelina, *Responding to Illegal Mining and Trafficking in Metals and Minerals. A Guide to Good Legislative Practices* (UNODC 2023) <https://sherloc.unodc.org/cld/uploads/pdf/Illegal_Mining_and_Trafficking_in_Metals_and_Minerals_E.pdf> (accessed 8 August 2024).

3. Benefits

3.1 AI and formally criminal harms

The first category in our taxonomy includes environmental harms that have been criminalised at the international, regional, and/or domestic levels. Those laws may target individuals, criminal organisations, or corporations. In general terms, the crimes in question tend to concern biodiversity loss, pollution, illegal waste trafficking and disposal, and natural resource depletion.[42] These activities are inordinately profitable,[43] which makes them attractive not only for domestic actors but also for transnational criminal organisations.[44] The international agreements that incorporate hard obligations for state parties to criminalise include the Convention on International Trade in Endangered Species of Wild Fauna and Flora,[45] the Basel Convention on the Control of Transboundary Movements of Hazardous Wastes and their Disposal,[46] and the Convention on the Prevention of Pollution from Ships.[47] These international agreements have been further implemented at the regional and the national levels. For instance, the 2024 EU Environmental Crime Directive criminalises a wide range of environmental offences, determines the content of specific criminal sanctions, and fosters cooperation between the Member States.

The capacity of AI to detect and predict environmental harm could improve the enforcement of the criminal codes and environmental or criminal statutes which have become the basis for the implementation of those instruments. AI finds uses across the whole spectrum of environmental crimes, primarily by enhancing monitoring and surveillance. Its employment has been particularly fruitful in wildlife, ocean,

42 See, for example guidance documents supporting the new 2024 ECD, such as European Commission, Directorate-General for Environment, *Combating environmental crimes and related infringements – Environmental compliance assurance – Guidance document* (Publications Office of the European Union 2021) <https://data.europa.eu/doi/10.2779/035969> (accessed 8 August 2024).

43 See, for example C. Nellemann et al. (eds), *World atlas of illicit flows. A RHIPTO-INTERPOL-GI Assessment* (RHIPTO-Norwegian Center for Global Analyses, INTERPOL and the Global Initiative Against Transnational Organized Crime 2018). See <www.rhipto.org> and <www.interpol.int> (accessed 24 March 2023). United Nations Environment Programme, *The rise of environmental crime: A growing threat to natural resources, peace, development and security* (United Nations Environment Programme (UNEP) 2016) <https://wedocs.unep.org/xmlui/handle/20.500.11822/7662> (accessed 11 August 2024).

44 D. Bank et al., *Environmental crime: A threat to our future* (Environmental Investigation Agency (EIA) 2008) <https://eia-international.org/report/environmental-crime-2/> (accessed 24 March 2024).

45 Article viii.

46 Articles 4(3) and 9(5) are to be read conjointly.

47 Article 4(4).

and land conservation.[48] For instance, researchers from a network of universities have developed an AI system that optimises patrol routes for rangers in national parks based on data from past poaching incidents and environmental factors.[49] AI can also be programmed to recognise specific sounds or shapes and to alert officers when it detects them. The Nature Guardians project, which is being run by the World Wide Fund for Nature (WWF) Italy with the support of Huawei and the start-up Rainforest Connection, leverages these functionalities.[50] AI can also recognise patterns of deforestation and illegal dumps, thus reducing the cost of monitoring large territories.[51] The Spanish Nature Protection Service (SEPRONA) is developing a smartphone app that can scan DNA and thus allow users to trace the origin of imported timber.[52] Similarly, AI has been used to combat crimes, such as arson, against particular ecosystems in Africa by employing image analysis and thermal infrared cameras.[53] AI is also instrumental in processing vessel-tracking data and radar satellite imagery to identify suspicious activities in international waters.[54] It has proven effective in identifying, tracking, and mitigating illegal pollution, particularly from chemical pollutants.[55] AI has also been used to pre-empt environmental crimes such as the illegal dumping of waste, illegal logging in rainforests, and poaching.[56]

---

48 D.A. Isabelle and M. Westerlund, 'A Review and Categorization of Artificial Intelligence-Based Opportunities in Wildlife, Ocean and Land Conservation' (2022) 14 *Sustainability* 1979.

49 F. Fang et al., 'PAWS — A Deployed Game-Theoretic Application to Combat Poaching' (2017) 36 *AIMag* 23.

50 For more information on this project, see <https://www.huawei.com/en/tech4all/stories/italy-biodiversity> (accessed 8 August 2024).

51 L. Colantoni, G.S. Sarno, M. Bianchi, *Fighting Environmental Crime in Europe. An Assessment of trends, players and action* (Istituto Affari Internazioanli (IAI) – Ambitus 2022) <https://www.iai.it/sites/default/files/ambitus_report.pdf> (accessed 23 March 2024), 75–6.

52 Ibid, 72.

53 See, for example R. Sigsworth, 'AI can turn the tide on organised environmental crime in Africa' (Institute for Security Studies 2024), <https://issafrica.org/iss-today/ai-can-turn-the-tide-on-organised-environmental-crime-in-africa> (accessed 23 March 2024).

54 See, for example J.A. Fernandes-Salvador et al., *Artificial Intelligence and the fisheries sector* (European Parliament, Policy Department for Structural and Cohesion Policies, Brussels, Research for PECH Committee 2022) <https://www.europarl.europa.eu/RegData/etudes/STUD/2022/699643/IPOL_STU(2022)699643_EN.pdf> (accessed 8 August 2024).

55 J. Wang et al., 'Identification of pollution source and prediction of water quality based on deep learning techniques' (2024) 261 *Journal of Contaminant Hydrology* 104287.

56 See, respectively, L. Du et al., 'Assessing and predicting the illegal dumping risks in relation to road characteristics' (2023) 169 *Waste Management* 332; I. Mporas et al., 'Illegal Logging Detection Based on Acoustic Surveillance of Forest' (2020) 10 *Applied Sciences* 7379; E. Castelli, *Enhancing anti-poaching efforts through predictive analysis of animals. Movements and dynamic environmental factors* (Umea Universitet 2023) https://www.diva-portal.org/smash/get/diva2:1777041/FULLTEXT01.pdf> (accessed 8 August 2024).

The second category in our taxonomy covers environmental harms that stem from integrated criminal activities. Here, the term 'integrated' refers to the interplay between environmental harm and other serious offences, such as murder, money laundering, tax evasion, corruption, piracy, forgery, corporate fraud, and the trafficking of drugs and firearms.[57] International environmental and law-enforcement agencies have used the terms 'crime convergence' or 'threat convergence' to highlight the dynamics of organised-crime groups that operate globally by harnessing recent innovations in technology and communication.[58] For instance, drug trafficking is not an 'environmental crime' per se, but law-enforcement agencies have demonstrated that the routes which have traditionally been used to traffic drugs can also be used to smuggle wildlife-derived products such as ivory.[59] Similarly, serious crimes like corruption, fraud, and money laundering may enable the illegal destruction of the environment. This wider and integrated representation of the phenomenon of environmental crime has prompted the United Nations (UN) and the Council of Europe to endorse the notion of 'crimes that affect the environment' as a replacement for the traditional and sectorial label of 'environmental crimes'.[60] This shift could pave the road to the expanded adoption of autonomous criminal offences that are linked to (higher) thresholds of harm to the environment and human health, and whose operation would be separate from that of extant civil- or administrative-law provisions.[61]

---

57 D.P. van Uhm and C.C. Nijman, 'The convergence of environmental crime with other serious crimes: Subtypes within the environmental crime continuum' (2022) 19 *European Journal of Criminology* 542.

58 A. Crosta et al., *Environmental Crime Convergence: Launching an Environmental Crime Convergence Paradigm Through Investigation of Transnational Organized Crime Operations* (Earth League International and John Jay College of Criminal Justice 2023) <https://earthleagueinternational.org/wp-content/uploads/2023/06/ELI-Environmental-Crime-Convergence-Report-June-2023.pdf> (accessed 8 August 2024); Interpol, *Environmental Crime and its Convergence with other Serious Crimes Environmental Security*, Report no 2015/999/OEC/ENS/SLO (Interpol 2015) available at: <https://www.interpol.int/en/Crimes/Environmental-crime/Our-response-to-environmental-crime> (accessed 8 August 2024); Wildlife Justice Commission, *Convergence of wildlife crime with other forms of organised crime: A 2023 review* (Wildlife Justice Commission, 2023) <https://wildlifejustice.org/convergence-wildlife-crime-organised-crime/> (accessed 8 August 2024).

59 Interpol (2015) (n. 58), 7. See also Angus Nurse's Chapter 8 The Global Illegal Wildlife Trade Crisis, in this volume.

60 Respectively, UN General Assembly Resolution Preventing and combating crimes that affect the environment, Resolution A/RES/76/185, adopted by the General Assembly on 16 December 2021; V. Jaworski, *Working paper on protecting the environment through criminal law*, CDPC(2020)9 (European Committee on Crime Problems (CDPC) 2020). See also E. Lyman and T. Wyatt, *Global Analysis on Crimes that Affect the Environment – Part 1: the Landscape of Criminalization* (UNODOC - United Nations publication 2024) <https://reliefweb.int/report/world/global-analysis-crimes-affect-environment-part-1-landscape-criminalization> (accessed 8 August 2024).

61 The recently adopted 2024 ECD seems to be moving in this direction. Whereas Article 3 'Criminal offences' requires that conduct, to be criminal, shall be unlawful, i.e.that is shall breach a law, regulation, or administrative provision, its paragraph 1 further

AI can certainly expose criminal convergences. Experiments have already been conducted in the context of the trafficking of drugs, cultural artifacts, and firearms.[62] AI can also reveal links between separate but interlinked illegal activities, including environmental crimes and other serious crimes. For instance, it could expose the environmental consequences of corruption by detecting irregular grants of licences that sanction the otherwise illegal clear-felling of forests.[63] These AI capabilities could contribute to the consolidation of an integrated notion of 'crimes that affect the environment', which the UN and the Council of Europe have proposed as a substitute for the sectorial approaches that currently predominate in legal discourses.

3.2 AI and non-criminal harms

We now turn to the last of our suggested categories of environmental crimes, that is, the special case of environmental harms that are not formally criminal. The activities that fall in this grey area, which are sometimes lawful and sometimes unlawful, are typically carried out by corporations. The Royal Institute of International Affairs suggests that enterprise crime 'is more effectively conceptualised as a market

requires that such conduct 'shall be unlawful even where it is carried out under an authorisation issued by a competent authority of a Member State … if such authorisation *is in manifest breach of relevant substantive legal requirements*' [emphasis added]. Arguably, this paragraph introduces a notion of unlawfulness that aligns with the entire domestic legal order, including human rights obligations. If this is the case, the 2024 ECD is, in effect, introducing specific qualified offences characterised not only by substantial thresholds of environmental damage (Article 3(3) thereof) but also by an expanded notion of 'unlawfulness', which appears to reflect a significant shift from the traditional use of criminal law as ancillary to environmental regulations towards an independent or autonomous environmental crime. For a discussion on defining a new environmental crime for breaching a general environmental duty of care, see R. White, 'Environmental Harms and Innovative Justice' in S.L. Smith and I. Sahramäki (eds), *Research Handbook on Environmental Crimes and Criminal Enforcement* (Cheltenham, UK and Northampton, MA: Edward Elgar Publishing 2024), 128.

62 I. Mademlis et al., 'The invisible arms race: digital trends in illicit goods trafficking and AI-enabled responses' (2023) *TechRxiv* <https://www.techrxiv.org/doi/full/10.36227/techrxiv.24288703.v1> (accessed 8 August 2024); N. Schörnig, 'AI for Arms Control. How Artificial Intelligence Can Foster Verification and Support Arms Control' (2022) *PRIF Spotlight* <https://blog.prif.org/2022/01/19/ai-for-arms-control-how-artificial-intelligence-can-foster-verification-and-support-arms-control/> (accessed 8 August 2024).

63 See, for example J. Baker, *Corrupt networks in the Indonesian forestry sector Politics and pulp in Pelalawan, Riau* (2020) *U4 Issue* <https://www.u4.no/publications/corrupt-networks-in-the-indonesian-forestry-sector> (accessed 8 August 2024). See also the Report by FATF, *Money Laundering from Environmental Crimes*, (Paris: FATF 2021) https://www.fatf-gafi.org/publications/methodsandtrends/documents/money-laundering-environmental-crime.html> (accessed 1 September 2024) on the interplay between money laundering and environmental crime. The 2024 ECD acknowledges the link between environmental crime and other crimes, as indicated for instance under Article 8 'Aggravating circumstances', (c)–(f).

than a form of social deviance: criminal activities are structured around multilateral exchanges involving producers, processors, retailers and final consumers where supply and demand for services interact in a free-market relationship'.[64] In these markets, unlawful and lawful economic activities converge. Some examples include the trade in e-waste, which often entails illegal disposal in destination countries and involves actors such as shipping companies, state officials, and intermediaries, all of whom may be acting legally.[65] This category also includes harmful corporate operations that are conducted with the authorisation of the state. A typical example is the ILVA case, in which a large multinational operated a steel production plant pursuant to licences that had been issued by the Italian authorities. Although these permits shielded the corporate actors involved from prosecution, the ECtHR recognised the tremendous harm that their operations had caused to the environment and, consequently, to the human rights of the local residents.[66]

AI can enhance corporate compliance with environmental obligations by enhancing deterrence. All punitive laws that apply to corporations, including criminal law, are premised on two assumptions. The first is that businesses are rational economic actors, and the second is that, the greater the severity and likelihood of a punishment, the stronger its deterrent effect. Both of these assumptions are underpinned by efforts to rationalise punishment that originates from the law-and-economics literature.[67] In brief, the idea is that corporations are 'rational actors' that are motivated by utility maximisation and therefore multiply the likelihood of detection by the severity of the prospective sanction, be it criminal or non-criminal. They then compare that prospective punishment to the expected benefits of embarking on an illicit course of action.[68] Yet empirical research has exposed the shortcomings of these law-and-economics models – 'compliance rationality' appears to vary from risk to risk for reasons such as information asymmetries and poor awareness of regulatory risk.[69] AI could arguably compensate for these deficits by enhancing the deterrence of 'rational' corporate

---

64 G. Hayman and D. Brack, *International Environmental Crime: The nature and control of environmental black market* (The Royal Institute of International Affairs – Sustainable Development Programme, Workshop Report, 2002), 6.

65 L. Bisschop and G. Walle, 'Environmental Victimisation and Conflict Resolution: A Case Study of e-Waste' in R. Walters, D.S. Westerhuis and T. Wyatt (eds), *Emerging Issues in Green Criminology: Exploring Power, Justice and Harm* (Palgrave Macmillan UK 2013), 34.

66 *Cordella and Others v Italy* (App nos 54414/13 and 54264/15) (ECtHR, 24 January 2019). On the harmful implications stemming from this plant, see also the recent *C.Z. e altri v Ilva SpA in Amministrazione Straordinaria e altri* (C-626/22) EU:C:2024:542 (CJEU, 25 June 2024), especially [132].

67 G.S. Becker, 'Crime and Punishment: An Economic Approach' (1969) 76(2) *Journal of Political Economy* 169; see also M. Faure and R. Partain, *Environmental Law and Economics: Theory and Practice* (Cambridge University Press 2019).

68 Ibid.

69 R. Baldwin, 'The New Punitive Regulation' (2004) 67 *The Modern Law Review* 351, 368–9. For criticisms of rational actor models and the control of corporate crime, see C. Parker, *The Open Corporation* (Cambridge University Press 2002), 34–5, 68–70.

actors. As Sabia has pointed out, AI can improve the rationality of corporate actors and corporate decision-making processes by improving corporate assessments of risk, the detection of its sources, and its management.[70]

Corporations should adopt responsive strategies that leverage the capacity of AI to detect complex interactions between events, such as the release of contaminants during industrial production and the dynamics of ecosystems. For instance, Eastwood and others developed an AI model that ties changes in biodiversity to historical environmental changes.[71] They found, on the basis of AI-generated data, that the presence of insecticides and fungicides could have accounted for up to 90% of biodiversity loss at the sites they studied. More generally, they showed that AI can learn from past data and predict future trends with unmatched accuracy, thus illuminating the connections between certain human activities and their environmental consequences. AI could therefore be particularly effective in rendering corporate compliance more forward-looking by enabling corporations to consider not only criminalised and non-criminalised harms but also environmental harms that are not yet known to science or are known in theory but have yet to materialise. This feature of AI is particularly significant in the context of the phenomenon of historical pollution, whereby the constant release of marginal quantities of contaminating substances causes harm over prolonged periods despite the emitters' compliance with the applicable standards. Unlike harm from single catastrophes or events, the environmentally detrimental effects of historical pollution emerge over long timespans and are due to the cumulative effects of pollution. From a criminal law perspective, historical pollution raises significant challenges because environmental harm may result from numerous occurrences which, when viewed in isolation, are either lawful or constitute minor administrative infractions.[72] AI may detect actual patterns of contamination and anticipate their cumulative effects, which may benefit both regulators and corporations when setting their enforcement or compliance strategies. In short, AI could bolster preventive efforts and enhance the effective imposition of sanctions in the environmental domain.

70 R. Sabia, 'Artificial Intelligence and Environmental Criminal Compliance' (2019) *Revue Internationale de Droit Penal - The Criminal Law Protection of Our Common Home* 179; D.N. Wagner, 'The nature of the Artificially Intelligent Firm - An economic investigation into changes that AI brings to the firm' (2020) 44 *Telecommunications Policy* 101954. For a critical assessment of automated criminal compliance, see W.S. Laufer, 'The Missing Account of Progressive Corporate Criminal Law' (2017) 14(1) *New York University Journal of Law & Business* 71. See also Carolyn Abbot and Gary Lynch-Wood's Chapter 3 Transnational Environmental Crime across Global Supply Chains - A Place for Due Diligence?, in this volume.

71 N. Eastwood et al., '100 years of anthropogenic impact causes changes in freshwater functional biodiversity' (2023) 12 *eLife* RP86576.

72 On the challenges to tackle historical pollution, see F. Centonze and S. Manacorda (eds), *Historical Pollution and Long-Term Liability: A Global Challenge Needing an International Approach*? (Springer 2017).

4. Tensions

We have thus far focused on the upside of AI. However, it would be absurd to argue that AI carries no risks or that it is wholly unproblematic – in fact, its interaction with the criminalisation of environmental harm also engenders tensions. In general terms, the advent of AI poses an accountability gap issue,[73] which is sharpened by the risks that attend reliance on AI decision-making processes. These risks may originate indirectly from symbiotic man-machine entities or directly from AI operating autonomously or as part of networks of AI systems.[74] Such decision-making processes raise criminal liability issues.[75] This is an emerging field of research, and it has two main pillars.[76] Firstly, scholars are exploring the possibility of introducing liability for humans for criminally relevant decisions that are made by AI. The assumption behind this argument is that humans exercise, or should exercise, control over the algorithms.[77] The recent EU AI Liability Act is germane to this line of reasoning because it establishes a liability regime that is based on the duty to ensure 'human oversight' of AI-related risks of different magnitude.[78] Secondly, other scholars propose a more innovative approach built on the premise that it is an oxymoron to speak of human control over a technology that is designed to perform tasks that are beyond human capabilities. These scholars are focusing on the possibility of establishing an autonomous criminal

---

73 The accountability gap refers to the failure to establish a link between a law or regulation, on the one hand, and a responsible decision or action, on the other. See K. Heine and A. Quintavalla, 'Bridging the accountability gap of artificial intelligence – what can be learned from Roman law?' (2024) 44 *Legal Studies* 65.

74 Ibid, 68. See also G. Teubner, 'Digital personhood: the status of autonomous software in private law' (2018) *Ancilla Juris* 35.

75 G. Hallevy, *Liability for Crimes Involving Artificial Intelligence Systems* (Springer International Publishing 2015).

76 M.C. Karlsson, *Artificial Intelligence and the External Element of the Crime: An Analysis of the Liability Problem*, student thesis (2017) <https://urn.kb.se/resolve?urn=urn:nbn:se:oru:diva-58269> (accessed 6 September 2024).

77 A. Giannini, 'Intelligenza artificiale, human oversight e responsabilità penale: prove d'impatto a livello europeo' (2021) *Criminalia* 249.

78 See, for example AIA, Recitals 66, 72 and 73, and Articles 14, 16 and 26. See also the EU Commission's Proposal for a Directive of the European Parliament and of the Council on adapting non-contractual civil liability rules to artificial intelligence (AI Liability Directive) COM/2022/496 final. In Recital 22 and Article 4 therein, the Commission proposes the establishment of a rebuttable presumption of causality against the defendant in order to overcome the difficulties of proving that a specific input by the potentially liable person has caused a specific AI system output causing the damage at stake. For a comment on the EU approach to ensuring the 'human oversight' over AI, see L. Enqvist, '"Human oversight" in the EU Artificial Intelligence Act: what, when and by whom?' (2023) 15 *Law, Innovation and Technology* 508. For a critique on the limits of turning AI governance towards risk regulation from a remedial perspective, see B.B. Arcila, 'AI Liability in Europe: How does it complement risk regulation and deal with the problem of human oversight?' (2024) 54 *Computer Law & Security Review* 106012.

liability regime that targets AI systems directly.[79] The breadth of these issues is such that they must remain outside the scope of the present chapter. It should suffice to say for now that, to the best of our knowledge, no AI-generated decisions are known to have criminally impacted the environment.[80]

However, a growing, albeit still small, corpus of literature points to the use of AI as a facilitator of environmental crimes, in particular crimes that fall into the first two

---

[79] A. Giannini, *Criminal behavior and accountability of artificial intelligence systems*, Doctoral thesis (Maastricht University, University of Florence - Eleven Publishers 2023); A. Nanos, 'Criminal Liability of Artificial Intelligence', Research Paper No. 2023/III/3 (Charles University in Prague Faculty of Law Research 2023) <https://papers.ssrn.com/abstract=4623126> (accessed 6 September 2024); Y. Hu, 'Robot Criminals' (2019) 52 *University of Michigan Journal of Law Reform* 487.

[80] We refer here to infringements of domestic criminal law frameworks. However, AI could also play a role in causing environmental harm that is relevant under different legal frameworks, such as international humanitarian law and international criminal law. AI-powered autonomous weapon systems (intelligent AWS) used in warfare may commit actions that contravene Article 55 of Protocol I to the 1949 Geneva Conventions, 'Protection of the natural environment', or constitute war crimes affecting the environment. Article 8(2)(b)(iv) of the Rome Statute is the only international criminal law provision that protects the environment directly, although some scholars advocate for expanding Article 7 of the Rome Statute to encompass environmental destruction (see, for example A. Dumont, 'A "Clear" War Crime Against the Environment?: The Destruction of the Nova Kakhovka Dam' (*Völkerrechtsblog*, 2023) <https://voelkerrechtsblog.org/a-clear-war-crime-against-the-environment/> (accessed 18 September 2024). When intelligent AWS commit environmentally detrimental actions related to prohibited attacks in warfare, including those not intended by the users, they should be considered as acts of state for the purpose of attributing state responsibility under international law. In this sense, see P. Gaeta, 'Who Acts When Autonomous Weapons Strike? The Act Requirement for Individual Criminal Responsibility and State Responsibility' (2023) 21 *Journal of International Criminal Justice* 1033. The interplay between intelligent AWS and environmental harms is a field still under-researched. The UN General Assembly draft Resolution, Protection of the environment in relation to armed conflicts, no. A/C.6/77/L.22, adopted on 11 November 2022, establishes 27 principles enhancing the effective protection of the environment before, during, and after armed conflicts. However, these principles do not make any express mention of intelligent AWS and their potential role in causing environmental devastation. Concerns regarding the environmental impacts of intelligent AWS are expressed in the UN Report of the Secretary-General, *Lethal autonomous weapons systems*, General Assembly, no. A/79/88, 1 July 2024 <https://documents.un.org/doc/undoc/gen/n24/154/32/pdf/n2415432.pdf> (accessed 18 February 2024), and in submissions to the Report from various actors listed therein, including the collective report *Challenges posed by autonomous weapons systems and ways to address them: a perspective from Latin American academia and civil society. Contributions to the United Nations Secretary-General's Report on Lethal Autonomous Weapons Systems*, para. 2.2.(xvii) <https://peruporeldesarme.org.pe/documento-colectivo/challenges-of-autonomous-weapons-systems-and-approaches-to-address-them-a-perspective-from-the-latin-american-academy-and-civil-society/> (accessed 18 February 2024).

of our suggested categories.[81] For instance, illegal loggers and poachers can use AI surveillance systems to avoid areas that the authorities are likely to be monitoring.[82] Similar arguments can be made about the use of AI to prevent or facilitate illegal fishing or wildlife smuggling; in fact, those arguments are likely to hold true for all forms of criminal conduct, and similar ones can be made about our third category of crimes-to-be, a context in which AI can generate novel means of exploiting natural resources.[83] As recognised by Europol, AI systems based on large language models (LLMs), such as Chat GPT, are built on deep learning techniques and the training of neural networks on significant amounts of data, which allows criminals to learn how to commit a particular type of crime.[84] In such cases, the resultant liability issues are not specific to AI because it serves as an instrument that is under the complete control of humans.

Several more nuanced liability-related issues emerge from the capacity of AI to generate an artificial representation of environmental harm by translating reality into the numbers on which algorithms run.[85] While this translation might result in assessments of empirical facts of unparalleled accuracy, the consistency between representation and reality depends on the specificities of the algorithm that is being used. This role of AI can become particularly problematic because of its well-documented shortcomings,

---

81 In this sense, AI is considered a mere technological tool fully under human control, and thus does not pose specific issues in terms of the criminal liability of the human perpetrator.

82 Cyber-poaching, that is the capacity of poachers map animal routes, is reality. See S.J. Cooke et al., 'Troubling issues at the frontier of animal tracking for conservation and management' (2017) 31 *Conservation Biology* 1205; K. Norton, 'The 21st Century Threat to Wildlife is "Cyberpoaching"' (*PBS-Nova Education*, 30 October 2020) <https://www.pbs.org/wgbh/nova/article/21st-century-threat-wildlife-cyberpoaching/ (accessed 8 August 2024).

83 Such as practices of biopiracy. See, for example V. Shiva, *Biopiracy: The Plunder of Nature and Knowledge* (North Atlantic Books 2016). On the capacity of AI technologies to accelerate resource extraction, see P. Dauvergne, 'The globalization of artificial intelligence: consequences for the politics of environmentalism' (2021) 18 *Globalizations* 285.

84 Europol, *ChatGPT - The impact of Large Language Models on Law Enforcement, a Tech Watch Flash Report from the Europol Innovation Lab* (Luxembourg: Publications Office of the European Union, 2023) <https://www.europol.europa.eu/media-press/newsroom/news/criminal-use-of-chatgpt-cautionary-tale-about-large-language-models> (accessed 18 September 2024).

85 AI makes this conversion possible through complex computations that humans cannot perform, at least not within the same time frame.

which include biased input data,[86] lack of transparency and interpretability,[87] and human rights concerns.[88]

We argued earlier that AI could enhance the compliance rationality of corporations, but the opposite outcome also holds true when AI-generated outcomes distort corporate decision-making processes and consequently expose corporations to serious risks. Entrusting compliance strategies to AI can have highly problematic consequences for corporations that are eager to avoid criminal liability. In legal regimes that impute fault on companies, such as the Italian legal system,[89] liability is ascribed on the basis of the capability of the company to prevent the commission of a crime by adopting due diligence compliance mechanisms. Arguably, a mistake by AI alone could hardly result in the liability of a legal person. However, such a mistake could reveal structural deficits that are of actual criminal relevance, such as a failure to institute precautionary measures to mitigate the unreliability of AI algorithms. Such findings might lead to the company being held liable for failing to prevent the commission of a crime.[90] Several other attribution doctrines, most of which originate from common law countries, pose thorny questions. For instance, in the US, corporate criminal liability is established on the basis of the *respondeat superior* principle. It has recently been pointed out that '[m]ost corporate liability requires corporate mental states, such as knowledge of falsity or intent to defraud, which the law presently defines in terms of employee mental states'.[91] Logically, when algorithms determine company behaviours, the corporate mind in question is not that of an employee but the algorithm itself.[92] Similarly, under the identification theory, which is most developed in the United Kingdom (UK), the condition for holding the company liable is that the acts and state of mind of those who represent the directing mind and will of the company can be imputed to the company itself.[93] Closer examination reveals that AI's lack of legal personhood prevents a straightforward application of these and other models of attribution of corporate criminal liability[94] to AI decisions. What is

---

86 E. Ntoutsi et al., 'Bias in data-driven artificial intelligence systems—An introductory survey' (2020) 10 *WIREs Data Mining and Knowledge Discovery* e1356. Considered biases include socioeconomic, racial, cultural, age-related, and gender ones.

87 B. Mittelstadt, 'Interpretability and Transparency in Artificial Intelligence' in C. Véliz (ed), *The Oxford Handbook of Digital Ethics* (Oxford Academic 2021).

88 A. Quintavalla and J. Temperman (eds), *Artificial Intelligence and Human Rights* (Oxford University Press 2023).

89 Legislative Decree no. 231/2001.

90 On these aspects, see P. Severino, 'Intelligenza artificiale e diritto penale' in U. Ruffolo (ed), *Intelligenza artificiale. Il diritto, i diritti, l'etica* (Giuffrè 2020), 538.

91 M.E. Diamantis, 'The Extended Corporate Mind: When Corporations Use AI to Break the Law' (2020) 98 *North Carolina Law Review* 930.

92 Ibid, 898.

93 On the identification doctrine, see C. Wells, *Corporations and Criminal Responsibility* (Oxford University Press 2001).

94 Such as the failure to prevent a crime from occurring emerging in the UK. On this model, see L. Campbell, 'Corporate Liability and the Criminalisation of Failure' (2018) 12(2) *Law and Financial Markets Review* 57.

needed instead is engagement with the accountability gap issue that we mentioned earlier, as well as with the related liability matters, in the specific context of corporate crimes. The capacity of AI systems to interpret data concerning environmental harm and even to predict its occurrence aggravates tensions in liability discourses. A flawed AI system can distort reality; and decisions about criminalisation that are based on such distortions can produce even graver social and environmental harm. A problem that is connected to the design of AI systems is that AI algorithms have been designed mainly by Western-based companies and personnel. If non-Western perspectives are marginalised, AI might entrench 'hegemonic knowledge'.[95] As a consequence, epistemologies from the Global South and Indigenous cosmovisions may be excluded from discussions about harms.[96] A techno-centric and efficiency-oriented approach to remedying environmental harm could obscure the relational and cultural factors that are at stake when decisions must be made about criminalisation. If victims are ignored, the idea that environmental harms are 'victimless' might be reinforced.[97] While this problem may affect discourse about any environmental harm, regardless of its legal status, it seems more disturbing in the context of non-criminal harms, in which victims lack the formal protection that is typically available under criminal justice processes.[98] Therefore, it is argued that a broader range of stakeholders should be able to participate in decision-making about the definition and creation of algorithms in order to mitigate these risks.[99]

We now turn to the actors who could attempt to exercise legitimate forms of control over the functioning of AI systems. Political groups, environmental associations, trade unions, and businesses all compete to determine the extent to which nature

---

95 R. Machen and E. Nost, 'Thinking Algorithmically: The Making of Hegemonic Knowledge in Climate Governance' (2021) 46(3) *Transactions of the Institute of British Geographers* 555.

96 A. Escobar, 'Thinking-Feeling with the Earth: Territorial Struggles and the Ontological Dimension of the Epistemologies of the South' in B. de Sousa Santos and M. Meneses (eds), *Knowledges Born in the Struggle* (Routledge 2019).

97 E. Skinnider, *Victims of Environmental Crime - Mapping the Issues* (The International Centre for Criminal Law Reform and Criminal Justice Policy, 2011).

98 The provision of a penal statute would, at least in principle, allow those who claim to be victims to seek the state's protection through the prosecution of the alleged polluter and to benefit from the victim of crime protective measures as well as the remedial measures available in some legal systems.

99 V. Keswani, *Algorithmic Decision-Making with Stakeholder Participation,* Doctoral dissertation (Yale University 2023) https://www.proquest.com/openview/9106fae46db6a354f207c50a7766dba9/1?pq-origsite=gscholar&cbl=18750&diss=y> (accessed 1 August 2024); C.F. Breidbach, 'Responsible algorithmic decision-making' (2024) 53(2) *Organisational Dynamics* 101031. For a pilot project in the UK, see I. Bouzguenda, 'Examining Stakeholders' Involvement in AI Policy Initiatives: The Case of the United Kingdome', ECPR General Conference 2022, Section: Towards a New Generation of Interest Group Studies – Panel: Digital & New Modes of Lobbying (ECPR Press 2022) <https://research.utwente.nl/en/publications/examining-stakeholders-involvement-in-ai-policy-initiatives-the-c> (accessed 11 August 2024).

can be exploited for economic purposes. When the problem is approached from this angle, it appears obvious that the cluster of interests that control AI can also shape the political ends to which it is directed, which may vary from increased environmental protection to enhanced economic growth through extraction.

Economic actors, particularly corporations, may use AI algorithms to manipulate public discourse to their advantage. This outcome would not be surprising given the present state of affairs.[100] The risk is that AI might be used to conceal rather than expose environmental harms: for example, corporations may present their activities as harmless by manipulating algorithmic representations of reality. Such a strategy could help corporations avoid prosecution for environmental crimes by creating false narratives of compliance. This risk is particularly acute when it comes to socially accepted logics of production and consumption. AI could bolster the ability of corporations to shield their permits from social stigma by downplaying certain forms of environmental damage. The exploitation of Mexican water by the international soft drinks industry is a case in point.[101] Industry spun a narrative of social acceptance by exploiting local culturally ingrained habit,[102] as well as by greening its presence through the provision of funding for reforestation programmes.[103] When used in this way, AI could enhance the effectiveness of the existing narrative based on schemes that shield vested interests. Conversely, it is also possible for public authorities to use AI – particularly its predictive capacities – to muster support for security-oriented approaches to environmental governance, potentially by manipulating public perceptions of potential harms and by making them appear more exigent.[104] Whatever the

100 See further C. Rikap, 'Dynamics of Corporate Governance Beyond Ownership in AI' (*CommonWealth*, 2024) https://www.common-wealth.org/publications/dynamics-of-corporate-governance-beyond-ownership-in-ai> (accessed 11 August 2024).

101 The Special Rapporteur on the human right to safe drinking water and sanitation, Mr Léo Heller, expressed concerns regarding the human rights implications of Mexico's water privatisation policies. See UN *Seguimiento a la visita oficial a México Informe del Relator Especial sobre el derecho humano al agua potable y el saneamiento*, Doc. A/HRC/45/10/Add.1, General Assembly, Human Rights Council, 45, Section, 2020 https://documents.un.org/doc/undoc/gen/g20/218/53/pdf/g2021853.pdf> (accessed 1 September 2024). On state-corporate complicity in pursuing water exploitation, see A. Brisman et al., *Water, Crime and Security in the Twenty-First Century: Too Dirty, Too Little, Too Much* (Palgrave Macmillan 2018).

102 See J. Nash, 'Consuming Interests: Water, Rum, and Coca-Cola from Ritual Propitiation to Corporate Expropriation in Highland Chiapas' (2007) *Cultural Anthropology* 621.

103 See, for example the Coca-Cola Femsa company Press Release on its reforestation programme in the State of Chiapas (Mexico) <https://www.femsa.com/en/press-room/press-release/coca-cola-femsa-joins-the-environmental-actions-of-san-cristobal-de-las/> (accessed 9 September 2024). This programme occurs in the same area where this company operates one of the biggest and most water-consuming bottling plants in Mexico.

104 On the use of AI for environmental security, see M. Francisco, 'Artificial intelligence for environmental security: national, international, human and ecological perspectives' (2023) 61 *Current Opinion in Environmental Sustainability* 101250.

motivation behind such uses of AI, from a criminal law perspective, the risk is that 'environmental protection' may be instrumentalised as justification for state repression. Such scenarios become conceivable when one takes into account existing state practices. For instance, South African policies to combat wildlife crime, which have included the employment of quasi-military agencies, strategies, and technologies, overlooked the cultural and societal issues that were at stake and eventually caused grave harm to the ongoing relations between local communities and protected park personnel, even if those measures were necessary, in principle, to combat wildlife crime.[105]

To summarise, AI could exacerbate the power imbalances that already typify the perceptions of and negotiations about the criminalisation of environmental harm. This possibility is magnified by the capacity of new technology to alter a fundamental element of democratic debate, namely the quality of information. Artificially distorted information about harm could foster epistemic power imbalances, thus undermining the democratic processes that should guide the criminal law.

5. Conclusion

This chapter began by pointing to the changes that AI has introduced to criminal law: a burst of technological progress has made it possible to automate and thus expand surveillance beyond what was previously imaginable and to forecast human law-breaching behaviour with much greater precision than ever before. We then introduced a taxonomy of environmental crimes that recognises three categories: environmental crimes in the strict sense, non-environmental crimes that produce environmental harm, and formally non-criminal forms of conduct that ought to become crimes in the future. The purpose of that taxonomical exercise was to enable a granular and structured examination of the implications of AI for environmental criminal law. Perhaps unsurprisingly, our analysis revealed that AI makes it easier to detect environmental crimes, as well as convergences between non-environmental crimes and environmental damage. Critically, we also showed that AI can identify lawful (or marginally unlawful) forms of conduct that cause or have the potential to cause grave damage to the natural environment in cumulation and that AI can be instrumental in the efforts of private companies to improve their environmental compliance. In the last substantive section of this chapter, we also explained that AI can, however, be used to hijack debates about the criminalisation of environmentally harmful behaviour, for example by entrenching Western worldviews or by furnishing misleading evidence of corporate green-washing practices.

---

105 A. Hübschle, A. Dore, and H.D. Mostert, 'Focus on victims and the community: applying restorative justice principles to wildlife crime offences in South Africa' (2021) 4(1) *The International Journal of Restorative Justice* 141.

We do not, of course, claim to have exhausted the topic of AI and environmental criminal law – as we noted in section 2, our objective was merely to sketch out an analytical scheme of the impact of AI on environmental criminal law. AI has opened several avenues for research, of which two appear especially promising. First, the ability of AI to revolutionise environmental criminal law depends on the data with which it is fed. The most popular AI applications of our day, LLMs, were trained on public data. However, AI can only solve problems of criminal law such as prediction and surveillance if it is trained on data on smuggling routes, hunting grounds, and the like, which is highly unlikely to be disseminated online, or at least on the open internet. State agencies might be able to plug this gap, but their efforts would likely aggravate problems of control of the kind that we discussed in section 4. Second, AI, despite all appearances to the contrary, is not omniscient – in fact, it 'hallucinates' and replicates all of the subtle biases that are coded into its training datasets unquestioningly.[106] Whether and how these problems can be overcome is a question that exerts a magnetic hold on those who develop and regulate AI, but, to date, their efforts are yet to yield a remedy to those problems. In the interim, 'artificial stupidity' can undermine the efficacy of AI as an instrument for preventing and combatting environmental crimes. Absent a technological solution to those challenges, it is policy-makers, judges, and lawyers who must determine when and to what ends AI should be deployed.

106 P. Domingos, *The Master Algorithm: How the Quest for the Ultimate Learning Machine Will Remake Our World* (Basic Books 2015).

13

Imprisonment as an alternative to financial punishments on corporations for environmental offenses

Gabriel Hallevy

I. Introduction[1]

After a corporation is convicted, most courts, for most offenses, impose financial punishments on the convicted corporation. Of course, these criminal punishments may be imposed on the corporation regardless of the punishments imposed on the corporation's officers in legal systems that accept the concept of corporate criminal liability. Yet in most cases the way in which these financial punishments are implemented are neither efficient nor effective. Careful analysis reveals that the chances for financial punishments to be effective, especially in environmental offenses, are not particularly high. This situation calls for a change in the way sentencing corporations is implemented.

This chapter starts by discussing the limited effectiveness of financial punishments on corporations. The chapter then explores the theoretical legal basis for imposition of imprisonment on corporations as an alternative to financial punishments for corporate environmental damage. Further, the chapter then explores the actual judicial methods for imposing imprisonment as an alternative to financial penalties on corporations. It is argued that there is a theoretical basis for imposing imprisonment as an appropriate corporate criminal punishment for environmental harm and that, in many instances, it is theoretically possible to convert certain non-financial physical penalties typically applicable to natural persons to corporate legal entities. It should be noted that as this chapter focuses on the theoretical case for imposing

1 Full Professor of Law, Ono Academic College. I thank Dr Ricardo Pereira for inviting me to participate in this project and for the fruitful editorial comments received on earlier drafts of this chapter. I also thank the anonymous readers for their comments. Of course, any errors remain the author's own.

imprisonment as an alternative to financial penalties on corporations, it will not place considerable emphasis on other non-financial penalties that are generally applicable in several legal systems for corporations for environmental damage (such as community services orders or environmental remediation) and have thus been the subject of previous research.

II. Motivation: the limited effectiveness of financial punishments on corporations

The most widely available and simple way to execute criminal punishment for corporations is the fine. The fine is the common form of financial punishment. When a corporation is convicted and a fine, at any sum, is being imposed, the execution of the punishment, from the corporation's point of view, is no different from the payment of taxes or bills to the authorities.[2] Fines are easily collected from corporations in the same way as taxes are. Although a fine is not supposed to be considered as part of the corporation's deductive expenses for tax purposes, there are so many legal ways to make it become one. Therefore, with the right accounting advice, it is no different from all other expenses of the corporation, even for tax purposes.

When the modern idea of criminal liability of a corporation was developed in English common law during the seventeenth century, the punishability of the corporation was associated with financial punishments.[3] It was considered the 'natural' punishment for corporations for two main types of considerations: *in personam* considerations and *in rem* considerations. First, the corporation is considered to be a legal entity which acts in the economic sector, therefore it was understood that punishing corporations should be based on financial measures. Second, most offenses related to corporations are financial; therefore, proportionality between the punishment and the offense may indicate financial punishments as both proportional and appropriate punishments from the perspective of both the offender (*in personam* considerations) and the offense (*in rem* considerations).

During the twentieth century, the increased use of imprisonment for human offenders by the courts came under sharp criticism. The criticism was triggered by the high expense needed to operate prisons, the side-effects of imprisonment on the prisoners (including the harm to their social status, chances of rehabilitation, and chances of reintegrating into society), and the high rates of recidivism among prisoners. This criticism gave rise to a search for substitutes for imprisonment in appropriate cases. One such substitute was the fine, which was already part of most penal systems.

---

2 Although fines may have further impacts on some corporations, such as reputational damage, in most cases such impacts are considered to be negligible side-effects of the fine. In most cases, the corporation is a local one and imposition of a fine attracts no public interest within the relevant local community.

3 Gabriel Hallevy, *The Right to Be Punished – Modern Doctrinal Sentencing* (Springer, 2013), 148–55.

The fine is considered to be a flexible punishment. It is easily matched to the offender and the offense, it does not share the negative effects of imprisonment, and requires much lower expense to impose than imprisonment does. Moreover, the fine creates income for the state, and in that way it may be considered beneficial. The fine has proven an effective deterrent for certain offenses.[4] As a result, the fine rapidly became the most common and frequent punishment in most Western legal systems, both as sole punishment in a verdict or accompanying other punishments.[5]

The availability and simplicity of punishment options do not necessarily indicate that they are effective. Since the generally recognized goals of sentencing do not include convenience of the process of imposing the punishment, these characteristics of financial punishments arguably become secondary in importance. One of the most significant examples for the limited effectiveness of financial punishments is with regard to environmental offenses.

The starting point is when a corporation is convicted for commission of an environmental offense,[6] for example a pollution-control offense. After evaluating the general sentencing considerations, the involvement of the corporation in the commission of the offense, the specific characteristics of the corporation and the consequences of the offense, in most cases the court may decide to impose a fine on the corporation as the most appropriate form of punishment. Under the assumption of solvency, the corporation is expected to pay the fine on time. However, different actual rates of the fine dictate different courses of conduct by the corporation.

If the fine is not excessive, the corporation would probably consider whether it is worth continuing in violation of the law, that is continuing the commission of environmental offenses, and occasionally paying a price for this in the form of a fine. The fine would be treated as a cost of doing business and hence would have limited deterrent effect. Where the fine is not excessive, there would not be a need for a company to pass on the costs of fines to consumers. Ironically, in this case the general taxpayer pays the costs for environmental damage, as the corporation is not punished with an appropriate fine that can cover, for example, environmental remediation. In fact, in this scenario, the general public ends up paying a double price. Not only has the environment been damaged, but public funds must be used to pay for environmental

4 Gail S. Funke, 'The Economics of Prison Crowding', 478 *Annals of the American Academy of Political and Social Sciences* 86 (1985); Thomas Mathiesen, 'The Viewer Society: Michel Foucault's "Panopticon" Revisited', 1 *Theoretical Criminology* 215 (1997).

5 Claire Whittaker and Alan Mackie, *Enforcing Financial Penalties* (1997); Hans-Heinrich Jescheck and Thomas Weigend, *Lehrbuch des Strafrechts – Allgemeiner Teil* (5 Auf., 1996), 766–82; MDR 1976, 626; MDR 1983, 341; MDR 1985, 76; BGH 26, 325; BGH 37, 226; BGH NJW 1990, 2897; BGH NJW 1995, 67; BGH NJW 1995, 1368; BVerfGE 77, 102.

6 In this chapter it is of course assumed that a corporation may be prosecuted and convicted within a criminal process in the relevant legal system. If not, criminal proceedings are irrelevant to the corporation, as well as fines and any other punishment.

remediation.[7] Even if, within the specific legal system, the fines collected from corporations for environmental offenses are used to fund projects aimed at pollution control and remediation of environmental damage, the fine would still be treated as a cost of doing business that can be passed on to consumers in the form of higher product prices.

It is arguable that in the above scenario an aggravated punishment would be called for, that is the imposition of a higher fine. In the event that courts impose fines at higher rates, there are two relevant scenarios. The first scenario assumes that the corporation is financially capable of paying the fine, for example by making its products more expensive while remaining profitable in a competitive market. Another scenario emerges when the corporation is incapable of paying the fine or competition with other corporations does not allow the fined corporation to increase the cost of its products while remaining profitable. In light of those financial constraints, the natural corporate decision in this scenario could be to relocate to a different country and a different legal system where the corporation is capable of remaining profitable in a less competitive market. For a corporation facing charges for environmental offenses in one jurisdiction, there are other alternative jurisdictions to which it could relocate where either the environmental regulatory regime or legal enforcement is weak.[8]

This situation is not unique to imposition of fines or other financial punishments on corporations linked to the commission of environmental offenses. In fact, this situation is common in relation to the use of most disproportionate penalties against corporations, both in criminal law and outside of it. In Anglo-American corporations law, for instance, the legal basis for piercing the corporate veil provides many examples of this.[9] When the domestic court uses the measure of piercing the corporate veil too many times to impose financial punishments, there is no reason for shareholders to keep on investing their property in the local market. They will probably search for alternatives, which minimize the risks for them, both financial and legal. This attitude is reflected in various situations, of which punishing corporations for environmental offenses is only one. Both *ex-ante* and *ex-post* considerations suggest that the effectiveness of financial punishments on corporations is, at most, limited. In many types of situations, it is completely ineffective. Of course, if environmental issues are important to the public, alternatives should be considered.

7 For the dynamics of the fine as a criminal punishment and its implications see Hallevy, n. 3, 191–200.

8 For an analysis of the extent to which corporations relocate to jurisdictions with lax environmental regulations, see further, for example Ricardo Pereira, 'Environmental Regulation, Business Competitiveness and Corporate Responsibility' in Karen Makuch and Ricardo Pereira (eds), *Environmental and Energy Law* (Wiley-Blackwell, 2012), 61.

9 For example the attitude towards piercing of the corporate veil in Anglo-American legal systems, see, *Adams v. Cape Industries Plc* [1990] Ch. 433; *Williams v. Natural Life Health Foods Ltd* [1998] 1 W.L.R. 830; *Berkey v. Third Avenue Railway*, 244 N.Y. 602, 155 N.E. 914 (1927); *Fletcher v. Atex, Inc*, 68 F.3d 1451 (2d Cir. 1995).

In the following sections, the theoretical case for the imposition of imprisonment on corporate legal entities as an alternative to financial penalties will be analyzed, drawing upon the existing practices in selected jurisdictions (in particular the United States (US) and Israel). In this context, I will analyze the potential implications of the imposition of imprisonment on corporate legal entities for the fight against corporate environmental crimes.

III. The theoretical legal basis for imposition of imprisonment on corporations

As change in sentencing corporations is required, it should be founded on legally stable and justified foundations. Sentencing in criminal cases, in general, is governed by the general principles of criminal law, regardless of the identity of the convicted person. That includes humans, artificial intelligence (AI) entities,[10] and, of course, corporations.

a. Fairness and equality for corporations under principles of criminal law

Modern criminal liability is not restricted to humans. The fourth fundamental principle of criminal law, the principle of personal liability, makes it feasible to impose criminal liability on non-human entities, such as corporations, and several legal systems have developed this idea thoroughly.[11] Accordingly, during the seventeenth, eighteenth, and nineteenth centuries, and part of the twentieth century, in some jurisdictions (chiefly the US) the criminal liability of corporations was imposed through a convoluted legal structure of vicarious liability, which is complex, ineffective, and, in very many ways, unjust.[12]

---

10 For the criminal liability of AI entities and sentencing these entities see Gabriel Hallevy, *When Robots Kill – Artificial Intelligence under Criminal Law* (UPNE, 2013); Gabriel Hallevy, *Liability for Crimes Involving Artificial Intelligence Systems* (Springer, 2015).

11 For the criminal liability of corporations under modern criminal law, see Gabriel Hallevy, *The Matrix of Derivative Criminal Liability* (Springer, 2012), 21.

12 *The case of Langforth Bridge* (1635) Cro. Car. 365, 79 E.R. 919; *R. v. Inhabitants of Clifton* (1794) 5 T.R. 498, 101 E.R. 280; *R. v. Inhabitants of Great Broughton* (1771) 5 Burr. 2700, 98 E.R. 418; *R. v. The Mayor, Aldermen, and Burgesses of the Borough of Stratford-upon-Avon* (1811) 14 East 348, 104 E.R. 636; *R. v. The Mayor&c. of Liverpool* (1802) 3 East 82, 102 E.R. 529; *R. v. Saintiff* (1705) 6 Mod. 255, 87 E.R. 1002; *R. v. Severn and Wye Railway Co* (1819) 2 B. & Ald. 646, 106 E.R. 501; *R. v. Birmingham, & Gloucester Railway Co* (1842) 3 Q. B. 223, 114 E.R. 492; *New York Cent. & H.R.R. v. United States*, 212 U.S. 481, 29 S.Ct. 304, 53 L.Ed. 613 (1909); *Old Monastery Co v. United States* 147 F.2d 905 (4th Cir.1945); *United States v. New York Great A. & P. Tea Co*, 67 F.Supp. 626 (E.D.Ill.1946); *Regan v. Kroger Grocery & Banking Co*, 386 Ill. 284, 54 N.E.2d 210 (1944); *State v. Western Union Tel. Co*, 13 N.J.Super. 172, 80 A.2d 342 (1951); *United States v. Thompson-Powell Drilling Co*, 196 F.Supp. 571 (N.D.Tex.1961); *United States v. Dye Construction*

For example, if the relevant officer of the corporation acted without explicit permission from the corporation, or if the establishment documents of the corporation (for example the articles of association) included provisions explicitly prohibiting its officers from committing an act considered an offense while on duty, no criminal liability could have been imposed on the corporation.[13] It was possible, therefore, for corporations to informally encourage officers to commit criminal offenses for the benefit of the corporation without the corporation being subject to criminal liability.

In modern criminal law, the principle of personal liability can accommodate the imposition of criminal liability directly on the corporation or on other non-human legal entities.[14] When a legal entity functions independently in the commission of an offense, the appropriate and just response would be to impose criminal liability directly on it. The principle of personal liability, through the secondary principle of legal participation, makes it possible to overcome the difficulties created by the requirements of the mental and factual elements. In fact, the secondary principle of legal participation may be applied not only to corporations but also to any other legal entity,[15]and redefines what legal personhood really means.[16]

In this fashion, the principle of personal liability leads to the general recognition of the possibility of imposing criminal liability on non-human legal entities. But the concrete implementation of the principle of personal liability through the criminal law is carried out using the legal principle of derivative criminal liability. Applying the criminal law principle of legality, the criminal law is considered to be of general

---

Co, 510 F.2d 78 (10th Cir.1975); *United States v. Carter*, 311 F.2d 934 (6th Cir.1963); *State of Ohio v. I. & M. Amusements, Inc*, 10 Ohio App.2d 153, 226 N.E.2d 567 (1966); *United States v. MacAndrews & Forbes Co*, 149 F. 823 (C.C.S.D.N.Y.1906).

13 *United States v. Alaska Packers' Association*, 1 Alaska 217 (1901).

14 In many legal systems criminal liability is imposed through the convenient legal doctrine of identity (the identity or identification doctrine), which has been developed under English law. See, for example *Director of Public Prosecutions v. Kent and Sussex Contractors Ltd* [1944] K.B. 146, [1944] 1 All E.R. 119; *R. v. I.C.R. Haulage Ltd* [1944] K.B. 551, [1944] 1 All E.R. 691; *R. v. McDonnell* [1966] 1 Q.B. 233, [1966] 1 All E.R. 193, [1965] 3 W.L.R. 1138, 50 Cr. App. Rep 5; *R. v. Robert Millar (Contractors) Ltd* [1970] 2 Q.B. 54, [1970] 1 All E.R. 577, [1970] 2 W.L.R. 561, 54 Cr. App. Rep 158, [1970] R.T.R. 147, 134 J.P. 240; *Seaboard Offshore Ltd v. Secretary of State for Transport* [1994] 2 All E.R. 99, [1994] 1 W.L.R. 541, [1994] 1 Lloyd's Rep 593; *Granite Construction Co v. Superior Court*, 149 Cal.App.3d 465, 197 Cal.Rptr. 3 (1983); *Commonwealth v. Fortner L.P. Gas Co*, 610 S.W.2d 941 (Ky.App.1980); *State v. Lehigh Valley Ry. Co*, 90 N.J.L. 372, 103 A. 685 (1917); *Commonwealth v. McIlwain School Bus Lines, Inc*, 283 Pa.Super. 1, 423 A.2d 413 (1980); Gerhard O.W. Mueller, 'Mens Rea and the Corporation – A Study of the Model Penal Code Position on Corporate Criminal Liability' 19 U. Pitt. L. Rev. 21 (1957).

15 For the criminal liability of AI entities, see n. 11.

16 See the classic article of Laurence B. Solum, 'Legal Personhood for Artificial Intelligences' 70 N.C.L. Rev. 1231 (1992). However, new theories on dynamic legal personhood seem to be prevailing in the context of AI.

application, since *all* legal personhoods are subject to it.[17] Generality, in this context, has the characteristic of equality. Therefore, all persons are equal under the (criminal) law. No person is deprived of any right to plead any argument in criminal proceedings. That does not ensure that the argument raised by the party will be accepted by the court, but that the court is obliged to check carefully whether it is relevant and acceptable in the specific case.

Depriving an indicted person of any right under criminal law, just for having a certain personal characteristic, is unfair, unequal, morally wrong, and most importantly, legally prohibited. This would be a violation of the principle of legality in criminal law. The legal personhood of the corporation is beyond doubt under modern criminal law. Being a legal entity rather than flesh and blood is, with no doubt, a personal characteristic. Therefore, when a person, human or legal, is charged with a criminal offense, the principle of legality is designed to ensure fairness and equality under the law and regardless any of this person's personal characteristics.

When this idea is applied to corporations, it becomes very interesting and thought-provoking. For example, a human defendant may plead insanity. Consequently, by extension a corporation as a separate legal entity should be able to plead insanity as well, but what is the meaning of insanity for corporations? This insanity is not the insanity of the corporation's officers, but the insanity of the corporation itself, that is of that very legal entity. Can a legal entity be insane, for example on the basis of its collective or aggravated fault or dysfunctional governance structures? The same question may arise for typical defenses in criminal trials such as intoxication, automatism, infancy and many more, which are considered to be quite common for human defendants but intriguing if not yet recognized as applicable to non-human defendants. As the answers to these questions, unfortunately, exceed the scope of this chapter, they will not be discussed hereinafter, especially when they have already been discussed elsewhere.[18]

It may be concluded that, as a starting point for the imposition of imprisonment on offending corporations, the fundamental principles of criminal law ensure that fairness and equality for corporations in criminal proceedings are protected by criminal law provisions. It is arguable that corporations should not be deprived of any right which is guaranteed under the criminal law just for being legal entities rather natural persons.[19] Of course, the other side of the coin is that corporations have no privileges

17 For generality within the principle of legality in modern criminal law see Gabriel Hallevy, *A Modern Treatise on the Principle of Legality in Modern Criminal Law* (Springer, 2010), 135–7.

18 Gabriel Hallevy, *Theory of Criminal Law*, Vol. III (Bursi, 2010) 887–906. However, it may be indicated that the answers to these questions are rooted in the basic concepts of the above legal arguments, and may be easily deduced from them.

19 Corporations are also recognized as having human rights. See further, for example Marius Emberland, *The Human Rights of Companies: Exploring the Structure of ECHR Protection* (OUP, 2006).

in criminal law just for being corporations. If, for example, principles of sentencing direct the court to impose imprisonment on the convicted defendant, corporations, in principle have no privilege that enables them to be excluded from the applicability of this punishment. However, one more legal step is required to provide the legal basis for setting the theoretical case for imprisonment as an appropriate and feasible punishment for corporations, and it concerns the general purposes of sentencing.

b. Applicability of the general purposes of sentencing to corporations

As aforesaid, corporations are legal entities in criminal law, and criminal liability may be imposed upon them as if they were human offenders.[20] Consequently, when a corporation is found criminally liable, the question of what could be an appropriate (criminal) punishment arises. In general, because in certain legal systems there is no difference between corporate and human offenders regarding the imposition of criminal liability, there is arguably no reason for substantive differences between them in sentencing, at least not from the point of view of the general purposes of sentencing.[21]

Retribution is a general purpose of sentencing, which relates to the subjective pricing of punishment and which is influenced by the social condemnation arising from the commission of the offense.[22] The social harm, that is the harm caused to society by the commission of an offense, is measured objectively, regardless of the identity of the offender. Although a corporation may cause greater harm with a lesser effort than natural persons, retribution considers the actual harm and not the offender's capabilities. Environmental offenses are committed by corporations, in many cases, during processes of production and there is not always an identifiable direct human offender. However, the human offender may also be an officer in the corporation, though the corporation is the primary offender.[23]

Yet for the subjective element of punishment, the court should also consider the personal characteristics of the corporation, together with the objective elements as may be applicable to a particular offense, in the same way it does in relation to human offenders. Retribution can ensure a high level of certainty in relation to the expected punishment, both in terms of the type of punishment (for example financial and non-financial punishments) and the level of punishment (for example the rate of a fine and the prison term).

---

20 If, in certain legal systems, such as in Germany and Austria, the criminal liability of corporations is not yet recognized, the case for law reform in these legal systems would be expected to be much more transformational.

21 In modern criminal law, four basic general purposes of sentencing are accepted: retribution, deterrence, rehabilitation and incapacitation.

22 For retribution as one of the general purposes of sentencing see Hallevy, n. 3, 16–24.

23 Sometimes the offense is defined as an omission, and the identity of the human officer may not be significant for the criminal liability of the corporation.

The actual damage caused by the offense is a factor which tends to be simpler to define and establish in sentencing than the potential damage, the offender's mens rea or the offender's personal characteristics. Retribution does not neglect the offender's personal characteristics and it aims to adjust the punishment to the offender's subjective attributes. Retribution aims to retain the connection between the consequences of the offense and the offender's fault, on the one hand, and the punishment being imposed, on the other. However, some environmental offenses are classified as strict liability offenses, therefore the offender's fault becomes of secondary importance. Retribution can thus assuage the thirst for revenge of the victims and of society as a whole, subject to the principle of proportionality.

In many instances of environmental offenses, revenge might be considered irrelevant as there are no direct human victims of the offense, besides the victims who suffer from long-term damages, such as diseases discovered after many years of exposure to pollution. It is most likely that a factory that pollutes the air in a certain town for a number of years will cause the inhabitants of that town to fall victim to the high levels of pollution.[24] It is only natural that human inhabitants of that town would seek retribution. Besides, society in general is suffering, either directly or indirectly, from the pollution released by the factory. Society would have to use more of its resources for the inhabitants' healthcare in the short-term, but also most likely in the long-term because the direct victims may include children and the elderly population, who are much more vulnerable in relation to environmental pollution. Society may also suffer other damages concerning general public goods or interests (for example damage to natural resources, damage to tourism and restriction of access to public funds or resources).

Conversely, deterrence fulfills a more general purpose of sentencing, and is concerned with finding a balance between the expected benefits from commission of the offense and expected punishment resulting from the commission of the offense.[25] On balance, in this context, the effect of deterrence through punishment is not that different between corporate and human offenders. Increasing the expected levels of the punishment affects their deterrent effects in the same way for both corporate and human offenders. The deterrent effect, when it comes to corporate offenders, is evidenced in the rationality in corporate decision-making processes.

Essentially, there are two types of deterrence: individual deterrence and public (or general) deterrence. Individual deterrence is aimed at deterring the individual human

---

24 They may become victims due to diseases related to the pollution, due to the inconvenience the pollution creates, and due to the damage to their quality of life.

25 For deterrence as one of the general purposes of sentencing see Hallevy, n. 3, 25–36. For different applications of punishment theories on environmental offenses, see Ricardo Pereira, 'Environmental Criminal Law in the First Pillar: A Positive Development for Environmental Protection in the European Union?' 16 Eur. Energy and Envtl L. Rev. 254 (2007); Richard Lazarus, 'Assimilating Environmental Protection into Legal Rules and the Problem with Environmental Crimes' 27 Loy. L. A. L. Rev. 867 (1994).

or corporation from recidivism. The natural or legal person to be deterred, in this case, is the offender. By contrast, public deterrence is aimed at deterring potential offenders (the public) by punishing the individual offender. The public as a whole, in this context, is considered to consist of potential offenders. Individual deterrence is the basis of deterrence as a general purpose of sentencing. General deterrence is a controversial expansion of the former.[26]

In the case of individual deterrence, society considers the realistic possibility that some offenders, who have just committed an offense, may continue to commit further offenses as long as the benefit they derive from the commission of the offense is higher than the sum of the costs of punishment (as anticipated by the prospective offender), and the likelihood of conviction. The seriousness of the offence committed by the offender is an adequate basis for assuming that the offender may commit further offenses if not appropriately punished, including through individual incapacitation. In this context, any offender may be considered a future potential offender. In the context of individual deterrence, a convicted offender may not commit further offenses in light of the offender's experience with the consequences of punishment.

As noted above, financial punishments for corporations who commit environmental offenses have very limited effectiveness. The limited effectiveness of fines and other financial penalties is most likely to be expressed in lower rates of deterrence. When the corporation is not deterred by a particular expected punishment – or even encouraged by that particular punishment to continue offending – there is no effective incentive for the corporation to stop offending. For many financial crimes committed by human offenders, courts around the world have preferred imprisonment over financial punishment for that very reason. Tax offenses and securities offenses are dominant examples in this context. Even though some statutes foresee the possibility of courts imposing dynamic fines or fines proportional to income as legitimate forms of punishment, courts still prefer imposing imprisonment in the context of tax offenses.[27] Although imprisonment is far from being an ideal punishment, it is still considered to have a stronger deterrent effect on an individual than financial punishments, especially when an offender is due to be imprisoned for the first time.[28]

---

26 Ibid, Hallevy, 33–34. It is controversial since it is difficult to justify why the individual should suffer more than retributive punishment just for the general public to be deterred, regardless the offender's individual deterrence.

27 In general, a dynamic fine is a fine by which rate is determined in relation to the damage caused by the offense. For example, Article 63 of the Israeli Penal Code provides that the court may impose a fine of up to four times the damage caused by the offense.

28 When offenders are imprisoned for a further offense, the rate of deterrence reduces dramatically, most probably due to their adaptation to the result. The first term of adaptation is sometimes called 'incarceration pains' by criminologists and the period of 'pains' appear to be very short. It is suggested that prison inmates eventually do adapt themselves to prison, although this point is controversial.

Rehabilitation is a general purpose of sentencing, which relates to the offender's personal rehabilitation potential and seeks an appropriate treatment that addresses the drivers for the offender's delinquency.[29] As a general purpose of sentencing, rehabilitation may be relevant whether the offender is human or a corporation. A corporation may have rehabilitation potential, depending on its 'personal' characteristics. This relates to its personal characteristics as a corporate offender and the use of appropriate measures which could have a rehabilitating effect on corporate delinquency. Occasionally the offense reveals a delinquent organizational subculture within a corporation that encourages offending and provides incentives for it, directly or indirectly (for example by disregarding offenses or by failing to prevent their commission).[30] This may happen, for example, when the corporate officers receive incentives to achieve better results without any question of how these results are actually achieved.

Basically, a similar idea is the legal basis for modern corporate insolvency law.[31] When the corporation has the required potential for economic 'rehabilitation', modern corporate insolvency law prefers economic reconstruction of the corporation over its liquidation. Only when the court has lost any hope of restructuring or reconstructing the corporation, does liquidation become a relevant solution (at least under modern corporate insolvency law). In criminal law, a similar question is raised in this context: does the corporation have the required potential for legal rehabilitation?

Imposing criminal liability on a corporate officer for the commission of a given offense while disregarding the root causes of the corporate delinquency cannot be effective in driving improvements in corporate governance. Financial punishments are rarely capable of initiating a rehabilitation process within the corporation. Often there is only a minimal difference between a corporation that is incapable of changing its delinquent subculture and associated decision-making processes, and a corporation that accepts that subculture and takes no action to improve corporate governance.[32]

At times, the reasons for delinquency are objective, for example internal power struggles among the shareholders or the board of directors that actually paralyze the operation of the corporation. In this context, rehabilitation may appropriately address the root causes of the delinquent subculture. Yet for rehabilitation purposes, financial punishments are far from effective. Although these financial punishments may be combined with other penalties to achieve this goal and to increase their rehabilitative effect, alone and in themselves their effectiveness in driving major changes to corporate governance is limited, as noted above.

---

29 For rehabilitation as one of the general purposes of sentencing see Hallevy, n. 3, 36–45.

30 Peter A. French, *Collective and Corporate Responsibility* (Columbia University Press, 1984), 47.

31 See, for example Vanessa Finch and David Milman, *Corporate Insolvency Law: Perspectives and Principles* (3rd edn, Cambridge, 2017), 26–50.

32 Stuart Field and Nico Jorg, 'Corporate liability and manslaughter: should we be going Dutch?' Crim. L.R. 156 (1991).

Incapacitation is another general purpose of sentencing, which seeks to physically prevent reoffending and the endangerment to society and the environment posed by the offender.[33] The evaluation of the social endangerment posed by the offender is done in the same way, whether the offender is human or a corporation. The opportunities to commit offenses are examined objectively based on the behavior of the offender, whether human or a corporation. For example, the extent of an opportunity to release a false report to the tax authorities is evaluated on the basis of the behavior of the offender, not on the offender's identity. In this context, the measures of incapacitation are determined based on the endangerment to society and the environment posed by the offender and not the offender's identity.

In the context of environmental offenses, incapacitation of the corporation requires appropriate measures to prevent and, in some cases, physically stop the commission of offenses. Rarely does the imposition of a fine achieve this effect. However, if the court could have the delinquent substructure of the corporation incapacitated, even if only in the very specific context of the particular offense, this could be much more beneficial to society and the environment. What if the court could prohibit the corporation from continuing in a certain production process which damages the environment, for example through an *in personam* specific injunction, rather than imposing a fine to be paid for an offense that happened in the past? Such an injunction would probably serve the purpose of incapacitation much more effectively than a fine.

IV. How to actually impose imprisonment on corporations for environmental harm

In light of the above analysis of the general purposes of sentencing in the context of corporations, it is argued that there is no substantial difference, legally, between human and corporate offenders as far as the general purposes of sentencing are concerned. Nevertheless, there may be some differences in the way in which certain punishments are actually applied. When a fine is imposed, there is not much difference between human and corporate offenders, as paying the fine is not actually different from paying taxes or bills, regardless of the identity of the offender.

However, there is the technical question of how imprisonment could be applied when the offender is a corporation. The same question may arise in the case of probation, capital penalty, public service and virtually all other penalties which are interpreted as 'physical' punishments.[34] In several legal systems around the world those non-financial or equivalent punishments may be imposed on corporations for environmental harm, even if, in practice, national courts often fail to implement them in favour of financial punishments. In most cases mere technical obstacles tend to deter

[33] For incapacitation as one of the general purposes of sentencing see Hallevy, n. 3, 46–54.
[34] For physical punishments in criminal law see Hallevy, n. 3, 121–87.

the court from implementing the arguably right, just, fair and needed punishment on corporate offenders.[35]

In one example, Israel Ports Co was indicted for commission of water pollution offenses in Haifa Port in Israel. The magistrate court in Haifa thought that the most appropriate punishment would be public service rather than financial punishment.[36] Indeed, cleaning the port might be more effective in the context of certain environmental offenses rather than the payment of a fine. Yet the district court, upon appeal, found that public service for a corporation could not be implemented, and therefore the punishment was converted into fine.[37]

The High Court of Appeal reaffirmed the principle that all punishments are applicable to both human offenders and corporations, even if they were originally designed for human offenders.[38] The High Court of Appeal then ordered a public service penalty on the corporation, as had been originally imposed by the magistrate court. Nevertheless, nearly three years later, the Supreme Court reversed the decision of the High Court of Appeal. Although the majority opinion has reaffirmed the principle that all forms of punishments available in the criminal law are applicable to both human offenders and corporations, the majority opinion did not accept the applicability of public service as a legitimate punishment for corporations merely for technical reasons (particularly concerning how the inspections of implementation of the punishment would be carried out). It is argued that the majority opinion could have, instead of reversing the High Court of Appeal decision, given specific instructions on how the required inspections could be carried out.[39] Indeed, the minority opinion thought that there was no reason to reverse the decision.[40]

As for the actual imposition of imprisonment on corporations, the general construction of this legal step and a workable algorithm for its practical imposition will be discussed hereinafter. In this context, this chapter will consider whether converting certain physical punishments generally applicable to natural persons to corporate legal entities is indeed appropriate and theoretically possible.

---

35 See Nick Werle, 'Prosecuting Corporate Crime when Firms Are Too Big to Jail: Investigation, Deterrence, and Judicial Review' 128 Yale L.J. 1366 (2019).

36 *State of Israel v. Israel Ports Ltd* Cr. (Haifa) 5525-09-09 (31 March 2011).

37 *State of Israel v. Israel Ports Ltd* Cr.App. (Haifa) 1314-06-11 (24 October 2011).

38 *State of Israel v. Israel Ports Ltd* Cr.App.Req. 8487/11, High Court of Appeals Judgments 65 (3) 845 (23 October 2012), para. 26.

39 Compare this with the US in Martin Harrell, 'Organizational environmental crime and the Sentencing Reform Act of 1984: combining fines with restitution, remedial orders, community service, and probation to benefit the environment while punishing the guilty' 6 Vill. Envtl L.J. 243, 260–67 (1995).

40 *State of Israel v. Israel Ports Ltd* Cr.Add.Sess. 8062/12 (2 April 2015).

a. The general legal construction

Since no physical punishments have been designed or planned *ex ante* for corporations, it has been argued in the past that they are inapplicable to corporations and therefore corporations cannot be punished physically.[41] This argument is incorrect, as noted above. In general, it is theoretically possible to apply similar punishments to both humans and corporations,[42] although, in the case of some punishments, it is necessary to make some adjustments. These adjustments, however, do not negate the applicability of physical punishments to corporate legal entities, but focus only on the way they are actually applied.[43]

Historically, not only has criminal liability been imposed upon corporations for centuries in certain legal systems, but corporations have also been sentenced in criminal prosecutions, and not only with fines. Corporations are actually punished in various ways in different legal systems. In fact, they are already punished by imprisonment in some legal systems, as will be shown below. It should be noted, however, that generally corporations are punished separately to their human officers (directors, managers, employees, and so on).[44] Arguably, in order to achieve the retributivist and utilitarian goals of punishment discussed above, there should be no dispute over the question of whether corporations should be punished using a variety of punishments (including a range of non-financial punishments which may include imprisonment), but a more pressing question concerns the way in which these penalties are applied.[45]

To answer the question of 'how' (that is how to punish corporations with imprisonment), a general legal technique of conversion is needed. This operation is carried out in three principal stages. First, the general punishment itself (for example imprisonment, fine, probation, death, and so on) is analyzed regarding its roots in social meaning. Second, these roots are considered in the context of corporations. Third, the punishment is then adjusted to take into account how its social roots are relevant in

---

41 Harry G. Henn and John R. Alexander, *Corporations and Other Business Enterprises* (3rd edn, West Publishing Company, 1983), 184; *People v. Strong*, 363 Ill. 602, 2 N.E.2d 942 (1936); *State v. Traux*, 130 Wash. 69, 226 P. 259 (1924); *United States v. Union Supply Co*, 215 U.S. 50, 30 S.Ct. 15, 54 L.Ed. 87 (1909); *State v. Ice & Fuel Co*, 166 N.C. 366, 81 S.E. 737 (1914); *Commonwealth v. McIlwain School Bus Lines Inc*, 283 Pa.Super. 1, 423 A.2d 413 (1980).

42 John C. Coffee, Jr, '"No Soul to Damn: No Body to Kick": An Unscandalised Inquiry Into the Problem of Corporate Punishment' 79 Mich. L. Rev 386 (1981); Steven Box, *Power, Crime and Mystification* (Routledge, 1983), 16–79.

43 Gerard E. Lynch, 'The Role of Criminal Law in Policing Corporate Misconduct' 60 Law & Contemp. Probs. 23 (1997); Richard Gruner, 'To Let the Punishment Fit the Organization: Sanctioning Corporate Offenders Through Corporate Probation' 16 Am. J. Crim. L. 1 (1988); Steven Walt and William S. Laufer, 'Why Personhood Doesn't Matter: Corporate Criminal Liability and Sanctions' 18 Am. J. Crim. L. 263 (1991).

44 That is criminal liability is imposed upon corporations separately from the criminal liability, if any, imposed on human officers within the corporation.

45 Field and Jorg, n. 32.

the corporate crime context. For example, in the case of imposition of imprisonment (and not necessarily incarceration) on corporations, first, imprisonment is traced back to its original roots and overarching goal of depriving individuals of their freedom; then, an equivalent concept is sought for depriving corporations of their freedom.

After the meaning of a corporate physical punishment is understood in that light, in the third and final stage the court imposes a punishment that is the equivalent to depriving a corporation of its freedom. This is how the general legal technique of conversion works in the case of sentencing corporations. At times, this requires the court to be creative in the adjustments required to make imprisonment applicable to corporations, but the general theoretical framework for this is arguably clear, workable and feasible. In fact, as was noted above, a range of physical punishments have been implemented and imposed on all types of corporations.[46]

An excellent example is the US case of *Allegheny Bottling Co*,[47] a corporation that was found to be guilty of price-fixing (that is in breach of antitrust laws). It was agreed by the justices that, under the given circumstances, if the defendant were human, the appropriate punishment would be imprisonment for a certain term. Hence the question was one of the applicability of imprisonment to corporations, that is a question of 'how' to convert penalties normally applicable to individuals to corporations. As a general principle, the court declared that it 'does not expect a corporation to have consciousness, but it does expect it to be ethical and abide by the law'.[48]

The court did not find any substantive difference between humans and corporations in this matter and added that '[t]his court will deal with this company no less severely than it will deal with any individual who similarly disregards the law'.[49] This statement reflects the basic principle of equalizing the punishment of human and corporate defendants.[50] In this case, the corporation was sentenced to three years' imprisonment, a fine of one million US dollars, and probation for a period of three years. The court proceeded to discuss the idea of corporate imprisonment based on the three stages described above.

First, the court asked what the general meaning of imprisonment was and accepted the definitions of imprisonment as 'constraint of a person either by force or by such other coercion as restrains him within limits against his will' and 'forcible restraint of a person against his will (n 47)'. The court's conclusion was simple and clear:

46 Lynch, n. 43; Gruner, n. 43; Walt and Laufer, n. 43.
47 *United States v. Allegheny Bottling Co*, 695 F.Supp. 856 (1988).
48 Ibid, 858.
49 Ibid.
50 Brent Fisse and John Braithwaite, 'The Allocation of Responsibility for Corporate Crime: Individualism, Collectivism and Accountability' 11 Sydney L. Rev. 468 (1988).

The key to corporate imprisonment is this: imprisonment simply means *restraint*

and

restraint, that is, a deprivation of liberty.

The court's conclusion was reinforced by several provisions of the law and case law as well.[51] Consequently, '[t]here is imprisonment when a person is under house arrest, for example, where a person has an electronic device which sends an alarm if the person leaves his own house (n 47)'. This concluded the first stage. In the second stage, the court searched for a meaning of this punishment for corporations and concluded that '[c]orporate imprisonment requires only that the Court restrain or immobilize the corporation',[52] and proceeded to implement the prison sentence on the corporation according to this insight.

Thus, in the third and final stage the court made imprisonment applicable to the defendant corporation and implemented it as follows:[53]

> Such restraint of individuals is accomplished by, for example, placing them in the custody of the United States Marshal. Likewise, corporate imprisonment can be accomplished by simply placing the corporation in the custody of the United States Marshal. The United States Marshal would restrain the corporation by seizing the corporation's physical assets or part of the assets or restricting its actions or liberty in a particular manner. When this sentence was contemplated, the United States Marshal for the Eastern District of Virginia, Roger Ray, was contacted. When asked if he could imprison Allegheny Pepsi, he stated that he could. He stated that he restrained corporations regularly for bankruptcy court. He stated that he could close the physical plant itself and guard it. He further stated that he could allow employees to come and go and limit certain actions or sales if that is what the Court imposes.[54]

The court in *Allegheny Bottling Co* then went on to note that:

> Richard Lovelace said some three hundred years ago, 'stone walls do not a prison make, nor iron bars a cage.' It is certainly true that we erect our own walls or barriers that restrain ourselves. Any person may be imprisoned if capable of being restrained in some fashion or in some way, regardless of who imposes it. Who am I to say that imprisonment is impossible when the keeper indicates that it can physically be done? Obviously, one can restrain a corporation. If so, why should it be more privileged than an individual citizen? There is no reason, and accordingly, a corporation should not be more privileged.

---

51 The court relied on the key cases of *Johnson v. Norfolk and W. Ry.*, 82 W. Va. 692, 97 S.E. 189 (1918); *Kress v. Musgrove*, 153 Va. 348, 149 S.E. 453 (1929); *Zayre of Virginia v. Gowdy*, 207 Va. 47, 147 S.E.2d 710 (1966).

52 *Allegheny Bottling Co*, n. 47, 861.

53 For its importance and the reader's convenience, full quotation of the relevant excerpts is directly quoted in the text.

54 *Allegheny Bottling Co*, n. 47, 861.

> Cases in the past have *assumed* that corporations cannot be imprisoned, without any cited authority for that proposition. ... This Court, however, has been unable to find any case which actually held that corporate imprisonment is illegal, unconstitutional or impossible. Considerable confusion regarding the ability of courts to order a corporation imprisoned has been caused by courts mistakenly thinking that imprisonment necessarily involves incarceration in jail. ... But since imprisonment of a corporation does not necessarily involve incarceration, there is no reason to continue the assumption, which has lingered in the legal system unexamined and without support, that a corporation cannot be imprisoned. Since the Marshal can restrain the corporation's liberty and has done so in bankruptcy cases, there is no reason that he cannot do so in this case as he himself has so stated prior to the imposition of this sentence.[55]

Thus, in that sense, imprisonment can be applied not only to human but to corporate offenders as well. Following the same approach, imprisonment is not the only penalty applicable to corporations, but other non-financial penalties can be 'converted' as well, even if they were originally designed for human offenders. And if this is true for imprisonment, which is an essentially human penalty, there is no reason for this not to be true for all other non-financial punishments.

A careful analysis of individual punishments shows how every type of punishment could, in principle, be applicable to both humans and corporations. Thus, in determining the type of punishment and its scope based on the general purposes of punishment, it is immaterial whether the offense was committed by humans or by corporations, although it is recognized that it may not be possible (or it may be more difficult) to convert certain punishments which were specifically designed for corporations to human defendants.[56] After the court decides to apply an appropriate punishment, it may be necessary to make some adjustments to some of the penalties. To make the process clearer, a simple workable algorithm in alignment with the theoretical framework proposed by this chapter may be developed, as will be discussed below.

b. A workable algorithm with examples for imposition of imprisonment on corporations

When the court's conclusion, after conviction of the corporation, is that a non-financial punishment is required in order to achieve the purposes of sentencing in the particular case, whether together with a financial punishment or not, a simple

---

55 *Allegheny Bottling Co*, n. 47, 861.

56 Examples are found in the new Directive (EU) 2024/1203 of the European Parliament and of the Council of 11 April 2024 on the protection of the environment through criminal law and replacing Directives 2008/99/EC and 2009/123/EC (the Environmental Crime Directive), Article 7(2): '(g) judicial winding-up; (h) closure of establishments used for committing the offense; (i) an obligation to establish due diligence schemes for enhancing compliance with environmental standards; (j) where there is a public interest, publication of all or part of the judicial decision relating to the criminal offense committed and the penalties or measures imposed, without prejudice to rules on privacy and the protection of personal data'.

algorithm,[57] based on the aforesaid, may be helpful. The algorithm forms a series of checks and actions due to the circumstances of the particular case. The basic question that the court should ask itself before sentencing the corporation is: what is the nature of the right or liberty that the corporation should be deprived of with the required punishment, regardless of the punishment's title?

In general, any punishment includes a deprivation of rights or liberties of the convicted person, whether that person is human or corporation. For example, in the context of environmental offenses, the court may decide that the most appropriate punishment is deprivation of the liberty to lawfully pollute the environment (for example pollution within a certain range), even within the permitted legal thresholds (for example under administrative law), for a certain period. In addition, the court may decide that the corporation's profits were achieved unlawfully due to commission of an offense, and it should be deprived of the right to possess that property. The court may decide that there is no chance that this particular corporation would be inclined to bring about the appropriate reforms to its corporate governance structures so that it acts in a law-abiding way; therefore, the court may decide that the corporation should be deprived of its right to exist through application of an appropriate sanction of license revocation (which is broadly equivalent to the corporate 'capital penalty').

In some cases, the court may decide that the commission of an environmental offense was not more than a bona-fide mistake of the corporation and that the damage may be repaired and restored for the benefit of the public and the environment. The court may also consider the corporation's sincere will to cooperate with the authorities to repair the environmental damage. In such cases, the court may decide that a temporary deprivation of the corporation's liberty to operate is the most appropriate punishment which may be expressed by imposition of a service for the benefit of the public to repair the environmental damage using its own officers, resources and funds.[58] Accordingly, the court aims at the appropriate action to be taken against the corporation which begins with the sentencing process, and that is where the suggested algorithm begins.

---

57 In mathematics, 'algorithm' refers to a finite list of rigorous instructions. A cake recipe, for example, is an algorithm of how to bake a cake. In the above context, it refers to the relevant instructions to impose imprisonment on corporations.

58 One may pose the question of the personal price that the corporation's officers and other related persons (for example workers, services suppliers) may actually pay in such cases. The answer is not different from the answer to the parallel question with regard to human offenders. When a human offender is convicted and sentenced to imprisonment carried out by incarceration in jail, the offender's family may pay a very high price accordingly, including loss of income, social status in their community and so on. If the offender is also an employer, the employees may also pay a personal price of losing their jobs. This is part of the imposition of any punishment on any person. Therefore, there is no substantive difference between human offenders and corporations concerning the impact of certain criminal penalties.

Stage 1: identify what the meaning of the particular punishment is in terms of the deprivation of rights or liberties (of human or corporation)

All punishments are designed to deprive the offender of certain rights or liberties. Thus, imprisonment is deprivation of the defendant's liberty, partially or absolutely. Incarceration is a particular type of such deprivation, but not the only one. Capital penalty is deprivation of the defendant's right to live. Confiscation is deprivation of the defendant's right to possess a specified property previously possessed by the defendant. A fine deprives the defendant of the right to possess part of their property, but not necessarily a specified property. Public service is deprivation of the defendant's liberty of occupation, as the defendant is obliged to perform a certain activity and nothing beyond that is allowed; and so on. This stage basically consists of a generalization of the punishment in terms of the rights and liberties impacted by the punishment, and therefore it is embedded in the social roots of and philosophical foundations for punishment.

Stage 2: identify what the meaning of the particular deprivation of right or liberty is for the particular corporation in the context of the particular offense

When focusing on financial punishments, their meaning is pretty much the same for all defendants. Depriving any defendant, whether human or corporation, of the right to property by imposing a fine, for example, is not dependent on their legal status. However, many other rights and liberties may be interpreted and considered differently due to the type or identify of different defendants. Indeed, liberty may be considered differently in various contexts. For example, the main liberty of a corporation which produces soft drinks may be different from the main liberty of a corporation which sells computers, publishes newspapers, transports people or makes movies.

In general, the right to live of a human defendant is interpreted intuitively, therefore depriving a human defendant of the right to live is interpreted as the death penalty, if this penalty is legitimate in the particular legal system. However, the 'life' of a corporation may be interpreted in many different ways. For some corporations, 'life' means their statutory registration, that is the recognition in law that these corporations are independent legal entities, whereas for other corporations 'life' means all of their property. For example, for a real-estate corporation life is its property, since without it, it is not recognized as real-estate corporation, and loses its right to act as an independent legal entity in that field.[59]

The meaning of the particular deprivation of right or liberty should be examined in terms of the particular corporation in the context of the particular offense, and not generally or conceptually. The court should ask itself what the meaning of the deprivation of right or liberty is for the particular corporation and only for it, in line with

[59] In some legal systems corporations, which own real-estates as their main property, under certain tests, have a special law applicable to them regarding corporate law, property law and tax law. See, for example in Israel the provisions of Article 1 of the Real-Estate Taxation Act, 1963.

the concept of 'individual sentencing'.[60] The relevant, exact and particular interpretation of this notion is crucial for matching the correct punishment to be imposed on a particular corporation. There is no point in depriving a corporation of the liberty of mobility when it is located in one place and has no need to move anywhere else or to mobilize its officers or economic activity elsewhere.

Stage 3: match and adjust the punishment to the meaning of the particular deprivation of right or liberty for the particular corporation

At this stage the court has the required information to complete the process of sentencing. The corporation is sentenced with the most appropriate penalty taking into account the characteristics of the particular offense (*in-rem* characteristics) and the characteristics of the particular corporation (*in-personam* characteristics). The penalty is not being imposed due to the lack of other appropriate alternative penalties, but is selected due to an in-depth consideration of the most appropriate penalty option. A few particular examples may illustrate how easy and simple the imposition of imprisonment on corporations may become following the appropriate law reforms, if required in the particular legal system.[61]

The following hypothetical example is given to illustrate how Stage 3 could be implemented by domestic courts when sentencing imprisonment on corporate legal entities. A transportation company supplies public transportation services in a certain area. It uses old vehicles which are fueled with diesel, so they pollute the air beyond the permissible legal threshold. The corporation is convicted of air pollution offenses. It appears to be that this is not the first time the corporation has been convicted of the same air pollution offenses. The court realizes that it would still be possible for the company to remain profitable after paying a fine and to continue using cheap vehicles and fuel. An excessive fine would lead to liquidation of the company and the general public and employees would bear the consequences. Therefore, the court decides that imprisonment may be imposed as an alternative penalty. The particular deprivation of liberty for this particular corporation in the context of that particular offense concerns the liberties associated with the mobility and occupation of the corporation.

In this hypothetical scenario, the court may decide that three months' imprisonment is the proportionate penalty, and that it is carried out by depriving this particular corporation of its mobility and occupation freedoms. That would mean that for three months the corporation is not allowed to continue in transporting people, it is not allowed to sell or hire the license to transport people to any third party (for example

60 See, for example Susan Easton and Christine Piper, *Sentencing and Punishment: The Quest for Justice* (2nd edn, Oxford Universitry Press, 2008), 72–110; Hallevy, n. 3, 64–101.

61 In some legal systems, this judgment may also be interpreted as an *in-personam* injunction against the shareholders which prohibits reassociation as a different corporation which has the same occupation as the first corporation at the time of imprisonment, which would thus bypass the punishment. As shown in *Allegheny Bottling Co*, n. 47.

by outsourcing) and it is not allowed to perform any act, which might result in air pollution over a certain rate, even within the permissible legal limits.[62]

Therefore, in this scenario the punishment is matched and adjusted to the meaning of the particular deprivation of right or liberty for this particular corporation, which suggests that the theoretical framework for punishing corporations with imprisonment proposed by this chapter could have significant practical implications if the appropriate law reforms are implemented in the relevant legal systems.

V. Conclusion

Due to the limited effectiveness of financial punishments for corporations, especially in the context of environmental offenses, it seems that there is no legal justification for domestic courts to keep on primarily using these financial punishments alone. Modern criminal law enables courts to impose non-financial penalties both on human offenders and corporations. The legal framework for this is simple, applicable and practical. Moreover, non-financial punishments (which arguably should also include imprisonment) for some types of corporate environmental crimes may be much fairer and just, for the defendants, the human victims and the environment.

Non-financial punishments enable the court to act in a much more flexible way compared to financial punishments, as the court has the power to match an appropriate penalty to circumstances of the case, taking account of both the *in-rem* and *in-personam* characteristics of corporate defendants. Of course, in some cases the financial punishment may reflect well the public reaction to and condemnation of a particular environmental offense. Using non-financial punishments – including imprisonment as per the theoretical framework discussed in this chapter - does not negate the option of courts imposing financial punishments or using an appropriate combination of both punishments. Whilst recognizing that there is need for further research in this field, this chapter has proposed a three-stage algorithm which would enable the practical imposition of imprisonment on corporations.

The conclusion of this chapter may be easily generalized. In line with the principle that it is theoretically possible to convert certain penalties applicable to human defendants to legal persons (and *mutatis mutandis*), it is argued that imprisonment should be one of the non-financial penalties available to domestic courts in order to deter and appropriately punish corporate offenders for environmental harm. It would also go a long way in fulfilling the symbolic and declaratory goals of punishment, given that prison sentences are widely regarded to be among the harshest possible penalties available to courts in criminal proceedings.

62 Ibid.

14 International institutions and the fight against transnational environmental crimes

Teresa Fajardo and Ricardo Pereira

1. Introduction: the rationales and legal bases for international and regional institutions to fight transnational environmental crimes

Environmental crime has become a global problem that transcends domestic borders. Since the environment has become a victim of transnational and organised crime, the criminality associated with it has been addressed by international agreements, yet mostly by *soft law* instruments promoted by international institutions and decisions of conferences of the parties (COPs) of multilateral environmental agreements (MEAs). There is, as yet, no treaty on environmental crime nor a common definition of environmental crime since states prefer to refer, in international forums, to 'crimes related to the environment'. Some MEAs such as the Convention on International Trade in Endangered Species of Wild Fauna and Flora (CITES),[1] the Basel Convention[2] or the International Convention for the Prevention of Pollution from Ships (MARPOL)[3] contain provisions on penalties for environmental offences. These instruments are not only a source of obligations for states to introduce into their legal orders the normative

1 Convention on International Trade in Endangered Species of Wild Fauna and Flora, 3 March 1973, 27 U.S.T. 1087, 993 U.N.T.S. 243; 12 I.L.M. 1085 (1973). Available online: https://cites.org/sites/default/files/eng/disc/CITES-Convention-EN.pdf.

2 Basel Convention on the Control of Transboundary Movements of Hazardous Wastes and their Disposal, adopted on 22 March 1989. Available at https://www.basel.int/TheConvention/Overview/TextoftheConvention/tabid/1275/Default.aspx.

3 International Convention for the Prevention of Pollution from Ships, 2 November 1973, 1340 U.N.T.S. 61; 12 I.L.M. 1319 (1973) (MARPOL 73/78). Available online: http://sedac.ciesin.columbia.edu/entri/texts/pollution.from.ships.1973.html. Amended by: Protocol of 1978 Relating to the International Convention for the Prevention of Pollution from Ships.

and operative tools to fight environmental crime[4] but they also establish the institutional mandate for cooperation between international organisations and states aimed at promoting implementation and compliance. Since several forms of environmental crimes are transnational, enhanced cooperation among international institutions and their member states is necessary.

The lack of an international environmental organisation not only exposes the institutional deficit in the field of international environmental law, but also calls for flexible multi-level governance that responds to the fragmented and sectoral institutionalisation that has emerged from MEAs and soft law instruments.[5] Synergies and cooperation between institutions at the national, regional, and international levels have produced a form of 'soft governance' with flexible institutional structures, networks, and programmes that have built up cooperation and trust amongst international organisations and the national law enforcement agencies ('LEAs'), despite the differences in legal traditions and resources for enforcement in the states of origin, transit, and destination of environmental crimes.

The role of international institutions in fighting environmental crimes depends to a large extent on how far they have a mandate to strengthen the implementation and compliance with the environmental rule of law, as established in MEAs and complemented by soft law instruments,[6] through the provision of twofold political and normative action. Political action is carried out through the adoption of international declarations, strategies, and programmes that seek to raise awareness of the seriousness of environmental crimes and thereby to mobilise state actors to adopt the necessary national and international cooperation measures. These soft law instruments, adopted as declarations by the UN General Assembly or by COPs of MEAs, become global policies on environmental crime when they bring virtually all states together, contributing to a common understanding of environmental crime. In contrast, normative action is undertaken by international institutions when they carry out legal processes concerning an array of social concerns such as crime prevention, prosecution, and punishment, and develop normative frameworks for reacting to environmental damage. This normative activity varies in intensity, depending on the mandate conferred upon them by states and if they are organisations primarily of cooperation or integration, as in the case of the European Union (EU). However, when most of these international organisations were created, the environment was not yet a common concern for states, so only after the reform of their founding treaties or an exten-

---

4 See B.-S. Cho, 'Emergence of an International Environmental Criminal Law?' (2000/2001) 19 *UCLA Journal of Environmental Law and Policy* 3.

5 As mentioned in Chapter 1 in this volume, UNEP is a UN programme, and not as such a fully-fledged organisation.

6 See UNEP, *Environmental Rule of Law, First Global Report* (2019), available online: https://www.unep.org/resources/assessment/environmental-rule-law-first-global-report?_ga=2.151172345.1355101735.1711627717-470208184.1698839616 and the second report, *Environmental Rule of Law: Tracking Progress and Charting Future Directions* (2023), available online: https://doi.org/10.59117/20.500.11822/43943.

sive and teleological interpretation of their goals has it has been possible to expand their jurisdiction and capabilities to deal with specific environmental offences related to their expressly mandated aims and purposes.

Those circumstances are the source of enormous challenges for international environmental governance, understood in a broad sense, as the numerous sectors affected by environmental crime call for the involvement of a wide range of international institutions and agencies. They are joined by civil society actors who have become the 'eyes on the ground' and have developed roles that complement those of international organisations in the investigation and prosecution of environmental crime.[7] The cooperation between institutions and non-state actors is essential to raise awareness of environmental crime risks, which have steadily increased due in part to the unrelenting demand of consumers and the perceived high profits and low detection and prosecution risks enjoyed by offenders.[8]

It is a maxim of international organisations that their organs are designed according to the functions they are intended to perform. In this light, the following sections review, firstly in section 2, the specific functions exercised by international institutions for fighting transnational environmental crime, including the cooperation among international organisations and national agencies in fighting environmental crime; then in section 3, we critically review the functions and mandates of a selection of international and regional organisations and the informal networks created between them. In this context, the chapter examines the current fragmented legal frameworks aimed at fighting transnational environmental crime at the international and regional levels, particularly through the UN bodies and agencies and international and regional agreements and their respective institutions. We then turn, in section 4, to an analysis of the frameworks for interstate environmental cooperation in the context of selected MEAs, while section 5 evaluates the role of non-governmental organisations (NGOs) in advancing the global fight against environmental crime through their active participation in the governance of international institutions. Section 6 concludes.

---

7 See L.A. Malone and S. Pasternak, *Defending the Environment: Civil Society Strategies to Enforce International Environmental Law* (Island Press, 2005), R. White, 'NGO Engagement in Environmental Law Enforcement: Critical Reflections' in R. White, *Transnational Environmental Crime* (Routledge, 2013), L. Smith and K. Klaas, *Networks and NGOs Relevant to Fighting Environmental Crime. Study in the framework of the Efface research project* (Berlin: Ecologic Institute, 2015).

8 See Chapter 6 The Effectiveness of Environmental Criminal Law Enforcement by Juan Fuentes Osorio in this volume.

2. The functions exercised by international institutions for fighting environmental crime

Specific functions to fight environmental crime were not foreseen in the founding treaties of intergovernmental organisations (IGOs) with competences in the field of environmental protection, insofar as they concern very sensitive issues related to sovereignty over which states have been unwilling to accept limitations through treaty obligations. We therefore need to consider how the general functions performed by IGOs can be adapted to the purpose of combating environmental crime. As was discussed above, IGOs have political and normative functions – which may or may not be supported by a treaty framework – that can be classified under the heading of cooperation,[9] and that often includes functions of harmonisation or coordination of the laws, policies, and behaviours of states. Moreover, IGOs have functions related to coordination of collective actions (such as those of INTERPOL) as well as functions regarding performance of institutional actions (such as those performed by the CITES institutions), as will be discussed in the folowing sections.

2.1 The formulation of global policies in the fight against environmental crime

Through their parliamentary diplomacy, IGOs contribute to the formation of global public policy on common problems, which, in the case of environmental crime, also means working with individual member state LEAs.[10] One of the most striking aspects of the global policies and actions adopted by IGOs is that they are directed at countering crimes affecting the environment, rather than specifically environmental crime. This approach is reflected in the policies adopted by international organisations and agencies that tend to refer to 'crimes related to [or that affect] the environment' in negotiated binding and non-binding instruments or studies.

According to their competences and mandates, IGOs might adopt new rules or processes aimed at combatting environmental crime with differing degrees of ambition depending on factors such as their global or regional scope, their nature as organisations of primarily cooperation or integration, and the political and economic support received from their member states. In the exercise of their functions, the United Nations General Assembly (UNGA) and the United Nations (UN) Economic

---

9 See M. Virally, 'La Notion de Fonction dans la Théorie de l'Organisation Internationale' in *Mélanges Offerts à Charles Rousseau, La Communauté Internationale* (Pedone, Paris, 1974), 283–8.

10 The diplomacy of LEAs, international organisations and NGOs has emerged out of necessity and practice to combat transnational environmental crime. With or without actual diplomats, they arguably perform similar functions to those of diplomats, initiate diplomatic demarches, such as the celebration of international conferences and seminars or discussions on the state of play of new environmental crimes, and have succeeded in getting all institutions and states to incorporate the fight against environmental crime into their agendas.

and Social Council (ECOSOC) may only adopt non-binding resolutions, while the Security Council can resort to binding resolutions and has done so for example in the context of armed conflicts and illegal natural resource extraction.[11] Moreover, as will be discussed further below, at the regional level the Council of Europe has proposed to its Member States a Convention on the protection of the environment through criminal law,[12] and the EU has adopted an instrument for the harmonisation of the national legislation of its Member States.[13]

2.2 Approximation and harmonisation of criminal offences and sanctions for the protection of the environment

The fact that criminals are able to exploit the differences in legislation and legal enforcement techniques in different states to their benefit is a main driver for the harmonisation of both substantive and procedural criminal law led by IGOs.[14] In general, the diversity of national penal systems allows criminals to select the legal system that is regarded as less effective and use it as a sanctuary or safe haven.[15] Moreover, one of the main justifications for interstate cooperation and legal harmonisation is that the comparability of legal norms is fundamental for effective transnational (criminal) control[16] of environmental offences with global or transboundary effects, such as the illegal trade in endangered species, waste trafficking, marine pollution, or the illegal

11 See, for example Resolution 1306 (2003) concerning the illicit trade in diamonds during the conflict in Sierra Leone; and Resolutions 1457 (2003), 1856 (2008), and 1952 (2010) concerning the DRC. See further L. van den Herik and D. Dam-De Jong, 'Revitalizing the Antique War Crime of Pillage: The Potential and Pitfalls of Using International Criminal Law to Address Illegal Resource Exploitation During Armed Conflicts' (2011) 22 *Criminal Law Forum* 3, and R. Pereira, 'After the ICC Office of the Prosecutor's 2016 Policy Paper on Case Selection and Prioritisation - Towards an International Crime of "Ecocide"?' (2020) 31 *Criminal Law Forum* 179–224.

12 See Council of Europe Convention on the Protection of the Environment through Criminal Law (1998), Strasbourg, 4.XI.1998, E.T.S. 172 (not yet in force). See further A. Vercher, 'The Use of Criminal Law for the Protection of the Environment in Europe: Council of Europe Resolution (77) 28' (1990) 10 *Northwestern Journal of International Law & Business* 442, 445.

13 Directive 2008/99/EC of 19 November 2008 on the protection of the environment through criminal law, OJ L 328, 28–37, and Directive (EU) 2024/1203 of the European Parliament and of the Council of 11 April 2024 on the protection of the environment through criminal law and replacing Directives 2008/99/EC and 2009/123/EC, OJ L 2024/1203.

14 R. Pereira, *Environmental Criminal Liability and Enforcement in European and International Law* (Brill, 2015).

15 See A. Weyembergh, 'Approximation of Criminal Laws, the Constitutional Treaty and the Hague Programme' (2005) 42 *Common Market Law Review* 1579.

16 Pereira (2015), n. 14. For example, the lack of a common definition of crime may have an impact on crime statistics, as the collection of data and statistics depends on the legal categorisation given by each legal system, and the comparability of the figures may be compromised by variations. In this regard, UNODC has proposed a typology of crimes related to the environment for the classification of information concerning

trade in ozone-depleting substances. Therefore, the progressive approximation and harmonisation of criminal offences and sanctions has become a task for some international and regional organisations. In the case of sanctions, harmonisation is also recommended in order to meet the requirements for cooperation, as in the case of the 2000 Transnational Organised Crime Convention (the Palermo Convention)[17] which requires that a maximum prison sentence of at least four years is foreseen under national law in order to trigger the mechanisms for interstate criminal-law cooperation and investigation of transnational organised crimes, including organised environmental crimes.[18]

2.3 Cooperation among international organisations and national agencies in the prosecution of environmental crime

In the fight against transnational and organised environmental crime, some of the main challenges are related to the lack of compliance with the environmental rule of law as shaped by MEAs and national rules relating to environmental protection, which may be a reflection of weak state and institutional governance. The lack of human, technical, and economic resources is at the root of compliance problems and stands in stark contrast to the criminal environment in which smugglers, white-collar criminals, poachers, criminal groups, and organisations are able to operate with more financial resources than most local, national, and international authorities. Thus, a 2016 United Nations Environment Programme (UNEP)-International Criminal Police Organization (INTERPOL) Report has pointed out that 'the sheer financial scale and sophistication of environmental crimes now require an entirely different scale of coordinated responses and international collaboration, working across ministries and jurisdictions at the national level, to international cross-UN and trans-border collaboration'.[19] In a coordinating effort to achieve synergies in common fields of action, the institutions of the UN family have launched initiatives between the UNEP, the Food and Agriculture Organisation (FAO), the International Maritime Organisation (IMO) and the COPs of the different MEAs. Their actions to combat transnational environmental crimes such as the illegal trafficking of ozone-depleting substances or illegal, unregulated and unreported (IUU) fishing are clear examples of this.

Although no international organisation has the function of enforcing international rules to combat environmental crime, IGOs play an instrumental role in promoting

environmental crime. See further, https://www.unodc.org/unodc/en/environment-climate/.

17 UN Convention against Transnational Organized Crime and the Protocols thereto, adopted by the UN General Assembly Resolution 55/25, of 15 November 2000.

18 See UN Convention against Transnational Organized Crime, Article 2(b).

19 C. Nellemann, R. Henriksen, A. Kreilhuber, D. Stewart, M. Kotsovou, P. Raxter, E. Mrema, and S. Barrat (eds), *The Rise of Environmental Crime – A Growing Threat to Natural Resources Peace, Development and Security. A UNEP-INTERPOL Rapid Response Assessment* (UNEP and RHIPTO Rapid Response–Norwegian Center for Global Analyses, 2016), 11, available online: www.rhipto.org.

international cooperation between the LEAs of different member states. Hence, international organisations have facilitated cross-border cooperation through legal instruments and frameworks that enable joint investigations, mutual recognition of sentences, or extradition of perpetrators of serious environmental crimes, as in the case of the Council of Europe[20] or the EU.[21]

2.4 To promote the progressive development of international environmental law in the 'global commons'

International organisations should consider the expansion of states' jurisdiction to protect the environment beyond national jurisdiction. One of the rationales for the criminalisation of environmental harm at the global level is connected to the fact that the conservation of natural resources found in the so-called 'global commons', that is areas that are beyond national jurisdiction such as the high seas or deep seabed,[22] transcends individual harm and concerns the protection of collective interests. As international environmental law incorporates *erga omnes* obligations, it includes obligations imposed on states regarding the international community as a whole.[23] The eventual entry into force of the 2023 United Nations Convention on the conservation and sustainable use of marine biological diversity in areas beyond national jurisdiction[24] would require regulatory and operational action to enforce the

---

20 See, for example the 1957 European Convention on Extradition, E.T.S. 24, 359 U.N.T.S. 273; 1959 European Convention on Mutual Assistance in Criminal Matters, E.T.S. 30; 1972 European Convention on the Transfer of Proceedings in Criminal Matters, E.T.S. 73, 72 U.N.T.S. 185.

21 See Council Framework Decision of 13 June 2002 on the European arrest warrant and the surrender procedures between Member States –Statements made by certain Member States on the adoption of the Framework Decision OJ L 190, 1–20.

22 However, there are limitations in this regard, as the enforcement of environmental law in the high seas is limited by the principle of the exclusive jurisdiction of flag states; and the unwillingness of flags-of-convenience states to enforce environmental standards on their own vessels in the high seas. See further, Y. Tanaka, *The International Law of the Sea* (CUP, 2012); and D.R. Rothwell and T. Stephens, *International Law of the Sea* (Hart Publishing, 2010); C. Costa de Oliveira, D. Diz, and T. Fajardo, 'Editorial: Oil Spill Prevention And Response: Introductory National, International, and Comparative Perspectives' (2024) 20(3) *Revista de Direito Internacional*, doi:10.5102/rdi.v20i3.9386.

23 See Pereira (2015), n. 14. In the *Seabed Chamber Advisory Opinion*, the International Tribunal on the Law of the Sea (ITLOS) upheld its recognition of the '*erga omnes* character of the obligations relating to the preservation of the environment of the high seas and the Area'. Responsibilities and obligations of States sponsoring persons and entities with respect to activities in the Area (Request for Advisory Opinion submitted to the Seabed Disputes Chamber), 1 February 2011, *ITLOS Reports 2011*, para. 180.

24 United Nations Convention on the Law of the Sea on the Conservation and Sustainable Use of Marine Biological Diversity of Areas Beyond National Jurisdiction (BBNJ Agreement), C.N.203.2023 TREATIES-XXI.10 of 20 July 2023. See S.L. Lothian, 'Transnational Maritime Environmental Crime and the BBNJ Agreement' (2024) 5 *Front. Conserv. Sci. Sec. Conservation Social Sciences*, doi: 10.3389/fcosc.2024.1406105.

obligations foreseen in that treaty for the exploitation and conservation of marine resources beyond national jurisdiction.[25] Therefore, unless cooperative frameworks are in place to govern the extraction of the natural resources in these common spaces, open competition between states or between private operators could ultimately have the effect of depleting these resources against the interests of present as well as future generations.[26] The 'global commons' are thus especially vulnerable to environmental damage and thus require interstate and inter-institutional cooperation for the effective enforcement of environmental law and management of natural resources, arguably also through criminal law cooperation frameworks and sanctions.[27]

3. International institutions and agencies fighting transnational environmental crime

3.1 The United Nations

The UN began to examine the role of criminal law in the protection of the environment in the early 1990s.[28] Since then, within the organisational structure of the UN, there has been a division of labour in which the main institutions such as the UNGA, the Security Council, and the ECOSOC have assumed responsibilities for incorporating environmental crime policy-making into their agendas and the UN agencies' mandates.

In 1994, the ECOSOC, in the realm of its competences,[29] recommended that 'national and supranational authorities should be provided with a wide array of measures, remedies and sanctions, within their constitutional and legal frameworks and consistent with the fundamental principles of criminal law, in order to ensure compliance with environmental laws'.[30] ECOSOC has also recommended that policy-making functions are exercised through expanded mandates of the United Nations Office on Drugs and

25 See also, R. Pereira, 'The Exploration and Exploitation of Energy Resources in International Law' in K. Makuch and R. Pereira (eds), *Environmental and Energy Law* (Wiley-Blackwell, 2012).

26 On the elaboration of the rights of future generations, see, for example UNGA Resolution 35/36 on International Development Strategy for Third UN Development Decade 1980, para. 41. See also the 1997 UNESCO Declaration on Responsibilities of Present Generations toward Future Generations.

27 See S.C. McCaffrey, 'Crimes against the environment' in M.C. Bassiouni, *International Criminal Law: Sources, Subjects and Contents* (Vol.1) (Brill, 2008), 985.

28 F. Mégret, 'The Problem of an International Criminal Law of the Environment' (2010) 36 *Columbia Journal of Environmental Law* 195, 199.

29 See Articles 62 and 66 of the UN Charter on its Functions and Powers.

30 ECOSOC, E/RES/994/15, The role of criminal law in the protection of the environment, 25 July 1994.

Crime (UNODC) and the Commission on Crime Prevention and Criminal Justice in order to counter environmental crime.[31]

The then UN Secretary-General, Kofi Annan, recognised as early as 2003, that illegal wildlife trafficking is a serious environmental crime with links to organised crime and with its own characteristics and *modus operandi*.[32] Later on, the UN Security Council adopted two resolutions in 2014 considering wildlife trafficking as a threat to international peace and security, finding links between wildlife trafficking and the funding of militia groups.[33] For its part, the UNGA adopted a resolution in 2015 which recognised environmental crime as part of other transnational organised criminal activities.[34] The adoption of those UN resolutions was a major step forward for UNEP and its partners' efforts 'in raising awareness of the growing threat that environmental crime poses to peace and security, sustainable development and environmental rule of law'.[35] UNEP made it clear that transnational environmental crime was a 'crime in need of better enforcement'[36] and adopted initiatives to expand international cooperation that soon went beyond the UN agencies to include a wider range of international organisations as well as NGOs. As an extension of UNEP, the first session of the United Nations Environment Assembly (UNEA) in June 2014 adopted a resolution on global wildlife crime, which broadened the issue to include marine and timber species and set targeted actions to eradicate supply, transit, and demand for illegal wildlife products.[37]

However, the discussions on environmental crime changed when states expressed themselves in favour of a different approach and preferred to refer to 'crimes affecting the environment' when considering options and measures aimed at combatting and preventing environmental crime. They did so in the framework of the United Nations Congress on Crime Prevention and Criminal Justice, organised every five years by the ECOSOC's Commission on Crime Prevention and Criminal Justice (CCPCJ). In its 13th meeting in Doha in April 2015, the CCPCJ adopted the Doha Declaration that recommended the introduction of effective measures to prevent and counter the serious

31 See ECOSOC, E/RES/2021/24, Preventing and combating crimes that affect the environment 22 July 2021, available online: https://documents.un.org/doc/undoc/gen/n21/206/44/pdf/n2120644.pdf.

32 ECOSOC, E/CN.15/2003/8, Illicit Trafficking in Protected Species of Wild Flora & Fauna & Illicit Access to Genetic Resources, 5 March 2003, 10.

33 See Security Council Resolution 2134 on the Central African Republic, S/RES/2134(2014), and Security Council Resolution 2136 on the Democratic Republic of Congo, S/RES/2136(2014).

34 A/RES/69/314 Tackling Illicit Trafficking in Wildlife adopted by the General Assembly on 30 July 2015, A/69/L.80 and Add.1.

35 See UN Secretary-General, 'Message on World Wildlife Day' (5 March 2015).

36 L. Coppens, 'Transnational Environmental Crime – a common crime in need of better enforcement', UNEP Global Environmental Alert Service (GEAS), January 2013.

37 UNEA Resolution 1/3 of 27 June 2014 on Illegal trade in wildlife.

problem of crimes that have an impact on the environment,[38] which manifested the lack of consensus on the concept of environmental crime.[39] In the 14th congress held in Kyoto in 2021, states renewed their commitment to fight 'crimes that affect the environment'[40] and in response to this, the UNGA adopted Resolution 76/185 on preventing and combating crimes that have an impact on the environment in which it urged member states to make:

> '[T]he best possible use of relevant international instruments and to this end strengthening legislation, international cooperation, capacity building, criminal justice responses and law enforcement activities aimed at, inter alia, tackling transnational organised crime, corruption and money laundering linked to such crimes and the illicit financial flows derived from them, while recognizing the need to deprive criminals of the proceeds of crime'.[41]

From then on, references to crimes 'related to' or 'that affect' the environment appeared in all global policy proposals developed not only by the UN institutions but also by other IGOs such as INTERPOL. The UNODC has undoubtedly played a key role thanks to ECOSOC's extension of its mandate through the creation of the CCPCJ, established in 1992 through Resolution 1992/22, which stressed the need to advance 'the role of criminal law in the protection of the environment'.[42] Subsequently, this mandate was extended by ECOSOC Resolution 2021/24, which calls for action by Member States and the international community to prevent and combat crimes that affect the environment.[43] The resolution attributes to UNODC the complex mission of supporting Member States in different areas, such as advancing the debate on a common definition of environmental crime (or 'crimes affecting the environment') and preparing instruments that serve as a guide to improve the enforcement against

---

38 See the Doha Declaration on integrating crime prevention and criminal justice into the wider United Nations agenda to address social and economic challenges and to promote the rule of law at the national and international levels, and public participation, April 2015, 11, available online: https://www.unodc.org/documents/congress/Declaration/V1504151_English.pdf.

39 See T. Fajardo del Castillo, 'Wildlife crime: The European Union's Approach in the Fight against Wildlife Trafficking: Challenges Ahead' (2016) 19(1) *Journal of International Wildlife Law and Policy* 1–21.

40 See the Kyoto Declaration on Advancing Crime Prevention, Criminal Justice and the Rule of Law: Towards the Achievement of the 2030 Agenda for Sustainable Development, 2021, para. 87, available online: https://www.unodc.org/documents/commissions/Congress/21-02815_Kyoto_Declaration_ebook_rev_cover.pdf.

41 A/RES/76/185 Preventing and combating crimes that affect the environment: resolution, adopted by the General Assembly, 16 December 2021.

42 ECOSOC, E/RES/1992/22 Implementation of General Assebly Resolution 46/152 concerning operational activities and coordination in the field of crime prevention and criminal justice, section VI, para. 1(a). See further, G. Broussard, 'The Evolving Role of the United Nations Office on Drugs and Crime in Fighting Wildlife and Forest Crimes' in L. Elliot and W. Schaedla (eds), *Handbook of Transnational Environmental Crime* (Cheltenham, UK and Northampton, MA: Edward Elgar Publishing, 2016).

43 See E/RES/2021/24 (n. 31).

these crimes, also taking into account their links with other crimes such as corruption and money laundering.[44] The latest report of UNODC, *Global Analysis of Crimes that Affect the Environment*, of May 2024 provides 'the landscape of criminalisation' globally, with the first global overview of where offences against the environment are criminalised, in which nine specific sectors are covered.[45] The report also sets UNODC's own agenda of future research, proposing further analysis of the geographic differences of criminalisation which could guide future projects aimed at harmonising legislation and ensuring that penalties are fit for purpose, as it has already done with its legislative guides.[46]

As regards the operation (by acting as the Secretariat) and updating of the 2000 Palermo Convention on Transnational Organised Crime ('the Palermo Convention'), the UNODC has played a major role in shaping organised environmental crime as a criminal offence at the international and national levels. At first, the environment was not considered among the relevant global issues for the purposes of this convention, unlike trafficking in human beings, smuggling of migrants, and illicit manufacturing of and trafficking in firearms, which later became protocols to the Palermo Convention.[47] Two decades later, the environment is considered a common concern of humankind that is threatened by organised and transnational crime, but states have not yet been willing to address it within the framework of a binding normative instrument, although the adoption of a protocol on illegal wildlife trafficking has been promoted by civil society organisations.[48] For example, thanks to funding from

---

44 UNODC, *UNODC Approach to crimes that affect the environment* (2021), available online: https://www.unodc.org/documents/Maritime_crime/UNODC_Approach_to_Crimes_that_Affect_the_Environment.pdf.

45 Deforestation and logging, mining, air pollution, noise pollution, soil pollution, water pollution, fishing, waste, and wildlife. See UNODC, *Global Analysis on Crimes that Affect the Environment – Part 1: The Landscape of Criminalization* (Vienna: United Nations publication, 2024), available online: https://css.unodc.org/documents/data-and-analysis/Crimes%20on%20Environment/ECR_1.Legislative_Review.pdf.

46 See further examples of UNODC legislative guides mentioned in footnote 49 below; and Ricardo Pereira and Teresa Fajardo's Chapter 1 Introduction: A Panoramic View of Global Environmental Criminal Law Research, in this volume.

47 This convention has three Protocols: The Protocol to Prevent, Suppress and Punish Trafficking in Persons, Especially Women and Children; the Protocol against the Smuggling of Migrants by Land, Sea and Air; the Protocol against the Illicit Manufacturing of and Trafficking in Firearms, their Parts and Components and Ammunition. The three Protocols were adopted and opened for signature, ratification, and accession by General Assembly Resolution A/RES55/25 United Nations Convention against Transnational Organized Crime, 15 November 2000.

48 As John Scanlon notes:

> This draft has been prepared in response to requests coming from States and organisations to offer some tangible ideas on the possible form and content of a potential Protocol and thereby help advance the discussion on this necessary reform. The draft has no formal status and it will be for States alone to negotiate the content of a new Protocol.

France and Japan, the UNODC has prepared non-binding guidelines on the regulatory and operational model for the better prosecution and sanctioning of environmental crime, providing states with best practice for combating the different types of crime associated with global environmental crises.[49]

On the operational front, the UNODC has worked to strengthen international cooperation between law enforcement agencies and national law enforcement, prosecutorial and judicial capacity through what was initially the World Programme on Combating Wildlife and Forest Crime and is now the Global Programme on Crimes that Affect the Environment (GPCAE). This programme also supports the classification of these crimes as serious transnational organised crimes and forms part of the UNODC's new Border Management Branch.

The UNODC has also led international cooperation efforts, both inside and outside the UN.[50] UNODC's leadership is particularly relevant in the case of the International Consortium on Combating Wildlife Crime (ICCWC). In 2012, under its direction, members of ICCWC developed the Wildlife and Forest Crime Analytic Toolkit that became the 'comprehensive guidance in analysing administrative, preventive and criminal justice responses to wildlife and forest crime and other related offences in

---

See Global Initiative to End Wildlife Crime, *Form and content of a possible Protocol on the illicit trafficking of wildlife*, available online on the End Illegal Wildlife Trade website: https://endwildlifecrime.org/untoc-wildlife-protocol/.

49 To date, the UNODC has developed five legislative guides on the regulatory and operational model for the better prosecution and sanction of environmental crime, providing states with best practice for combating the different types of crime associated with global crises. These guides to combat trafficking in flora and fauna species, waste, illegal mining, illegal fishing, and marine pollution are examples of the UNODC's contribution to strengthening the application of the environmental rule of law by states with soft law instruments. See https://www.unodc.org/documents/treaties/WG_TA_2024/Briefings/3_GLOTOC.pdf.

50 Thus, UNODC must:

> ... within its mandate, to further enhance and expand its cooperation and coordination with the United Nations Environment Programme, the United Nations Interregional Crime and Justice Research Institute, and, in close consultation with Member States, enhance its cooperation with INTERPOL, the World Customs Organization, the International Union for Conservation of Nature, the secretariat of the Convention on International Trade in Endangered Species of Wild Fauna and Flora, the secretariat of the Convention on Biological Diversity, the World Bank, the secretariat of the Basel Convention on the Control of Transboundary Movements of Hazardous Wastes and their Disposal and other relevant international and regional organizations, within their respective mandates, in supporting Member States, upon request, in their efforts to effectively prevent and combat crimes that affect the environment, including through inter-agency partnerships, such as the International Consortium on Combating Wildlife Crime and the Green Customs Initiative.

See UNODC, E/RES/2021/24 (n. 31).

a given country'.[51] Ten years later, this Toolkit has been revised by the UNODC to update its mission statement to reflect the need to protect nature and ensure sustainability, which are some of the distinguishing features of environmental crime in relation to other transnational crimes.[52]

3.2 INTERPOL

INTERPOL is an international organisation whose aim is to help the police in its 196 member states work together to make the world safer. The environment has been on its agenda since it was first addressed in the 1970s – almost half a century later, the fight against environmental crime is one of its Global Policing Goals which seeks to unite security[53] and sustainable development.[54] According to Goal 7, INTERPOL seeks to 'strengthen environmental security and support the promotion of sustainable livelihoods by countering crimes that affect the environment and climate'.[55] In line with this goal, INTERPOL's operational actions stand out for conducting collective operations, supporting national LEAs in the fight against environmental crime through its operational tools and services, facilitating cross-border police operations, intelligence gathering and analysis, as well as promoting partnerships with stakeholders.

Even though it does not have direct enforcement competences in the territories of state parties, INTERPOL leads global and regional operations aimed at dismantling the criminal networks behind environmental crime through intelligence-led investigations under its Environmental Security Unit, whose task is to lead 'lthe global effort to bring players together to fight crimes against our planet'.[56] Thus, INTERPOL has, over the past few decades, developed criminal intelligence analysis studying data and uncovering the structure, scope, and dynamics of criminals and the organisations involved in environmental crimes. The Environmental Security Unit has conducted operations related to different environmental crimes in order to identify the *modus operandi* of criminal groups and, in turn, to assist law enforcement agencies

---

51 UNODC, *ICCWC Wildlife and Forest Crime Analytic Toolkit* (2nd edn, 2022).

52 See UNODC, *ICCWC Wildlife and Forest Crime Analytic Toolkit* (2nd edn, 2022), 13.

53 See Chapter 1, 'Environmental crime has become the largest financial driver of conflict' in C. Nellemann, R. Henriksen, R. Pravettoni, D. Stewart, M. Kotsovou, M.A.J. Schlingemann, M. Shaw, and T. Reitano (eds), *World Atlas of Illicit* Flows, RHIPTO-INTERPOL-GI Assessment (RHIPTO – Norwegian Center for Global Analyses, INTERPOL, and the Global Initiative Against Transnational Organised Crime, 2016).

54 'The Global Policing Goals focus on the collective efforts of the international law enforcement community to create a safer and more sustainable world for future generations', see INTERPOL, *Global Policing Goals, Security as a Foundation for Sustainable Development*, October 2023, INTERPOL website: https://www.interpol.int/Who-we-are/Strategy/Global-Policing-Goals.

55 Ibid.

56 See further, INTERPOL, *Our response to global crime*, INTERPOL website: https://www.interpol.int/en/Crimes/Environmental-crime/Our-response-to-environmental-crime.

in combatting and preventing different forms of criminality.[57] This way of fighting environmental crime is now applied by national LEAs on a daily basis in the context of wildlife crime and other types of environmental crimes. With the intelligence gathered by the different LEAs, these coordinated operations are the basis for developing appropriate prevention and repression policies to deal with a type of criminality that adapts and mutates in the face of repressive measures. The operations carried out by INTERPOL have also fostered the necessary trust between LEAs to overcome the many obstacles to the development of international cooperation.

With its pros and cons, INTERPOL's environmental crime activities have proved to be impactful in developing interstate cooperation in particular contexts. For example, this includes externally funded activities which are dependant on successful partnerships with other organisations, such as that of the Countering Waste of Electric and Electronic Equipments Illegal Trade (CWIT) project funded by the European Commission. In the context of the CWIT project, INTERPOL's role was to facilitate dialogue among LEAs and various recycling stakeholders who were seeing recyclable e-waste disappear down the chain of collection and at recycling points, hence frustrating attempts to implement the circular economy.[58]

INTERPOL set up an Environmental Crimes Committee in 1992 that has since been reformed into an Environmental Compliance and Enforcement Committee (ECEC), which now coordinates the work of four Working Groups on Wildlife Crime, Pollution Crime, Fisheries Crime, and Forestry Crime.[59] Each INTERPOL member country has a National Central Bureau (NCB) which connects its national police to the I-24/7, the secure global police communications system. INTERPOL's system of notices can be used to alert member countries and share information on environmental crimes. In this vein, Red Notices are used to find wanted environmental criminals; Blue Notices to collect information on suspects; Purple Notices for information on *modus operandi*, and finally Green Notices to provide warnings and intelligence about environmental criminals likely to repeat offences in other countries.[60] INTERPOL also recommends that member countries develop a National Environmental Security Task

57 One of its first operations, Operation COBRA, called on the police forces of the participating countries to carry out month-long monitoring operations of species trafficking to identify the practices of traffickers, breeders, pet shop owners, as well as mail, transport, and shipping companies. See T. Fajardo, *Study on Wildlife Crime in Spain, Report to the European Parliament*, IP/A/ENVI/2015–10, PE 578.962 (April 2016), 1–36.

58 INTERPOL played the role of Coordinator in the Project Countering WEEE Illegal Trade (CWIT). See CWIT, *Deliverable on Recommendations related to the EU Legal Framework* (2015), available online: https://weee-forum.org/wp-content/uploads/2019/11/CWIT_WP6_D6.1_Recommendations_EU_Legal_Framework_Submit20151014.pdf.

59 See further, INTERPOL, *Environmental crime*, INTERPOL website: https://www.interpol.int/en/Crimes/Environmental-crime.

60 See INTERPOL, *Our response to global crime*, INTERPOL website https://www.interpol.int/Crimes/Environmental-crime/Our-response-to-environmental-crime.

Force (NEST) to ensure a coordinated multi-agency response to tackling environmental crime and enhancing environmental security.[61] It is the task of the INTERPOL Environmental Security Sub-Directorate to strongly encourage NESTs to set up Memoranda of Understanding with other countries and international organisations.[62]

Lastly, it is worth noting that as a member of the International Consortium on Combating Wildlife Crime, INTERPOL also coordinates and develops manuals, guides, and other studies and resources on 'best practice' in law enforcement.

3.3 Regional organisations

Because of their significance as models, in this section we will examine the Council of Europe and the EU as examples of regional organisations which have developed initiatives and legal instruments aimed at fighting environmental crime. Although, to the best of our knowledge, a comparative study of the mandates and policies of a range of regional organisations to fight environmental crime has not yet been carried out, it is likely that future studies will find that the policy outcomes of each regional organisation will be proportional to their respective competences and economic resources and to what extent environmental crime is regarded as a political priority. Even though their member states are among the most affected by transnational and organised environmental crime, the Organisation of American States (OAS), the Association of Southeast Asian Nations (ASEAN), and the African Union (AU) lack assigned competences in this area and have only relatively recently incorporated environmental crime into their political agendas.[63] These organisations are indebted to the proposals of the UN and have made use of the programmes aimed at promoting the

---

61 INTERPOL, *National Environmental Security Task Force. Bringing Compliance and Enforcement Agencies Together to Maintain Environmental Security* (2014).

62 Ibid.

63 On the ASEAN context, see further, for example G. Broussard, 'Building an Effective Criminal Justice Response to Wildlife Trafficking: Experiences from the ASEAN Region' (2017) 26(2) *Review of European, Comparative and International Environmental Law* 118; on the OAS context, see further B. Garcia and R. Pereira, 'International Environmental Law in the Americas' in L. Obregón, L. Betancur-Restrepo, and J. Amaya-Castro (eds), *The Oxford Handbook on International Law and the Americas* (Oxford University Press, online, 2024); M. Ungar, 'Prosecuting Environmental Crime: Latin America's Policy Innovation' (2017) 8 *Latin American Policy* 63; in the African Union context, see, for example D. Lambrechts, 'Reflections from Africa: Limited State Capacity and the Rise of Environmental Organised Crime' in S.L. Smith and L. Sahramaki (eds), *Research Handbook on Environmental Crimes and Criminal Enforcement* (Cheltenham, UK and Northampton, MA: Edward Elgar Publishing, 2024); and more generally, D. Mystris, 'Transnational Crime in the African Union' in V. Mitsilegas, S. Hufnagel, and A. Moiseienko (eds), *Research Handbook on Transnational Crime* (Cheltenham, UK and Northampton, MA: Edward Elgar Publishing, 2019).

environmental rule of law through the Montevideo Programme,[64] which has served to raise awareness of environmental law through training courses for public officials. Moreover, these regional organisations have been the main recipients, through the Montevideo Programme, of manuals and toolkits for the application and enforcement of environmental law by their member states. They have developed operative actions in the context of their cooperation frameworks with other international organisations such as the UNODC, INTERPOL, or the EU, which have enabled them to make use for instance of the ICCWC Wildlife and Forest Crime Analytic Toolkit. They have also participated in diplomacy initiatives thanks to capacity building and intelligence sharing projects such as the Jaguar Network project with Latin American countries financed by the EU and its agencies.[65] These diplomacy initiatives have also inspired other initiatives tailored to the needs of their participants, such as the South Asia Wildlife Enforcement Network (SAWEN), a regional intergovernmental wildlife law enforcement support body of South Asian countries that has as its main purpose to promote regional cooperation to combat wildlife crime.[66] As is the case with the other regional initiatives, SAWEN focuses on policy harmonisation, the strengthening of institutional capacity through knowledge and intelligence sharing, and collaboration with regional and international partners to enhance wildlife law enforcement in the member countries.[67]

3.3.1 *The Council of Europe*

The Council of Europe was created in 1949 with the mission to promote democracy, human rights, and the rule of law across Europe and beyond. It has been noted that, 'the task of promoting adherence to the rule of law becomes particularly important when developing environmental regulation and the protection of the environment is a priority'[68] for this organisation. Within the framework of its cooperation competences, one of the main functions of the Council of Europe has been to propose to its member states the adoption of international treaties that serve the objective of developing a common normative framework aimed at harmonising and improving their legislation. In the case of environmental crime, specific efforts towards the harmonisation

64 See Resolution UNEP/EA.4/Res.20 adopted by the United Nations Environment Assembly on 15 March 2019, Fifth Programme for the Development and Periodic Review of Environmental Law (Montevideo Programme V): delivering for people and the planet, available online: https://wedocs.unep.org/bitstream/handle/20.500.11822/28483/English.pdf?sequence=3&isAllowed=y.

65 This network is one of the results of 'El PacCTO', The Europe Latin America Programme of Assistance against Transnational Organised Crime, which was a five-year international cooperation programme funded by the EU that seeks to contribute to security and justice in Latin America by supporting the fight against transnational organised crime. See https://elpaccto.eu/en/about-el-paccto/what-is-el-paccto/.

66 See further, S. Sinha, 'Wildlife trade in South Asia' in Elliott and Schaedla (2016), n. 42.

67 See its website at https://www.sawen.org/.

68 European Committee on Criminal Problems, *Draft Feasibility Study on the Protection of the Environment Through Criminal Law* (25 February 2022), CDPC(2021)9 rev, 8.

of environmental criminal law began when, in 1978, the Committee of Ministers of the Council of Europe adopted Resolution (77) 28 on the contribution of criminal law to the protection of the environment.[69] It concluded that criminal law should be used as an '*ultima ratio*' when other measures were ineffective or inadequate and recommended a possible future harmonisation of the Council of Europe member states' legislation in this field. Thus, in 1994, the Council of Europe proposed the adoption of the Strasbourg Convention on the Protection of the Environment through Criminal Law.[70] This Convention aimed to establish a minimum standard for a common criminal policy and the adoption of effective administrative and criminal sanctions for the protection of the environment, on the basis (as stated in its Preamble) of the fact that harmonisation of legislation in this area also enhances international cooperation. Yet this Convention has never entered into force because it has not received the minimum number of ratifications.[71]

Three decades after the failed attempt to bring into force the 1998 Strasbourg Environmental Crime Convention, on 23 November 2022, the Committee of Ministers of the Council of Europe adopted the Terms of Reference for a new Committee of Experts on the Protection of the Environment through Criminal Law (PC-ENV),[72] and entrusted it to elaborate a new Convention on the Protection of the Environment through Criminal Law, which would lay down a legal basis for pan-European environmental criminal law cooperation, providing a common framework for tackling

---

69 See further Vercher (1990), n. 12, 445.

70 See Council of Europe Convention on the Protection of the Environment through Criminal Law (1998), Strasbourg, 4.XI.1998, E.T.S. 172 (not yet in force). See further, F. Comte, 'Protection of the Environment through Criminal Law: Destiny of the Various European Union's Initiatives' in M. Odina (ed), *Europe and the Environment* (Groningen, 2004), 46. For an analysis of the relationship between the 2008 Environmental Crime Directive and the 1998 Council of Europe Convention on the Protection of the Environment through Criminal Law, see further R. Pereira, 'The External Dimensions of the EU Legislative Initiatives to Combat Environmental Crime' (2016) 19 *Spanish Yearbook of International Law* 1; and Pereira (2015), n. 14.

71 Although its entry into force was dependent on the receipt of only three ratifications, the convention was only ratified by Estonia. See 'Chart of signatures and ratifications of Treaty 172', available online: https://www.coe.int/en/web/conventions/full-list?module=signatures-by-treaty&treatynum=172.

72 The terms of reference were valid from 1 January 2023 up to 30 June 2024; however, at the time of writing this chapter, there has been no communication regarding its results. See European Committee on Crime Problems (CDPC) – Terms of reference of the Committee of Experts on the protection of the environment through criminal law (PC-ENV), 23 November 2022, CM(2022)148-add2final: 'In its work, the Committee should take into account the documents "Feasibility Study on the Protection of the Environment through Criminal Law CDPC(2021)9-Fin", "Model Provisions for Council of Europe Criminal Law Conventions CDPC(2014)17-Fin" and "Draft Elements for an Explanatory Report CDPC(2014)24-Fin"'.

the current and emerging transnational environmental challenges.[73] One of the first steps taken by this committee was to conduct a survey of the Council of Europe member states on the factors that were at the root of its initial failure to bring into force an environmental crime convention. Among the underlying factors that emerged from this survey was that some states could not accept the proposal for certain environmental offences to be treated as autonomous from administrative offences.[74] Other factors may also have been influential in the failure of the Council of Europe convention to enter into force, such as the fact that in practice states have proved to be generally averse to ratifying environmental liability treaties that they have negotiated.[75] The final text of a new Council of Europe treaty will certainly be the subject of any future research agenda on environmental crime – and especially so if, unlike its predecessor, the new treaty eventually enters into force. Of particular interest will be whether or not the new treaty will aim to criminalise ecocide. Although draft Article 27 was previously titled 'Ecocide', it was renamed by the Committee as 'particularly serious offence'.[76] While all offences in the draft Convention are meant to be serious, it will be interesting to follow how the convention drafters will come to define (perhaps in an Explanatory Memorandum) 'particularly serious offences', and whether the definition of those offences will bear any resemblance to the much debated 2021 Independent Expert Panel's proposed definition of ecocide.[77] Moreover, since the European Commission represents the EU Member States in negotiating the new Council of Europe Environmental Crime Convention,[78] an evaluation will be due of the syner-

73 In the ongoing debates, the importance of international cooperation has been emphasised since:

> the effectiveness of the fight against environmental crime, in all its dimensions and in particular across borders, depends *also* and amongst others on effective international co-operation between states. Such co-operation is essential to ensure that the relevant national authorities involved in the prevention and the fight against environmental crimes 'speak the same language'. A new legal instrument would be an opportunity to lay down common rules for such enhanced international co-operation, drawing from existing international instruments of the Council of Europe (emphasis added). (CDPC (2022), n. 68).

74 CDPC (2022), n.68, 25 and 26. There is one autonomous offence in the 1998 Council of Europe environmental crime convention, under Article 2(1)(a) concerning the discharge of substances or ionising radiation into the environment that causes death or serious injury to any person, or creates a significant risk of causing death or risk of serious injury to any person.

75 See further discussion in Pereira (2015), n. 14; and Pereira (2016), n. 70.

76 See further, Committee of Experts on the Protection of the Environment through Criminal Law, 4th Meeting, Meeting Report of 4–7 June 2024, PC-ENV(2024)03, 10 June 2024, available online: https://rm.coe.int/pc-env-2024-03-eng-4th-meeting-report-2768-9392-3849-v-1/1680b05fe2.

77 See further, Thomas Obel Hansen's Chapter 4 Towards a New Agenda for Ecocide Norms-Adoption and Enforcement, in this volume.

78 See Recommendation for a Council Decision authorising the European Commission to participate, on behalf of the European Union, in negotiations on a Council of Europe Convention superseding and replacing the 1998 Convention on the Protection of the

gies between the text of a Council of Europe convention and the 2024 Environmental Crime Directive (ECD).[79] On this note, we turn to discuss developments in EU environmental criminal law and the EU cooperation with third countries and other international organisations in fighting transnational environmental crime.

3.3.2 *The European Union*

The EU is the regional integration organisation that best reflects the assumption of an institutional mandate to implement policies and legal instruments for environmental protection through criminal law, even though it initially required an extensive interpretation of its competences (particularly through the Court of Justice of the European Union (CJEU) case law) and then a reform of its constituent treaties to introduce new legal bases.[80] At the beginning of EU action to fight environmental crime, there was a dispute between the European Commission and the Council of Ministers (representing the Member States) on the correct choice of legal basis of a legal instrument aimed at strengthening the implementation of and compliance with EU environmental legislation through criminal law.[81] The final shape and scope of the adopted legal instrument was indebted to two seminal judgments of the CJEU. The judgment of 13 September 2005 first recognised the competence of the European Community under the former first pillar to protect the environment through criminal law,[82] and subsequently, the judgment of the CJEU of 23 October 2007 reiterated that, although the European Community could propose the adoption of criminal measures to its Member States for the protection of the environment, it did not have the power to harmonise specific types and levels of criminal penalties.[83] In the aftermath of those ECJ rulings, the 2008 Environmental Crime Directive ('2008 ECD')[84] was adopted

Environment through Criminal Law (ETS No. 172), as well as a draft Explanatory Report thereto, COM(2023) 419 final.

79 Directive (EU) 2024/1203 of the European Parliament and of the Council of 11 April 2024 on the protection of the environment through criminal law and replacing Directives 2008/99/EC and 2009/123/ECPE/82/2023/REV/1,2009/123/EC PE/82/2023/REV/1, OJ L 2024/1203.

80 T. Fajardo, 'European Environmental Law and Environmental Crime: An Introduction' in A. Farmer, M. Faure, and G.M. Vagliasindi (eds), *Environmental Crime in Europe, Modern Studies in European Law* (London: Hart Publishing, 2017), 1–14.

81 R. de Rijck, 'Believing in criminal law. On how the European legislator of Directive 2008/99/EC deems strict criminal law necessary for the functioning of environmental legislation, but Member States consider it an expression of their sovereignty' (2013) 4 *Tijdschrift voor sanctierecht & compliance voor ondernemingen*.

82 *Commission v Council* (C-176/03) EU:C:2005:542, Judgment of the Court (Grand Chamber) of 13 September 2005.

83 *Commission v Council* (C-440/05) EU:C:2007:625, Judgment of the Court (Grand Chamber) of 23 October 2007, [70].

84 Directive 2008/99/EC of the European Parliament and of the Council of 19 November 2008 on the protection of the environment through criminal law, OJ L 328, 28–37. As a directive adopted under the former first pillar, it should be noted that the opt-out clause in the area of freedom, security and justice (AFSJ) was not available to Ireland, Denmark, or the UK.

under the former first pillar establishing a framework for the harmonisation of nine environmental criminal offences, but with weak provisions on criminal penalties and no provisions on interstate cooperation in criminal matters.[85] Subsequently, the Lisbon Treaty introduced the legal bases that conferred competences upon the EU to further advance the harmonisation of Member States' criminal legislation,[86] although Denmark and Ireland have the option (as did the United Kingdom (UK) pre-Brexit) to trigger their opt-out clause.[87] Despite its significance, it should be noted that the 2008 ECD was not instrumental in the birth and shaping of the basic core of environmental criminal law in most EU Member States, a process that started in the early 1970s.[88] However, it played an important role in two respects: as a brake on movements to decriminalise environmental harm and as a stimulus for constant improvement of the criminal justice systems of the Member States.[89] The recast of Directive 2008/99/EC has led to its substitution by the Environmental Crime Directive 2024/1203 ('2024 ECD') which requires Member States to incorporate 21 offences (in addition to two so-called 'qualified' offences),[90] also including shipping pollution, that was first addressed through a separate directive that incorporated the MARPOL standards[91] on enforcement against shipping pollution discharges.[92] Moreover, as per the post-Lisbon Article

---

85 See further, for example T. Fajardo (2017), n. 80; and Pereira (2015), n.14.

86 R. Pereira, 'The Development of Environmental Criminal Law Enforcement in the European Union: From Institutional Fragmentation to European Environmental Criminal Justice Governance?' in R. Pereira, A. Engel and S. Miettinen (eds), *The Governance of Criminal Justice in the European Union: Transnationalism, Localism and Public Participation in an Evolving Constitutional Order* (Cheltenham, UK and Northampton, MA: Edward Elgar Publishing, 2020).

87 Thus:

> in accordance with Articles 1 and 2 and Article 4(1) of Protocol No 21 on the position of the United Kingdom and Ireland in respect of the area of freedom, security and justice, annexed to the TEU and to the TFEU, and without prejudice to Article 4 of that Protocol, Ireland is not taking part in the adoption of this Directive and is not bound by it or subject to its application.

and

> in accordance with Articles 1 and 2 of Protocol No 22 on the position of Denmark, annexed to the TEU and to the TFEU, Denmark is not taking part in the adoption of this Directive and is not bound by it or subject to its application.

88 See further Michael Faure and Sjoerd Lopik's Chapter 2 Methods for Environmental Criminal Law Research, in this volume.

89 See J.L. Fuentes Osorio, 'Environmental Criminal Law in Spain', in Farmer, Faure, and Vagliasindi (2017), n. 80.

90 2024 ECD, Article 3(3). See further, R. Pereira, 'A Critical Evaluation of the New EU Environmental Crime Directive 2024/1203' (2024) 2 *EUCrim*.

91 Convention on the Prevention of Pollution from Ships (MARPOL 1973/1978). See Directive 2009/123/EC of the European Parliament and of the Council of 21 October 2009 amending Directive 2005/35/EC on ship-source pollution and on the introduction of penalties for infringements, OJ L 280/52.

92 See Directive 2005/35/EC of the European Parliament and of the Council on Ship-Source Pollution and on the Introduction of Penalties for Infringements, OJ L 255/11, Preamlble, Recital (3).

83(2) Treaty on the Functioning of the European Union (TFEU) legal basis, the 2024 ECD prescribes specific types and levels of criminal penalties for both natural and legal persons[93] and also brings other significant improvements to the previous legal frameworks such as, for example, rules on jurisdiction,[94] crime prevention,[95] public participation in criminal proceedings,[96] limitation periods,[97] the protection of environmental defenders[98] and cooperation between Member States and EU agencies.[99]

These EU directives exemplify the regulatory capacity of an international organisation that has been given the necessary powers to harmonise the legislation of its Member States. However, the evaluation carried out by the European institutions of the implementation of the 2008 ECD has highlighted that cooperation between the Member States is among some of its main weaknesses. Notably, the outcome of the evaluation showed that while some Member States have made use of the law enforcement cooperation tools available to them under the framework of the European agencies – particularly the European Union Agency for Law Enforcement Cooperation (Europol), the European Union Agency for Criminal Justice Cooperation (Eurojust), and the European Anti-fraud Office (OLAF)[100] – others have not yet done so.[101] In order to address these perceived weaknesses, the 2024 ECD reinforces the obligation of cooperation at four main levels – between the LEAs of a Member State; between

---

93 See 2024 ECD, Articles 5 and 7.

94 2024 ECD, Article 12.

95 2024 ECD, Article 16.

96 2024 ECD, Article 15. On the case question of participatory governance in EU criminal justice, see further R. Pereira, A. Engel, and S. Miettinen (eds), *The Governance of Criminal Justice in the European Union: Transnationalism, Localism and Public Participation in an Evolving Constitutional Order* (Cheltenham, UK and Northampton, MA: Edward Elgar Publishing, 2020).

97 2024 ECD, Article 10.

98 2024 ECD, Article 14.

99 2024 ECD, Article 20.

100 See further, V. Mitsilegas and F. Giuffrida, *The Role of EU Agencies in Fighting Transnational Environmental Crime: New Challenges for Eurojust and Europol* (Brill, 2017).

101 The European Commission and the Council of Ministers undertook a parallel process of evaluation of the results obtained through consultations with Member States, academics, and actors involved in the implementation of the 2008 ECD and the general public. As a result, the reform of the directive has gone far beyond what was initially envisaged. The European Commission's initial proposal of 2021 has undergone changes due to contributions made not only by the European institutions in the framework of the legislative procedure but also due to the feedback received by stakeholders from different sectors of civil society. See Commission Staff Working Document Evaluation of the Directive 2008/99/EC of the European Parliament and of the Council of 19 November 2008 on the protection of the environment through criminal law, SWD(2020) 259 final, 28 October 2020, and EU Presidency, *Final report of the Eighth round of mutual evaluations on environmental crime*, GENVAL, Doc. 14852/1920195 (2019).

the LEAs of all Member States; between Member States and EU agencies (particularly Europol and Eurojust) and enhanced international cooperation with third states and international organisations.[102]

As Gerstetter,[103] Farmer,[104] Chin, and Veening[105] and Smit and Klaas[106] have shown in their referential work and reports for the European Union Action to Fight Environmental Crime (EFFACE) project, cooperation among Member States can take place through formal compliance channels or, as they have favoured, through networks that have been formed with LEAs. The main networks of relevance to the fight against environmental crime at the EU level are the European Union Network for the Implementation and Enforcement of Environmental Law (IMPEL), the European Union Forum of Judges for the Environment (EUFJE), and the European Network of Environmental Prosecutors (ENPE). The fourth network, the European Network for Combating Environmental Law Crime (EnviCrimeNet)[107] has recently become an institutionally independent, not-for-profit association offering advice and training to both European and non-EU police forces. Each of these networks, because of the specialisation of its members, have their own approach to the major issues to be addressed: in particular, harmonisation, implementation, and enforcement.

Cooperation can also be more formal, based on EU instruments for police and judicial cooperation, such as the Council Framework Decision 2002/584/JHA of 13 June 2002 on the European arrest warrant and surrender procedures between Member States. However, the evaluation of its implementation suggests that it is under-utilised for

---

[102] See 2024 ECD, Preamble, paras 17, 21, 51, 62–5 and Articles 19–21.

[103] C. Gerstetter, Chapter 4 'Functioning of Enforcement Institutions and Cooperation Between them (MS/EU level)' in A. Farmer et al., *Evaluation of the strengths, weaknesses, threats and opportunities associated with EU efforts to combat environmental crime, EFFACE Project* (Berlin: Ecologic, 2016).

[104] A. Farmer, 'Networking' in *Handbook of Environmental Protection and Enforcement: Principles and Practice* (London: Earthscan, 2007), 249–62; A. Farmer, *IMPEL Project 'Practicability and Enforceability of the IPPC Recast Proposal'* (IMPEL, 2008).

[105] S. Chin and W. Veening, *Actors and Institutions Relevant to Fighting Environmental Crime. Study in the Framework of the EFFACE Research Project* (The Hague: Institute for Environmental Security, 2014).

[106] L. Smith and K. Klaas, *Networks and NGOs Relevant to Fighting Environmental Crime. Study in the Framework of the EFFACE Research Project,* (Berlin: Ecologic Institute, 2015), available online: www.efface.eu.

[107] Following the expert-level conference of the Augias Project held in Budapest on March 24 and 25 March 2011, an informal platform for countering environmental-related crimes called 'EnviCrimeNet' was launched. EnviCrimeNet, supported by Europol, had as its overall aim combating environment-related crime, including improving the exchange of information and the gathering of criminal intelligence, training officers, and exchanging best practices. See Draft Council Resolution on the creation of an informal network for countering environmental crime - 'EnviCrimeNet' 8011/2/11 REV 2 ENFOPOL 70 ENV 221, Brussels, May 2011.

political and technical reasons,[108] with limited evidence of its implementation in the cross-border environmental crime context.[109] A more structured cooperation is channelled through the EU institutions for police and judicial cooperation, insofar as they deal with environmental crime within the scope of their competences. Particularly significant is the role of Europol as the EU's law enforcement agency with the aim of assisting the EU Member States in their fight against serious crime and terrorism.[110] Among Europol's best practices, the one that stands out is the EnviCrime Analysis Project (AP) which produced intelligence-led investigations and information-sharing via Europol's Secure Information Exchange Network Application (SIENA), which allowed for successful cooperation between Member States and with third countries, for example in Latin America. Eurojust is the EU agency dealing with judicial cooperation that facilitates cooperation in criminal investigation and prosecution in the 27 EU Member States. Its joint investigation teams (JITs) have been set up to coordinate the work of police officers from two or more Member States, for example the 'Bird-Egg' investigations in 2013 involving illegal trafficking in wild bird eggs in which Eurojust assisted the authorities of Finland and Sweden in setting up and funding a JIT.[111] In addition, the EU Member States also participate in police cooperation as members of INTERPOL. They coordinate their actions according to the priorities set by the EU Policy Cycle that is implemented by the European Multidisciplinary Platform Against Criminal Threats (EMPACT). EMPACT introduced a specific priority focused on 'combating environmental crime'[112] in the 2018–21 EU Policy Cycle, and in the new 2022–25 EU Policy Cycle, which was later renewed with the aim '[t]o disrupt criminal networks involved in all forms of environmental crime, with a specific focus on waste and wildlife trafficking, as well as on criminal networks and individual criminal entrepreneurs with a capability to infiltrate legal business structures at high level or to set up own companies in order to facilitate their crimes'.[113] It should be noted, though, that the European Public Prosecutor's Office's current mandate relating to environmental crime is very limited and restricted to certain financial crimes linked to the financial interests of the EU with an environmental dimension.[114]

---

108 See *Joint report of Eurojust and the European Judicial Network on the extradition of EU citizens to third countries* (2020), available online: https://www.eurojust.europa.eu/publication/joint-report-eurojust-and-ejn-extradition-eu-citizens-third-countries.

109 The EAW was used for the first time by the Environment Agency in the UK in a case involving illegal waste dumping in which the defendant had flown to Ireland, as a result of a three-year investigation codenamed 'Operation Huron'. See https://www.gov.uk/search/news-and-communications?organisations%5B%5D=environment-agency.

110 Under the Lisbon Treaty, all EU Member States are automatically members of Europol.

111 See further, Mitsilegas and Giuffrida (2017), n. 100.

112 EU Presidency (2019), n. 101, 67.

113 See Council conclusions on the permanent continuation of the EU Policy Cycle for organised and serious international crime: EMPACT 2022+, Doc. 7100/23 (9 March 2023), at https://data.consilium.europa.eu/doc/document/ST-7101-2023-INIT/en/pdf

114 Thus, the EPPO 'is the first European body with coercive powers in the field of criminal law and has a potentially significant role to play in the fight against environmental crime, as long as the latter is related to the offences falling within its current mandate',

In the case of EU cooperation with third states and international organisations, the diplomacy deployed to influence the fight against organised crime and operational cooperation actions with non-EU countries stand out, particularly involving countries of origin, destination or transit of proceeds and products of environmental crime.[115] This thus calls for a future mapping of the ramifications of the environmental crime cooperation between the EU and third countries.[116] As stated by the first author in previous reports for the EFFACE project, the EU has tried to promote the fight against environmental crime on the global stage before the UNGA and the UNEA, but its position on environmental crime is not shared unanimously by third countries that consider that this is not a clear concept or believe it could lead to interference with their natural resource exploitation policies.[117] However, at the operational level, the EU has secured cooperation through the funding of UNODC and INTERPOL operations or projects, as well as projects in collaboration with countries in Latin America, Africa, and Asia that contribute to nature conservation through the prevention of environmental damage and prosecution of environmental crime. The EU renewed its 2016 Action Plan on Wildlife Trafficking (WAP2016)[118] in 2022 particularly to deepen efforts aimed at improving international cooperation with third states and the specialised international organisations whose projects are supported by European funding.[119]

V. Mitsilegas, E. Fasoli, F. Giuffrida, and M. Fitzmaurice, *The Legal Regulation of Environmental Crime: The International and European Dimension* (Brill Nijhoff, 2022), 6. On a possible extension of the competence of the EPPO over environmental crime, see further C. Di Francesco Maesa, 'EPPO and Environmental Crime: May the EPPO ensure a more effective protection of the environment in the EU?' (2018) 9(2) *New Journal of European Criminal Law*.

115 See General Secretariat of the Council, Operational Action Plan 2018 related to the EU crime priority 'Environmental Crime', 12 December 2017, Doc. 14484/1/17 REV 1 RESTREINT UE/EU RESTRICTED.

116 EU Presidency (2019), n. 101, 71.

117 T. Fajardo, Chapter 6, 'External dimension of environmental crime – what can the EU do (EU only)' in A. Farmer et al., *Evaluation of the strengths, weaknesses, threats and opportunities associated with EU efforts to combat environmental crime* (EFFACE Project, Berlin: Ecologic, 2016), available online: https://www.ecologic.eu/sites/default/files/publication/2016/efface_swot_analysis.pdf.

118 See Communication from the Commission to the European Parliament, the Council, the European Economic and Social Committee and the Committee of the Regions, EU Action Plan against Wildlife Trafficking, COM(2016) 87 final. See also, Ludwig Krämer's Chapter 5 Biodiversity Crime, in this volume.

119 See T. Fajardo, 'The European Union's Response to the New Strategic Vision of CITES 2021-2030' in M. Campins, X. Fernández-Pons, M. Abegón, *Cambio climático, biodiversidad y salud pública global en el Derecho internacional* Tirant Lo Blanc, 2025.

4. International cooperation in selected MEAS

International cooperation in the framework of MEAs also concerns the implementation and enforcement of environmental law, as highlighted in UNEP's reports on the Environmental Rule of Law.[120] Some MEAs contain obligations for states to introduce penal sanctions for violations thereof, but, generally, they do not go as far as establishing detailed mechanisms for police and judicial cooperation in criminal matters similar to those found in international criminal law instruments. Most commonly, these instruments require the contracting parties to take 'appropriate measures to ensure the application of the provisions of the agreement [in question] and the punishment of infractions against [those] provisions'.[121] Despite the fact that only a few existing MEAs call on states to introduce criminal and non-criminal penalties to counter environmental crimes, future MEAs could require states to take more specific action to criminalise activities highly harmful for the environment.[122] Even though this possibility could increase compliance with MEAs, it would create a responsibility on state parties to provide the required human and financial resources to fight environmental crimes, a burden which would be particularly high on developing countries fighting transnational environmental crimes. These environmental crimes strain the weak governance of these states and are linked to other serious crimes such as corruption, money laundering, and traditional forms of organised crime such as drug and human trafficking.[123] This helps to explain why, in the context of international cooperation and diplomacy, states and international organisations such as UNODC tend to speak of 'crimes that affect the environment', insofar as this gives states greater scope for intervention according to their mandate, interests, and resources.

The aim of provisions on penalties in international treaties such as CITES or the Basel and MARPOL Conventions is for states to introduce sanctions - administrative or criminal – against infringements of the measures transposing these agreements into domestic law, as they are *non-self-executing* international treaties. To this end, state Parties to CITES shall introduce appropriate national legislation to prevent and punish illegal wildlife trafficking, and in particular '*to penalise* trade in, or possession of

120 See UNEP's 2019 and 2023 reports on the Environmental Rule of Law, n. 6.

121 See for example International Convention for Regulation of Whaling, 161 UNTS 72, 62 Stat. 1716, TIAS 1849 (1946), Article 9; the Convention for Prevention of Marine Pollution by Dumping from Ships and Aircraft, 932 UNTS 3, 11 ILM 262 (1972), Article 15(3); the Convention on Prevention of Marine Pollution by Dumping of Wastes and Other Matter 1046 UNTS 120, [ATS] 1985 16, 11 ILM 1294 (1972), UKTS 43 (1976) (1972), Articles 4 and 7; the Convention for the Prevention of Marine Pollution from Land-Based Sources (1978) (replaced by the OSPAR Convention 1992), 2354 UNTS 67, 32 ILM 1069 Article 12; the Convention on the International Trade of Endangered Species 993 UNTS 243, Article 8(1). See further, S.C. McCaffrey, 'Crimes Against the Environment' in C.M. Bassiouni, *International Criminal Law*, (Brill, 2008), n. 27, 1104.

122 See T. Fajardo, n. 117, at 64.

123 Ibid.

[...] specimens...' (emphasis added).[124] These 'penal' provisions in MEAS are, as Byung-Sun Cho stated, 'only a source of obligation, not a source of law'[125] and as such, they must govern interstate cooperation and be developed and transposed into national law to appropriately sanction environmentally harmful conduct, including environmental harm that transcends national borders. However, 'the prosecution of environmental crimes that international environmental conventions have introduced is only possible before national courts'.[126] Moreover, these penal provisions in international agreements illustrate how the effective law enforcement against environmental crimes at the national level is a prerequisite for transnational crime cooperation. These penal provisions in certain MEAs thus represent one of the foundations for transnational environmental criminal law cooperation, given that they pursue the protection of environmental common goods that the international community 'has come to recognise as so important that criminal sanctions must be employed'.[127]

On the other hand, for LEAs,[128] one of the main challenges remains how to monitor and enforce international and national laws and regulations related to MEAs and international conventions with environmental chapters such as Part XII of the United Nations Convention on the Law of the Sea. In this latter case, this includes the fact that the enforcement of environmental law in the high seas is limited by the principle of the exclusive jurisdiction of flag states; and the unwillingness of flags-of-convenience states to enforce environmental standards on their own vessels in the high seas.[129] In this regard, some international agreements contain 'policing provisions' allowing signatory parties to take action on the spot to enforce the rules of the agreement, but they are often constrained to a limited geographical area, or to a specific environmental resource or media.[130] This is the case of a number of regional fisheries agreements which tend to contain enforcement provisions requiring parties to oversee the management of shared fish stocks, while recognising that interstate concerted action and common management are necessary to give effect to the conservation of those high seas resources. Yet there are notable weaknesses in the enforcement provisions present in specific regional fisheries agreements, including the fact that they do not generally apply to third-country vessels.

The lack of solid institutionalisation of international environmental law through a global environmental organisation has meant that the application and implementation of international environmental law falls on a fragmented array of national,

---

124 See CITES, Article VIII.1.
125 B.-S. Cho (2000/2001), n. 4, 2.
126 Ibid.
127 Ibid.
128 Pereira (2015), n. 14.
129 *See* further, Tanaka (2012), n. 22; and Rothwell and Stephens (2010), n. 22.
130 See, for example the 1911 Convention for the Preservation of Fur Seals in the North Pacific, Articles 1 and 7; and the 1937 International Agreement for the Regulation of Whaling, Article 1, n. 121.

regional and international institutions. With a few exceptions,[131] it is UNEP that provides the secretariat for MEAs. Each of these MEAs has, in turn, developed its own institutions to give effect to its objectives and these, alongside individual states, submit reports and proposals to the Conference of the Parties (COPs). Moreover, the COPs meet periodically to develop the MEA's normative framework through resolutions and recommendations as well as to monitor and promote compliance. To give effect to these actions, MEAs depend on their state parties enacting national legislation to sanction environmentally harmful conduct through administrative and criminal laws. In addition, for their effective implementation states must develop a national institutional system to combat environmental crime through the provision of the necessary resources to set up dedicated environmental police and enforcement officers and specialised prosecution and judiciary.[132]

CITES was the first convention to call for sanctions to tackle problems related to the illegal trade in wildlife.[133] However, as suggested by John Scanlon, it is an over 50-year-old trade-related convention, not a crime-related convention.[134] Nonetheless, until there is a thorough reform of CITES, or the adoption of a new convention or protocol, the present version of CITES remains the regulatory framework of reference as regards illegal wildlife trade. To fight wildlife trafficking crimes, state parties to CITES are expected to adopt national legislation to build a system of export and import permits that enable national authorities to control wildlife trade and to foster interstate cooperation channelled through international institutions or partnerships such as INTERPOL, the UNODC, and the ICCWC. The perpetrators of these crimes typically have been, and continue to be, organised criminals, companies,[135] and even the public authorities of state parties to CITES, who often operate transnationally across physical borders and the largely lawless internet space.

---

131 Such as the 1971 Ramsar Convention on Wetlands of International Importance that developed its own secretariat; see T. Fajardo, 'The Ramsar Convention and the Convention on Biological Diversity: Proposals for Enhanced Cooperation, Synergies, and Interoperability for the Kunming-Montreal Global Biodiversity Framework' in R.C. Gardner, R. Caddell, and E. Okuno (eds) *Wetlands and International Environmental Law: The Evolution and Impact of the Ramsar Convention* (Cheltenham, UK and Northampton, MA: Edward Elgar Publishing, 2025).

132 See G. Pring and C. Pring, *Environmental Courts & Tribunals: A Guide for Policy Makers* (UNEP, 2016) and UNEP, *Environmental Courts and Tribunals: A Guide for Policymakers* (Nairobi, 2022).

133 See further, Angus Nurse's Chapter 8 The Global Illegal Wildlife Trade Crisis, in this volume.

134 See Global Initiative to End Wildlife Crime, *Form and content of a possible Protocol on the illicit trafficking of wildlife*, available online on the End Illegal Wildlife Trade website: https://endwildlifecrime.org/untoc-wildlife-protocol/.

135 See further, Carolyn Abbot and Gary Lynch-Wood's Chapter 3 Transnational Environmental Crime Across Global Supply Chains – A Place for Due Diligence?, in this volume.

The CITES COP is responsible for monitoring and promoting compliance with its obligations. In the event that a state party fails to act due to a lack of resources or a tolerance of illegal wildlife trade, the COP and the other CITES institutions can adopt measures ranging from aid to sanctions. For example, the CITES Standing Committee recommended a suspension of all commercial trade in CITES-protected species with Mexico because it had failed to submit an adequate plan to control totoaba fishing and the illegal trafficking that threatens the vaquita.[136]

CITES is also the first convention that has demonstrated cooperation and synergies between biodiversity-related conventions that can put environmental crime on a wider agenda. In addition to strengthening cooperation for the implementation and enforcement of both conventions, CITES and the Convention on Biological Diversity (CBD):

> are jointly responsible for the new Target 5 of the 2022 Kunming-Montreal Global Biodiversity Framework, which calls for ensuring that the use, harvesting and trade of wild species is sustainable, safe and legal. This Target 5 dovetails with the CITES Vision Statement 2030 which seeks to ensure that all international trade in wild fauna and flora is legal and sustainable, consistent with the long-term conservation of species, and thus contributes to halting the loss of biodiversity, ensuring its sustainable use and achieving the 2030 Agenda for Sustainable Development.[137]

Despite calls for further institutional coordination under the frameworks of CITES and the CBD for the achievement of coherent strategies and goals, regretably the 2022 Kunming-Montreal Global Biodiversity Framework does not have any specific targets or goals aimed at combating illegal wildlife trade.[138]

5. NGOs

Article 71 of the UN Charter offers non-governmental organisations (NGOs) the possibility of having a formal role within the UN structure. This is the legal basis for 'inclusive multilateralism' in the UN,[139] which has enabled NGOs to participate in

---

136 CITES Secretariat, Notification to the Parties No 2023/037 concerning: Compliance action plan of Mexico on Totoaba (Totoaba MacDonald), Geneva, 27 March 2023.

137 See T. Fajardo (2025), n. 119.

138 See the Decision adopted by the Conference of the Parties to the Convention on Biological Diversity, 15/4. Kunming-Montreal Global Biodiversity Framework, CBD/COP/DEC/15/4, 19 December 2022, available online: https://www.cbd.int/doc/decisions/cop-15/cop-15-dec-04-en.pdf.

139 The current UN Secretary-General, Antonio Guterres, considers that inclusive multilateralism:

> in addition to intergovernmental organizations, this can include parliaments, subnational authorities (cities and local and regional governments), civil society, faith-based organizations, universities, researchers and experts, trade unions, the

international normative procedures – from the negotiation of international treaties to the adoption of soft law instruments – and also in environmental monitoring and advocacy functions, such as overseeing state compliance with MEAs. Through NGO participation, the UN bodies and agencies gain invaluable support in terms of legitimacy, intelligence-sharing[140] and scientific knowledge.[141] Thus, non-state actors from civil society organisations[142] complement states in their fight against environmental crime, through different functions ranging from proposing new and emerging categories of environmental crimes (such as ecocide) to the collection and processing of information on the impacts of environmental crime and the *modus operandi* of criminal groups.

The role played by NGOs such as the Trade Records Analysis of Flora and Fauna in Commerce (TRAFFIC), the International Fund for Animal Welfare (IFAW), Greenpeace, and World Wide Fund for Nature (WWF) is essential in complementing the fight against environmental crime carried out by both states and international organisations. It is necessary to emphasise that NGOs act as the 'eyes and ears on the ground' – whether in a country of origin, transit, or destination, or on the internet. They not only assist national authorities in enforcing their legislation,[143] but also contribute to national policy-making in their advocacy capacity. They also collaborate with international organisations in the fight against environmental crime, for example WWF participated in joint research efforts with the UNODC that led to the adoption of a 2021 *Crimes that Affect the Environment and Climate Change* report with the overall aim of 'working in partnership to reduce the occurrence of crimes that affect the environment and their impact on marine and terrestrial ecosystems'.[144]

---

private sector and industry, and local and grass roots movements, including those led by women and young people. This vision recognizes that States remain central to our collective ability to meet global challenges and have unique responsibilities in the multilateral system, while also acknowledging that solutions increasingly depend on the private sector and non-State actors, who should therefore be part of the deliberations and accountable for their commitments.

See the General Secretary of the United Nation, *Our Common Agenda*, available online: https://www.un.org/en/content/common-agenda-report/assets/pdf/Common_Agenda_Report_English.pdf.

140 See T. Fajardo, 'La sociedad civil internacional y el multilateralismo inclusivo en la CoP26 de Glasgow' (2022) 26 *Anuario de la Facultad de Derecho de la Universidad Autónoma de Madrid* 157–81.

141 The IPBES reports, the Red List of the International Union for Conservation of Nature (IUCN), and the criteria they establish serve to characterise environmental harm and crimes.

142 See A. Colás, *International Civil Society* (Polity, 2002).

143 See further, for example A. Nurse, 'Privatising the Green Police: the Role of NGOs in Wildlife Law Enforcement' (2013) 59 *Crime Law Soc Change* 305–18.

144 UNODC and WWF, *Crimes that affect the Environment and the Climate Change* (2021), available online: https://www.unodc.org/res/environment-climate/resources_html/Crimes_that_Affect_the_Environment_and_Climate_Change.pdf.

6. Conclusions and future research directions

The triple planetary crises of global warming, biodiversity loss, and pollution bear a close relationship with environmental crime, or 'crimes related to the environment' more generally. The fight against environmental criminality needs the joint efforts of international organisations and civil society actors who act as environmental stewards on the ground. They must therefore work together to achieve regulatory action to harmonise or coordinate responses to environmental crime and the efficient implementation and enforcement of regulations adopted at both international and domestic levels.

Yet the lack of a global environmental organisation and the sectoral nature of international environmental law obligations have led to the fragmentation of the work, programmes and strategies of institutions and agencies responsible for the development, implementation, and enforcement of MEAs. In a coordinated effort to increase international cooperation and achieve synergies in common fields of action, the institutions of the UN family have launched initiatives between the UNEP, as the secretariat of most MEAs, together with the UNODC and other IGOs with common interests in fighting crimes that affect the environment.

Although states would be less amenable to the adoption of a global environmental crime treaty that limit their sovereign competences, they have accepted a more limited role for international organisations to continue their missions through the adoption of soft law instruments that serve to establish policies on 'crimes that affect the environment' while proposing guidelines and manuals that states can adapt to their national circumstances and respective capacities. In addition, at the operational level both formal and informal cooperation networks with NGO participation are expected to expand with the growth of transnational (organised) environmental crime.

However, these institutional actions remain insufficient insofar as IGOs not only lack the legal mandates and competences to enhance action in the face of the growth of transnational and organised environmental crime, but also because they depend on funding from their member states, other international organisations (such as the EU or the World Bank), and from private donors. Therefore, it should be in the interest of states to expand the competences and resources of IGOs so that, with autonomy, they can pursue the common environmental protection interests of humanity.

Index